Praise for *Compassionate Reasoning*

"In presenting his idea of Compassionate Reasoning, Marc Gopin takes us on a journey from neuroscience to democratic theory, from the plasticity of neurological pathways as keys to habituating prosocial thinking and behavior—*compassion*—to the dangers of 'reasoning' from the amygdala and blind obedience to tyrants and autocrats, to the degradation of our planet. The theory—and the *practice* and *training*—of Compassionate Reasoning is voiced in terms of conflict management and peacebuilding, but more profoundly in the language of moral philosophy and ethical traditions, spiritual and secular. It calls forth the beneficent conjoining of compassion as a healing and joyful emotion, with the power of human reason to challenge the most intractable problems of our species and societies, most especially violence. Like all of Gopin's work, it is based on over three decades of deeply personal engagement with peacebuilding in war-torn and seemingly hopeless places. When he writes against 'empathy' and for compassion as an antidote to trauma and burnout, this comes from his life. Yet in the end, this is a hopeful book, marrying habits of the heart with habits of the mind, offering a theory and a practice toward a humane and sustainable future."

—Kevin Avruch, former Dean, Rosalynn and Jimmy Carter School for
Peace and Conflict Resolution, George Mason University

"In *Compassionate Reasoning* Marc Gopin brings together practical wisdom and reflection, gained from a lifetime of engaging in and teaching global peacebuilding, with deep and cutting- edge theoretical research into the brain to offer a remarkably clear understanding of how social cooperation can be developed across the starkest differences and conflicts. Bringing to bear the most current science, Gopin offers an effective strategy that individuals and groups can implement to come to work together for constructive solutions to urgent problems. Analyses abound of what has gone wrong in America and the world to create such pressing problems as the threat to the climate, the growth of political violence, and extremes of poverty and wealth, yet proposed solutions are few and often more wishful than realistic. Gopin's breakthrough book shows how rational thinking and dialogue can be infused with the prosocial emotion of compassion, internalized and habituated through practice, to open up possibilities for working together toward the peaceful resolutions and constructive solutions we all yearn for."

—H. M. Ravven, Ph.D., Professor of Classical & Religious Studies and
Professor of Jewish Philosophy, Hamilton College; author of *The Self Beyond Itself:
An Alternative History of Ethics, the New Brain Sciences, and the Myth of Free Will*

"Marc Gopin has the intellectual capacity to coherently integrate wide-ranging research, theory, and philosophical inquiry. But that integration only scratches the surface of how he holds and brings forth both his practical experience in the work of protracted conflict, and the wisdom emergent from decades of deep listening leading into reflective action. In this volume, perhaps more than any other, he has gifted to our peacebuilding community a clear understanding of how compassion links not just the heart and the head but the hands and the feet—and the imagination to hold human pain in ways that engender a sense of hope and joy, and ultimately unfold into collective initiative with capacity to shift people and structures, mindsets and embodied ethics away from harm, toward respect and flourishing."

—John Paul Lederach, Senior Fellow, Humanity United;
Professor Emeritus of International Peacebuilding,
Kroc Institute, University of Notre Dame

"Here we have a truly exceptional, even vitally important book. Marc Gopin has drawn upon his vast personal experience inside the politics, spiritualities, and cultures across the globe to gauge and understand how people in all walks of life are now able to build up the abilities to listen and reason together. Gopin has discerned truths and synthesized ways that will enable us to become our true and, yes, happier selves."

—The Rt. Rev. Shannon S. Johnston, XIII Bishop,
Episcopal Diocese of Virginia (retired)

"An eloquent plea, drawing on personal experience, neuroscience, and public health methods, to argue that training in compassionate conduct can bring about beneficial change in the lives of individuals, communities, and society as a whole."

—Dr. Sissela Bok, Professor Emeritus, Harvard University;
author of *Exploring Happiness: From Aristotle to Brain Science*

"'Compassionate Reasoning.' What a wonderful concept, putting reason, which has become for some an unquestioned idol and for others a suspect threat, in its rightful and honorable place, as a partner to the compassion and care that make us fully human. And what a wonderful book Marc Gopin has written, guiding us in bringing the wisdom of the concept to our individual and collective understanding and to action in the service of healing and peace."

—James S. Gordon, M.D., author of *Transforming Trauma:*
The Path to Hope and Healing

Compassionate Reasoning

Changing the Mind to Change the World

MARC GOPIN

OXFORD

UNIVERSITY PRESS

OXFORD
UNIVERSITY PRESS

Oxford University Press is a department of the University of Oxford. It furthers
the University's objective of excellence in research, scholarship, and education
by publishing worldwide. Oxford is a registered trade mark of Oxford University
Press in the UK and certain other countries.

Published in the United States of America by Oxford University Press
198 Madison Avenue, New York, NY 10016, United States of America.

Library of Congress Cataloging-in-Publication Data
Names: Gopin, Marc, author.
Title: Compassionate reasoning : changing the mind to change the world / Marc Gopin.
Description: New York, NY, United States of America : Oxford University Press, [2022] |
Includes bibliographical references and index.
Identifiers: LCCN 2021033936 (print) | LCCN 2021033937 (ebook) |
ISBN 9780197537923 (hbk) | ISBN 9780197537947 (epub)
Subjects: LCSH: Compassion. | Ethics. | Conduct of life. | Reasoning.
Classification: LCC BJ1475 .G67 2022 (print) | LCC BJ1475 (ebook) |
DDC 170–dc23
LC record available at https://lccn.loc.gov/2021033936
LC ebook record available at https://lccn.loc.gov/2021033937

DOI: 10.1093/oso/9780197537923.001.0001

1 3 5 7 9 8 6 4 2

Printed by Sheridan Books, Inc., United States of America

Contents

Acknowledgments   vii

1. Compassion, Reasoning, and the Urgency of Healing Divided Societies   1

2. The Theory and Practice of Compassionate Reasoning   37

3. Compassionate Reasoning, the Mind, and Moral Choice   79

4. Violent Ideas Treated as Disease and Compassionate Reasoning as Treatment: A Public Health Analogy   131

5. The Applied Ethics and Habits of Compassionate Reasoning   170

6. Summary of the Argument of *Compassionate Reasoning: Changing the Mind to Change the World* and Implications for Training   221

Notes   243
References   261
Index   281

Acknowledgments

This book, more than any of my other books, centers on the creation of a new idea and a new approach to thinking, feeling, and doing that might help transform human relations for the better. I have encapsulated that in the phrase "Compassionate Reasoning," which is founded upon an exploration of and devotion to compassion as one of the most amazing and important emotions and ethical principles that brings healing and hope to human relations. The "reasoning" part rests on the importance for human reasoning, and moral reasoning in particular, as it is expressed and described over the centuries in at least five different approaches to virtue and moral decision-making.

I have asked myself how I can acknowledge the roots of this journey toward this new idea and combination of skills and practices. When did I begin my love for these strands of feeling and thinking, and who influenced me? Whom do I acknowledge for making me want to figure out how to be more of a "compassionate reasoner"? I have to begin that journey with my Jewish grandmothers: European immigrants, neither of whom had any schooling, one of them having had a very, very hard life of poverty, both speaking an English that was heavily mixed with Yiddish. All I know from my earliest memory was what they did with words. Both generously would offer blessings of good fortune, of health, of happiness at every meeting in a mixture of Yiddish, English, and Hebrew. As they showered me with these blessings, they would look at me as if I was a precious gift to this world. Both uttered a simple phrase from time to time as they spoke to me in ways I could barely understand, but they said, "*Hott Rachmanus,*" "Have Compassion." And I heard them deeply. They would use the phrase plaintively. They tilted their heads slightly to the side as they uttered these words, their eyes glistening with kindness, and it was usually a request to have compassion on someone who was suffering. It is my earliest and most enduring memory of them and other elders when I was a small child. I learned two things from them: the centrality of compassion for the meaning of life on this earth, and the power of positive words like blessings to transform us, to have power and reality, to change everything.

Training in and comfort with reasoning, with philosophy, with the study of ethics came to me also by way of important teachers, and I am especially mindful of Rabbi Dr. Joseph Soloveitchik who taught me that reasoning and use of the mind was the most profound spiritual experience of all. I still sit before him as I did from the age of 10 to 30. He taught me an endless love of exercising the mind for the good of this world. I remember my high school teacher Michael Schockett introducing me at a very young age to psychology, philosophy, and the analysis of profound ethical dilemmas. That put me on a lifelong journey to understand the nature of human suffering, the sins of blind obedience implicated in the Holocaust, and how to use our minds and hearts to escape obedience to tyranny and undercut the potential for human barbarism.

This background has guided me for decades into a professional exploration of peacebuilding, healing conflict, neuroscience, and compassionate reasoning. I also must acknowledge with gratitude the lifelong mission of the Dalai Lama, whom I met only once in extended conversation in Caux, Switzerland. He has stimulated a global commitment to the serious intellectual work and neuroscience research on compassion, in addition to being such a persistent and creative teacher of compassion ethics and compassion habits over many decades.

As a professional I have been most fortunate to occupy the founding Chair and to be the Director of the Center for World Religions, Diplomacy, and Conflict Resolution (CRDC) at the Jimmy and Rosalynn Carter School for Peace and Conflict Resolution, George Mason University, for 18 years now. Among those older and younger colleagues who have nurtured and continue to nurture my work I include Professors Kevin Avruch, Chris Mitchell, Rich Rubenstein, Daniel Rothbart, Susan Allen, Karina Korostelina, Doug Irvin-Erikson, and Charles Chavis. Daniel Rothbart and I have known each other the longest, and he has been a career-long friend in our passion for philosophy and ethics together with conflict resolution. We also engaged in a major project together on compassion that has since spurred both of our writings. Béatrice Pouligny was the wonderful chair of that project on compassion, neuroscience, and peacebuilding, funded under Melanie Greenberg's leadership of the Alliance for Peacebuilding.

My journey in my years of practice now on compassion was also stimulated by my dear friend Rabbi Bruce Aft, who is a Senior Fellow at CRDC. None of CRDC efforts would have been possible without the mentorship for decades of Mr. Joseph Montville, a most humble pioneer of the field of psychology and conflict resolution. Fellow travelers have included Dr. Lisa Schirch and her husband Mr. Bill Goldberg, who have been such key pioneers in peacebuilding research, practice, and education. Rabbi Dr. Daniel Roth, whose own book on peacebuilding has been recently published by Oxford, has been a wonderful colleague and student on the journey of building a field of religion and peacebuilding. I am indebted to him for our constant learning together in theory and in practice. Dr. Heidi Ravven has become a wonderful colleague and collaborator on ethics, neuroscience, and peacebuilding. I continue to learn more from her, and this has helped me persist in my writing and finishing this book.

In my world of peacebuilding practice, there are many colleagues who helped me along the path of discovering and experimenting with Compassionate Peacebuilding. These include the wonderful folks of Charlotte, NC: Mr. Joel Segal, Reverend Dr. Rodney Sadler, Reverend Dr. Sheldon Shipman, and former Mayor Jennifer Roberts, among many other new friends in Charlotte, where we have pioneered a commission to address reformation of American society and specifically its sins around the subject of race. Other influences include my work with the very noble and kind Dr. Tory Baucum and Bishop Shannon Johnston, now fellows at CRDC and whose care for the poor and the oppressed of the United States continues to press me forward in research and practice. Bruce and Wynne Busman have been a deep support to all of this work and such good friends in expanding all of these alliances. John and Karen Willams were supremely helpful in facilitating this great work that has led to so much expansion of the practice of Compassionate Reasoning, as has the kind and honorable Mr. Charles Scheidt. Reverend Charlie Reynolds has been a lifelong companion in the work of compassion around the world, and I am grateful for our work and experiments together in this field.

I want to thank two PhD students who have played an excellent role in helping with the manuscript of this book, and some of their comments are included in the text: Nicholas Sherwood and Naomi Kraenbring. I have begun teaching and training on Compassionate Reasoning, and I would like to thank the Vancouver School of Theology and Rabbi Harold Kravitz, Adath Jeshurun Congregation of Minnetonka, MN, who have hosted my teachings and training. This also includes Reza Soltani's wonderful teaching sessions globally on peace and tourism, where I also explored these ideas with thousands of listeners who participate in his wonderful music festivals. And this includes my many students at the Carter School who have been in my classes as we continue to describe and explore the ethics and neuroscience of Compassionate Reasoning, as well as elicitive peacebuilding.

My partner for 18 years of work on behalf of Syrian citizens and survivors of terrible oppression of war against them, Hind Kabawat, has been invaluable in the joint exploration of the true practice of compassion, teaching, and training. Dr. John Paul Lederach, a dear friend, is the pioneer of elicitive peacebuilding which I have practiced for 30 years, and it is elicitive peacebuilding's theory and practice that gave rise to my search for the inner personal workings and outer practices of Compassionate Reasoning. Michele Everson Gentry has been my partner in building CRDC and especially the phenomenal set of overseas classes and interventions that have made it possible for me to practice and experiment with Compassionate Reasoning in teaching, training, and interventions in the conflict zones in which we work, offering aid and support to thousands of refugees in severe conditions of conflict and trauma.

I want to thank my children, Ruth Gopin, Lexi Gopin, and Isaac Gopin, whose lives as young adults fill me with pride. It is a joy that I have lived to see them grow and flourish into compassionate, caring, responsible citizens of this sacred earth, and a testimony to the wonderful parenting of their mom. Everything I have done, I have done to contribute in some small way to a better earth for them to inherit. They have been there for my successes and my failures, and blessed me with respect, love, and patience. Every time I look at them it takes my breath away, more so every year, as gratitude fills my eyes with wonder, and I can feel my eyes toward them becoming the eyes of my grandmother toward me.

My mother, who is 98 in 2021, has always been the major support and stimulus for me to work hard, to think hard, to use my brain to its utmost, to reason with the world and bend it toward goodness. She expected much from me, and I have tried and achieved—and failed to achieve—much for this world. I am indebted to her model of sharp analysis and sharp thinking, creative problem solving, and her very high hopes for a better world.

It is a joy that my sister Reissa Leigh, my backbone for much of my life, can witness me publishing this book. We continue to help and coach each other decade after decade, and there is no one in my life for this long who has been there with me through thick and thin, through success and failure, always giving me a way forward. She is the epitome of Compassionate Reasoning, and I am so grateful for her and all of the people in my life who have been mentioned.

I want to dedicate this book on Compassionate Reasoning to my partner in love and my partner in life, my dear wife Christel. Christel Gopin has guided me every step of the way to be a better person than I was just a few years ago, to be kinder, wiser, more controlled, more reasonable, more ethical, more loving, and more responsible than I ever was before she came into my life. She is an extraordinary light to this world, as everyone attests who meets her, and as her Hebrew name "Meira" attests to. We learn from each other every day, as I can safely say that I would not have completed this book without her, and my life would be incomplete every day were it not for Christel. Blessings to you, dear Christel—and all of our friends and fellow travelers—for long life, health, happiness for everyone you love, as we pursue our journey toward a more compassionate, more reasonable, more ethical world of the future.

1

Compassion, Reasoning, and the Urgency of Healing Divided Societies

The Time Is Now

Today, it is common knowledge that humanity faces the unprecedented and steadily increasing destruction of the earth through our own behavior. In our human past, there have been specific societies that have faced total collapse due to their own fatal errors (Diamond 2004). These societies collapsed forever, buried beneath their mistakes, in far-flung places such as Easter Island and the Mayan civilization in Central America. By contrast, other societies of the past flourished as they managed better to control greed, loss of self-control, and abuse—tendencies that doom nature and people to exploitation and destruction.

As is often asked: what was the person thinking who chopped down the last tree on Easter Island in order to drag pointless, lifeless statues to a high point at the edge of the island? His counterpart today might be thinking, "It's a living, who gives a damn, and pass the beer."

Rather than apathy toward our behaviors and their consequences, survival depends on communal consciousness, planning, cooperation, self-control, and the cultivation of compassionate cooperation (Hublin 2009; Goodall [1971] 2000). These are not utopian ideas for the naïve, but rather the proven basis for determining which communities and societies will live and which will die in our shared human history, which will decline and which will recover.

For thirty years, I have been counseling people around the world who are living through catastrophes in their civilization. I remember once sitting with a wonderful pastor who had barely escaped the genocide of his tribe and the destruction of his African country by bloodthirsty extremists, funded by greedy corporations who were intent on using war to loot diamonds. We pondered what could possibly help his people recover, and we came up with a symbol of rebirth and the practical need that they all had for water. We used

Compassionate Reasoning. Marc Gopin, Oxford University Press. © Oxford University Press 2022.
DOI: 10.1093/oso/9780197537923.003.0001

our compassion, and then we used our reasoning to find how we could put that compassion into the practice of rebuilding his civilization.

That is why, in this study, I propose a unique combination of psychological, social, cultural, and ethical skills as the building blocks of future survival. Within this study, I am concentrating these skills into one term: *Compassionate Reasoning*. The book explains why Compassionate Reasoning is a combination of mental and social abilities that are critical to our human future.

Compassionate Reasoning is *a combination of the best lessons of human ethical reflection and practice from across the centuries and diverse cultures, together with the best of the emotional capacities in the higher mind, namely compassion.* Unlike ages past, where emotions were seen only as a phenomenon that gets in the way of intellect and reason, it turns out that compassion is a critical adaptation for survival (Goodall [1971] 2000; Thorpe 2017). I will explore why the most effective exercise of compassion is when it combines with reasoning skills, especially moral reasoning of specific kinds that will be outlined.

Put another way, the question of our future survival depends on whether: (a) our lower brain (namely, our brain stem and amygdala) governs politics, policing, governance, and finance; or (b) our higher brain (namely, our cerebral cortex) and higher thinking cultivate joint planning and highly coordinated, disciplined collaboration on the use, control, and protection of the earth, air, water, and animals that we oversee. In terms familiar to students of the Bible, the survival of humanity depends on whether the gifts of Eden have been overseen, managed, and lovingly tended, or abused and squandered for the purposes of greed and grudge.

Global collapse or progress is the choice we face, and the training of our minds and bodies, in truly collaborative approaches to ethical challenges, is essential for the future. In too many modern societies, the difficult questions and choices of ethics, and the debates and conversations about them, are shunted aside in favor of professional and transactional uses of rules for mere mutual gain. But collaboration in the exploration of ethical dilemmas is essential to the future, especially across progressive and conservative divides.

People need more faith in a system—in a political entity, in what they put their heart and soul into—rather than just learning to abide by rules for mutual gain. Instead, the capacity to collaborate across moral divisions, across political and class divides, across secular and religious divides, across ethnic, gender, and racial divides, is going to be the litmus test of our future. The future of most species on the planet depends on us humans to control ourselves as we struggle with each other. The life or death of the oceans and of the earth is in our hands at this moment.

History suggests those who make strenuous efforts to use their brains well, with both cognition and affect, with moral reason and moral sense, will collaborate and work out their differences in non-destructive ways (Diamond 2017, 2019; Lopez-Carlos and Nakhjavani 2018; Mitra, Bang, and Biswas 2015). Adaptive survivors seem to be the ones to thrive on inclusion and diversity, and the essential search for common moral values across differences so that thriving and flourishing is possible. They collaborate with the most diverse set of other humans, actively learning from everyone and everything—constantly. These are the ones to make life better and better on the planet, to make human survival possible again.

Why Compassionate Reasoning

In the next chapter, I will present Compassionate Reasoning as a solution for our currently divisive approaches to moral differences and the deepest conflicts dividing our societies. Compassionate Reasoning will be seen to manage profound ethical differences in a more productive way. One may legitimately ask, however, why does our future depend on this new approach to ethics, and why do we need to resolve our problems based on education, training, and fluency in ethical schools of thought? Why should fluency in the diversity of ethical decision-making approaches be expected from kindergarten to university, and even as a continuous professional development requirement? Why not just focus on social justice warriorship? Why not righteously fight against what is wrong or destructive, with no effort at understanding others or working with them? Why accept multiple approaches to discerning what is true, what is right, what is kind, or what is a fair compromise? Why search for an ethical way of negotiating between people of different cultures, beliefs, religions, and secular constructs of the world? Perhaps this war of all against all is inevitable and simply must be won by whatever means necessary in terms of argumentation and political struggle?

In previous books, I have mapped out the challenges of coexistence in a world of (1) unprecedented variation in lived religions, (2) contradictory secular political and economic philosophies, and (3) endless nationalities, each with their own aspirations (Gopin 2000, 2002). We have seen in our lifetimes what history taught us to anticipate: how easy it is to weaponize secular ideologies, and equally weaponize religions, in ways that destroy whole civilizations and set back peace, prosperity, and progress for generations. But we have also seen that heroic religious people are often at the forefront of the most humane movements in history, such as slavery abolition, human rights expansion, poverty reduction, child protection, and torture criminalization.

In a word, ideology, culture, and religion all seem to be agnostic in the determination of how much a person commits herself to peaceful relations on this planet; the ideologies and religions can be pushed in either direction. On the other hand, whether they be religious or secular, female or male, white or of color, the people who are the heroic bridge-builders from war to peace, the heroic creators of peaceful societies, have a predictable set of cultivated moral character traits and psychosocial skills. *They are kinder, more reasonable, more self-controlled, and more goal-oriented to peace.* Most of all, *they are united by a particular set of moral values and the emotional skills to practice them.*

Our aim is to uncover the "secret sauce" of those skills and values, the best combination of those values and skills. The reason we must do this is straightforward: Future generations of humans and all living creatures depend upon our discovery of this special formula. As a human community, we need to discover how to make those skills of peacebuilding healthier, more sustainable, and more ingrained—at all stages of the evolution of the human mind in social contexts. We need the peacebuilders and social change-makers to be stronger and happier so that millions of young people are attracted to and want to take up the calling of peacebuilding in every culture. That is the goal of this book in its articulation of a new combination of skills and values in the form of Compassionate Reasoning.

Compassionate Reasoning and the Field of Peace and Conflict Resolution

This book brings several fields of analysis together with the practical interests and practices of ethics and social change—especially peacebuilding. We will explore the specifics and emphases of five ethical schools of thought—especially the role of reasoning, calculation, and moral feelings (such as empathy and compassion). Our goal is to outline why and how Compassionate Reasoning can form the basis of a new way of thinking, feeling, and acting that will contribute to the positive transformation of societies.

I have worked for decades in the field of peace and conflict resolution, and this field's terminology should be outlined here.[1] *Peace and conflict studies* is a literature designed to look at the deep roots of conflict—often cutting across the realms of interpersonal, family, communal, national, and international conflict. This literature integrates many fields (e.g., psychology, sociology, political science, anthropology, philosophy, religious studies, health science, geography, economics, international relations, gender and sexuality studies, and history) in order to search for patterns and generate theories of peace and conflict. Peace and conflict studies, at its best, aspires to be transdisciplinary, multi-level, multicultural, critical, both analytic and normative, in intellectual solidarity, and both theoretical and applied (Reychler 2010).

In its most basic sense, *conflict* occurs when individuals or groups have competing goals, objectives that are not aligned. Conflict can be both destructive and constructive, engaged through violent and/or nonviolent action (Kriesberg and Dayton 2017). *Conflict prevention* refers to interventions designed to undermine and prevent the generation of deep-rooted systemic conflict (Wallensteen 2019). *Conflict management* refers to methods of managing conflicts in such a way as to prevent escalation and encourage de-escalation (Wallensteen 2019). *Conflict resolution* refers to efforts to bring destructive conflict to conclusion (Wallensteen 2019). *Conflict transformation* looks beneath and around the situation at hand, examining contributing factors and preexisting patterns, the context and content involved, in order to "envision and respond" or perceive the constructive opportunity that might emerge from the conflict and actively engage it (Lederach 2003). *Peacebuilding* is the broadest term we use, encompassing all efforts to (a) transform society in terms of social relationships and social structures, (b) encourage the most peace and justice possible, and (c) reconcile former enemies and heal local populations. These aspects of peace do not proceed in any linear fashion; sometimes deep reconciliation may occur between some (but not most) enemies, and these special folks become role models encouraging the improvement in relations among others. In this space, "peacebuilding" is not limited to the manner in which the United Nations and the broader international community employs "peacebuilding" (usually referring to peace processes occurring after the cessation of conflict, and contrasted with "peacemaking" and "peacekeeping"; Reychler 2010).

Finally, we will also refer to *elicitive peacebuilding*, the form of peacebuilding and social change that is most respectful of and adherent to the wisdom and emotional intelligence of cultures, religious communities, and civilizations, as well as native or indigenous peoples in any conflict context (Lederach 1996). Elicitive peacebuilding assumes empowerment comes from active listening and provoking questions more than imposing answers. Change is only possible through honor, respect, compassion, and care for those in all sides of conflict. This book explores Compassionate Reasoning on the basis of elicitive peacebuilding. Compassionate Reasoning is designed as an ethical skill, cultivated inside the person intrapsychically, and is strongly influenced by interpersonal and communal verbal and nonverbal communications that generate compassion and reasoning together (as we shall demonstrate in the coming chapters). Compassionate Reasoning is designed to create more sustainable peacebuilders and a peacebuilding field, because this approach generates more joy and less burnout, in the ways we shall soon explore. I hope this exploration stimulates not only a deeper understanding of the practical skills and ethics of social change, but also the application of neuroscience to practical individual, social, communal, political, and global change.

The Marriage of Compassion and Reasoning

There are so many noble moral skills and values. But compassion represents the flower of human ethics that reaches beyond mere civility, and beyond universal principles such as honesty. Compassion is an eagerness to care and love others, to love the world, and to do this in a way that is kind in practice and fulfilling emotionally. It is fulfilling for both the agent of compassion, the compassionate person, and those cared for. The eagerness, zeal, and joy of the doing of compassion are what we might call "pursuit of compassion." The eagerness expresses itself in using all the faculties of the mind and body for the purposes of care and love of the other person, and love of the world.

Compassion Always Leads to Reasoning, but Empathy Does Not Necessarily

Here is the key linkage of compassion and reasoning. The more compassionate you are as a person, the more you are energized to use logic and reasoning, the whole of your mind and capacities, in order to care for others in the best way possible. You will talk to many people, you will study, you will consult with experts that you may know, and you will work on yourself, step by step, to help the people to whom your compassion is directed.

By contrast, you can have empathy for someone you love while they are lying in the hospital. You can feel their pain, you can lie on hospital floors next to their bed, feeling their agony literally in your body. You can rush to bring them their favorite things, talk to them even when they are unconscious, hold their hand even if it is puffed up and filled with a deadly illness; you can pray your heart out, and you can visualize their recovery and health. You can worry day and night about your kids wherever they may be, and whether they are safe. You can make yourself immobilized with fear when all your kids are in different places vulnerable to every imaginable accident. You can even feel like you are dying a little when they are hurt.

All of this is empathy and deep love. Billions of people throughout history have felt this way for those they love, and often humans feel this way for total strangers, as many of us have in refugee camps. It tore my heart out there, and wherever I went afterward, for they stayed in my heart. This level of empathy is a pinnacle of human decency and goodness. It is us at our best in many ways. *But this level of empathy is not always helpful, fulfilling, sustainable, or even good for those whom you have come to love.*

If you are too empathic with suffering people, you can become so angered by the pain you are suffering because of their pain that your empathy and suffering may become overwhelming and paralyze you, thus preventing the kind of compassionate care they actually need. *You* are the one who could end up needing more care. If you do not think and plan how to help them, how to speak constructively on their behalf, then is your empathy hurting you and them more than helping? If someone is sick and you feel terrible for them, but in despair you do not talk to their health providers; if you do not ask questions about challenges and obstacles to their health and happiness, medically or emotionally; if you alienate everyone with rage in your pain and grief at the pain of those you love, then is it really helping? Can we then, in such circumstances, honestly say we have acted *compassionately* in the ethical sense of the term? Additionally, if you do not seek answers to what is going on in the surrounding environment; if you do not use your mind, your reasoning, and your communication powers, all because you are in such despair, then you could end up not doing all you could have done to take care of those who suffer. You could even hurt them by what you did *not* know or failed to do, due to naiveté or a withdrawn state of depression, or a reluctance to "deal" with other people. This is not very compassionate, ultimately. You could be so caring, and yet not say and do the right thing to make sure those you care about survive and flourish.

Learning, thinking, planning, sometimes asking the tough questions—these are also basic aspects of how we show our compassion for others, how we struggle for each other's survival and basic needs, especially when a person or a community of people cannot do this for themselves. But this aspect of true human compassion requires a careful combination with higher reasoning, a marriage of heart and mind, an alliance of emotions and reasoning.

Compassionate Reasoning as I am proposing it in this volume is a combination of the best lessons derived from a long history of ethical schools of thought, schools which we will study in coming chapters. Compassionate Reasoning combines the best of our reasoning with the most refined of our positive emotions. It embraces the supreme importance of principles but also outcomes, of calculus of costs and benefits, of wise and experienced foresight into *both* dangers and opportunities of the best moral path, but also the long-term project of the cultivation of moral character.

The commitment to compassion leads to a passion for inquiry, learning, and reasoning. The combination of compassion and reasoning helps the mind discover the best ways to aid and serve those we love and to aid and serve a world that we love. Compassionate Reasoning is put into practice through research and analysis, but also by studying the world directly: observing the circumstances around you, analyzing the situation and the people. Sometimes it involves active listening at great length to others and inquiring with a humble ear and heart close to the ground of human experience. Sometimes it involves networking and learning on social media, with friends and strangers alike, all in order to figure out with one's reasoning the best way to pursue a compassionate path in a complicated world of difficult choices.

Whether someone's compassionate path to care for others and to care for the world is more academic or more practical, compassion and reasoning are wedded partners for the improvement of life and for building a peaceful world in which we can flourish.

Compassion and Reasoning Are Essential for a More Ethical Future

I have been engaged for decades with compassion and moral reasoning as subjects of study, as methods of experimental practice in conflict resolution, and as key components of training. The cultivation of compassion and reasoning, and their increased importance in human education in recent centuries, have been essential for moving people globally to become less violent,[2] more kind, and more just. Many studies point to compassion as the core of a long, slow human evolution toward less violence over many centuries. Other studies point to the importance of reasoning and higher brain function leading to more self-reflection and more self-control that works together in some combination with compassion. This is detailed in extensive research, most recently outlined by Steven Pinker in his seminal study, *Better Angels of Our Nature* (Pinker 2011a).[3]

I am arguing in this book that Compassionate Reasoning should become an essential component in the study and practice of applied ethics, as well as the practice of peacebuilding. Ethics training for coexistence, conflict resolution, and the best practices of sustainable planetary life, is an essential step forward for humanity. It is essential for habit formation and for both formal and informal education at all ages.

Education in Compassionate Reasoning is also critical for human beings in all of their cultural and ethnic diversity and across society's divides between secular and religious worlds. There are many cultural, religious, and ethnic ways of expressing applied compassion and reasoning, many texts and traditions, rituals, and ethical precepts that resonate with and enhance the effectiveness of Compassionate Reasoning as we are defining it. These need to become a key part of training for citizens of each country and for citizens of the planet who hope to collaborate internationally. It is the only way to affect the whole of society and to move societies in a direction toward less violence and more peace.

I have engaged in peacebuilding across the lines of conservative and progressive citizens, secular and devout, in many troubled countries of the world (Gopin 2000, 2002, 2009, 2012). Compassionate Reasoning in its ability to imagine and care for those who are different is essential to the stability and flourishing of any society. While the moral habits of the mind and body are universal in nature, they require an embrace of and patience with a wide variety of cultural expressions. There are ways to interpret traditions and cultures in such a way that compassion and reasoning not only resonate with all citizens but even become central passions and pursuits. A flexible and interpretive engagement with compassion and reasoning leads to more peace and less violence in both secular and religious worldviews, in conservative worldviews and progressive worldviews. Accomplishing this in a way that integrates and unites citizens is an essential goal of the methodology we undertake in this study.

Compassion in Neuroscience Research

Moving beyond the vantage point of ethics and ethics training, we will engage psychology and neuroscience in terms of Compassionate Reasoning. Recent studies in neuroscience provide a revolutionary understanding of compassion that is clearly distinguished from empathy or empathic distress. When the human mind is trained in compassion visualization, for example, the brain forges unique neural pathways that can be seen from observation of functional MRI brain scans (Klimecki et al. 2013). A specific set of areas light up, suggesting compassion has its own unique signature in the mind. In particular, *compassion pathways are different from empathy pathways and regions. Feeling the hurt of others, which causes great distress, lights up a very different and separate set of areas and pathways, and stimulates a very different set of biochemical effects on the body and mind.*

We will explore the promise of training in compassion that generates greater health. We will also explore the neuroplasticity of the brain and its capacity to shift our responses *away* from destructive emotions and behaviors and *toward* prosocial emotions and behaviors. In particular, we will explore how to reinforce the sustainable and healthy responses of compassion through training, through habit formation, through education, through personal modeling, and through other innovative educational and cultural techniques that infuse the mind experientially with ethical teachings.

The process of actively moving the mind and heart in the direction of compassionate neural pathways not only strengthens the ethical pursuits of social change, but it also invests in personal health due to the metabolic and personality changes associated with increased compassion reactions (Bluth et al. 2015; Dunne, Sheffield, and Chilcot 2018). Compassion reactions and pathways of the brain are strongly associated with being more social, engaged with people, and even joyous, causing great health benefits. Compassion training, compassion habits, and compassion commitments can thus be a boon for the successful embrace of ethics and for the embrace of social change work and conflict resolution.

Too often, the work of positive change is experienced as debilitating and disheartening due to challenging or tragic circumstances of conflicts, disaster, and war. This has discouraged many people from a long-term commitment to the work of positive change. We can change this aversion by changing the nature of what the mind experiences when engaging in work to help others in tragic situations. We can dampen the destructive effects on health and happiness by reframing what we do and how we think about it. We can transform the experience itself by focusing on the contrasting mentalities of empathic distress versus compassion. We can train people to direct the mind toward compassionate thinking, feeling, and best practices, and away from an over-focus on the tragic condition of those we engage.

For example, we can learn how many doctors facing patient tragedy cope well, and even are resilient and joyful in their everyday practices as they lead a compassionate life of professional engagement (McKinley et al. 2020). The reason why some cope better than others is due in part to a state of mind, an attitude that is based on many years of thinking and feeling that have established healthy neural pathways. Neuroplasticity suggests the power of our minds to shape what we see and focus on, how we frame and feel what it is that we are doing and why we do it. This is how neuroplasticity becomes a key component of the positive evolution of the self.

Compassionate Reasoning and neuroplasticity have implications not only for the empowerment and health of individuals but also for the health of society as a whole, through education and the contagion of good practices. This is the path from the individual to the society and back again. Once this approach becomes a basic part of education, for both children and adults, it can shift us away from the fatigue associated with feeling the tragedy of others and toward the powerful feelings of accomplishment when we aid others. These are competing neural pathways, and ultimately, we can steer ourselves with the power of our thinking in a direction of more ethical treatment of others that is also healthful for ourselves.[4]

A major motivation for this book has been to establish a healthier, more enjoyable, and sustainable approach to the work of social change and social justice. Healthy metabolic responses, such as lower blood pressure, are strongly associated with compassion training in many tests (Sirois and Rowse 2016). This is accompanied by a move away from the debilitating effects of empathic distress and withdrawal from people, more commonly known as "burnout."

This stark contrast between, on the one side, neural pathways associated with increased socialization and happiness, versus neural pathways associated with deep stress and antisocial feelings, on the other, will be a central focus of our inquiry. Effective Compassionate Reasoning practices solidify a better direction for the brain, for the happiness of the individual, and for all of society through social networks of mutually enforcing practitioners of Compassionate Reasoning. I am exploring both personal health and public health models of Compassionate Reasoning that together can affect all of society through education, through social networks, relationship building, and innovative techniques of compassion.

Neuroscience compassion research affirms many insights of classical and applied ethics that we will see outlined in the coming chapters. The same research is confirming much received wisdom from sacred traditions on the ethics of peacebuilding. The joy of compassion and love stimulates good critical thinking about how to aid those you love, those who need our help and compassion. This demonstrates a vital and interesting relationship of the mind's natural capacities for compassion, on the one side, and, on the other, the classical lessons of ethics and wisdom tradition. There is also a clear mental health benefit to moving ethical decision-making of all citizens in the direction of Compassionate Reasoning. This is especially valuable for the development and training of caregivers of many kinds, as well as peacebuilders and social change makers. This would entail a conscious move away from empathic distress and burnout that leads to withdrawal, antisocial tendencies, and a failure therefore to build sustainable social changes and changes to the nonviolent progress of society. Thus, ethics, mental health, and compassionate intervention coalesce into a seamless whole of a new approach to personal and social change.

The dichotomy of compassion and empathic distress helps explain much of what has been inadequate in the practice to date of altruism, of peacebuilding, and of social change efforts. It explains the weaknesses of relying on empathy to motivate behavior. It also explains how mental health exercises and training in compassion can induce joy, love, and great happiness even while engaged in a life of service to others in need.[5] We know this can work, since we see at least a significant number of caregivers who, with a very specific frame of mind, flourish even while caring for very sick or terminal patients. We are now able to study this and generate practices that will allow many more of us to become more effective and happier while engaging and serving those in distress. The capacity to be healthy and happy while giving compassionate care will be critical to developing ethics and moral habits of the future that are sustainable and effective for the society as a whole.

Religious and Secular Practitioners Need to Contribute Together to the Evolution of Compassionate Reasoning

Both religious and secular sources of ethics and rituals are crucial in the development of and training in new practices of social change. These changes will engage the whole of society in a way that strengthens the social contract of governmental entities, both local and national. This effort must be invitational to religious and secular citizens alike in order to be viable. In the field of religious peacebuilding, there is increasingly an exchange of rituals between faiths and a healthy emulation of compassionate practices.[6] Religious and secular people can and do learn from each other to cope better with the emotional challenges of building peace in regions of war, for example. I have witnessed this myself in many conflict regions of the world. Secular/religious bridges of understanding and ethical agreement between religious communities, between secular and religious worlds, between worlds of citizens divided by politics, are indispensable to a less violent and ultimately nonviolent future. Compassionate Reasoning is a bridge across many tribal ways of thinking that bind us into binary divisions and destructive polarization.[7]

Implications of Compassionate Reasoning for the Study and Practice of Ethics

The study and practice of ethics is the key foundation of the "reasoning" side of the Compassionate Reasoning methodology. Ethics is divided into a number of schools of thought with intriguing implications for practice and social change. Neuroscience research has added important nuances, not only to the understanding of compassion but also its application to moral decision-making. Lessons from research in neuroscience and psychology concerning compassion and reasoning have intriguing implications for the field of ethics. There is a range of ethical schools of thought and practice, from Aristotle to Kant, Shaftesbury, and Mill. From virtue ethics to deontology, from moral sense theory to consequentialism and utilitarianism, there exist an array of important schools of ethical theory, ethical practice, and ethical training. Compassion plays an important role in several of these schools, and reasoning is part and parcel of all of them. We will explore exactly how this is the case and how reasoning and compassion working together play a unique role in stimulating social change.

An inclusive and appreciative approach to all the ethical schools of thought has direct relevance to peacebuilding and conflict resolution practice. The ethical schools, in all their diversity and debates, have a variety of strengths that have proven useful to me and other peace practitioners as we confront difficult arenas of conflict and war zones. Taken together, these schools of ethics give us tools, ways of thinking and coping, on the front lines of tragic situations. As Viktor Frankl (1959) noted so poignantly from his own horrific experience in Auschwitz, it is the search for and discovery of deep meaning for one's existence that sometimes provides the saving grace of sanity and survival in impossible situations. For him, that meaningfulness often expressed itself in the ethics of compassion.

Care for others gives meaning even to the most absurd and horrific circumstances of life. This lesson applies to many places of conflict and failure in which I have worked with thousands of others around the world. These victims were not in Auschwitz, but they witnessed and lived through remarkably similar horrifying days and weeks of their lives, witnessing many similar atrocities and experiencing similar assaults on their bodies. The vacancy in their puffed and watery eyes spoke volumes to me as I met them, so much so that I too felt as if I was with them in that chamber of horrors.

What could I do for them? How could I help them with a way of being in this world after what they had seen? This question always haunts me, and it is the reason I went searching for a way for the mind itself to recover, for the mind to be a core solution, for the mind to heal the body. I was in search of what kind of mind could build a different world.

Compassion and Ethical Reasoning as Connectors to a Diverse and Divided World

Peacebuilding often entails strenuous efforts to help people in dire situations to generate better moral decision-making, which in turn would lead to more healing and health. The diverse ways of ethical reasoning we will study have important resonance with a number of texts, traditions, laws, and rituals of many cultures and traditions. Compassion training is actually central to Tibetan Buddhism, for example (Dalai Lama 2000). As another example, compassion as a frame for the sacred is essential in all three Abrahamic faiths in their description of core divine qualities that the human believer is supposed to emulate. Compassion is the beginning of citations in all sections of the Quran. In Judaism, compassion is a foundation to the world itself, essential to the divine/human encounter and the emulation of the most sacred behavior and feelings (Gopin 2000). *Imitatio Dei* guided the life of pious Jews and Christians for thousands of years, and core to that emulation has been emulating the compassionate and merciful image of God. All of this makes the experience and practice of compassion a powerful bridge-builder across many approaches to human ethics.

Let us think for a moment about the power of motivation for the psyche when the motivations originate from *many* sources of your identity, based on many things most important to you. If a person sees compassion spiritually as the foundation of the world, and then they also learn that compassion gets a nod from neuroscience as good for you, the habitual practice of compassion can form the basis of health, and that finally, many secular approaches to good citizenship involve compassion for the poor or disabled, then this leads to a far more sustainable set of motivations for behavior. It also suggests multiple forms of training in care and social change that resonate culturally and psychosocially. The aim is to move people toward the greater use of compassion in daily life through training, but with the aid of a reasoned appeal to their highest cultural values and to the meaningfulness of compassion for the person and the community.

With the right frames and forms of intervention, compassion training based on neuroplasticity research could become a vital support for the best ethical and spiritual practices around the world. This kind of Compassionate Reasoning and framing of the mind then becomes an opportunity to develop respectful parallels between the secular universe of best ethical practices and mentally healthy and sustainable ways of interacting. But for those who are traditional, it will also resonate deeply with their identity in sacred ethics, rituals, meditations, habit formation, holidays, and observances. The combination suggests the possibility of a far better approach to cosmopolitan ethics today, in building equal societies comprised of a majority of willing participants to the construction of the compassionate society—secular, religious, and spiritual citizens who need a common ethic and a common "social contract" to live in peace with each other.

Human Habits Are Sealing the Fate of the Planet

Neuroscience and psychology emphasize that individuals do not evolve or change, and their neural pathways do not alter in a plastic way, *without* repetition and habit (Malvaez 2019). We will explore educational and training practices demonstrating the power of inducing new ways of thinking and behaving. This too is a vital bridge to the best assets of cultural traditions around the world in terms of habitual ethical practices that will play a vital role in generating better human dispositions and better societies.

Today, we face a world where there are vastly greater consequences to our habits than ages ago, and the reason is that the human power to create and destroy has increased to unimaginable levels. With the power to destroy the world instantly through weapons—or gradually through environmental destruction—we humans are the only species to hold the fate of life on earth in our hands.

There have also been many mass extinctions in earth's history, although this is the first man-made mass extinction, and this indicates how fragile and miraculous life is on the planet. In the recent past, there have been massive human-induced extinctions of plant and animal life due to our choices (Diamond 2004; Sánchez-Bayo and Wyckhuys 2019; Stone, Goring, and Kretch 2015). But today birds, bees, and insects are dying at unprecedented rates, by the trillions. There has been a 40 percent decline in insects, including bees (Sánchez-Bayo and Wyckhuys 2019).

At the same time, life is longer and the quality of human life is better than in any previous centuries, and in that sense, we have been learning how to sustain human life better. We have made some wise choices to become, on average, less violent and more self-controlled than we used to be. We live today therefore with paradoxes of unprecedented human accomplishments and unprecedented catastrophes in terms of life sustainability. We have become less violent to each other than we used to be, but far more violent to all other life forms on earth by our overwhelming presence and exploitation, as never before in history. Their extinction is also portending our own extinction, even extinguishing the atmosphere that makes life possible. You could say that our increased success at longevity has directly contributed to the overall demise of the system of life on the planet.

The power once imagined in ancient stories to be possessed by the gods that could destroy everyone and everything in an instant—we moderns now possess that. Now we wipe out so much life simply by making seemingly practical choices, such as single-use plastic, which we all grew up with and which made human life so much easier, while the plastic actually destroyed life all over the world, even into the deepest depths of vast oceans (Romer 2012). Even as we are becoming more civilized, we have so much power that our mistakes of negligence or lack of foresight or greed are deadly to trillions of life forms on earth.

To Prevent Extinction, We Need to Train Ourselves in a New Way to Live

We must find a way to do more of the good and the right for the sake of all life on the planet, of which we are custodians due to our vast intellectual power. This requires us to control ourselves more than ever as our power augments, to become wiser on this journey of power. This takes an evolution of our thinking and habits, which takes training. We are having a hard time keeping up with our power and the responsibility to wield it wisely. How to do what is good and right then becomes infinitely more consequential today for each of us individually, and for us together as a species.

What is the "Good" That Makes for Good Habits?

How to do that which is good is the simplest of questions and the hardest to answer, in part because "good" is defined in very different ways. Throughout the centuries and across every civilization, this question has led millions of people on journeys of personal discovery. The quest to do what is good has been a deeply personal search, but it has also been the goal of many political and spiritual communities throughout history.

Over the course of a lifetime, I have wanted to explore the great secular and religious wisdom traditions, the schools of philosophical ethics, and the sciences of the mind to see how their interconnections and combinations might lead to a better guide on being good, especially on making urgent ethical decisions. I wanted to see how ethics have been applied by heroic people to complicated realities and difficult circumstances, and so I sought out the wisdom of extraordinary people facing harrowing circumstances (Gopin 2012). I sought out very educated people whose minds and hearts have been trained in scholarship, but I especially sought out simple people in conflict zones, in every taxi, and in every refugee camp I have been to, because wisdom can be found in all humans—when you ask the right questions. In addition, refugees are an increasingly educated and informed group all over the planet. We all have far more wisdom than we think, more capacity for heroic ethical gestures, and we underestimate the manifestations of goodness all around us that we will see if we have the courage to look and ask.

The Lessons of Heroic Empathy

We also tend to be too overcome by bad news and attention to the dark side of human behavior (Soroka, Fournier, and Nir 2019). We are strongly habituated over the millennia to look for danger and ignore what is positive. If we dare to look, there is generous and heroic behavior all around us to see. Just as one example, I was looking over the masterful work and contributions of James Baldwin. In 1965, in a major debate at Cambridge University, Baldwin spoke in this astonishingly empathic way about his oppressors (Regas 2015). I quote the significant excerpts demonstrating his extraordinary psychological insights:

> In the Deep South, you are dealing with a sheriff or a landlord, or a landlady or a girl of the Western Union desk, and she doesn't know quite who she's dealing with . . . .
>
> What is happening in the poor woman, the poor man's mind is this: they've been raised to believe, and by now they helplessly believe, that no matter how terrible their lives may be, and their lives have been quite terrible, and no matter how far they fall, no matter what disaster overtakes them, they have one enormous knowledge in consolation, which is like a heavenly revelation: at least, they are not Black . . . .
>
> Now, I suggest that of all the terrible things that can happen to a human being, that is one of the worst. I suggest that what has happened to white Southerners is in some ways, after all, much worse than what has happened to Negroes there because Sheriff Clark in Selma, Alabama, cannot be considered—you know, no one can be dismissed as a total monster. I'm sure he loves his wife, his children. I'm sure, you know, he likes to get drunk. You know, after all, one's got to assume he is visibly a man like me. But he doesn't know what drives him to use the club, to menace with the gun and to use the cattle prod. Something awful must have happened to a human being to be able to put a cattle prod against a woman's breasts, for example. What happens to the woman is ghastly. What happens to the man who does it is in some ways much, much worse. This is being done, after all, not a hundred years ago, but in 1965, in a country which is blessed with what we call prosperity, a word we won't examine too closely; with a certain kind of social coherence, which calls itself a civilized nation, and which espouses the notion of the freedom of the world . . . . And I suggest further, and in the same way, the moral life of Alabama sheriffs and poor Alabama ladies—white

ladies—their moral lives have been destroyed by the plague called color, that the American sense of reality has been corrupted by it.

Baldwin here demonstrates a critical feature of the most advanced minds of human history: the capacity to empathize, in a deeply affective way, with the moral tragedy of other human beings who wish you ill, and who indeed have tormented you. Baldwin became a towering American historical figure who not only portrayed the inner life of the black man and the black woman but also the inner life of the kind of white man and woman who embodied the oppression that continues to plague our society to this day.

Baldwin's psychosocial and ethical capacity for compassion and reasoning in this quote demonstrates much of the theory of change I am suggesting in this book. It implies the foundations for a new approach to education, enlightenment, positive change, and even repentance. Such gestures of heroic empathy, displayed toward both victims and oppressors, leads to greater self-understanding and self-reformation for the person who works on creating this kind of mental and social disposition, and it implies a way to shift society as a whole.[8] Indeed, that night in Cambridge, in an almost all-white audience at the most elite university of England, Baldwin received a standing ovation. He easily won the debate with a leading voice of American conservatism, and in my opinion established a unique place for himself in the history of conservative/progressive debates on race.

The Challenges of Empathy

Such heroic kindness, grace, and empathy, makes life more complicated. From the moment you are bitten by the bug of witnessing heroic kindness and generosity, it drives you forward to uncharted waters. It is an exciting journey but there are also potholes, because empathy is quite challenging to us. It is hard to look straight at moral heroism, radical empathy, and generosity because the very seeing of them makes demands upon us. Once we see it, we are called to it, urged by what we see to rise to our own highest potential—and that is daunting. Cynicism, by contrast, is a relief from heroic empathy, and it is an escape from the call of responsibility.

Here is an even bigger challenge for awakening to empathy. There are some built-in human dangers of empathically feeling the pain of others on a regular basis. For example, we tend to get very invested emotionally in the people we are helping. This, in principle, is a good thing from an ethical perspective but not necessarily from a health perspective. Some of us get easily overcome by an *excess* of empathy, an uncontrollable over-identification with the pain of others. This then leads to stress, trauma, and ultimately withdrawal from doing good (Newcomb and Hymes 2017). Thus, ill health can lead to less ethical and prosocial behavior, thus defeating the purpose of empathy-driven ethics.

Empathy can lead to burnout and emotional disorders,[9] which can also lead to rage, and then we stop being motivated to act ethically (Lo 2016). Furthermore, over-identification with those we love leads to empathy for some people over others, for our family or nation or race over others, due to the intense solidarity we feel (Rothbart and Korostelina 2006). What begins as ethical empathy can lead to the preferential treatment of some over others, hatred and even incitement to violence. It is easy to see this devolution of positive sentiments as people get more and more invested, get angrier and angrier, and more ready for aggressive confrontation.

After three decades of volunteering in war zones, I can attest to the fact that it takes every ounce of my energy to not hate those who are maiming and killing those I have come to love on one side of a civil war, for example. This happened to me in the 1990s during the suicide bombings in Jerusalem. This negatively affected me during much of my European work long ago, due to being haunted by the Holocaust memories of my teachers and family. This has happened to me every year from 2012 to 2020 as I watched 12 million Syrians forced from their homes, hundreds of thousands killed, thousands tortured to death, and so many of those I worked with raped and deprived of all their relatives. Some victims I knew personally, and many a night I could not sleep. I knew at least one of the perpetrators, and this also can eat away at your soul. It takes extensive work on the self to prevent this kind of empathy from turning into hate for perpetrators or an unbalanced approach to ethical interventions and peacebuilding.

Our empathy can lead also to cynicism, isolation, or partisan embroilment in the wars of those we are trying to help. Selective empathy, or love only for our own, for our tribe, for our family, or for our nation, even for our adopted family and friends in war zones, can become dangerous. *Empathy is a key motivator of moral practices, but it can also lead to its opposite unless we cultivate compassion in very particular ways that we will explore in this book.*

Empathy That Provokes Moral Confusion

I also discovered empathy can lead to great confusion and frustration over how to distinguish bad from good. How do you examine situations that are morally complicated and invite dialogue that respects differing moral opinions and gray areas? How do you distinguish them from situations that demand resistance to something categorically bad? Confusion over definitions of what is ethical, over the methods of making ethical decisions, and over the fine line between gray areas of moral choice versus clear cases of black-and-white choices—these all lead to stress within the psyche and between people. This is acute when your empathy for those who are suffering is overwhelming. The stress of empathy itself has led many otherwise decent people into impulsive and destructive conflicts with others who come to different conclusions on complex moral matters. It all stems from the powerful impact of the empathy that we feel for victims, and then the emotional confusion of identifying with victims on more than one side.

When we are stressed by moral confusion, we tend to either get depressed or, on the contrary, we get overinvested in impulsive choices and absolute certainty of our righteousness. When you are excessively convinced that you are in the right, that your cause is just, that you are doing only the good and others are doing evil, you can be driven to radical behavior that stimulates spiraling cycles of anger. In terms of neuroscience, our moral reflections and deliberations may *begin* as higher brain reasoning about what is right. But quickly, and in the context of too much empathy, what starts out as reasoned thinking can turn into lower brain impulses of righteousness, hatred, isolation, paranoia, and rage. The human brain is filled with contradictions, and very good people can fly into rages when they feel deeply the pain of victims.[10]

This confusion over how to even debate and discuss the good and bad of situations has also led many people I respect into disastrous paths involving loss of life in war. They made these mistakes not only due to typical causes of destructive conflict described by my field of conflict analysis: miscommunications, struggles for power, mixed motives, fear. I started to discover a deeper reason for destructive conflict at the personal and global level. I noticed seriously flawed ways of thinking about *the act of ethical choosing, in and of itself.* There was almost no attention to how to decide what is good and what is not, how to intuit the good and how to intuit the bad.

In general, even among social change-makers, we are barely communicating well as to how to use our minds to choose good from bad, and which part of our mind to exercise the most in that process.

- Should feelings dominate or logic in the search for the good and the right?
- Do principles matter more than the specifics of the situation, or does the situation matter more than principles?
- Are likely consequences of actions the key moral consideration, or should the focus be on the acts themselves that are being contemplated?
- Who should be in on our decisions about what is right? Family and friends? Coworkers? All employees of a company equally, or none? Only fellow citizens? Never "enemies"?

On and on, the moral confusion magnifies our frustration, and then, once mentally exhausted or frustrated, we make impulsive decisions that spiral into truly bad behavior.

Tension around moral choice is pervasive among even the most educated of human beings. Most of us walk around, including leaders of countries and billionaires, cab drivers and shopkeepers, without any clear idea of how to make simple ethical choices. As opposed to the sophistication of our education for STEM,[11] for careers in law, medicine, and business, we have elected to have no training at all in ethics. This allows problematic behavior to emerge all the time as we interact with others and as we make decisions as citizens on a host of fateful policies and political choices, especially when we get tired or frustrated (Appiah 2006).

Muddled thinking, confused emotions, and impulsive anger around moral discussions and decisions seem completely at variance with the incredible genius of *the same people* when it comes to their math or business talents, for example. The lack of training in ethics flies in the face of the increasing competence of most humans today in terms of their *technical* skills, or that side of their brain that deals with technical matters of STEM. I have seen brilliant people, functioning at a genius level in one part of their brain like math, acting far worse than animals in another part of their brain the second their young toddler refuses to move. We must face the fact that some parts of the human brain are super-developed as moderns, and some parts are still dangerously underdeveloped and undertrained.

Moral Courage under Fire, Brain Plasticity, and Ethics Training

Truth be told, all of this human ethical underdevelopment is tantalizing to me as an optimist, because we now know from a significant and growing literature how "plastic" the brain really is, how much it is like a muscle, with strong and weak parts. We can in fact teach ourselves to do remarkable things and recover lost brain abilities in remarkable ways *if* we have the will and intention to do so with the right training methods (Su, Veeravagu, and Grant 2016). "Will" and "intention" are two words with a rich history in philosophical discourse. They hold a special place in the minds of great thinkers who intuited, long before the discoveries of neuroscience, that we refashion ourselves very often with two things: strong intention and strong willpower.

If the brain can recover and refashion through neuroplasticity, why can we not retrain our brains in ethical thinking and practice? Why can we not build new neural pathways and new habits that turn into lifelong moral habits of thinking and doing, deliberation and deeds? Essentially, why can we not evolve ourselves and our behavior with sheer intention and will? The phenomenon of neuroplasticity, with all of its promise, led me to conclude that today's unprecedented global advances in literacy and technical education for our species are in remarkable contrast to the poverty of brain training in how to think about and practice ethics, how to understand and cope with moral quandaries, and how to make challenging moral decisions at every moment.

On the other hand, I have seen *some* very courageous people in the most dangerous of circumstances making sophisticated calculations of ethical principles. They make those calculations on a continuing basis, such as in a war zone as they tend to victims, or as they tend to patients in an emergency room. It is as if we humans have this capacity for moral genius, but it is atrophied in too many of us, like a weak muscle, because human civilization has chosen not to frame it as an advanced skill at the present time. But life in the extreme circumstances of war, or life-and-death situations, can free some of us to fashion our brain for moral engagement in profound ways, and this challenge turns some people into moral geniuses. I have explored the moral genius and inner lives of such peacemakers (Gopin 2012), but in this book, we will look into the mechanics of how we can generate such inner lives and outer behaviors in all of us through Compassionate Reasoning.

Sometimes a horrible war seems to bring out the best in some people, and they find their moral genius from within; under pressure, they develop an extraordinary brain capacity for ethics. The violence-based scoundrels and sociopaths of war are better known, however, even more lionized and romanticized by popular culture. We know them very well, and we even make them adorable, such as in the movie *Butch Cassidy and the Sundance Kid*, with two heartthrobs, the young Paul Newman and Robert Redford, playing the scoundrels and making them sympathetic characters. We can ask ourselves why so many writers and directors fixate on scoundrels, why they can count on popularizing their lack of self-control, as reflected by our affection for the many characters of Robert Downey Jr. and Johnny Depp.

The fact is, however, this picture of lawlessness is at variance with the true moral complexity of violent realities. Some violent situations do provoke extraordinary moral genius and courage in some, and yet we have studied very little as to why this happens and to whom. There is much to be studied here as to how morally courageous behavior, heroic behavior, arises, and what we can learn from it. Let me get more specific about this by drawing more from what I have witnessed in my own journey.

I have spent decades in war zones with survivors and peace activists, soldiers and healers, witnessing both the worst and the best in humanity under the trying circumstances of immediate danger and ultimate loss. I have studied professionals in emergency care in search of their unique lens upon doing the good and the right in very confusing circumstances. I learned on this journey one of the greatest barriers to being good or doing good is *despair over moral confusion itself*, confusion over the grey areas of life where there *is* no clear separation between right and wrong.

Every day, in fact, we are faced with bewildering choices around what is right or wrong to do for ourselves or for others, and we see right and wrong on both sides of choices. Depending on limited information, we go back and forth between competing moral evaluations, sometimes at a dizzying pace. Our thinking and feelings can become muddled as we struggle with such complexity.[12] Frustrated by this, we can impulsively choose based on ill-informed instincts of fear, frustration, aggression, or bias (what we will see later is our limbic system, especially the amygdala).

In frustration, we lurch impulsively toward one direction and then rationalize it with some mindless sentences muttered to ourselves or others. Our impulses drive these moments, and our wordy justifications are not reasoned conclusions at all but mere verbal expressions of inner impulses. At such times, we often alienate others when our tongue is not controlled by the neo-cortex; rather, we speak our impulses and then think later. Any of us can, by habit, fall into sloppy moral thinking and sloppy moral actions. In such times, we numb ourselves to the consequences for our relationships.

We humans, seen from one angle of the brain, are a kind of "genius team," like bands of superheroes in popular films. We have actually gone to the moon as a team of superhuman achievers, and we have massively increased the human lifespan through medical sophistication, doing things to the body and for life preservation that were pure miracles just fifty years ago. Should we not be able to do much better at this thing called "moral choice," some-thing better than muddled, contradictory, and impulsive feelings?

We must do better at moral choice and moral courage if we want to over-come our present massive problems of life on earth. Our descendants would want us to overcome decades of fatal industrial mistakes promoting fossil fuels that are presently destroying the climate. If we want our descendants to have the cognitive and moral tools to shepherd life on this planet to long-term survival, we must consider moral training in decision-making to be an essential skill going forward. This skill will require great training in self-control. Now we have the tools to train for this, to inspire this, but we have not applied those tools to our educational and cultural outlets. We must work on our civilization so that every young member learns from experience, learns to examine herself and her life—so that we each become lifelong learners and lifelong teachers of an ethically engaged way to live.

Every Moment a Teacher: From the Floor of a Hospital

Life's troubles are the best teacher of ethics, the most demanding instructor of how to make complicated ethical decisions. I remember one night of my life in 2014 at the Massachusetts General Hospital in Boston. The world-famous, massive hospital is right next to the Charles River and right across from Phillips Street on Beacon Hill, where my great-grandparents lived in 1910 when they first landed in the United States from Ukraine.

I had been almost living in the halls of the hospital, for several days in fact, rarely leaving my sister's side in the intensive care unit. On one fateful night, I was bewildered and disheveled. My family had to decide whether to try an extremely risky method to save the life of my sister, who was in a coma and dying from H1N1 swine flu, a case written about some months later (Lamas

2014). I can still see in my mind the hospital hallways near the intensive care unit. I can still hear the desolate quiet in the middle of the night where I lay down on the floors under gurneys for some rest and quiet reflection. I didn't care how I looked or who saw me. Deep into the night, I was searching for answers to the situation and what could be done. Death can make me enraged, and at times it can turn me into a warrior determined to defeat a nemesis. And so, I roamed the halls in search of a way out of the situation. I would not let her go; I just refused.

To this day and this moment as I write, my heart races with palpitations as I visualize the hospital meeting of the family and the doctors that night. The doctors knew how impossible the ethical choice was between two highly risky options, with death very possible in both directions, and so they left the moral decision to the family as a group. Continue to medicate but let her lungs steadily collapse to less than 10 percent capacity, or operate with a radical operation to attach the experimental ECMO machine, to take a risk with a new machine that would take all the blood out of her body and then put it back in, in a last attempt to defeat the disease. This is a simplification of the process, but it was indeed that dramatic and that dangerous.

I am still in that room right now in that meeting. I can still see everyone gathered around; I can still feel myself barely able to sit in my seat from agitation to rush, to rush like a madman to save her. My chest heaves as I write these words six years later, and I know I have trauma. I can see the meeting room turn glossy through wet eyes. I can hear my voice cracking. Moral choices are weighty and hard, and their consequences last forever. I hesitated. I knew the words coming out of my mouth could lead to courses of action that would either save her or kill her. We seemed to agree as a family to aggressive intervention—at least this is what I sensed from the room, and then I just blurted out, "Let's go!" And so, we did. It was a night of hell on earth, medical disaster combined with astonishing medical technology, heroic efforts by medical personnel, seeming miracles, all wrapped into moments of terror.

Just a few hours later she died. They actually gave us the bad news of her death, pupils dilated and fixed. I was called into a room for the grim news, alone, as my family had gone home for some sleep. And then somehow they came back to the room, and they could not believe it, as it never happens. The pupils were no longer fixed and dilated, and with a miraculous resuscitation that still makes no sense, she was saved by hours of medical staff labors to do things to her that I will not describe here. People do not understand the level of heroism of many doctors and nurses.

I stood over her bed that night, after her resuscitation, after this heroic struggle, the ECMO machine pumping at her side, the technician at attention 24/7, the nurses coming in every few minutes to adjust machines, in this constant battle with death. My sister was now a cause. We never knew, moment-to-moment, when the entire experiment with the ECMO machine might fail over weeks, but especially that first night.

I remember one moment that night when I stood beside her bed in the darkness, my hands spread wide, clutching the guardrail of the bed at either end. I was clutching so hard that my hands turned white, and I felt as if I might crush the metal. I breathed in and out deeply and ferociously, I shook and quivered, I kept my eyes clenched tight, I faced toward Heaven, and I felt as if I was physically at war with the Angel of Death. I knew her death was wrong, that it was not her time, and I would not let go. Something inside me became fierce, and from that fierceness, I found a strength in me that I did not know existed.

People are not supposed to fully recover all their faculties after such a long stay in intensive care, with the exception of my sister. The ECMO machine, together with amazing nurses, technicians, surgeons, and doctors, saved her. With thousands of constant interventions and endless medications, with some antibiotics almost killing her from an allergic response, it was a battle of weeks after that strange night. It felt like a supernatural struggle with an angry virus that wanted this one life. My sister made a full recovery, and she leads a healthy life today, working and happily married.

Ethical Choices Come in an Instant and We Must Be Prepared

That night embodied just one moment of the dramatic world we live in, a world in which billions of people every day must seize upon and struggle with their biggest challenges. And they must use their ethical values, their deepest ideas about what is right, in order to do the good in difficult and often strange circumstances. They often find inside themselves a place of deep strength and a level of mental concentration they did not know they had. They find a space of higher thinking and heroic compassion, and in those moments, a miraculous human capacity for the good emerges. This capacity emerges sometimes quietly but also sometimes with the ferocity of a guardian angel. We are all called upon at times to be guardian angels of precious life all around us, lives that are or become completely dependent upon us without warning.

None of us ever know when these moments come. There was a group of humans in that hospital on that night, a random gathering of professionals, family members, and family friends, who all formed an unlikely team in order to struggle with the right and the good and the compassionate. The team came together for but a few moments in time, then dispersed to each play their fateful roles in what would end up being the saving of one life.

This is typical of the strange contexts in which we humans must struggle for values, for reasoning, and for compassion, that we engage in together. These instants come and go millions of times every day, everywhere in the world, and it is up to each of us whether, in those moments, we are or are not ready to work with our highest expression of compassion, reasoning, and communication, in order to do the good and the right. We are called upon to do this in the context of all of the messiness, imperfection, and creativity that comes from human beings as a team.

Every Moment a Teacher: A Stranger's Fate in a Hotel Room on the Border of War

I remember another time when I had minutes to convince a young man to not go over a border and into a war. He felt driven to seek out the murderers of his brother, who were part of one of the worst terrorist organizations in history. I was begged to intervene by his friend, but without any advice on how to save this complete stranger. I agreed to see him, and he entered my hotel room. I looked him in the eyes, this underweight and agitated, oddly smiling and barely twenty-something survivor of absolute horror that I will not describe here. Considering who he wanted to go up against, I was certain that he would die if he left my room and went over the border, despite his considerable intelligence and strategic ability, which was obvious after I listened to his story. I had no idea how to organize my questions and my thoughts.

The moral choice was what to say to him and how to say it in order to save his life. It was clear to me that although he was very intelligent, strategic, and capable, he was making a decision driven by survivor guilt and desperation to join his brother in likely death, as atonement. I had many confusing thoughts instantly about the ethics of the situation. How do I convince him to not die, to not join his brother? How do I convince him to spare his own life? Do I lie or bend the truth in order to convince him to not cross the border, in order to save his life at that moment, and then build a relationship of trust with him later? What are my moral priorities at that moment? What are my goals? What are the methods of deciding what is right for me to say or do? Is it a focus on principles I should stick to, or do I focus on the likely consequences of my advice? What was more important, his independent rights to choose autonomously or his life?

So many choices I felt inside of me in that darkened hotel room. I felt his pain. I had no time to reflect, and I started to literally shake from too many choices in too short a time. I felt agitated with emotions of radical empathy, a sense of responsibility, and a fear of loss for this complete stranger. As is so often the case with me, I am in an agitated state because I feel all the emotions of the person in front of me *in addition to my own* (Salinas 2017; Ward, Schnakenberg, and Banissy 2018). I frequently faced these fateful moments and choices, as many of us working in war zones do.

When confusion rooted in overly active empathy affects us about serious matters, it can lead to despair and withdrawal. Science tells us we human beings can deal with *some* confusion, but the more that confusion piles on, the more tired we get. And the more tired we get, the more we lose our ability to reason through problems and difficult decisions. An agitated moment of empathy triggers memories of other agitated moments, and they together build to a traumatic paralysis and social withdrawal.[13]

The Need for Training in Ethics, Empathy Management, and Internal Conflict Management

How to confront situations such as this requires intensive training on making better choices, more preparation for fateful moments and sudden choices, and means of anticipating and coping with the challenge of empathic distress. Practicing better decision-making, and feeling better about the process of making those decisions, generates good habits of the mind and heart and good practices for directing the will to act in an ethical way. This way, the habits of one's will and good intentions take over the mind in difficult moments rather than the paralysis of too much empathy.

Another strategy of resilient coping in such situations is to seek out the wisdom of others when there is time to do so.[14] This elicits productive debate and brainstorming, and it joins the highest part of our thinking to that of others with whom we engage in relationships of trust.

Seeking out the wisdom of others for complex moral moments can become a habit and even a sacred meaningful practice. This is why the Jewish Talmud advises people to work hard at making friends with those people whom one will consider to be like teachers. This is because connecting more than two people together in reflection and debate, like the cords of a strong rope, makes unbreakable bonds of wisdom and trust.[15] There is power, joy and mental strength to be found in collective thinking with those who are working as hard as you are on fateful ethical decision-making. Such thinking soars above the thinking of only your own mind.

Clarity Is Not Simplicity

The goal of clarity in moral thinking in this book is not to have simplistic answers for every situation because that is (a) impossible and (b) unwise. It is impossible and unwise to pretend that there are simple moral prescriptions for every situation, just as surely as we would never train a doctor or any diagnostician in such a primitive way. Rather, the goal is to discover a way for us to work dynamically with the mind and heart, and then for more of us to make better decisions together for each situation—"better" in the sense of decisions that are the "most good" that they can be, that maximize goodness.[16]

We will present a better way to think and feel in reaction to life's moral challenges and choices. This way of thinking and feeling will lead to a more effective engagement with the best of human wisdom on the art and science of ethics throughout the ages. It will empower those who take this journey to find a path to their own conclusions. Those conclusions will be based not on anger or confusion or cynicism, but on an increase in moral clarity rooted in the wisdom of ethics traditions combined with various scientific approaches to health.

Most of us choose to believe in certain truths and in certain paths of right and wrong, but we are unprepared for the task of wading through the confusion of everyday choices in light of the values we hold dear. From personal choices to political ones, from local choices to global ones, we need help with the confusion over how to *practice* and *apply* our values, how to make them part of our lives. This is a lifelong challenge that will have its successes and failures, but we can become better at the habits of thinking and feeling that will make those choices more consistent and more satisfying. In so doing, we will contribute to making a better society by providing a model of ethical thinking and action for ourselves as individuals, as well as for our role as part of collectives of citizens.

Ethical Reflection Is a Means to a Goal but Also an End in Itself

Here is the most important point of this book. Human ethics has always yielded many principled conflicts and radically different choices, but we do not need to all agree on ethical and political paths of society in order to make society better. *The very act of calm reflection and discernment on how to feel, think, and act, the very experience of principled deliberations with each other, will steer us in a far better direction as communities and societies.* The more we deliberate and debate these matters together in reflective ways, the better our decisions and debates will become. It will sharpen our higher thinking and intuitions. It will train our prosocial emotions and use of reason to work in concert with one another while depressing our worst instincts for fear and paranoia. It will favor those parts of our mind geared toward prosocial emotions and logical thinking.

This social habit, in and of itself, even when we disagree, will steel us against blind obedience to charlatans. The quality of our disagreements will increase, and the compromises we come to will depend less on fatigue or corruption and more on the considered reasoning of reflective minds in concert.[17] Our governance will truly be reflective and interactive, and less subject to manipulation.

Experience suggests the more time we spend on reflection about ourselves and about our choices, alone and in concert with others, the more all of us come to ways of thinking and behaving that are better in terms of moral quality.[18] In other words, impulsivity is almost a guarantee of poor moral behavior, but the reflection that becomes second nature leads to independent and collective actions that are far more morally good, even when we must agree to disagree about the application of principles to grey areas.

From Reflection to the Compassionate Embrace of Others

After careful reflection, it often becomes apparent there is more than one legitimate way to argue for the goodness or badness of a course of action, and this leaves us respecting differences when principles contradict each other and the consequences of each course of action are honestly unclear when analyzed. The embrace of compassion concomitant with reasoning compels us to listen and truly hear multiple perspectives, which in turn positively sharpens our collective effort at reasoning. This way, all parts of the mind work in concert to discover the good and the right in complex situations.

The cognitive recognition by the individual that peers come to very different moral conclusions about a situation, all based on reasoning, positive moral intuitions, and calculations, is the beginning of nonviolent coexistence, conflict resolution, and compromise. Out of those compromises comes a greater valuation of and attention to principles of goodness seen from many angles.

Turning Ethics into an Experience That Is Second Nature

The result of such moral deliberations between many people is imperfect and messy. But the act itself of engaging in such deliberations shuts down impulsive, violent, or destructive behavior. The act of engaging others leads to far greater public and private respect for ethics, and for shared paths to social decency, both for groups and individuals.

Our goal, then, is to get ourselves used to these ways of thinking, intuiting, and deliberating so they become second nature. This will lead to better human beings, better communities, and political societies. The doubt we develop when having to confront ethical choices is that there are too many extreme opinions and approaches, and we fear we can never solve our conflicts and dilemmas. So, we yearn for simpler instructions, fundamentalist instructions perhaps, authoritarian guidance. But life has never been as simple as simplistic instructions. We run from complexity to simplicity because we have not developed enough comfort and skill at managing complex approaches to moral disagreement.

The Source of Blind Obedience

All that truly happens with expressions of fundamentalism and authoritarianism—be they of a religious or secular political variety—is that we surrender our choices to someone else. In particular, we surrender to their interpretations of authoritative legal codes, be they sacred religious codes or secular national codes. It is a surrender of the rule of law to an arbitrary manipulative leader. It is a surrender of freedom and a false solution to eth-ical problems. In the end, some authoritarian leader will decide right and wrong *for you*, with no checks and balances on whether, in fact, that leader's decisions are ethical or corrupt, biased or objective, in everyone's interest or only in the interest of the few—or the one narcissist.[19]

This is a major source of blind obedience to authority. Blind obedience undermines a broad range of both secular and religious values. Blind obedi-ence becomes tempting for us as a way to surrender moral and political de-liberation and debate to authorities, as we face challenging, opaque choices we have not become skilled at making. Our lack of training and willingness to courageously debate moral complexity has serious consequences. Our exhaustion under pressure, our excessive empathy, our sadness and with-drawal, all leave a vacuum filled only by the most unscrupulous and the most predatory, and this is something humanity can no longer afford and should no longer abide.

We must make a bold conclusion from this line of reasoning: Our lack of training in ethical decision-making is a mortal threat to democracy, human rights, and the good society. A lack of generalized ethics education and training leads to far too many citizens who surrender their rights and respon-sibilities to others, to the few who cannot be trusted. A new commitment to ethics education is imperative, for it is a vital component of democracy's fu-ture and essential to the construction of just societies. It must be an ethics ed-ucation focused on creating experiences of service and practice that generate moral thoughts, feelings, habits, and sophisticated forms of moral reflection in concert with fellow practitioners.

Ethical Deliberation Supported by Science is the Foundation of the Good Life and of Sustainable Democracy

I propose in this book that part of the answer to the crippling doubt and ex-hausted thinking in complex moral situations is ethical study and training, combined with deliberation and debate in education, in traditional cultural contexts, and with friends. These practices then lead to strong habits and ways of thinking for the individual and her circle of friends and colleagues. The more comfortable we become with the variety of approaches to ethics, and the more we utilize those ways of thinking to deliberate with each other, the more we will build habits of good thinking and best moral practices together.

In this way, we will become less fearful at moments of uncertainty and less prone to surrender our freedom to charlatans, bigots, and frauds. We will learn to ask simple, deep, and clarifying questions of our own mind and the minds of others. Questions such as: What is the principle behind what you are proposing? Is what you are proposing for yourself actually valid for everyone else? Are you okay with everyone behaving in the way you propose? Is this a kind thing to do? Will it make you and everyone else happier? In the short run, will the results be better, or in the long run? How do you decide what is the "most fair"? All of these questions stimulate the mind toward higher, more noble, less selfish, more visionary thinking, and they discourage shouting matches based on fear, anger, resentment, and hidden biases.

We will explore in coming chapters important parallels between the schools of ethical practice on the one side, and on the other, positive emotions and habits emerging from health sciences, psychology, and neuroscience. This will help to evaluate what courses of action and what trainings will lead to the most effective forms of ethical training and guidance. We will see the way in which ethical schools of thought each have their strengths in terms of what we know about the mind and body.

I propose that all ethical deliberation is good deliberation. All the schools of ethical deliberation involving self-examination, reasoned calculation, use of the higher brain, the search for universal principles, inculcation in the nonviolent prosocial emotions (such as compassion) over the violent emotions— all of these approaches become constructive for ethical growth. They all contribute toward a healthy evolution of the human mind toward less violence, more just relations, and the mitigation of impulsive retreats into anger and fear-based actions. The less moral deliberation within ourselves, however, the less debate between ourselves and others, the more prone we become to the baser instincts of fear, paranoia, impulsivity, and authoritarian blind obedience. This is where all manner of crimes become attractive, habit-forming, and even construed as morally righteous.

The Embrace of Respect and the Dignity of Complexity

One objection both political extremism and religious fundamentalism often raise against an approach of complexity to ethics involves the charge of "moral relativism." It is argued that considering more than one moral point of view as possibly valid is to compromise the truth, it is to shake patriotism, and it is to dilute loyalty to a single way of acceptable being or acting. But an embrace of multiple ethical schools of thought, of ethical dilemmas and deliberations, is not a nihilistic, relativist surrender to confusion. On the contrary, it is an embrace of respect for the human mind, an embrace of the value of all people's opinions, and a sharpening of our capacity to manage moral complexity in new and changing circumstances. It is also a critical way to clarify and even deepen one's own moral commitments. Exploring differences not only builds tolerance, it can also build a deeper and more substantial set of moral and spiritual commitments.

Engaging multiple schools of ethical deliberation represents an embrace of time-tested wisdom, which leads to complex thinking, entertainment of multiple moral emotions, flexibility, and productive deliberation. This has led, at various points in history, to less violence, more justice, more altruism, more compassion, and more happiness for all, *even when there were serious ethical dilemmas that could not be resolved.* Considering multiple points of view on ethical dilemmas is the surest way to make us better ethically, to make our minds more self-controlled, more disciplined, more able to listen to others and live with them in peace and mutual respect. Those who can entertain and understand multiple ethical positions generate less violence and cycles of revenge, and in neuroscience terms, they live more in the neocortex and less imprisoned in the brain stem and amygdala.

There is another important way to see the advantage of diversity in ethical discourse and conclusions. Fundamentalism and authoritarianism tend to distort moral discussions by demonizing differences, especially despising outlier positions getting in the way of pure obedience.[20] In doing so, they betray their true intention—not ethical betterment, but authoritarian obedience. What people share in common is suppressed, and what makes them different becomes a clarion call of conflict in order to divide, to despair, and to conquer.

For example, when everyone in society agrees all life, regardless of religion or color, must be valued and protected, but there is disagreement on when precisely life begins, then you are already in 99 percent agreement over most ethical behavior. True valuation of all life makes you come to broadly similar conclusions on many issues of care for others, as well as a broad range of human rights. But when your goal is not the value of life as an ethical value but the value of obedience for control, you tend to search for what divides, for what threatens obedience. True deliberation over ethics freely engaged in by as many people as possible will reveal far more in common that binds most people to common values, despite places of disagreement.

We can educate ourselves and educate our children to imagine each other as moral agents with far more in common than where we differ. With greater training, we can focus the mind's eye on what we have in common, and this training can prevent our fragmentation and vulnerability to demagoguery and division—demagoguery from within, and destructive interference from without. Armed with a recognition of each other as moral agents, and equipped with a less polarized and hateful psyche, we can learn the art of principled compromise.

A neuroscience lens on ethical choices, studying each school of ethical thinking in terms of its healthful cognitive parallels, demonstrates the deeper unity of the mind and heart, reason and emotion, when it comes to reflecting on goodness. It will help us also respect our differences as we comprehend the inherent moral worth of a variety of progressive and conservative theoretical positions. We will also learn to hammer out compromises in practice that embrace the diversity of our values.

Debating goodness should be seen as an activity of the higher mind that all our cultures, at their best, can model. Society-wide respectful debates on goodness will lessen existing problems of moral relativism and chaos, problems that stem from out-of-control political tribalism, not the diversity of opinions. Instead of seeing diverse schools of ethical thought as a threat to morality or as embracing relativism, the study of all of them will put us into a higher unity of commitment to *ethics and ethical reflection itself as a civic duty (and a sacred duty for religious people)*. This kind of moral practice and joint reflection strengthens the higher brain function of the prefrontal cortex and pushes us away from the "fight or flight" instincts of the brain stem, and even farther from the regressive, infantilized reactions of obedience to demagogues and charlatans. This in itself will prove to be a major victory for personal and collective morality, even when we disagree on some issues.

Even when we disagree on thorny ethical problems, the very act of joint reflection and debate steers participants away from the most destructive anti-ethics of the human psyche, namely the fear, hatred, and contempt of neighbors, of fellow citizens. Hatred of the other is a basic danger stemming from the amygdala and is ameliorated by the calming effects of prefrontal cortex reflection and self-examination. Reflection and debate in the context of humble respect, when done well, preempts the angry spirit of fear and rage, as well as the infantilized need to be obedient to an angry overlord. It also is an essential prerequisite to care for the self and care for others.

2

The Theory and Practice
of Compassionate Reasoning

In this chapter I will introduce a theory and practice of *Compassionate Reasoning*. I want to build this step-by-step as a critical tool of personal change, conflict resolution, and peacebuilding. I will map this out first as a tool for the mind, second as a tool for personal behavior, third for society and social change, and fourth for transforming the earth.

Operational Definitions of *Compassion* and *Empathy*

Let us begin with the base of the tool: compassion. I define *compassion* for the purposes of this book as the following: thoughts, feelings, and actions that express a joyous, abundant care and love for persons or other sentient beings. This sentiment and practice is often expressed in the most universal and expansive terms as applying to everyone. In that sense, compassion is radically prosocial in thought, emotion, and practice.

Compassion, as I am defining it, is *not* the same as *empathy*, which I am defining for the purposes of our inquiry as feeling the pain of specific others, feeling sadness at the sadness of specific people. This is a reaction that does not necessarily extend empathy to everyone. I will explain below the important distinction of empathy and compassion in terms of brain science, and why that distinction is central to the psychosocial approach, the ethical path, and conflict resolution methodology I am outlining in this book. "Empathy" is a term used interchangeably with compassion in common usage, and in addition there is literature in psychology that also uses it with a different definition than I am using here (Lanzoni 2018). Lanzoni's *Empathy: A History* offers a detailed analysis of how empathy has been defined and redefined within the field of psychology. A definition of empathy emerging from her text is "*affective resonance* with the others' feelings and *to become cognitively aware of his* [sic] *situation* (italics in her original text, p. 276)." My purpose

Compassionate Reasoning. Marc Gopin, Oxford University Press. © Oxford University Press 2022.
DOI: 10.1093/oso/9780197537923.003.0002

here is to make a plain distinction between the neural pathways of what is called "empathic distress" versus the neural pathways of compassion, evidence for which I will outline shortly.

This distinction of compassion from empathic distress is critical for the theme of the book. A central challenge of social change is to make change-makers healthier, more sustainable, and more transformational. This is accomplished through a crucial emotional path *away* from personal distress and its contagious effects and *toward* a joyous embrace of and service to others. That pathway is what we are exploring in this book.

The experience of empathy, as I have observed it among peacemakers and victims in conflict zones, is very specifically directed, intense, and targeted toward specific persons and moments in time. Empathy is a feeling in these circumstances, *not practice or action*. It is specific to certain others and not generalized to humanity. Compassion, by contrast, is generalized and geared toward behavior and interaction with others. Compassion is a pervasive positive feeling leading to practice and to behaviors that emanate from those feelings. Empathy can be intensely sad, whereas compassion is often happy. Empathy is often painful, while compassion is joyous. Empathy leads often to withdrawal and isolation, whereas compassion is engaging and loving.

As I have witnessed and experienced it in decades of peacebuilding, empathy seems to be involuntary, seizing the subject who experiences it, whereas compassion can sometimes be involuntary but is just as often rooted in training, practice, and intentionality. Both empathy and compassion can lead to moral acts of care for others, but the two phenomena actually emanate from very different cognitive and emotional foundations and with very different neural pathways, as we will show. They also have distinguishable psychological and metabolic effects, such as on blood pressure. This will be important for understanding their respective effects on individual and collective efforts at peacebuilding and social change.

Sometimes empathy with the pain of others can paradoxically include its opposite, antipathy, namely a great hostility to others who have caused pain to chosen loved ones or to pitied strangers. Empathy does not necessarily extend universally, and it can be accompanied by strong feelings of hatred or desire for revenge. While it is a powerful motivator of ethical feelings and actions, (a) empathy can also be enervating since it is so focused on pain, and (b) it can generate anger, frustration, and even violence. Compassion, by contrast, has a joyful and grateful quality to it, making it harder to become an agent of violence.[1]

Operational Definition of *Reasoning*

I am defining *reasoning* in fairly standard philosophical terms as the process or faculty of logically inferring one thing from another, with *practical reasoning* referring to the use of that process or faculty for the sake of making decisions regarding behavior.[2] (More on *practical reasoning* below.)

Reasoning as a critical component of Compassionate Reasoning theory is also important for social network theory.[3] One of the great popularizers of social network theory has been Malcolm Gladwell (2002) in his classic text, *The Tipping Point.* Gladwell points to several key qualities that make for virality, that is, qualities of particular kinds of people who make things go viral. One such person he refers to as The Maven.

Maven is a Yiddish word that entered into the English language as a person who is an expert, but Gladwell makes it into a typology, a kind of person who makes it his/her business to know everything about everything, or how to get anything done, including finding a bargain.

The Yiddish word *maven* comes from the Hebrew word *may-vin. May-vin* means to understand in a deep way. The concept has a much more noble history than simply Gladwell's bargain hunter. In ancient rabbinic literature, one of the key intellectual qualities that makes for a righteous and wise human being, a scholar—that is, the highest spiritual person in rabbinic Judaism—is the person who is a *"may-vin davar mi'tokh davar,"* literally a person who derives one thing from the other, or who understands one thing from *within* another. This is not explained exactly, but in several sources it refers to erudite knowledge of the deep secrets of the universe.[4] It alludes to a notion that all knowledge is related and that all things can be derived from basic and deep truths about the world. This meaning of *may-vin* has important parallels to reasoning in the philosophical sense, seeing deeply into one phenomenon, into one observation or text or truth, in such an insightful and logical way that it leads to a deep understanding of another phenomenon, on and on, in an ever-deepening pattern of acquiring the wisdom of the universe.

Our goal here is to work on an operational definition of Compassionate Reasoning that leads to the practical paths of peacebuilding and social change that we have outlined. But we need to do this in a way that can traverse the boundaries dividing cultures and societies. Compassionate Reasoning must be effective across many cultural and national divides, offering a path that can bond people together, not tear them apart or oppress them.

We will explore further on the nature and applications of Compassionate Reasoning as a tool of personal wisdom, personal transformation, and social transformation. We will explore why and how the combination of compassion and reasoning into one practice of Compassionate Reasoning makes sense, in terms of integrating many reason-based approaches to ethics into an applied method of decision-making. We will also investigate an important parallel process of combining psychological and neuroscientific insights into both compassion and reasoning, and how (a) ethics, (b) traditional wisdom, and (c) neuroscience, when taken together, can make for powerful allies to move the human psyche in the direction of less violence and more prosocial behavior.

Operational Definition of *Practical Reasoning*

The cultivation of Compassionate Reasoning is the key to a less violent planetary future, depending upon the positive participation of both conservative and progressive communities, secular and religious communities, in every society. Every community has distinctive patterns of "practical reasoning." By this I mean their own cognitive and ethical conceptions of the world, and their own way to implement prosocial moral feelings and values. Let me explain this through my conceptual definition of *practical reasoning*.

Practical reasoning, for the purposes of our deliberations, is conceptually defined as those aspects of the mind involved in reflecting on (1) what is real and what is true, and (2) what plans can be implemented in order for a person, persons, or the world to move from point A to point B, situation A to situation B. Whereas *compassion* is a state of cognition focusing on a joyous and loving feeling to care and be kind to others, *reasoning* concentrates on how acts of care can happen practically in a challenging, complicated, and sometimes very dangerous world.

In order to better explore Compassionate Reasoning, we will specifically delve into several areas of human inquiry, including philosophical ethics as well as contemporary psychology and neuroscience. Human communities will need to collaborate across religious lines as well. Religions across the world have a vast reservoir of practices that can either enhance reasoning and deepen compassion or suffocate them, all depending on their interpretations. Thus, advancing communications between religions and within religions on ethics, reasoning, and compassion is a crucial parallel process to secular exploration of Compassionate Reasoning. These processes will ultimately need to be in dialogue.[5]

Definition of *Compassionate Reasoning*

Having defined both compassion and practical reasoning, I want to hone in on a new construction that I am calling Compassionate Reasoning, which assumes the definition of compassion that I stated above. Therefore, I will purposely use "compassion," previously defined, as part of this definition. *I define "Compassionate Reasoning" as compassionate thoughts, experiences, and habitual practices leading the mind toward higher practical reasoning about ethical principles that can maximize compassion in one's own life and in earthly existence.* The deeply rooted human feeling of compassion motivates the mind to consider practical reasoning regarding how to implement compassion in the entire world, and not just for one's immediate loved ones. Practical reason guides us to how to maximize compassion in one's personal, family, and community life. This is a move toward principles, meaning that the mind is led by the experience and habit of compassion to a practical search for applied principles that apply universally.

This is the quality of practical reasoning in search of universal principles for ethical treatment of all sentient beings. In other words, the cultivation of feelings of compassion and actions of compassion leads the mind toward a search for *how compassion for all can be maximized* (in the consequentialist sense of ethical choice[6] that we will examine later) and also *how compassion can be universalized as a duty to all* (in the Kantian sense of ethical choice[7]). Both of these pathways, consequentialist and Kantian, lead toward the search for universal applications of compassion.

A compassion that is overflowing and deeply meditated upon tends to lead to repeated compassionate actions; then those actions and habits lead toward a desire to see more and more of it in the world. Repeated thoughts and actions turn into habits, and thus we can speak of habits of compassion generalized into a way of being, a way of relating to the world as a whole. The more a person indulges in compassionate feelings and actions, the more that these feelings, thoughts, intentions, and actions tend to extend outward to all.

The most important point is that this extension of compassion to all supports the mind's search—based on reason—for universal ethical principles and commitments, as well as political constructs that can enshrine compassion in sustainable institutions. Compassion leads the mind naturally to use reasoning to employ moral principles that can apply compassion to oneself and to all beings. This extension to all is also emotionally contagious, in the sense that compassion instigates compassion in others who are recipients or witnesses.[8] This contagion makes it far easier to go from an individual's compassionate habit and experience to reasoning and collaborating with others on universal principles and commitments.

Compassionate Reasoning therefore constitutes:

(1) the cultivation of a state of mind;
(2) a mode of ethical practice;
(3) an ethical practice, through repetition and habit, leading one's own mind toward a search to establish universal moral norms;
(4) a way of reasoning that calculates how compassion can be extended to the most people through the structures of one's own life, one's community, and the structure of society itself;
(5) a social contagion inducing others to give and receive compassion; and
(6) a social contagion leading to reasoned debate and the calculation of universal principles of compassion.

The experience and practice of compassion often leads the mind to build principles for compassion that can be applied to all sentient life, not just humans. The mind, influenced by the moral sense and experience of compassion, then uses reasoning to apply those feelings toward building universal principles for treatment of all people and even all of nature.

This extension of logic and prosocial feeling interacts naturally with a host of stubborn challenges facing a diverse, divided, and conflicted world. We have always lived in a world where resources are scarce, accidents are many, and the unknown future induces uncertainty and anxiety. But with the help of a disciplined mind and heart, compassion combined with reasoning leads toward less violent and more sustainable paths of collective survival and even flourishing. We will also see later that the Compassionate Reasoning combination flourishes only with habit formation that is crucial for neural pathways and ethical habits of thinking, feeling, and doing.

The move from feelings to intentions, from emotions to will and intentions for the world, is essentially what Kant referred to as a "good will" that forms the bedrock foundation of Kant's enormously influential school of ethics; this means the will and intention to extend good in all directions. Compassionate Reasoning as a theory is proposing that the feeling or moral sense of compassion—when it is cultivated and habituated by thought and action—is critical as a support for the Kantian concept of a good will that desires to treat all human beings the same. This is the intention to treat people as ends, not only as means, and to insert ethical principles into a conflicted and divided world. This is why Kant, the great philosopher associated so often with ethics as a rationally constructed duty, was in fact deeply affected by the rather sentimental writings of Jean-Jacques Rousseau. Kant knew that prosocial sentiments for humanity, such as compassion, are essential for building a good will for universal commitments (Cavallar 2014). A person needs to wish kindness for everyone as a step toward exercising the higher mind to build policies and principles that apply to everyone.

I am arguing in this book for a path combining the mind's emotional capacity for compassionate feelings and actions *together* with the mind's rational capacity for reason-based will and behavior. With proper guidance, one leads to the other in a steady direction that combines what traditionally and allegorically was referred to as "heart, mind, and body."

The Feeling of Compassion and the Process of Reasoning Increase the Likelihood of Peaceful Means and Outcomes

Let us now introduce the next crucial step of this scaffold. A careful combination of the science of the mind, neuroscience, while also drawing upon the wisdom of a variety of schools of philosophical ethics, establishes an interesting alliance. The combination suggests that the cultivation of the human will to develop universal principles of reason for ethics is connected to prosocial emotions, especially compassion. Positive emotions and the mind's evolution of principles of reason are inextricably related. A combination of (a) compassionate feelings and behaviors with (b) reason's development of universal principles is the only sure way to achieve a less violent world shared by all, regardless of race or creed. Let me explain why this is the case.

Human beings are constantly competing for scarce resources, and we get embroiled in a great variety of conflicts, sometimes reaching tragic proportions. Negative emotions, such as fear, greed, and jealousy, push the mind to only violent solutions of scarce resource challenges. But prosocial emotions, such as compassion, love, and hope, induce the mind to search for new approaches to survival and flourishing, as well as toward trust, solidarity, and shared enterprises with fellow human beings. There exists, then, a kind of competition between emotions in terms of best paths to survival. But reasoning tends to prompt the mind to rules of rational engagement in order to flourish with others, and thus aligns itself closely with the prosocial emotions.

A combination of compassion and reason can be and often is the genesis of political reflection and debate around the best nonviolent solutions to our struggles with each other. As we struggle with each other about rational rules of coexistence, it is compassionate understanding and engagement that gives the mind the bandwidth to move toward understanding the others with whom we are in competition or in outright conflict over principles of living, of governance, of commerce, and much more. A true understanding of conflict management and resolution must devolve into forging an alliance between compassion and universal reasoning in the search for common ethics, principles, and policies.

The more compassion is cultivated, the greater the possibility that competition becomes healthy and constructive as people search for shared principles. But when compassion is absent, rational debate often degenerates into a stubborn, arrogant, and narcissistic "winner-take-all" struggle. This is the most important reason that Adam Smith, the father of capitalism and a champion of the virtues of economic competition, was also one of the major intellectual enthusiasts of compassion-based moral sense theory.[9] The only way that the competition for scarce resources can proceed *without* descending into a Hobbesian state of war of all against all[10] is through the cultivation of compassion from an early age, so the argument goes, and where I completely agree with him. Only in this way does competition for scarce resources not descend into greed and barbarism. Capitalism *without* the requisite cultivation of compassion at every level of engagement leads to barbaric and hateful philosophies of so-called social Darwinism (unfair to Darwin) that rationalize the death of the many by suffering so that the few can flourish. This eventuality in turn prompts violent revolutionary and counter-revolutionary spirals of chronic warfare, as has been proven over many histories across global cultures. Absurd binaries of vulture capitalist private ownership versus Communist destruction of all ownership become attractive in a violent and fearful atmosphere of class struggle and identity-based hatreds.

The proper cultivation of compassion, by contrast, leads the mind—*and the body politic by extension*—toward healthy competition coupled with profound collaborative commitments embraced by the compassionate citizen. A compassionate citizen, for example, is eager to pay taxes for the sake of the common good and the common welfare, hence the word "commonwealth" as a designation for the good society. The compassionate citizen sees the common good as a place to practice cultivated compassion in the largest possible venue, literally with everyone that she or he will ever meet. Cultivated compassion depresses self-destructive instincts of endless fear and conflict within society and war with those in other societies; hence the notion of the "commonwealth of nations" as an ideal to be achieved.

Why Compassion Is Superior to Empathy

Let us explore compassion further from the perspective of science of the mind, in order to demonstrate compassion's centrality to building a theory of personal moral change and society-wide moral change. A psychological analysis of the evolution of nonviolent human ethics was gathered into an exhaustive study in recent years, with the aim of isolating the most essential elements of moral behavior that lead to a less violent society (Pinker 2007, 2011a). This analysis discovered the prevalence of compassion as the most important emotion for ethical feelings and actions that leads to less violence, and this held true across cultures and societies.

Empathy with pain, as I described earlier, has its virtues also, and it does help us to be ethical. In fact, if more people of wealth and power had more empathy, then many global and domestic problems would be immeasurably improved. Stabilizing social justice initiatives and laws would be an automatic outgrowth of empathy with the pain of the less fortunate by the powerful few. Indeed, this has happened to some degree several times in the history of democracies, such as the rise of the laws of the welfare state and the New Deal after the Great Depression. The welfare state of the 1930s was also preceded by decades of voluntary efforts to liberate care for the poor, which translated into social and religious movements of social responsibility. This is where the creative of progressive religious communities in one generation can strengthen the body politic that can turn compassionate moral gestures into essential public services, such as Social Security, unemployment benefits and more, all referred to as a social safety net. [11]

The 1920s with all of its conspicuous greed and corruption led to a defining turning point, a crash and an utter defeat for social Darwinist approaches to greed and power.[12] Thus, the earlier American social movements for the poor and the downtrodden led—fortunately in the nick of time—to broad reforms in America, forestalling the extremes of both fascism and communism in the 1930s and 1940s that were sweeping Europe. Empathy leads to excellent social policies that are both stabilizing and just (Gault and Sabini 2000).

Empathy has many problems, however. In addition to how narrowly we can feel empathy for some and not others, and how overly specified pain identification can become, it is also the case that it is destructive to feel the pain of others for great lengths of time. It debilitates and depresses (Smith and Rose 2011), and it may sour people on positive social change when they are exposed constantly to the pain of others.

There is also another problem. Some violent people actually have a great capacity for empathy but use it badly. Predators can have empathy to the degree to which they use an empathic understanding of victims *in order to destroy their victims*, often with great acumen. It pains me greatly whenever I think that in World War II the Nazi regime collaborated with many anthropologists to understand the Jewish community empathically—in order to break them and destroy their spirit (Schafft 2004). The use and abuse of psychology for interrogation and torture involves the same "skill."[13]

Empathy with pain can be abused. Compassion, however, is the experience of empathy *plus* an intense identification with the other that results in thoughts *and* actions of kindness, benevolence, solidarity, and joyous care. It seems harder to hijack compassionate actions for violent purposes than it is to do the same with empathic feelings or cognitions.

The Nature of Compassion Contrasted with Empathy

Turning now to explain the roots of compassion and how it can be strengthened, the biochemical and neurological foundations of compassion are not so simple to isolate. Classical moral sense theory (Blackburn 2016) and many a religious tradition sang the virtues of compassion and emphasized the importance of habits of compassion for thousands of years, but we still do not have a full picture of it in the brain. Some have posited a particular kind of neuron referred to as "mirror neurons" as the basis of compassion, but this is not conclusive. Mirror neurons explain much of the human and animal tendency to copy each other and mimic each other which is critical for socialization, but this does not yield the results always of compassionate feelings and moral actions (Pinker 2011b). Others have searched for particular neurotransmitters that seem to be especially associated with compassion, such as oxytocin.

At the same time, empathy with pain by itself has *not* been shown to be enough to develop the moral human being who is capable of being peaceful, for the simple reason that empathy for some and not others is often a *catalyst* for violence rather than an inhibitor. Sometimes the more empathy I feel only for my own family, group, or nation, the more deeply I feel the injustice to them, and the more violence I wish upon their enemy. I have lived these feelings myself and been part of many communities where the intense pain of the tortured others from the community, the empathy that this evokes, does lead to collective rage and a desire for justice that includes use of force. Often deep empathy with pain propels the motivation for wars in endless cycles, so that fellow soldiers and victims "would not die in vain."

If Empathy Has Antisocial Potential, Then Social Change Movements' Fixation on It Is Mistaken

Empathy with pain, empathic distress, is thus not the critical factor in creating the peaceful person—or the good society. Sometimes empathy is, quite the contrary, a heavy contributor to polarization, exchanges of rage and demonization, and cycles of violence. Yet most progressive political mobilization in modern times, which often has the stated intention to make a more compassionate society or a more compassionate foreign policy, tends to focus on making us feel radical empathy with certain victims. The mobilization campaigns and fundraising frames focus on citizens feeling deep pain and even horror as others suffer. Feeling the pain of victims is a premium, and it is the preeminent form of fundraising and motivation, working on our guilt, making us angry enough to "do something." I want to suggest that this has been wrong-headed. Empathic distress sums up most advertising and promotion for thousands of peace, development, and human rights organizations. Yet this engendering of painful empathy may produce the wrong results, such as depression and despair for activists or witnesses, but also a polarizing anger at those causing the pain of those you see as innocent. This has led to depression and burnout of countless activists, but also a backlash from those who are demonized as the oppressors.

By contrast, compassion as a motivator, together with the reasoning it engenders in the formation of reformed policies, tends to build motivation from a more joyous emotional foundation (Breines and Chen 2012; Friedman and Gerstein 2017). Compassionate action is self-reinforcing and sustainable, and also far more useful in building bridges across polarizing political divides. Compassion prepares the path to develop reasonable policies that can be agreed upon by as many citizens as possible in any given civilization.

Yet our efforts at social change and peacebuilding have not internalized the fact that empathy leading to rage is not constructive and rather builds massive burnout and massive backlash. We seem to have a habit in the name of peace to build dramatic polarization that leads to the opposite of peace and justice. Without proper understanding of, training in, and commitment to habits of Compassionate Reasoning, we tend to undo our best intentions for the realization of peace and justice.

Compassion Needs Reason to Develop Personal and Collective Self-Control through the Evolution of Principles

Compassion left to itself, however, does not push the brain far enough toward creating less violence and more peace in a complicated world. *For compassion to embed itself in the mind and generate civilized nonviolent life, reasoning is essential. It is reason that transforms positive emotions into internal principles, and it is reason that moves principles into a social phenomenon of people collectively advocating for laws that apply to all.* In other words, the mind, influenced by compassionate feelings, wishes, and habits, moves toward the search for internal, self-regulating rules that expand compassion into a personal and social program. Along the lines of the teachings of philosophical ethicists from Aristotle to Kant, as well as religious traditions, this direction of the mind from compassion to reason is first and foremost a search for rules that apply to all equally, or an embrace of the Golden Rule. This then leads to compassionate and reasonable actors joining forces in an ever-expanding social and political evolution that can be called the social contract or the good society.

It has also been demonstrated time and again that self-control is the core of mental health (Black, Semple, Pokrhel, and Grenard 2011). Thus, from cultural wisdom traditions to philosophy to the sciences, there is a critical role of self-control and self-regulation in the process of creating *internal law*.[14] For the religious person, these are laws commanded or inspired by sacred traditions and leaders, or inspired by emulation of a sacred being, such as God or the Buddha or a saint or a prophet. With or without emulation of ideal beings, *the critical step for the mind in its direction toward nonviolence is a law that is internalized and self-regulating*. It is in this way that we move from habitual feelings and intentions of compassion for others toward rules about how I ought to behave or not behave to *all* people. The mind moves from positive compassionate feelings and actions toward others to a higher brain thought process reflecting on actions and deciding what I will do and what I will not do, what I will *always try to do* and what I will *try to never do*; this is internalized negative and positive law.

The embedding of compassionate feelings and habits that generate reasonable principles in our minds and in our social constructs does not happen automatically. Rather, it takes habit formation, great training, in which only some people and some family units engage (Grusec 2011). It is essential for the good person and the good society to move from positive feelings to habits and training for internalized rules that govern our way of thinking; these become like a foundation bedrock of society.

This way of thinking proves stronger with practice and training to overcome constant triggers to our fear and rage that happen in everyday life, and especially during times of great deprivation or danger. Deprivation, danger, and perception of danger are an ever-present stimulus to our amygdala, our lower brain stem. This stimulus is a primordial necessity of survival, but it is also a problematic space of automatic response to perceived dangers. When compassion leads to internal rules, and when those rules become hardened by habit into principles that give life ultimate meaning, it then becomes harder and harder for anger and fear to undo these bedrock foundations of personality.

Ultimately, however, even such great internal rules cannot keep all human beings good in all circumstances, especially when the human mob becomes agitated by fear. In order to protect against the ravaging effects of mass hysteria or paranoia, the internal rules many good people conceive and live by must lead, with the aid of reason, to *externalized* rules, to transformative *public laws*. This is the essential move from ethical constructs to political constructs. That is why we all need the good society, the commonwealth, to be a space governed by unshakeable rules of the good, even when we do not want to be good.

The move from personal ethical constructs to political legal constructs can only happen through engagement with others, through powers of political persuasion, brainstorming, and constructive debate. This necessary move from the ethical to the political must have a clear commitment to adhere to ethical principles as much as possible, as one moves necessarily to compromise with others. Thus, compromise is sometimes a danger to universal ethical principles—but compromise itself, and the peace that comes with it, is also essential to ethics. This is a paradox that must be engaged. There is no peace without compromise; compromise with others is, in fact, an ethical rule in and of itself for the sake of peaceful relations. But compromise as an ethical practice does involve complex calculations that the higher human brain must continually undertake.

From Internal Self-Controls to External Obedience and the Rule of Law

This leads to another crucial step of the scaffolding we have built of the ethical person and the ethical society. Externalized laws are the essential next step in generating less violent societies through an important neural pathway: the interaction of law, obedience to authority, and the human mind. To generate compassion-based external laws applicable to all is to fix those laws back into the human mind through obedience to external law.

Human beings in groups are radically prone to obedience, and this has destroyed many societies (Janis 1972). In fact, overcoming populist obedience to demagogues and dictators is perhaps the most central challenge of the good society. Compassionate Reasoning as an internalized capacity is designed as much as possible to make the human being less prone to the manipulations of demagogues and their corrosive impact on the individual's moral capacity.

Nevertheless, obedience is a core human tendency, and we must see ways to utilize it to embed compassion and reinforce it. I am proposing a very different and redeeming side of our tendency to obedience. I am suggesting that there is a subtle and profound use of obedience that has actually liberated human beings throughout history from (a) the tyranny of others and (b) the tyranny of their own worst impulses. It is obedience to the rule of compassionate law, understood in a particular way, that I will frame. Let me explain this in greater detail.

A rule that I feel embedded in me, forged in my cultivated habits of thinking and doing, is a culminating victory over tyranny, the expression of true freedom for the individual and her good will. This was Kant's great aspiration for the "categorical imperative" and its liberating effect on the mind.[15] For most of us, internalized rules need to be externalized into social and public rules we habitually obey. Most of us are not strong enough to act on internal rules alone, as we are too prone to social conventions and peer pressure. We search too much for external sources of authority, and this is when we dangerously invest too much hope and power into human leadership. This is how we tragically succumb to demagoguery or authoritarian unjust systems.

We can manage collectively and democratically, however, to make compassionate universal laws into the laws of the state, the laws of the land. We can then enshrine these laws with enforcement—such as, for example, legally enforced tithing for the poor in the Bible, or taxes in modern society for universal healthcare, or anti-discrimination and anti-hate laws. *Then the rule of law makes external obedience to authority into an ally of compassion rather than an enemy.* Obedience to the rule of law is essential for the survival of any social contract and any society. It is also true that a tendency toward obedience is a powerful human trait with disastrous consequences due to its essential role in totalitarianism and genocidal behavior (Milgram 1974). But obedience to universal moral laws, especially when internalized, is a powerful ally of peace, violence prevention, and justice. Compassionate Reasoning can thus generate prosocial internalized commitments that lead to externalized universal laws that commit us to external obedience to compassionate universal laws.

Ideally, we want people to come to thoughts such as this: We *want* to pay taxes to help everyone with their health. In this way we satisfy our tendency to obedience through obedience to external democratic law, but exactly *not* obedience to authoritarians, rather only to universally fair law. *Obedience to fair law is the ultimate liberation of the body politic, as well as the individual's good will.*

Liberating Obedience and the Human Mind

Obedience to good laws is the culmination of a neurological system, a set of thought and feeling patterns that move from compassion to internal universal laws, and from there to obedience to the rule of law. *This enshrines compassion not only in our higher feelings but also in our lower brain stem that craves obedience to parental figures as a way to protect us from danger.* This is the true victory of human rights and democracy inside the human psyche. We use higher reasoning, but we do not depend on its everyday function since so many of us cannot stay in that realm of higher reasoning. (We would rather run that red light when no one is looking!) *With (a) practice in compassion, (b) cultivation of internal laws that we decide firmly to live by, and (c) our lower brain afraid to break democratically agreed-upon laws, we are then ready to create and solidify the good society.*

This model draws, then, on external obedience and the pressures of the lower brain stem. Thus, our prosocial feeling centers of the brain, our higher brain's functioning of reasoning, *and* our lower brain stem, all work *in tandem* "to do the right thing," to obey internal external laws of goodness and decency and thus create the good citizen and the good society.

We move from (1) contemplation upon and practice of compassion and compassionate habits, to (2) the generation of reason-based internal laws applied to everyone, to (3) external laws applied to all, to (4) obedience that stimulates the lower brain further into a reinforcing cycle of reason and compassion, from the neocortex all the way to the brain stem. Enforced rule of law completes the circle of higher and lower brain cooperation in embedding universal and compassionate laws into the entire human personality.

Correcting Limitations of the Enlightenment Paradigm: Habits of the Whole Mind

There is a more solid path to society-wide enlightenment that was not fulfilled by the Enlightenment philosophers. The Enlightenment pointed the way, but it did not enforce deeply enough inside the citizen a full higher and lower brain commitment to nonviolent compassionate citizenship. Today we can choose to educate ourselves and our minds into neural pathways reinforced in the whole mind, both in the higher mind and the more primitive mind. This requires constant education and reinforcement.[16]

Habits are not popular in intellectual and academic circles. They are not higher brain intellectual activities, and therefore elite forms of education now and in the past have tended to underestimate their importance. But habits are central to the formation of a well-regulated mind and heart. Educated people tend to overestimate their capacities to act reasonably, especially their capacities to remain independent moral agents. For nonviolence to embed itself in human behavior, a whole-brain approach is essential. Self-control is a critical human capacity associated with higher reason, and it is strongly associated with various parts of the neocortex, especially as they regulate and control the amygdala, the latter being most associated with "fight and flight," fear and violence (MacLean et al. 2014). But this self-control is based on a necessary process of habit formation and repetition of compassion that is consistently underestimated in intellectual formations of education and civil society.

Here is the essential point: The less violent person, and the peaceful society that she/he aspires to make, requires a subtle combination of compassion education, reason education, and habits of obedience to the common good. These taken together are critical for the generation of the peaceful human being who conceives and adheres to universally applied ethical principles. This is the good person who calculates his/her ethical actions with prudence, caution, and a careful attention to all possible consequences, but also with an embedded commitment internally and externally to universal, enlightened law based on compassion.

Compassionate Reasoning, the Enlightenment, and the Classical Schools of Ethics

A synchronicity of compassion and reasoning has its exact parallel in the history of ethical philosophy. Let me explain how, but first I must add a crucial critique of the European Enlightenment. The Enlightenment was a pivotal moment in the history of human evolution in which Western civilization was turned upside down by unprecedented scientific discoveries and empirical investigations never before experienced by the human species. This led to a reconsideration of everything about the human being and humanity as a whole. The Enlightenment had profound effects as well on our evaluation of and recommendations for human behavior, in other words, our ethics. All thinkers of the Enlightenment came out of civilizations steeped in religious traditions, yet the Enlightenment itself was severely in tension with fundamentalist or anti-scientific dogmas and worldviews dedicated to religious particularism.

So far, so good. But despite rebellious and independent origins, Enlightenment thinkers had many embedded biases, as it turned out, particularly toward non-European and non-Christian peoples (Bouie 2018). These biases call into question the alleged universal commitments of the Enlightenment. The *intention* of universality in ethical commitments accomplished a great deal, but the scope of its extension *in practice* failed in many cases (Kellner 2019). At the same time, the effects of Enlightenment thinking on ethics was to rededicate a commitment to searching for *universal* approaches to ethics, to human goodness, to universal responsibilities and rights that apply to every single person regardless of skin color, religion, or background. This search was always present (even if hypocritically applied) in classical ethical traditions from Greece, but the Enlightenment placed particular emphasis on universal principles that paralleled universal rules of science. Liberal religious ethicists of the Enlightenment followed a similar path in Jewish and Christian philosophy (Moore 1912).

There are interesting parallels between the evolution of this universalist trend in philosophical ethics, religious ethics, and today's neuroscience and psychology. By definition, the quest to map the brain's capacities is a search for absolute universality, a way to learn what applies to all human minds— what are the neural pathways for compassion, for example, that would be seen in a functional magnetic resonance imaging or functional MRI (fMRI) of anyone on the planet. These parallels of brain research and normativity, neuroscience, and ethics, hold the seeds for a new alignment of viewpoints between philosophy and psychology on the ethics of violence reduction. There is a common search between science and ethics for what applies to all human beings, and this aligns with our search for what is Compassionate Reasoning and how it should be applied by human beings to the world.

The Schools of Ethics

Let us delve into the ethical schools of thought in order to explore the relationship between science, ethics, and Compassionate Reasoning. Five relevant schools of ethics include:

(1) moral sense theory,
(2) consequentialism/utilitarianism,
(3) virtue ethics or the ethics of character,
(4) natural morality or natural law theory, and
(5) deontology, or Kantian ethics.

All these schools were important to the development of modern global political institutions that arose out of the Enlightenment. All these schools together are, in part, responsible for the world of 2021 in which people of great diversity of religiosity and culture can sit around the table as equals in many societies across the earth, inside countless governmental and nongovernmental agencies, and in millions of businesses. This was not the case not too long ago, and there is indeed a global revolution of equality never seen before in these numbers. The earth is hardly completely equal today, and in many parts of the world there are gross injustices of authoritarianism and gross inequality. Nevertheless, never before have so many hundreds of millions of people been given *legal* equality in endless national and international institutions, despite their differences of religion, ethnicity, or skin pigmentation.

Moral Sense Theory

Moral sense theory, with its perception of prosocial emotions as the foundation of ethics—especially sympathy—has had a major influence and positive effect on universalizing human ethics beyond the differences of race, religion, and nation. Many theorists explaining the steady, centuries-long decline in Western Europe of murder rates and public torture suggest that the movement toward compassion for all, even the most difficult and dangerous human beings, culminated in the runaway success of who we may call "compassion" novelists, such as Dickens, Hugo, Clemens, and Proust.[17] Transformational moral empathy was provoked for the common person and for the complete stranger through the complete immersion experience of great novels. These novels shifted from a traditional focus on kings and queens and elites toward the common person. More should be studied in terms of establishing a causal connection between a transformation approach to empathy for strangers and immersion in select novels and films.[18]

This massive moral move led toward identification not with aristocratic elites, such as in Shakespeare. It was a move toward the poor and toward simple uneducated strangers. This led to legislation and democratic movements to lessen the violence of society as a whole, and to lessen the horror especially of abject poverty, slavery, and cruel punishment. This movement was particularly focused on those who were traditionally othered, such as the poor. It is true that divisions of race and nation became more prominent in the modern period as a competing illiberal trend that divided bitterly and caused ultimately deadly wars. But the average levels of domestic murder and violence continued to decline over time in a way that suggests a significant increase in compassion, self-control, and respect for law.

Consequentialism

Consequentialism and utilitarianism, pioneered especially by Jeremy Bentham, James Mill, and John Stuart Mill, had the effect of taking positive feelings of compassion for others to the next level of ethical practice, namely calculation of the maximization of happiness for all. Consequentialism was very different from moral sense theory, but the calculus of "the greatest happiness for the greatest number" was an expression of clear commitment to a compassionate, highly inclusive way to care for all people. Utilitarianism was not a contradiction to the importance of prosocial emotions, but it was suggesting a necessary rational focus on planning and anticipation, based on reasoning, that is designed to maximize good outcomes and good consequences for all. This moral calculus was intended to extend compassion to all citizens who experience happiness and suffering, even, for example, prisoners. This innovation of Bentham and the Utilitarians was new in European life and the opposite of rampant torture and abuse that still haunts prison systems across the world.

Utilitarianism explored what kind of rehabilitation of prisoners would reduce the most suffering and create the most happiness for all in society; it extended compassion to perpetrators as well as bystanders and victims. How different this was from thousands of years of sport watching prisoners incarcerated for the smallest of crimes and tortured to death in public! A concern for criminals was a mental and moral revolution in human history (Bentham [1791] 2020). Consequentialism championed human rights for all, including many who had been abhorred by society. This is how torture of prisoners came to be frowned upon. Put the way the Dalai Lama (2020) might express it in his ethics of compassion, utilitarianism's goal is the minimization of suffering for the greatest number of human beings.

As the West became more and more committed to this approach to ethics, the sentiments of compassion extended to all life. The prevention of animal suffering through rights legislation is seen already in Ireland in 1635, and in 1641 in the Mass Bay Colony, well before abolition of human slavery.[19] It seems that the evolution of compassionate feelings had a universal quality to it, extending to all sentient life, but it was tragically selective considering the lives and feelings of animals before the lives and feelings of African slaves, indentured servants, and certainly prisoners. Nevertheless, progress must be seen and studied for what it can teach us about how human beings become more compassionate, more self-controlled and less cruel.

Calculation

Classical utilitarianism encouraged a somewhat vaguely defined but morally motivated *calculus* to anticipate future consequences of our actions. By this I mean that it was a focus on weighing in the balance all the possible consequences of behavior and then inventing moral rules that led to the greatest happiness for the greatest number. This gets very complicated when you get into how to decide what exactly is "happiness" *and* how to measure it. This is an issue that has spawned an entire subfield of psychology today, and even legislation to promote happiness in several countries (Seligman and Csikszentmihalyi 2000).

This kind of calculation of consequences and inferences from present facts to future possibilities directly involves the critical role of higher brain functions and neural pathways, including the neocortex (Mumford 1991). But it also entails a certain prosocial human passion to bring happiness to oneself as well as to others. Thus, consequentialism assumes a certain passion for making oneself and others happy, and a moral sense of compassion is necessary for that. But then it leads reasoning through the calculus of the greatest happiness to the most people.

Virtue and Character Ethics

Virtue ethics or character ethics, from Aristotle to our own day, emphasizes that the focus of ethics should be more on developing character based on a series of virtues, and less on how to figure out what is moral in the given moment of choice. There is an implicit critique of what is often called "situational ethics," namely that it is difficult to anticipate the problems of each moment's moral choices in life due to the incredible complexity of each situation and countervailing principles or moral feelings that could be applied.

Character ethicists or virtue ethicists are aware of (a) the complexities of consequentialist calculus, (b) the contradictions of universal laws and norms, and (c) the way in which making decisions based on a feeling of compassion or other moral senses can sometimes lead to contradictory moral choices.

For all those reasons, virtue ethicists emphasize and prefer a steady life-long development of moral character as the best way to generate the good human being who makes good choices in entirely unpredictable situations of choice. This approach explores the cultivation of courage, honesty, balance in virtues, generosity, and many more traits, all achieved through study, reflection, training, and habit formation.

Natural Morality Theory

Natural morality or natural law theory embraces a presence in the natural world of the "good." It is a way of looking to the good in the natural world, and to the good in human nature as well, as a guide to what the moral "good" should be. This can also be referred to as intuitionism. It is a search into the nature of how humans and animals act in good ways in order to understand what the good should be. Following many wisdom traditions, it is an assertion also of searching one's conscience as a way to define what is good and what are good choices.

There is a certain kinship between this ethical school on the one side, and on the other, the fields of psychoanalysis, psychology, and neuroscience. They all focus on the study of human nature. This is a fruitful comparison for our purposes of developing a theory and practice of Compassionate Reasoning, despite the critique of Moore ([1903] 1922). Moore argued against what he called the "naturalistic fallacy" in ethics, by which he meant any attempt to define the word "good" in terms of some natural quality—that is, a naturally occurring property or state such as pleasure. Despite Moore's critique, wisdom traditions throughout history, as well as psychology research today, continue to search for an understanding of the good through what is found in human and animal nature, and what is in the mind (Haidt 2007). Also, the faith positions of millions of spiritual people coalesce in an ongoing commitment to the self's own search for what is "good." In other words, they search for the voice of the "higher self," the voice of conscience, or the soul. They search by way of processes of self-reflection, discernment, and social processes of confession, repent-ance, and penance.

All of this buttresses the idea that at least one source of discovering the good in this world can best be defined by "natural morality." Now, it is also true that what is considered "natural" and "good" varies to some degree from culture to culture, place to place, and time to time. This is another critical reason why "natural morality" as it appeared in Western literature has been critiqued as an unreliable, culturally biased guide for ethics. But I place this trend in ethics before us anyway because there persists, from the religiously faithful to the scientists, some significant drive to discern what human beings—in all their variety, to be sure—label as "good," and as "right." This is not a search for uniformity of definition of the "good," which will not be found, but for a way of thinking about ethics and practicing morality. We must at least keep this in mind, along with the other ethical schools, as we work in this book to define the best practices of Compassionate Reasoning. We must keep in mind that one very significant way in which the good in ethics has been defined as (a) the voice of the human conscience and (b) the ways in which ethics appear in the natural world, such as compassion and al-truism among animals (De Waal 2019; Wohlleben 2017).

Deontology

Finally, Immanuel Kant and the deontologists insisted that the truly unas-sailable good is "the good will" and the "categorical imperative." Many other seemingly positive phenomena, such as happiness, are not *unconditionally* good. They are not reliable as a source of the good, because when, for ex-ample, happiness is achieved with bad intentions and violent behavior, we do not call the results morally good. Only good intentions leading to a good will can be considered moral.

Morality, however, is a step-by-step process. The good will of the human mind with its capacity for reason formulates a set of strictly universal or "cat-egorical imperatives." Their essence is that they treat all human beings as ends in themselves, not means. Deontology argues for the discovery of universal principles that apply to all humans equally, emerging from the good will of the human being. This path from the good will to the categorical imperative is the *only way* to discover what is unconditionally "good," what is ethical.

From Enlightenment Ethics to the Revolutionary Evolution of International Human Rights

The path from these five approaches of ethics to the revolutionary international documents of civil and human rights emerging out of the Enlightenment period is long, circuitous, but recognizable. There are thousands of international human rights laws today, and this has been a complicated but unmistakable progression for the safety, security, and flourishing of billions of human beings. There has been much inconsistent thinking and not a small number of hypocritical lapses, but there is no doubt that modern Enlightenment ethics changed the way we all relate to each other across the globe today and across every culture and religion.

Enlightenment ethics have gone from mere ideas of erudite philosophy and penetrated the foundational law codes of the international civilization of today. Tens of thousands of domestic and international laws of human rights exist today that never existed before in human history, and these laws affect in some way almost every person on the planet, as well as all animals. These laws were consciously developed as universal imperatives and the means of universal governance that were anticipated by Kant's masterpiece, *Perpetual Peace*. The means of arrival at consensus on these documents involved many approaches to reasoning and moral argumentation, often drawing on several of these ethical schools of thought, but also on many wisdom cultures across the world by scholars representing many traditions (United Nations 2020).

The Psychological Impact of the Universal Human Rights Agenda

In my experience of over thirty years in war zones, working with survivors, and teaching, I can testify to the surprising and absolutely hypnotic effect of the human rights idea. From secular to fundamentalist, from simple to highly educated, from poor to privileged, people are entranced by these human rights traditions and ways of thinking (Pritchard 2007). These ways of thinking seem to be immensely compelling to the human mind across many cultures. This even applies to people I work with facing the worst possible disruptions of their existence and unimaginable loss. The ones who hate the death and destruction of war, whom I have come to know so well, the ones who fight only because they are up against the wall—they actually thirst the most for the alternative of a human rights-based society, a human rights conception of the world; they are even ready to fight and die for it. Some fight violently and some only nonviolently, but millions put themselves in harm's way in order to try to establish some kind of human rights-based governance.

Here is the remarkable thing that we must contemplate: Just as racist ideas are rather hypnotic to the human minds of many but have no basis in science, so it is the case that the concept of human rights itself is rather new in history and has no basis in reality, in nature itself. It is not a scientific idea but an assertion about what *should* be and a belief about what is right. The question is why was the idea of human rights so hypnotic? Why has it become an aspiration of billions of people to possess and assert their rights?

I would suggest that people have come to love human rights because we humans, over time, *willed it to become a tangible idea*. We willed it to become a part of reality, a cognitive and then a legal construct of our world. The idea of international regimes of human rights was a twinkle in the eye of writers like Grotius (Forde 1998), but once generated even in miniature form and incomplete form, human rights seemed to take on a life of its own. It had a powerful and hypnotic effect on our imaginations as human beings that has multiplied with each passing decade for the last couple of hundred years.

The Mind's Construct of Human Rights as an Embodiment of Compassionate Reasoning

The idea of human rights embodies Compassionate Reasoning. Human rights constitute a combination of compassionate intentions toward others, together with the reasoning it takes to imagine laws that should protect every one of us, regardless of gender, religion, race, or creed. The idea of human rights has become embedded in the human mind as an absolute good, as a commonsense institution embodying the idea of compassion for all, but evenly distributed by way of universal law. Human rights are not real in nature. There is nothing tangible one can point to that affirms their reality. But the passion with which they are embraced by billions of people suggests a kind of collective will of humanity to make them real, a positing of reality by the human mind. Human rights may in fact be one of the most successful artificial constructs of the human brain in all of history. Such is the power of our minds to construct our reality. It may be that racism is also a durable construct of the mind, a habit of cognition and a common neural pathway. But human rights constitutes a remarkable example of the opposite, of the ability to construct a neural pathway that becomes so habituated in so many people that it is felt to be real. It became so real that the framers of the American Bill of Rights were so audacious as to believe they can construct an entire society based on these rights, and that they can framed as "inalienable."

Any decent person will be frustrated with the glacial pace of progress on the enforcement of human rights in these centuries, but there is no question that, when viewed historically, the contrast from today to even seventy years ago is astonishing in terms of how human rights violators are seen and treated by the end of their lives. Witness the leaders of war in Bosnia and former Yugoslavia, or Sudan, and many other war criminals. It is true that the span of time between crime and punishment seems agonizingly long, but there is no question that we are witnessing a lightning trend in terms of treatment of war crimes and war criminals.

Even the lionization of heroes has evolved. The masses may still love the fictional characters of Bruce Willis or Mel Gibson, for example. But when Gibson in real life utters just a few drunken, racist expletives against one group, such as anti-Semitic words that would have been commonly accepted parlance just fifty years before, he is shunned in real life, not worshiped as a hero (Kille 2005). Thus, even our violent movie heroes are held to standards of strictly nonviolent ethics when it comes to real life. This is not a linear progression, as there are constant relapses such as in Bosnia, India, Rwanda, or the United States. But the trend is clearly away from lionizing war criminals as heroes on the global scene. The exceptions in terms of war criminal lionization are in the heat of war and bloodshed, in particular in the hot spots of hatred and violence. This is a phenomenon that Compassionate Reasoning must be designed to address.

Compassion and Reason Need Each Other

Here is the most important point for the psychology and philosophy of ethics: *compassion and reason cannot exist without each other; compassion and reason need each other*. Let me explain this. Compassion needs reason, for compassion as an emotion is too easily confused with a narrow empathy and excessive love for a limited number of people. Compassion needs reason for the logical extension of prosocial emotions to all people, all sentient beings, even to the earth itself. Reason helps to bring out the logic and rational self-interest of principles of compassion applied to all.

This is the logical way to guarantee the survival and flourishing of all, by taking a very positive emotion that is rooted in the mind and subjecting it to great enhancement through habit and training. But then one extends its power by reason, extending the intentions and practices of compassion into principles for the individual and policies for communities and societies. It is reason that brings compassion into the realm of necessary principles to govern oneself and all of society.

Religious Reason and Compassion in Concert with Secular Reasoning

We have seen many organized religions fail at exactly this critical juncture, namely the failure to extend prosocial emotions as a matter of principle to all people regardless of their standing in the religion. Compassion is centralized, practiced, and inculcated in many religions—or so they think. But then religious institutions limit compassion to only the "saved," to only members, to only the tribe, and suddenly compassion turns into a narrow and contorted version of itself that descends into hypocrisy. Only reason can guarantee the flourishing sustainability of compassion.

The human capacity for reason can include religious reasoning based on religious ethics—either through the deontological development of universal principles or through consequentialist moral calculus and pragmatism. Religious reasoning, in addition to secular reasoning, is capable of channeling the prosocial emotion of compassion as a sacred experience into universal moral principles. Religion can also rationally justify joining religious moral principles of the compassionate society together with secular principles. This happens all the time today in the expression of modern religious values across the planet (Jones 2008). Religion can be—when religious representatives are ready and willing—an intellectually compelling peace partner in making society less and less violent (UNICEF 2021). Both religious and secular people need this vital bridge from compassion to higher reasoning and universal principles. They need it in their personal lives, in the evolution of their minds; and they need it for the societies that they share.

There is no turning back now from societies that are completely and permanently mixed between secular and religious, liberal and conservative religious, and infinitely diverse across religions. This embodies the reality of every major large city on the planet today, and there is no going back. Our relationship between compassion and reason going forward must be based on ways of cognition and emotion that are workable in this fundamentally pluralistic reality.

From this perspective, Enlightenment philosophy has provided humanity with an irreplaceable service, moving us from exclusively tribal and exclusively religious structures of governance to a steady evolution of universal principles that oversee governments and international systems. This was Kant's dream in *Perpetual Peace,* and such dreams have produced impressive results in terms of international regimens of coexistence through local human rights and international law.

This regimen is also impressive from the vantage point of old tribalistic realities on every continent. Severe hierarchies within religions and between religions used to be the norm across every continent. Secular people and nonconformists, male or female, gay or straight, used to be killed straight out with impunity. Although there are still many pockets of this, it no longer dominates the legal structures of most countries. Billions of people in major cities the world over now coexist nonviolently in the most egalitarian mixture of peoples, cultures, and religions ever in cosmopolitan history.

Where the Enlightenment and the Great Philosophers Failed to Prepare the Modern Citizen

Every moral sense theorist knew that habits and education were critical to compassion exercising its power over human life. Furthermore, it is a basic fact of psychology that self-control is one of the central challenges for human beings, no matter how educated we become (Strayhorn 2002). The amygdala can be easily driven to violence without the habituated positive effects of a well-trained and independent habit of moral reasoning and moral emotions.

The twentieth century history has taught us that secular political constructs are insufficient protection from the dangers of obedience. Powerful secular leaders can also make us subordinate to their deadly will; totalitarian regimes, their wars, and organized genocides have proven this beyond a shadow of a doubt. Unless our minds and bodies are trained in the habits of independent ethical thought, we cannot escape the ravages of political obedience and barbarity that drives us humans well below the behavior of animals. It is habits of the mind that are key to a less violent and more compassionate human future, a future that will also protect the rest of sentient life from our human problems with self-control.

Yet we have neglected the crucial step of habituation for enlightenment and human evolution. The Enlightenment propounded an historic universal application of ethical values, but did it prepare us as a global community for the challenges to democracy from totalitarianism, nihilistic abandon, and demagoguery? History is offering a decisive "no" as the answer.

Where today is the Enlightenment's effect on childhood and adult education? Where is education for enlightenment? Education for compassion? Education for the evolution of universal reason ethically committed to all? The Enlightenment fell down completely when it came to education for self-control, for compassion, for universal commitments of citizenship based on habits of the mind and the inculcation of clear and common values.

The Enlightenment was utilized instead by empires and states for acquisition of power through math and science, for the technical concentration of unprecedented human power and wealth in Western nations; this has now been emulated by advancing countries across the planet. The elements of enlightened education that we have today in Western public education, focused heavily on math and science in state or corporate employment, has little to do with the enlightened mind working in the service of a nonviolent, compassionate society or a rule-based society and global community. These ends may be implicit in some curricula, implicit in the minds of some teachers, but not explicit, self-conscious, and forthright.

Without an explicit ethical goal, there are no metrics of progress or success, and there is no grappling with the invariable moral conflicts between the good society and the powerful society. The part of the Enlightenment vision dedicated to creating the good society, the part of the Western democratic intention to create democracies based on human rights, has been jettisoned or never truly arrived, in part because the Enlightenment itself became instrumentalized for empire building.

The advance of the mind in terms of math skills or physics has no established causal effect on personal ethics, especially in atmospheres of stress, fear, or authoritarian pressures. Logic and science skills do not necessarily lead to the more ethical person or the more ethical society. You can be a math genius and a domestic terrorist, and you can be intellectually disabled and a paragon of prosocial emotions.[20] For enlightened ethics to build a less violent, more democratic society, you need, in addition, a very specific kind of ethics education that has not been offered. It requires an exploration of and habituation to (1) universal moral commitments and (2) moral practices and habits so compelling you want to practice them and believe in them as if it were fundamental to what your community is or who you are as an individual and (3) a community of fellow practitioners.[21] This is what is necessary for deep commitment to universal ethics and human rights that has a better chance of withstanding authoritarian, economic, and peer pressure in hard times.

How Culture, Religion, and Spirituality Can Contribute to Compassionate Reasoning

Compassionate Reasoning, as we have defined it, is a trainable methodology of the mind and of society to arrive at universal moral commitments that resist negative group behavior. However, for Compassionate Reasoning to be inculcated in the individual and in society itself, there needs to be a broad commitment to cognitive and behavioral habit formation, especially through formal and informal education. This must be a fundamental task of the society.

Here is a most important point: Education and habit formation can become a joint venture between traditional, spiritual, and secular members of society. Spiritual people and religious societies can mine the depths of their traditions and orient education toward two things: (1) compassion and (2) universal commitments to all people, to all sentient life.

Rabbi Samuel David Luzzatto, for example, perhaps the only traditional Jewish moral sense theorist of the Enlightenment period, understood this very well and therefore embraced "compassion for all" as the centerpiece of his religious philosophy (Gopin 2017), despite his other critiques of the Enlightenment. Oddly enough, Luzzatto and Immanuel Kant, one a Jewish religious moral sense philosopher and the other a Christian pietist deontologist, had in common one thing despite very different approaches to ethics and religious texts. They both searched for one sure component of human nature that could be relied upon to build ethics, something that would withstand all of the emotional distortions of life's sorrows and all the violent peer assaults of the mob or authoritarians on the ethical personality. For Kant, it was the good will, as we have studied. For Luzzatto, it was compassion. But compassion is not just a moral sense for Luzzatto but rather a sacred experience, a profound pleasure and an empowering act. The experience and practice of altruistic compassion was the one pleasure that even the worst sufferings could not take away from any person.

A person could be as poor and miserable as could be (as Luzzatto was), but nothing could stop compassion for others, and no person could take away the joy of helping another human being. Despite his fame across Europe in the first half of the nineteenth century as the foremost Jewish Biblical scholar of the age, Luzzatto lost most of his eight children to poverty and disease in Padua, Italy. The death of the children destroyed his first wife, who died of severe depression. When Luzzatto searched for a foundation to ethics that could not be shaken by life's sorrows, he was speaking of his personal experience. He adored his wife and children, but he discovered for himself the invincibility of compassion. There was at least left to him the joy of compassion and caring for them during those terrible years.

Dr. Viktor Frankl, the brilliant and courageous founder of logotherapy, and a survivor of Auschwitz, had very little in common with Rabbi Luzzatto. One was a highly assimilated Viennese Jew in the twentieth century, and the other a highly conservative Italian Jewish theologian in the nineteenth century. But in one regard they had much in common. Luzzatto anticipated by a hundred years Viktor Frankl's ingenious discovery of a path to meaning, purpose, and life fulfillment that even a concentration camp could not take away. When Frankl spoke at length of his own experience in his immortal classic, *Man's Search for Meaning*, he spoke of what it means to find life's purpose in giving away half of your last morsel of bread. He spoke of how this can give you a will to live even in hell. He spoke from the depths of his soul and not just his scientific observations (Frankl [1946] 2006).

To figure out a philosophy of life and a psychotherapy at Auschwitz—this was Compassionate Reasoning at its most noble and tragic hour. Both Frankl and Luzzatto believed altruism is a gift to others, but a gift even more so to the self, a source of ultimate and triumphant happiness that no physical misery can eliminate. Today, there is very good evidence that discovering a meaningful life leads to the deepest and most permanent kind of human happiness (Frankl [1946] 2006; Seligman and Csikszentmihalyi 2000). The deontologists, such as Kant, found their answer to a meaningful life and an ethical life in the good human will, a good will that develops categorical principles applying to all human beings, no matter what the circumstances.

The theory of Compassionate Reasoning argues, based on the science of the mind, that both moral sense theorists like Luzzatto, building off of

Hutcheson and Shaftesbury, and deontologists, building off of Kant, have been correct in their foundations for ethics. Both (a) highly developed compassion and (b) a strong, self-controlled good will that commits to universal ethics are necessary to create the good person and the less violent, more peaceful society. This is exactly why I have combined compassion and reasoning into one skill, Compassionate Reasoning.

One thing is missing from the formula, however: deeply ingrained cultural habits of the mind, body, and heart that will make prosocial human thoughts, intentions, and emotions to be victorious over the antisocial ones, the higher thinking mind victorious over the more fear- and rage-based parts of the mind such as the amygdala. This is where religion has seen its finest successes in history *when, and only when,* religion and culture make compassion apply to all human beings. For this to work, we must begin to rethink education at every developmental level, including public education of everyone through messaging and social media.

The Golden Rule, Compassionate Reasoning, and the Cognitive Embeddedness of Human Rights

The legendary Golden Rule of Leviticus 19:18 refers to loving your neighbor as yourself, which could be legitimately translated as either, "And you shall love your neighbor as (you love) yourself," or "And you shall love your neighbor, he/she is (like) you." It also has a later rabbinic formulation, "Do *not* do to others what is hateful to you" (*Talmud Bavli* Sabbath 31a6). Rabbi Akiba (first century CE) made the Golden Rule into the foundational rule of Judaism (*Genesis Rabbah* 24). Ancient formulations of the Golden Rule had a massive influence on the formation of Jewish, Christian, and Muslim ethics, and they are classic expressions of "Compassionate Reasoning" as we have defined it. Today the Golden Rule has been adopted and claimed by dozens of global religions and is likely to have old roots across the world (Rockwell 1961; Global Ethic Foundation 2021).

Let's analyze the Golden Rule more deeply. The Golden Rule assumes a love for oneself and care for one's own needs, but it extends that sense of love to all neighbors by making a compassionate identification between yourself and your neighbor who is like you, or who *is* you. The bonds of compassionate identification lead to a bond of love, and the love leads to compassionate action based on that love. Beginning with Aristotle, but continuing into major

Enlightenment moral sense theorists who were also deeply versed in the Bible, self-love and self-care are critical for any system of ethics (Maurer 2006) and are an assumption of this understanding of the Golden Rule. There is a reasoned analogy made by the mind, an analogy between love of and care of oneself and love of others, even of complete strangers who share a common humanity.

Here is the most important part: The Golden Rule is an appeal to our reasoning capacity in the following way. It stimulates our minds to draw a remarkable conclusion: that love of self extends to love for all others because they are just like you. *Then* this, in turn, leads toward a rational universal rule, a principle of ethics, a principle that makes my neighbor's needs vital to my legitimate needs. My needs that I care about so deeply, my care for myself, must be the logical foundation of universal rules that apply to *all* my neighbors. You can plainly see the anticipation of Kant by a few thousand years.

The Golden Rule is a combination of self-love, compassionate identification with others, and the embrace of rules for life based on reasoning. Versions of the Golden Rule express themselves in numerous major religions across the planet, and for this reason such a religious ruling could in principle be a tremendous asset to the formulation of universal ethics that we are exploring in this study (Neusner and Chilton 2008; Wattles 1996). The more we get "buy-in" to a universal commitment to care for neighbors from a variety of traditions and cultures, the easier it will be to constitute national/international social contracts and human rights commitments across the spectrum of law-abiding citizens.

The expansion of human rights commitments has been astronomical *if viewed* from the lens of 300 years ago. But from the lens of today, this expansion is agonizingly slow in its enforcement, and often faces backlash in the seesaw of nativist politics; that makes countless people suffer terrible discrimination and harm. Our ideological divisions around optimism or pessimism about human rights expansion is confusing and counterproductive, in my opinion. Our perspective often depends on how long a view of history we internalize. On the optimistic side, human rights as a concept has become embedded in the minds of billions of people today and is on a steady march upward. You can focus your mind on the success of the idea and the enforcement of it for millions of people, or you can focus your mind on its rejection by some and its lack of enforcement for billions. The very success of the human rights idea over our minds, however, has sensitized us to its every violation, to every bad leader who embodies the opposite, to every loss of life, and to every violation of dignity. This sensitization can skew us toward depression, impatience, cynicism, and destructive polarization, as we have seen in the United States in 2020.

Such empathy with victims is remarkable, but it also leads to painful frustration and exaggerated pessimism. I celebrate the frustration as a spur to deepening the human rights agenda, but without a good plan of incremental change, the frustration leads to despair and abandonment. There needs to be a better way forward for universal human rights than the endless battle between progressive and conservative camps, which only retards the evolution of human rights.

A key way to deepen universal commitments is to better embed them in every conservative culture around the world, inside every conservative bastion of every nation's heartland. This takes patience, tolerance, and some compromise. Religion is a well-trodden path to the conscience and worldview of the conservative heartland of every nation and community. That is why a deeper alliance on human rights and traditional values is a desirable end (Appleby 2000; Dubensky 2016; Johnston and Sampson 1994; Little 2007; Philpott 2012).

The Indeterminacy of Religious Ethics

Here is the challenge, however, to the Golden Rule's contribution to universal ethics and human rights, and a real problem with conservative religion's contribution in general. Although Compassionate Reasoning has *some* presence in numerous cultural traditions and religions, it has only dominated those traditions in the minds of select people and communities. Moral ideas are only as dominant as those who have the will and the power to act on them.

Religions are what religious people think they are. The *lived* religions of the world express themselves in infinite ways depending on what believers are thinking (Fry 2009; Moore 2014). Only some believers, and only some clerics and followers, have embraced versions of the Golden Rule and applied them to *all human beings*. Often, the opposite of the Golden Rule has dominated. Put a different way, a single sacred text like loving neighbors as yourself only dominates a culture to the degree to which the believers and community leaders *decide* that it will, and only to the degree to which they create educational and ritual atmospheres build upon a text like the Golden

Rule. This is precisely why Kant—as a Christian pietist surrounded by imperial expressions of violent confrontation and conquest in the name of
Christianity—made "the good will" into the centerpiece of his ethics. He understood one thing clearly: a religious ethical principle is only as good as its
absolute internalization inside the conscience of every individual which then
must extend to the moral practices of everyday society.

For example, you can be a great leader of a community, and you can decide
that the Golden Rule is the essence of your tradition. But it is just as possible
that you can take Leviticus 18:22, *just three verses after* the Golden Rule—
and even worse, 20:13 requiring the death penalty—and decide that banning
and outlawing homosexuals is the centerpiece of your sacred mission, thus
completely undermining the Golden Rule when it comes to LGBTQ human
beings.

This is the unfortunate freedom that people have to construct and reconstruct religious priorities in their minds, drawing at will from thousands of
years of accumulated texts and rituals. This is the power of the brain's ability
to construct reality through the prism of culture, tradition, or the prevailing
zeitgeist of a moment in history. Put another way, the Golden Rule is deeply
present in religious history, but the *scope* of the traditional Golden Rule is
often severely circumscribed in the history of religions. It can be limited to
certain people "worthy" of being called "neighbors," which can mean "the
faithful in good standing" or "anyone that I, or my cleric, or my king, *interpret* as being in "good standing" on any given day or decade."[22] You can
actually righteously order people to hate everyone else who is not from the
beloved club in good standing. The smaller the club of the beloved, the more
danger of violence against others. As a scholar of religion, I see the struggle
over this very issue constantly in global religious debates, debates that go on
in each religion, even as it also divides countries and regions along sectarian
lines of who is in and who is out, who is beloved and who is hated. And yet all
continue to claim the Golden Rule.[23]

Generating Religious Frames That Serve the Higher Mind of Reason

This is a problem of mandated religious love and its limitations. It bothered a
Jewish rabbi by the name of Ben Azzai in the second century of the Common
Era. He happened to be a leader of his generation, and he differed from Rabbi

Akiba, a century before, who had suggested that the Golden Rule was the core principle of Judaism. Ben Azzai, having witnessed the ravages of religious sectarianism, learned from experience that we often hate one another, and we get into serious wars, sometimes even amongst our closest relatives and sometimes with foreign peoples.

"Love" as a mandated foundation of ethics is unreliable, Ben Azzai argued. If we do not or cannot love due to various circumstances, then we may lose all self-control and become utterly barbaric if love is the sole foundation of our ethical system. At the same time, Ben Azzai did not want to let go of the spirit of the Golden Rule, even though it seems hard for people to love in all circumstances.

Ben Azzai landed on another religious principle as the essence of Judaism, and it centered not on prosocial ethics but on a theological belief as to the definition of humanity itself. By virtue of his position of authority, he tried to make this theological principle into a fact for the religious mind, a reality to perceive and to accept. To borrow contemporary language, he proposed a basic cognitive construct of the world for the religious brain, a fundamental way to look at and reframe every aspect of experience as such.

As one of the great leaders of his generation, Ben Azzai instructed all believers to remember that every human being, without exception, is created in the image of God.[24] Ben Azzai adapted this from a curious turn of phrase in Genesis 1:26 about how God created the human being, but Ben Azzai made this phrase into a core universal foundation of Jewish ethics, a core construct of the religious mindset and existential outlook.

Ben Azzai wanted to plant in the thought of the practitioner and into the atmosphere of every socially constructed situation the basic assumption that each of us is "the image of God," "tselem Elohim." Whether you love people or not, whether you have enemies or not, whether you believe in the same God or not, whether someone else is a believer or not, never forget that every human being is sacred, every life is sacred, argued Ben Azzai. Therefore, behave accordingly, control yourself accordingly, act and feel as if you were standing not before a fellow human but before God. Be in awe and be in control. Respect, honor, unconditional love, infinite gratitude, loyalty, compassion, solidarity, care—all the spiritual reactions that you would feel toward God who created you, do unto every human, whether that human is rich or poor, black or white, male or female, saint or sinner, someone you love or even someone you could not bring yourself to love. It was a bold moral move by Ben Azzai 2,000 years ago, a revolutionary reconstruction of human perception itself.

As we can see in these interpretive struggles of religion, it is difficult to discover and implant in the religious consciousness an unconditional motive or duty of compassion extending to all *without exception*, but it can be done. We need to make space for creative interpretive ways in which religious devotion rises to the challenge of Compassionate Reasoning and is universally applied (Gopin 2000, 2002, 2009, 2012). The Golden Rule, for example, can overcome dangerous descents into lower brain tribalism, hate, and murder if, and only if, this rule is taught by religious communities in a way that applies to all people.

This universal love need not supplant, contradict, or replace special love for one's own community of faith or practice. But there must be a place in every conservative community for some love for all of humanity, or valuation of their sacredness following Ben Azzai, regardless of who they are. It is only in this way that practice of the Golden Rule in the religious community will feed and support the higher mind. The higher mind is indispensable for its expertise in rational universal rules, prudent planning for a society shared by all, as well as its control of irrational fears and hatreds.

This is our task today in terms of the future of religion and society. Society needs to include a redemptive expression of religion that inculcates Compassionate Reasoning. Together with many dear colleagues, I have spent a lifetime working on integrating traditional religious sources with universal expressions of compassion and reason, while also encouraging such conversations across religious denominations in many contexts of war and peace (Gopin 2000, 2002, 2009, 2012). We must make an intentional effort between religions as a collaborative effort.

We must also make it a more intentional campaign between secular and religious citizens, to save the earth together from climate calamity, for example, to embrace humanity and help it evolve to its highest potential. We are divided by the behaviors of religious militants of all stripes, but we are also divided by bitterly opposed secular and religious constructs of the world that have made it difficult to combine energies and talents to create the good society for all. The liberal/conservative divide is allowing religion to be weaponized by extremists, making it very difficult to carry on bipartisan progress. It will take a self-conscious secular/religious covenant to effect a combination of energies and talents.

Back in 1795, Kant knew society was facing an uphill battle as it strug-gled with tribal psychology and intergroup struggles that could tear the globe apart, something realized about 120 years later in two horrific world wars and genocide. Writing in *Perpetual Peace* ([1795] 2016), he seemed un-impressed with the absolute rule of monarchs in terms of tribal selfishness. But he would not be impressed today either by democratic nation-states and superpowers when they behave as selfish tribes. Kant focused rather on the essential importance of a universal moral vision of the future, universal moral constructs of the future, developed first inside the human psyche and then translated into universal laws.

Kant's vision as a human being was critical to the future, but it was also buttressed by his liberal spiritual faith. This built the basis of the United Nations and all the legal foundations of nonviolent global civilization today. That civilization has now become embodied in thousands of international laws and treaties that apply to all nations equally, and these have kept the lid on world wars for an unusually long stretch of history (Pinker 2011a). People like Kant and Grotius were critical to building an international civilization today with thousands of human rights laws in place.

Kant's conception of law was based on his "categorical imperative," a form of philosophical reasoning that had strong roots in the biblical Golden Rule we analyzed above. The categorical imperative insisted no law is truly a law of ethics unless it applies to all without exception. Other visionary thinkers, such as Grotius and John Locke, shared Kant's grand vision of a globe ruled through universal laws. All these thinkers were pro-phetic in that they did foresee a world that was slowly coming into being, a world in which thousands of treaties and laws would come to govern many areas of the world and interactions of the world that must adhere to basic human rights. As grossly imperfect as our modern world is, it is neverthe-less far less plagued by massive death from war than just a century ago. It is in no small part due to these treaties that they argued for and foresaw as a *nonviolent* regime of international legal haggling, competition, struggle, and *nonviolent* cooperation.

These thinkers were moderately religious but also understood the severe dangers of fundamentalism and sectarian abuse of religion when we humans are not governed both *internally and externally* by universal commitments and reasoning. They read history well; they read its disasters and its strengths as they envisioned a better future. A peaceful future would necessitate a com-passionate embrace of the needs and interests of total strangers, and even enemies. Thus, they understood the necessity of combining universal religious values together with compassion, reasoning, and universal law.

The Missing Link: Education and Habit Formation of the Mind

There was one overarching flaw of these thinkers' ethical and political vision of the future: the failure to institutionalize, at the mass level, a regime of education and habituation of the mind toward universal commitments. From Aristotle to Mill, philosophers understood the critical importance of training, of habituating both the mind and body for reasoning and for self-control. And these Enlightenment thinkers we just cited—unlike Aristotle or the great medieval thinkers—understood in principle that rights and responsibilities needed to be extended to the masses of humanity. Although these thinkers did succeed in fomenting revolutionary political constructions of democracy and human rights embodied in bills of rights, they failed, as we mentioned above, to extend these insights to all genders and all people regardless of skin pigmentation.

In principle, advanced struggles have greatly expanded human rights regimens (Viljoen 2021). But the Enlightenment figures also failed as a matter of policy and law to inspire the creation of resources and institutions embedding these commitments into the mind of each modern citizen of society. They could not anticipate how much future studies of psychology and neuroscience would substantiate the critical role of habit in the formation of the independent self.[25] Many moral sense theorists and utilitarian consequentialists, such as Bentham and Mill, did emphasize the importance of habit formation, as did Aristotle and Confucius thousands of years before them (Nederman 1989). But they all failed to embed their ethical principles in a curriculum for citizen education of every single human being that would generate a completely new and truly egalitarian society.

Part of the reason for this failure is that the Enlightenment and democratic movements have been also rightly about freedom of thought and escape from tyranny of the mind. But this radical freedom of thought left the door open for someone or something else filling the mind with habitual ways of thinking. They did not pay enough attention to how fragile the democratic idea really is, but which we now, after a century of totalitarian regimes and wars, know very well.

No one anticipated just how badly masses of people tend to fall prey to demagogues—demagogues of religion and demagogues of antireligion, demagogues of nationalism who would fool people into surrendering their own rights, coax them to polarize and demonize the stranger, to even commit unspeakable slaughter and genocide, all while possessing education in the classics of literature and higher degrees in law and medicine. We have learned that higher education in the classics and in STEM turned out to be no preventive to millions of young educated European men lining up in World War I and committing mass slaughter of each other by the millions, with the aid of fabulous state-of-the-art gas and STEM-based technology.

Modern Western enlightened citizens failed to weave moral reasoning, moral self-control, and universal compassion into the cognitive fabric of the democratic citizen. They failed to teach the centrality of Compassionate Reasoning for human and planetary survival and flourishing. They failed to appreciate the need to inspire the young and to *model* Compassionate Reasoning in their every classroom behavior with children. In fact, even the most enlightened figures were still raising children in brutal ways (Mill 2008). They failed to see that a commitment to universal values needs to be inculcated at every stage of education, from birth to late adulthood, and in every institution of modern culture, including both religious and secular culture. Everywhere this commitment was lacking should have been seen as a project incomplete, as a detriment to the peaceful enlightened society, and as a direct threat to democracy and enlightenment itself. The well-intentioned early visionaries of democracy failed to see that democracy, human rights, and prosperity for all are delicate structures that only survive to the degree to which the mind of every citizen is habituated to an essential combination of (a) compassion for all and (b) higher reasoning.

These thinkers especially forgot compassion for all. The disciplined enlightenment and evolution of the self through STEM was only part of the job. They denigrated "savages" around the world, undoing their own teachings while at the same time turning a blind eye to the savagery in themselves, the savage work of robbing the world to "enlighten" human beings of color. They were so eager to liberate STEM from the Church within their Anglo-European context, they forgot that STEM was only one part of enlightenment. In all the great thinkers, from Socrates and Confucius on throughout the history of ideas, conquest of the self was the far harder goal of enlightenment, the one most prone to failure, the one most in need of moral habit formation.

Even more poignantly, Enlightenment thinkers did not look into their hearts and their own personal behavior to realize that higher reasoning and science *without compassion for all* is a dangerous mutation leading to very efficient and brilliant machine guns to mow down the best-trained minds of an entire generation of World War I, or genocide throughout Europe, or mass slaughter for profit in the empires, or omnicide of nuclear weapons and climate destruction. In our ignorance and arrogance, we continue to draw ourselves closer to omnicide by several means, through uncontrolled moral behavior of states and individuals and through a lack of training in compassion for all.

The Task at Hand That Is Urgently Upon Us

Considering the planetary climate challenges upon us that require unprecedented human collaboration, it is our task today to go further than these thinkers went, to formulate *shared education and habits* to move the mass of humanity away from demagogues and toward internalization of universal laws, toward shared compassion and reason, across cultures, across religions, across the globe itself, to an embrace of all of sentient life on the planet.

Today's liberalism places too much emphasis on championing freedom as the only ethical value of importance. There are many values, such as compassion for all, that are a core foundation of nonviolent society, as even the classical father of capitalism, Adam Smith, understood. Championing the moral value of freedom alone is a libertarian nightmare that is making extreme forms of capitalism ever more destructive to the stability of society and the future of planet Earth. By contrast, the jettisoning altogether of compassion for strangers by nationalists and populists is an even more direct threat to the global future. The absence of compassion for nonhuman sentient life has also led to greedy structures of power and energy acquisition that are creating the largest die-off of species in many millions of years, a mass extinction event (Carrington 2017).

Many organized religions have decent educational structures and crosscutting, global ties that can help move us forward ethically through their social networks, a topic we will take up later. But for this to happen we need more conciliatory efforts to occur between secular and religious visionaries of the good society. Adam Smith ([1759] 2005) made it very clear that the freedom given by capitalism depended on the inculcation of compassion.

We took his capitalism, married it to secular libertarianism, jettisoned the compassion training, and got uncontrolled greed alone to guide the logic and ethos of big business. This will kill our future if we do not adopt Compassionate Reasoning into the cognitive framework of more CEOs and leaders of nations.

Alternatively, if people of wealth, secular and religious alike, start to see the economic advantage of long-term sustainable survival, then together we can evolve human habits of consumption and production in a new direction. This will create a cascade effect of education and habitual behavior toward a new paradigm of sustainable human life.

We need representatives of world religions and secular social leaders to join forces in a common bid to generate Compassionate Reasoning as the way to think and behave. That means we need to privilege and lift up those movements in religious communities prepared to do this, no matter how conservative they may be. Progressives and conservatives need the courage to see each other's common values in the light of compassion and reason, learning how to negotiate and compromise where necessary.

We need social and educational systems that will collaborate to work on the implications of Compassionate Reasoning for policies, shifts in human behavior, economic activity, and engagement with the earth itself. But for this to happen, many constituencies of society, rich and poor, secular and religious, will need to manage their conflicts better, learning how to focus on a passion for issues rather than passionate hatred and rejection of people, learning how to argue constructively without polarization and demonization.

This is the only way to collaborate in time to save all of life on earth. We do not need all extremists on board, although we must develop methods of conflict resolution and reconciliation that can reach anyone potentially (Gopin 2012, 2016). Minimally, though, we do need enough people from conservative and progressive orientations, from the richest to the poorest, to hear each other, to build together a society of compassion and reasoned values and policies. That will create enough leadership to guide the masses away from demagoguery and toward compassion for all and reasoned approaches to sustainable life.

3

Compassionate Reasoning, the Mind, and Moral Choice

The purpose of this chapter is to explore distinct parallels between the neuroscience of compassion, the classical ethical schools of thought, and the method of change I am promoting through Compassionate Reasoning. We will explore the neuroscience of compassion and suggest an important working relationship between the psychology of empathy, compassion, and reasoning on the one side, and traditional schools of ethics on the other. This chapter will take a deeper dive into the mechanics of Compassionate Reasoning and how it can be practically implemented.

The Neuroscience of Compassion, Empathy, Self-Control, and Reasoning

As mentioned earlier, there has been a global range of interdisciplinary studies into the reduction of violence over the last few hundred years, but especially the reduction in violence in the last seventy years. In the same time period, there has been a vast increase in lifespan, a massive expansion of laws governing peaceful international transactions, human rights conventions outlawing a variety of cruelties that were common in the past, and a significant reduction in violent crime rates by comparison to previous centuries.

Despite dips and reversals, this historical set of patterns has also correlated on average with a significant increase in:

- literature and films that empathically portray the lives, the hopes, the triumphs, the sorrows, and tragedies of complete strangers from foreign cultures,
- compassion for and acceptance of strangers in the increasingly common large cosmopolitan centers around the world,
- personal and collective self-control in compliance with the rule of law,

Compassionate Reasoning. Marc Gopin, Oxford University Press. © Oxford University Press 2022.
DOI: 10.1093/oso/9780197537923.003.0003

- the power of reasoning to create shared principles for moral governance, and
- nonviolent democratic constitutions and civil rights emerging across
  many countries.

Thus, increases in compassion, self-control, and reasoning, as reflected in
our habits and our laws, have become increasingly important as vehicles to
accelerate nonviolent megatrends. These positive changes are of central importance to the ethical and political goal of making us a less violence-prone
and kinder species. Drawing upon the 80/20 rule of work, we want to look at
what has gone right and strengthen it, abandon what has not worked, hone
in on what has worked to make us less violent, while also envisioning what
could be even better.[1]

Especially important for our subject of Compassionate Reasoning, there
have been important developments in recent years of neuroscientific and
medical research on brain plasticity regarding compassion, and medical research regarding metabolic responses to empathy and compassion (Eisler
and Fry 2019; Regehr, Goldberg, and Hughes 2002).

There is now also a keen interest in and documentation of the *destructive*
aspects of excessive empathy. This also entails the feeling of powerlessness
that is experienced while feeling the pain of others over long periods of time
(Bechtoldt and Schneider 2016; Foruschani and Besharat 2011). *Empathic
distress*, as it is known, stands in marked contrast to studies of compassion.
Training in compassion, through the active joy of imagining the embrace of
and help to others, has a completely distinct effect on brain neural pathways
and is utterly different from the neural pathways of empathy and empathic
distress.

I have been interested in compassion as a foundation for ethics, religion,
and human psychology for much of my life, having written my PhD dissertation in 1993 on moral sense theory and compassion (Gopin 2017). Brain
research on compassion has made tremendous advances since my dissertation, and this has come to occupy my thinking centrally as a practitioner
and a theoretician of conflict resolution and peacebuilding. Thirty years
of experience in over a dozen countries with students from conflict zones
around the world gave me a certain perspective on compassion. I saw time
and time again that the only durable peacebuilding in any zone of conflict
was pioneered and sustained by those who demonstrated the deepest levels
of empathy and compassion. Otherwise, the efforts never lasted. All of this,

I realized, had implications for my conflict resolution practice experience and theory building. I started to discover that a neuroscience approach to empathy and compassion—thanks to the amazing discoveries through fMRI direct observation of the active brain—was a watershed moment of discovery for the connection between the brain and the practice of peacebuilding.

This research was uncovering what for me was the key to sustainable versus unsustainable peacebuilding: trauma, burnout, despair, and withdrawal based on too much pain and empathic distress on the part of peacebuilders, on the one side, and, on the other, the joy of giving and loving as lifelong gifts of caring for others. There was a basic distinction emerging between positive and negative aspects of feeling the emotions of the other, something that has been glossed over by compassion studies in much of classical ethical philosophical and wisdom literature. Research on the distinction between compassion and empathy is just beginning, but this research will change the way we do work on healing conflicts, and it should produce a powerful link between ethics (both secular and religious) and cutting-edge science. Facts elicited from both practical experience and from empirical science will allow for more effective applications of moral principles and values that can become embedded in the way society operates.

New lessons of science should stimulate both religious and secular formulations of ethics to consider the somatic and health effects of moral senses, moral feelings, and moral expressions of duty. In other words, we should develop better and better moral habits based on what we are learning from the sciences of the mind and body, "better" in terms of (a) moral effectiveness and (b) *personal* and *public* health.

The Neuroscience of Compassion

In order to analyze this further, let me highlight the pioneering work of Dr. Olga Klimecki (2020). Let me begin by quoting, at length, from Klimecki and her colleagues' (2013) recent research on the brain's response to feeling or practicing empathy versus the brain's response to feeling or practicing compassion:

> The development of social emotions such as compassion is crucial for *successful social interactions* as well as *for the maintenance of mental and physical health*,[2] especially when confronted with distressing life events. Yet, the

neural mechanisms supporting the training of these emotions are poorly understood. To study affective plasticity in healthy adults, we measured functional neural and subjective responses to witnessing the distress of others in a newly developed task (Socio-affective Video Task). Participants' initial *empathic* responses to the task were accompanied by negative affect and activations in the anterior insula and anterior medial cingulate cortex— a core neural network underlying empathy for pain. Whereas participants reacted with negative affect before training, compassion training *increased positive affective experiences*, even in response to witnessing others in distress. On the neural level, we observed that, compared with a memory control group, compassion training elicited activity in a neural network including the medial orbitofrontal cortex, putamen, pallidum, and ventral tegmental area—brain regions previously associated with *positive affect* and *affiliation*. Taken together, these findings suggest that the *deliberate cultivation of compassion offers a new coping strategy that fosters positive affect even when confronted with the distress of others.*

These results are further simplified by the authors (Klimecki, Leiberg, Lamm, and Singer 2013) with the following analysis of the subjects in question:

EMPATHY ⇒ COMPASSION ⇒ other-related emotion; positive feelings: e.g., love; good health; approach and prosocial motivation

EMPATHY ⇒ EMPATHIC DISTRESS ⇒ self-related emotion; negative feelings: e.g., stress; poor health, burnout; withdrawal & non-social behavior

Empathy is critical in the relationship between the subject and those who are viewed as suffering. But the pathways from empathy diverge with radically different results for human life and health, depending upon whether empathic distress emerged or compassion emerged. The experimenters traced these differing responses to the pain of others to different neural pathways and parts of the brain that light up in the fMRI.

I also had noticed, based on many years of peacebuilding practice globally, that empathic distress for one's own group and community actually was responsible for more hatred and antisocial behavior. Thus, empathic distress by itself was not only hurtful physically; it also seemed to lead to antisocial feelings and behavior that were the opposite of peacebuilding.[3] In other words, empathy that translates into a generalized care and eagerness to express compassion leads into an entirely different ethic than empathy for one's own group that becomes so strong and painful that it leads to brutality and endless cycles of violence and revenge. I also started to notice a radical difference among survivors of violence, war, and genocide who took two utterly contrasting paths emerging from their empathy for their beloved victims.

That is why I found that compassion, when properly defined and outlined, was a far more reliable foundation of peacebuilding thinking and training than empathy. Training in compassion through these neuroscience experiments has been seen to work even when people are confronted by the extreme distress of others. Parts of the brain light up most associated with love and relationships, as well as higher brain functions of the neocortex. Any part of the brain that "lights up" means that it is being stimulated and strengthened over and against other parts of the brain that might be strengthened by negative feelings of anger, fear, and paranoia, for example. Strengthening a part of the brain in this way has a significant effect on what parts of the brain develop and dominate.

What exactly was this training in compassion that led to these crucial areas of the brain lighting up and being strengthened? This compassion training involved extended meditations on compassionate feelings for loved ones, with a steadily increasing intentional application of those feelings toward others—*and even adversaries*—through feelings and thoughts. It also involved meditation that is expressed through visualization, such as imagining powerful scenes of love and compassion in one's life.

Here is the most important point: The compassion group consistently displayed completely different pathways in the brain lighting up, and a very different set of *reported* experiences that emphasized three things: (1) positive feelings, (2) increased social engagement, and (3) better health. This is remarkable in terms of the brain's simple and elegant capacity to develop new neural pathways that have such strong benefits for oneself and for others.

Revolutionary Implications for Human Flourishing

The potential of this line of research and practice is extraordinary. Training in compassion can change pathways in the brain, strengthen what brings us joy, deepen paths of a meaningful life, *and at the same time* strengthen good health, *even* when dealing with the pain of others. This takes a subtle combination of Compassionate Reasoning—namely, cultivated compassionate feelings and habits, in one part of the brain—and then the logical and planning steps it takes to act on those feelings by helping others with enthusiasm and pleasure. It is the difference between being a grieving, burned-out, ex-peacemaker versus an oncologist who daily bounces down the hospital hallway to treat his next cancer patient. (I am contrasting with deliberate stereotypes just to sharpen the point.) The mind has an overwhelming impact on how we react to the pain of others and what we do about it. Systems matter, systems of violence and oppression matter, and much that the social change maker deals with is impossible for any one individual to fix. But Compassionate Reasoning can help one react to impossible systems with far greater power and effectiveness. The mind is never the only factor in what makes some work meaningful and some work impossible, some work filled with successes and some work doomed to failure, but it plays a remarkably powerful role.

Compassionate Reasoning as a practice should pave the way to be better professionals, better change-makers, and healthier people. I suggest this should lead to a revolutionary approach to the ethics of care and the way we practice conflict resolution and peacebuilding in every society. It is not right or proper or ethical or logical that the change-makers should suffer and burn out, even as they are offering such vital aid to others. It is unfair to those doing the most, and it is an illogical waste of a precious social resource.

Training in ethics, therefore, should dovetail these neuroscience discoveries in order for the ethics of care to be strong, sustainable, and based on reason's training in the full range of moral theories and best practices. This way the reasoning part of Compassionate Reasoning can be at its peak performance in the mind. This kind of training can lead to significantly altered brain structures over time, and this is a remarkable testimony to the power of brain plasticity (Amen and Amen 2017; Klimecki 2019; Ramachandran 2010).[4]

Being ethical has always been seen by most people as something "nice," even "noble," not something that lengthens your life or that leads to a successful and happy life. That there are health benefits to being ethical through compassion and compassionate actions, in particular ways that bring more happiness and social engagement, is a tremendous incentive to both individual behavioral change and cultural evolution as a whole. This research also suggests that the teaching and practice of ethics may be at a watershed moment of history, since there is a meeting of paths here between brain plasticity, the teaching and practice of compassionate ethics, personal fulfill-ment, and positive social change.

The important ramification for our current study is that there are many ways of improving wellbeing while engaging in Compassionate Reasoning. For example, extensive research is underway on a range of neurological and biological markers of empathic distress, and some researchers are looking into many other measures of metabolic distress, such as blood pressure and sweat (Neumann and Westbury 2011). The research cited on neuroplasticity training associated with compassion suggests that many other stress markers can be improved as we learn how to switch empathy away from distress and toward the prosocial and health-inducing expressions of compassion. We are therefore on the edge of learning how to train people in compassion in a sci-entifically supported way that can take them from empathic pain to exhila-ration and joy. This means that instead of compassionate actions and social change globally being an arduous task, wearing people out through burnout, we may be on the brink of learning how to marry physical health, mental wellbeing, and the most advanced forms of moral altruism.

Ethics

There are a variety of prominent ethical schools of thought to go over in this context, in order to deepen our understanding of the relationship between ethical ways of thinking and doing on the one side and, on the other, the healthful and health-inducing characteristics of Compassionate Reasoning.

Let's take a sample of significant schools of ethics.

Moral Sense Theory and Deontology

Moral sense theory[5] is the most obviously connected to the brain research on compassion and prosocial emotions. Moral sense theory embraces the prime emotions of benevolence and compassion as the central basis for a sound ethical system.

Deontology refers to a focus in ethics on principles and rules. Deontology derives from the Greek words duty (*deon*) and science of (*logos*). It is strongly associated in recent centuries with Immanuel Kant's ([1797] 1991; [1788] 2004) focus on duty and universal rules, referred to as "categorical imperatives," which are internalized into the self by the exercise of the good will of the human being. This formulation of ethics speaks directly to the prominent role of the higher brain functioning areas of reasoning, logic, and inference. This is a part of the mind that develops rules to govern life and make rational choices which can be steered by the good will toward rules that apply equally to all human beings, thus constituting ethics.

Compassion, as we have seen above, stimulates prosocial engagement and is the opposite of antisocial stimulation provided by fear and paranoia, the latter being located in the base of the brain stem, the amygdala (Fox and Shackman 2019). Compassion leading to extensive socialization with others, in turn, stimulates the social interest in common principles and standards that form the basis of human units as small as the family and as large as states and civilizations. The cultivation of compassion as we have defined it makes it much easier to develop the motivation of the good will to create universal rules. There is thus a natural complementarity between compassion and reasoning.

Kant's focus on developing universal rules of what is right directly engages human prosocial tendencies and thought patterns. The search for a universal rule that applies equally to all is, by definition, a prosocial move in the mind. With Kant, all legitimate ethics begins inside the mind with (1) the sense of duty, (2) the good will, good intentions, (3) the categorical imperative, and (4) the treatment of others when developing ethical rules as ends in themselves, not as means. Rules become a "kingdom of ends," an absolute realm of the good where human beings are seen only as ends in themselves, not objects to be used by the more powerful.

Prosocial emotions were essential to Kant's understanding of how ethics needed to ultimately work. According to the great historian of the Enlightenment, Ernst Cassirer, Kant thought that Jean Jacques Rousseau's work on compassion and pity was vitally important as an entrée into the search for categorical imperatives, for universal rules (Cassirer 1945). After all, a good will was essential to the generation of categorical imperatives in Kantian thought, and a good will depends upon a positive disposition and feelings toward other human beings.

Kant mapped out in his classic, *Perpetual Peace* (Kant [1795] 2016), the peaceful foundations of an international society, and he thus sketched out and anticipated the role of the United Nations and the Geneva Conventions by two hundred years. Kant was thus an architect of the mind's pathway from *internal* universal rules to the generation of *external* law and social contracts.

These, in turn, have very slowly turned into global legal constructs that have steadily lessened the incidence of interstate wars.

Kant, however, as the visionary of reason-based international law, was also indebted to Rousseau, the quintessential sentimentalist of the Enlightenment period (Cassirer 1945). Rousseau emphasized in *Émile* ([1762] 1921) the supreme importance of prosocial emotions in the nature of the moral person. The only time that Kant was ever known to have broken his daily ritual walk at a precise time was when he was finishing Rousseau's *Émile* (Ziccardi 2014). It is in this connection between Rousseau and Kant on emotions and reason that Cassirer argued for the important interdependency in Enlightenment thought between emotions and reason. Compassionate Reasoning, then, is the perfect combination of moral sense theory, which champions emotions such as compassion, and deontology, which champions universal rules and duties based on the good will of the human being. Compassion and reason working together dovetails the important foundations of Kant's conceptualization of a less violent person and a less violent social order alongside Rousseau's belief that positive sentiments are at the core of human decency. There are, thus, important philosophical roots for the idea of compassion as central to the prosocial human moral psyche, and this provides an important foundation for contemporary neuroscience interest in the pivotal role of compassion for human happiness, health, and prosocial affect and behavior.

Consequentialism and Utilitarianism

With Jeremy Bentham, as well as James Mill and John Stuart Mill, we move to utilitarianism, a very different system of ethics but one that also is deeply related to the theory and practice of Compassionate Reasoning. Utilitarianism takes it as a given that: (a) ethics is about the calculus of likely outcomes and (b) the singular moral guideline to seek the greatest happiness for the greatest number of human beings in the calculus of moral choices.

There is in this position a basic compassionate solidarity with all human beings, with their welfare and happiness. The ethical method is a higher reasoning proposal for the act of calculating the most amount of happiness for the most number of people. This position assumes that the person is a calculator of consequences, and that he or she has basic compassion for all, even those whom society has rejected or left at the bottom.

Utilitarians are a subset of consequentialists, philosophers of ethics who also focus on outcome and calculus, but not necessarily on a "happiness" calculus. What they hold in common is calculus and prognostication of maximization of something inherently good. For example, one could want to maximize general wellbeing, or compassion, or saving of lives, or economic security, or human rights. Or one could want to minimize suffering, and that too would involve calculation. For some the calculus includes all sentient beings, and therefore the calculus must include animal welfare in addition to human welfare (Singer 2005).

This approach culminates—for both the utilitarians and consequentialists—in a complex use of the higher mind and higher reasoning in order to calculate something good for the greatest number possible. The optimal ethical thinking and ethical practice, in terms of the construction and governance of society, is to prognosticate the most good through the rules you come up with, whatever those rules may be in the ever-changing circumstances of the future. Consequentialists come to rules of governance finally, just like deontology, but the rules of consequentialists are focused on calculation and prognostication and could change at any time based on calculations. This requires sophisticated higher reasoning and debate. It also requires earnest learning from history, sociology, economics, psychology, medicine, and many other sciences as a way to predict, for example, what is the best approach to crime and punishment, what is the most ethical approach that causes the least harm and creates the most good. We can see that this entails compassion for all parties and reasoning through the best possible outcomes.

Consequentialism and utilitarianism perfectly align with the social change methodology of Compassionate Reasoning because calculation of possible futures—and a future orientation in general—is critical to a true consideration of compassionate acts and their lasting effects. It also is the case that reason and planning must be employed to build possible futures.

The other major strength of consequentialism is that it highlights the practical, lived reality of moral contradictions of principle at every turn when you are in the middle of destructive conflict. This is a weakness of Kantian systems that do not easily cope with many rules and values contradicting each other in ambiguous moments of conflict, especially violent conflict and systematic oppression.

Consequentialism is a crucial moral tool and methodology for the individual facing complex choices, from family to war zones, as to how to do the right thing. Consequentialism has been critical to my work, and that of countless colleagues, in navigating the uncertain minefield of peacebuilding, lifesaving, and caregiving in war zones.

Virtue Ethics

Let's move on to *virtue ethics*.[6] From Aristotle (1999) to Viktor Frankl ([1946] 2006) to Martin Seligman (2012), the search for the meaningful life based on good character and personal fulfillment is intertwined with the development of a virtuous character. Rather than a focus on moral choice in any one situation, such as in deontology, virtue ethics emphasizes ethics as character development and life fulfillment, and what Aristotle called "human flourishing" or *eudaimonia*.

This framing of character or virtue ethics in the philosophers has great symmetry with modern psychologists from Frankl to May (1975), and from Erickson (1969) to Seligman. It is the search for a meaningful life. What is interesting is how often this research leads to the fulfillment and flourishing that comes from helping others. In recent work of social psychology, a life of meaning and giving turns out to be the best path to a happy life.

We see, once again, an interesting parallel between an approach to ethical fulfillment that also leads to personal fulfillment and mental health. It is the happiness that comes with good health, a good metabolism, and compassion for others. The wisdom to know how to help leads to a good life, a meaningful life, even in trying circumstances. This is quintessential Compassionate Reasoning as we have defined it in this study. Compassionate Reasoning is a training of the mind, but a training of the mind that is for the sake of positive social change and a healthy and sustainable life journey.

Each of the approaches to ethics outlined above has a slightly different way of grappling with the question of ethics in the moment of life's challenges. Yet I am arguing that they all, in their best practices, contribute to what we are calling Compassionate Reasoning. Whether they can cohere in their approaches and be helpful for the practice of Compassionate Reasoning is something we will address shortly. In other words, it is invariable and normal for ethical schools of thought to come to contradictory conclusions, especially regarding specific situations. But becoming a student of all of them is part and parcel of becoming adept at Compassionate Reasoning. *For it is in the struggle to be good, with all of its uncertainties, that one cultivates natural capacities for both compassion and higher reasoning.* Let's look into this further.

The Centrality of Habit to Neuroscience, Ethics, and Traditional Value Systems

A common characteristic of both neuroplasticity analysis of the brain and the schools of ethics we have outlined is the critical importance of habit formation. A habit is effectively a strengthened neural pathway. Cognitive and behavioral habit formation is of central importance for both neuroplasticity theory, as well as for behavioral and cognitive psychology (Lakoff and Johnson 1980). Contemporary behavioral psychology and behavior modification has been built on habit formation,[7] and today's fMRIs track neural pathways lighting up more and more with meditation and practice (Taren et al. 2015). This refers to habits of the mind, or the forging and strengthening of neural pathways. But it also refers to habits of the body or habits of action, such as charitable behavior, which includes body and emotion signals to the brain, forging and strengthening neural pathways of the brain. In other words, moral habits of thinking *and* doing, suggested or mandated by numerous wisdom traditions going back thousands of years, affect the physical evolution of the mind itself on a daily basis.

There is extensive research today into changes in cortical thickness, neural sheath thickness, based on learning. There is a literal and measurable thickening with the frequency of neural pathway usage, and parts of the brain actually become larger with practice (Schnack et al. 2015; Goriounova and Huibert 2019). We are in an exciting era of brain research into mental and physical habits. But it is important to acknowledge that ancient wisdom literature, for thousands of years, and modern moral sense philosophers, for hundreds of years, understood the importance of strengthening a moral sense and creating habits and rituals that would do just that. What we will explore later is exactly what habits of the mind and body would lead to a strengthening of Compassionate Reasoning.

Multiple Approaches to Ethics in Debate Actually Strengthens Compassionate Reasoning

Another important theme of this chapter is that embracing and knowing all the ethical schools, even in a basic introductory way, will sharpen the mind when it comes to Compassionate Reasoning. This is actually what I have taught in my classroom and training in conflict resolution for many years.

Truly honest reasoning does not dictate singular dogmatic truths because—especially when it comes to ethics and politics—there are no simple answers. But when informed by these ethical schools of thought, *debating* multiple approaches to ethical and political dilemmas, both inside the self and with others, sharpens the mind for improvement in Compassionate Reasoning. My experience in the field suggests that good deliberations, which involve (1) a great deal of self-examination (2) a compassionate inquiry into multiple narratives and points of view, and (3) a basic understanding of ethical reasoning such as what we have outlined above, lead to far better results when confronting the moral challenges at hand.

I am proposing that *all ethical deliberation is good deliberation for the purposes of Compassionate Reasoning*. All the schools of ethical deliberation that involve (1) self-examination, (2) reasoned calculation, (3) habitual use of the higher brain, (4) a search for universal principles, and (5) inculcation in and habituation to the nonviolent prosocial emotions such as compassion over the violent emotions—all of these become constructive for ethical growth. They all contribute toward a healthy evolution of the human mind toward less violence and more just relations.

Reflection on and training in these approaches together tends to mitigate impulsive retreats into anger and fear-based actions. *The less moral deliberation within ourselves, however, and the less debate between ourselves and others, the more prone we become to the baser instincts of fear, paranoia, impulsivity, and authoritarian obedience.* The baser instincts and the loss of self-control are where all manner of personal and political crimes become attractive, habit-forming, and even construed as morally righteous. There is personal crime that is a fundamental challenge to the compassionate society, to the flourishing self, and it is the opposite of Compassionate Reasoning. But political crime through demagoguery, mind manipulation, and obedience inducement are all the opposite of Compassionate Reasoning and deeply destructive to far greater numbers of people.

Here is the most important point: As we struggle with ethics, as we explore moral debates with others, and as we explore together the structures of our own minds, we will also discover the ethical principles that bind us together *despite* our moral differences. We will see these common principles and virtues emerge from our discussion, but they include: the compassionate embrace of all life, the embrace of reason, the embrace of self-control, the embrace of fairness, and the embrace of positive vision and imagination. They will not include impulsivity, cruelty, manipulation, or blind obedience.

Disagreements will abound on *how to apply and balance* those virtues and whether they are, for example, established universal virtues or simply helpful guides for rational calculation of future costs and benefits. Some may consider these to be sacred virtues while others see them as secular values or exercises in enlightened prudence. But this difference will matter less than the commitment to ensconce them firmly within our habits of deliberation, within our educational structures from cradle to grave, and within the human psyche itself.

Managing the Differences

Let's go deeper into the nuanced differences in virtues and how to manage those differences. Some ethical approaches have emphasized justice and fairness as the principal basis of ethics, and others have emphasized compassion as the basis of ethics. Some have based personal ethics on acting justly and fairly to all, whereas others have combined all of these emotions and habits in a way that is focused on good consequences. Others begin the foundations of ethics with the use of reason that leads to justice and fairness. Still others have focused completely on happiness and pleasure, with the goal of ethics and politics being the greatest happiness for the most people. Yet others have found that principles that apply equally to everyone, regardless of the consequences, is the only true way toward the good and toward cultivating the good human being.

Most schools of ethics have emphasized human responsibility to other humans as the core of ethics, but since ancient times many moral traditions have included compassion for animals. In view of new understandings of climate science and the fate of the earth, some are arguing for a new and interdependent relationship between compassion and care for humans, on the one side, and care for and responsibility for all sentient beings taken together. This would enlarge ethical calculations and deliberations to include the fate of all of life.

Some require a sacred foundation to these deliberations as the only way to guarantee a moral outcome, whereas others, on the contrary, see organized religion as the basis of most of history's violence. Some argue that *nature* teaches us what we need to know about what is good and rational, whereas others argue that *ethics based on observation* of nature proved to be a terribly biased projection onto nature of personal and socially constructed biases.

Still others argue that the vagaries and uncertainties of life circumstances make these methods impossible for judging morality in the moment but that, by contrast, the *cultivation of character* and moral intuition is the key. Long-term cultivation of goodness in ourselves, our higher selves, is the best path to deal with real life circumstances in the moments that they present themselves. Still others cut through all of the complexity and contradictions of moral deliberation, and instead they focus on the *preservation of life* as the highest principle of ethics. Therefore, saving the most lives is all that matters in their moral calculations.

All of these schools of ethics have strengths and weaknesses that we will explore in the coming chapters as they confront real life circumstances. Here is why I think the study, teaching, and training of ethics is the key to the future: *All schools of ethics have crucial insights that will leave us stronger and more thoughtful if we study them and incorporate them into our thinking and day-to-day moral practices. All schools of ethics have advantages in terms of strengthening vital parts of the brain associated with less violent and more compassionate human behavior.* Familiarity with, and habituation to thinking in, all schools of ethics taken together will strengthen our ability to mold the human mind for less violence and more compassion.

The Embrace of Ethical Deliberation Is a Key Antidote to Authoritarianism and Violence

What I am proposing, therefore, is that the very study, discussion, and deliberation of diverse approaches to ethical dilemmas, the deliberative process of seeking to discover what is the *good,* is inherently healthful for the mind and heart. It is also productive in that all these diverse ways of thinking lead to a better engagement with social collaboration. This effort in itself is a cognitive shift for the mind, a habituation of the brain to thinking through ethical dilemmas with compassion and reason, and better equipment with which to negotiate with others at the moral level. This state of mind and behavior, in and of itself, is healthful, and it can lead to more agreement on agreed-upon paths to action, to human goodness, to less violence, and to more kindness.

The opposite of Compassionate Reasoning—and the opposite of every major school of ethics—is blind obedience. One thing that has become clear in the history of many civilizations is that the opposite of ethics is blind obedience to manipulators and demagogues. Demagogues, mafiosos, and charlatans enslave themselves and their followers to the lust for maximum power. All other considerations, principles, moral calculations are cast aside and not even allowed to be uttered. It all must be replaced by the artificial moral righteousness of the will to power of the demagogue and his gang or in-group.

Demagogues accomplish maximum power by a simple, tried and true method of instilling fear and uncertainty in massive amounts of people who are prone to believe habitual liars. This is a deep conditioning from childhood for simple mythical progressions of the story of life and the story of the world. There must be saints. There must be innocents. There must be absolute villains. The villains in children's tales usually resemble in vague ways some outgroup of any given society (Volkan 2013, 2017, 2020). Demagogues tap into the regressive need in adulthood for leaders that will treat you like children, that will take care of you like children, and therefore such leaders do very well by emphasizing simplistic bedtime stories. They are putting people to sleep, that is, their basic conscience.

Repetition of stimulation of such narratives hardens neural pathways in whichever direction they are stimulated, through expressions of love and empathy but also by constant lies in the context of fear, insults, bullying, and intimidation. Stories can take you in either direction, and often both: villainy is designated for the chosen scapegoat, and love is used to create a yearning for the absolute idealized self or heroic symbol embodied in the demagogue.

Very quickly most people learn to fear the bully, but they also learn that if they join the bully through obedience they will avoid victimhood themselves. This happens in the most astonishingly quick ways in terms of skin color or misogyny. Very quickly people change themselves and change their looks to seek the approval of bullies and leagues of bullies. The neural pathways stimulated by the bully, by ingroup/outgroup designations, fear, and paranoia strengthen the brain stem and the amygdala. This further readies people for mass obedience and mass hatreds, scapegoating, and ultimately violence or passive acquiescence to violence. This is the story of all genocides I have studied or worked on with survivors (Staub 2011, 2015; Irvin-Erickson 2017).[8]

To counter demagoguery, and for democracy and human rights to protect us and this planet's habitability, we need billions of people to be schooled in independent thinking and reasoning that specifically culminates in ethical reflection and practice with a built-in resistance to demagoguery and bullying. In particular, compassion education must play a central role due to its self-reinforcing prosocial and healthful qualities. This strengthens very particular pathways of the brain (Schneider and Koenigs 2017). It is time for the Enlightenment-rooted global commitment to universal education to stop its focus on STEM only, and to also see the virtue, the efficacy, and the logic of universal training for compassion and moral reasoning, from the youngest age to the oldest. I am proposing that Compassionate Reasoning education would embody the best qualities and aspects of most of the ethical schools of thought.

Training in ethical thinking and practice strengthens what science has demonstrated already exists within all of us in nascent form. We see in small children (1) a thirst for practical reasoning and empirical experimentation, and (2) a tendency toward kindness.[9] These exist within human beings from early on, but they can easily be suppressed and destroyed. Moral sense philosophers argued this centuries ago, and now neuroscience is showing us the neural pathways themselves (Gopin 2017; Klimecki, Leiberg, Lamm, and Singer 2013).

Demagogues, Decent Folks, and the Moral Mind

The greatest task that unites the diverse approaches to ethics that we have outlined is to *cultivate moral agency*, meaning the power that comes from making your own ethical deliberations and decisions. It is to cultivate the capacity of each and every human being to:

- *be kind* and
- *utilize reason* to work out the complexity of *applying* kindness in the natural and social world.

Kindness includes kindness to the self and to family, while balancing that care for self with care for strangers and for the world as a whole. This is a task of great complexity that rivals any complex physics in terms of confronting multiple variables. But a conscious commitment to lifetime learning and practice could yield far better results, positively in terms of strengthening a person's ethical practices, and negatively in terms of their ability to resist manipulation. This is what we propose to do with Compassionate Reasoning theory building and practice.

The opposite of Compassionate Reasoning is to be found among charlatans, authoritarians, and narcissists. Charlatans and authoritarian leaders completely fail at a balance of kindness for oneself, one's own group, and the world. They pass this failing on to millions of others through appealing to the lower brain in the way we have described. They completely lose control of their minds, in a certain sense, in that they allow their basest impulses to suppress completely their capacity for compassion, and they dominate all calculations and planning for the sake of the basest satisfaction of personal pleasure and power.

By contrast, those who work at balancing personal needs, family needs, community needs, and global needs are in some ways in touch with all parts of their mind. Specifically, they know and accept the normal fear of not providing for themselves, and they know and accept the normal fear for their family in danger, both strongly associated with the lower brain. They look at their own minds, all parts of it, as this is the advice of wisdom literature from time immemorial. But they also know the natural compassion they feel for others, and they know well the paths of their mind dedicated to rationally balancing their loves and their fears. They balance love and fear through planning, calculus of outcomes, keeping in mind the principles by which they live. Narcissists cannot do that, and when narcissists become demagogues through politics or violence, they inflict this brain dysfunction on all who are hypnotized by them.

Narcissism does not allow people to think of the good of all or compassion for all, since their only thought is of themselves, and often with the illusion that they embody all people inside of them. They *are* their people; "the state is me." Thus, they can act with impunity: they can steal all, they can kill all, because they embody the whole. This is the opposite of the natural capacities we human beings have for collaboration, for reasoning with others, for compassion for those around us, and for kindness exercised in such a way that leads to group survival and flourishing. But as moral sense theorists and wisdom traditions have noted for centuries, even the best of natures require cultivation and habituation. This is what we now can actually see from the explorations of brain science. We should not be surprised that just as the body has immense capacity for endurance and muscular power but only with endless practice, the same is true of the compassionate and reasoning parts of the brain.

We have not evolved enough as a human community when it comes to the practical need to cultivate virtue and ethical decision-making; we have not made it fundamental to how we build our personalities, our natural capacities—or our democracies. Billions of us have excellent qualities of resilience, and extensive compassion is in great evidence at the individual and communal level. But we need to develop a system of lifelong training for better thinking and for collaborative action toward the good of societies as a whole.

Thus, developing a serious education and training program in Compassionate Reasoning could help to tackle some of the most significant weaknesses in democracies and emerging democracies. Citizens require a more cultivated ability to create the good society and resist those who would manipulate them away from their best human capacities.

Toward an Integration of Schools of Ethics and Neuroscience through the Practice of Compassionate Reasoning

Different philosophical schools of ethics favor some parts of the brain over others. By this I mean that a focus on compassion, for example, as the basis of ethics (*moral sense theory*), might suggest an approach to training the mind through reinforcement of neural pathways for compassionate feelings. But a school of ethics that emphasizes rational calculation of the greatest happiness for the greatest number (*utilitarianism*) might emphasize training in:

(a) cognitive reasoning,
(b) scientific and in-depth investigation into human happiness and flourishing that is being explored now in the field of positive psychology, and
(c) optimal methods of governance.

These reason-based studies would be a prelude to choosing and recommending actions[10] as well as developing social and political rules[11] as to how to create the greatest good for the greatest number.

Integrating All the Schools of Ethics through Compassionate Reasoning

For the practice of Compassionate Reasoning, I am suggesting an integration of all of these schools in conversation with each other and in debate with each other. As an example of an argument for integration of ethical approaches, let's take the challenge of *rule invention*.

To really calculate the creation of good rules, a basic activity of reason and essential component of the good society, you also need to have enough compassion for everyone—in all their diversity—to even figure out how to make rules for society that would actually work. Rules are essential, but training in compassion is essential to build realistic rules across lines of difference and opposition.

Another important point is this: The very process of debating these approaches creates far more creativity of the mind that will integrate the schools of ethics into collective thinking and choosing (Mercier and Sperber 2017). The very effort of all in conversation with each other to persuade to their points of view sharpens the mind and leads to creative integration of rules and plans. These rules lead to communal collaboration, coexistence, trust, safety, and even solidarity and love when done very well.

This deliberative process integrates and harmonizes the person herself, in the sense that a positive approach to the whole mind unites all parts of the mind and body, including the following: areas of the brain governing reason, the emotional mind governing affect, interests of personal happiness and health, and the altruistic pleasures of compassion in seeking the happiness of strangers. These taken together present a vital integration of different parts of the mind's workings. From self-oriented designs to altruistic ones, from pleasures and happiness of the self to the happiness of the collective—considerations of all of these through debate and deliberation energizes the peace of society and also the mind itself. Thus, a good exercise in integration of people through ethics is also a good exercise in integration of the body and the mind, the self and the social, the personal and the communal.

A Clear Map of the Argument for Ethics, Neuroscience, and Compassionate Reasoning

This chapter is exploring an interaction between neuroscience research, neuroplasticity, and the foundations of our ethical theory, and therefore I want to map out clearly the argument we are making. Here is the course and direction of the argument:

(1) There are short-term benefits of empathy and perspective-taking for ethical relations, but empathy without training leads eventually to what scientists refer to as *empathic distress*, what is more popularly referred to as "burnout." This state of stress is destructive over the long term as a mental and physical condition, as it causes antisocial withdrawal and even hatred of selected others, in some cases. Empathic distress and antisocial withdrawal make it difficult to engage society with reason, with hope, and with moral intentions.

(2) There is a specific neuroscientific understanding of compassion's importance (as opposed to empathy) and its crucial role in neuroplastic training of the mind and body for healthy ethical interactions and social change. Training the mind and body for compassion and compassionate action is demonstrable and achievable as an alternative to empathic distress.

(3) Reasoning is critical to ethics but is dependent on compassion cultivation for the following reason. The cultivation of reasoning in ethics must be the ultimate goal of training and practice, since it is the mind's reasoning capacity *in engagement with fellow human beings and fellow citizens* that helps generate and uphold universal, fair rules. Empathic distress, however, leads to withdrawal from others, not engagement, whereas compassion by definition leads a person beyond the reaches of one's immediate circles to engagement with others. At the same time, *only with the aid of inference and reason does compassion move toward reasoned paths of responsible policy and human political progress.* Therefore, compassion must be favored over empathy, not only because it is healthier, mentally sustainable, and pleasurable, but because compassion is the foundation of prosocial interaction.

(4) Compassionate interactions lead to the use of the neocortex to create rules. If I have training in compassion for all, then it naturally leads my higher mind to search for policies and rules that result in the most compassion for all. These neural pathways lead to agreed-upon, well-reasoned universal rules of fairness for communities, for nations, and for the globe.

(5) Compassion as the basis of behavior and reasoning needs to pull together all segments of society, including religious and secular citizens who may have different worldviews. Secular and religious systemic

commitments to compassion need to collaborate more in creating the good society. Secular and religious approaches to truth can come to similar conclusions about compassion's value, when this is worked on collaboratively. The human rights tradition emerged out of hundreds of years of religious people moving away from absolutist hierarchies and toward an agreed-upon set of common principles. Following along the historical lines of the human rights tradition, there is a way to keep expanding the scope of ethics and the universe of moral concern. This can bridge not all but many secular/religious divides in ethical reasoning and habit formation, which will be satisfying for the mind and good for society.

(6) The key is to search for what can be agreed upon rather than let the mind go down the rabbit hole of negative fixations and polarization. Polarization is an ever-present possibility of minds controlled by the lower brain stem in search of enemies and danger. The opposite of this is the higher mind's search for consensus-based rules that apply to all.

(7) There is a basic need to nurture the brain through the body and mind, and in particular to pull the body and mind toward greater self-control, less impulsivity, less cruelty, and more compassion for all. Brain training in compassion has been demonstrated successfully, and it can be a key to further development of ethical practices.[12]

(8) The assertion of universal rules, the control of the mind by the will, provides conditioning toward self-control. These move the brain away from prejudice, polarization, fear, and flight.[13] Practice in thinking about universal rules (following neo-Kantian thinking), together with schooling and habituation in compassion (following moral sense theory), training in balancing of virtues (Aristotelian character or virtue ethics), moral consequentialist training in the calculus of outcomes and goals (consequentialism), all make the brain ready for being less prone to an impulsive or violent life.

(9) This combination of ethical schools of thinking and training is a vital protection against the most dangerous threat to ethics, justice and peace, namely excessive obedience by the masses to bullies and demagogues who are the authors of all kinds of ideological extremism. Compassionate Reasoning consciously integrates the best of all the ethical schools and traditions as a bulwark against excessive obedience to bullies and dictators.

(10) It is beneficial to frame ethics education, Compassionate Reasoning, and peacebuilding education as a part of public health education. We will explore in subsequent chapters how *human progress depends on a new approach to severe cruelty and hate, conceptualizing them as sicknesses in need of healing by drawing upon medical and public health approaches to healing.*[14] This can entail, for example, seeing Compassionate Reasoning progress through the following frames: markers of health maintenance and avoidance of disease; symptoms and patterns of habits, substances, and circumstances that lead either toward or away from the spreading of disease. For example, we will explore below a case study of the ethics of countering hate. We will see "hate" as a phenomenon of the human psyche and an ongoing hazard of human psychology, and more precisely as a social disease that can be prevented, managed, kept from spreading, and even cured.

(11) We will study below some fascinating moral-psychological examples of youth interventions regarding the problems of alienation and destructive conflict. These include the "buddy bench" and the "mediation corner" that are specific practices that affirm the basic tenets of Compassionate Reasoning and stem the tide of alienation, anger, and conflict through new habits of the mind and the body—especially the young mind in formation from earliest memories and global constructs. These new habits of thinking and practice change the mind and work to undermine alienation and destructive hate.

(12) The new literature on brain plasticity may suggest that not only meditation and visualization but habits and rituals can reconstruct the "plastic" brain and generate moral improvement for a lifetime. This is a reasonable extrapolation from current experimentation on mental states and their physiological effects (Turner 2019).

(13) We need to think more about the construction of mental maps at a young age, the kind of lens through which we want young people to see the world. In a similar vein, we need to explore the power of repetitive language to morally transform. Such practices and frames could be powerful tools for preventing the social disease of bullying and obedience to bullies, for example. We need a competitive outlook. By this I mean that we need to see the diseased lure of obedience to bullies, demagogues, and ideological extremists, and then compete with these destructive frames through alternative ones.

Obedience to bullies occurs very early on in social life, and we need to explore how to counteract or reconstruct a worldview through the eyes of bullying (Jolliffe and Farrington 2006).

(14) Essentially, the mental and physical health of society depends on a greater collaboration between health and healing disciplines with ethical commitments to compassion and reasoning training that are taught from the earliest age. One of the great challenges to the future of progressive institutions of society, such as nonviolence, human rights, and democracy, is the inculcation of these mental constructs and values from an early age. In other words, we need, for the sake of our personal health and our collective health, a rather revolutionary approach to the centrality of Compassionate Reasoning education for our future.

Now let's enter into greater detail.

Perspective-Taking as a Key Foundation of Ethics and Democracy

Some of the most inspiring experiences of my peace work in war zones have been while teaching the deceptively simple exercise of perspective-taking (Gopin 2009). The idea of the exercise is simple, but its execution and learning process is very complex and dramatic in terms of cognition and affect. This is essentially a practice of peacebuilding that has its roots in the Golden Rule, as it is understood by many cultures across the world. This is to love one's neighbor as oneself, to treat your fellow human being as you yourself would want to be treated, and many other formulations of reciprocity in ethical relations, feeling, and care (Neusner and Chilton 2008). Competent participants in peacebuilding go beyond pious sayings and affirmative ethical statements about loving their neighbors, however. Instead, they set up trainings between adversaries to play each other's roles, to explore personalities, longings, and sufferings in a dramatic fashion, a theatrical practice of adopting each other's perspectives. The mind does something wondrous as perspective-taking proceeds: It moves with amazing speed toward what we have been calling Compassionate Reasoning.

Perspective-taking is a labor-intensive form of peacemaking between adversaries, however, in that when millions of people are at odds with each other, it is a rather difficult suggestion that perspective-taking could be implemented on a large scale. Because it is labor-intensive, it has not been possible to scale up this practice sufficiently. To stop wars on a grand scale between millions of people, who are often subjected to mass propaganda and manipulation by their respective war leaders and political demagogues, it is necessary to think about dramatically expanding peacebuilding practices. If and when we get the chance to be more evolved as a species, then we will spend somewhat less on policing, incarceration, and war, and instead invest in labor-intensive but fruitful practices of evolving our behavior through such practices. We will especially extend these trainings to police, military, and prison officials.

Perspective-taking also does amazing things with former enemies who participate in post-conflict reconciliation work.[15] I have witnessed many adult students of mine from adversarial and competing sides of Syrian society come together in deep moments of compassion, as they listened to each other's stories and understood the depth of the other's inner life and personal suffering. The talents they displayed involved compassion and reasoning in conversation and debate—Compassionate Reasoning. This prepared the way for establishing common values, common principles of living, and building society together again, following the trainings that we created. Often they have had these encounters and trainings even in the midst of bombs raining on their heads from Syrian regime forces. We have established schools across Syria in 2019 and 2020, for example, that use basic ethical principles of conflict resolution that I have developed elsewhere, and perspective-taking is a critical part of that learning process (Center for World Religions, Diplomacy, and Conflict Resolution 2021; Tastakel 2021; Gopin 2016).[16]

For the purposes of exploring Compassionate Reasoning, it is important to ask how perspective-taking actually happens in the mind. First comes the emotional identification with the other and a recognition of many similarities in core values, fears, and hopes.[17] Deep experiences of empathy, feeling the pain of the other, have distinctive impacts on various systems of the body and mind, and this in turn creates powerful bonds between people that simultaneously light up various parts of the brain associated with empathy.

Bonds of empathy build strongly, and then comes a compassionate interest in the welfare of the other and a practice of care for the other that involves the body and the mind in profound prosocial engagement. With the proper guidance and training, this can stimulate the neocortex, the higher mind's interest in fair rules that govern relations. This is the essential progression of Compassionate Reasoning. Through the search for agreement upon common values governed by higher reasoning, compassion and care can become a basis for all relations. Thus, empathy with pain—*if it extends outward to all*—turns into positive compassionate care—a more joyous experience. This in turn stimulates the brain's interest in positive political relations and rule-making between all the disparate people with whom you now have some degree of empathy. This is a progression from empathy with pain, then toward a generalized compassionate care, and this in turn stimulates an ethical and political direction of rule-making and social contract or covenant.

In other words, the mind with these habits and neural pathways moves away from the fear/flight/fight instincts of the lower brain stem and toward the more sophisticated experiences of what we are calling Compassionate Reasoning. This in turn lights up and strengthens the development of several parts of the brain at once that involve prosocial affects and prosocial reasoning and rule-making. The mind moves to abstract reasoning in search of what principles and values could create fairness, happiness, nonviolence, for all the people with whom one now feels empathy.

Reasoning alone cannot get you there, which is why training in STEM by itself does not create the peaceful society. We are talking about a very specific type of reasoning for the creation of universal ethical and political rules, a good will that emerges out of powerful habituation to compassionate feelings and compassionate behavior. Returning full circle to Rousseau and Kant, it is the cultivation of compassion that sets the critical stage for human higher reasoning to take a critical turn toward universal ethics and universal political constructs of fairness and nonviolence or less violence.

The Evolution of Democratic Struggle as a Parallel to the Inner Workings of Moral Reflection

I want to take a cognitive and philosophical leap here. The process that I have just described is another way of saying that the brain recreates the evolution of democratic theory and practice. The brain's evolution from (a) empathy to (b) compassion, and from there to (c) moral reasoning and (d) political democratic reasoning, is the kind of enlightened reasoning that informed several hundred recent years of democratic theory and human rights theory building and experimentation. Various societies across the world sought in recent centuries to move beyond autocratic and aristocratic rule and the latter's obsession with the needs only of the king or the select few. This very important moral leap was based on an appreciation of the inherent worth of all citizens and empathy with all their needs and rights. Then out of that consciousness came an imperfect but increasing effort to create rules that would be fair to all.

Simple but profound questions emerge in the higher brain when properly induced by compassion. These questions include: What are our goals that are commensurate with compassion? What world do we envision[18] that is reasonable, practical, and compassionate at the same time? Will it be fair to all of us? How can we all flourish? Now that we have some basic sense of care for each other's pain and happiness through empathy, how can we also be safe and take care of each other at the same time? Rules begin to emerge, and exceptions also emerge. Contradictions between rules emerge, which then lead to more brainstorming and rational debate. Thus, Compassionate Reasoning gives birth to democratic legal discourse and debate at an advanced level. This demonstrates a perfect example of Compassionate Reasoning at work, and the way in which perspective-taking is an essential skill and precursor to progress.

We in peacebuilding and conflict resolution have seen perspective-taking work as a technique of enhancing and speeding up this approach to compassion, even in the most difficult places in the world. I have done this work with thousands of students from war zones over the past twenty years, and I have seen it work in powerful ways. We need all of modern education to move in the direction of consciously inculcating perspective-taking, with a particular emphasis on the cultivation of the elements of thinking, feeling, and doing, that I have encapsulated in Compassionate Reasoning. Perspective-taking needs to become not just a peacebuilding tool between enemies, but rather a fundamental building block of any society that hopes to be ethical, democratic, peaceful, and fair to all.

Perspective-Taking in Bosnia and the Challenges of Empathy

I want to illustrate with a story from June of 2017 in Bosnia. I run classes in different parts of the world, including Turkey, Syria, Jordan, and Israel, as a form of field education for peacebuilding, conflict resolution, and reconciliation. But I also make these education classes into a peace intervention to support overwhelmed and overtaxed peacemakers who are survivors of war. The class becomes a way for me and my wife, for my Center's team, and for my students every year to support peaceful change-makers who are often under great stress. We do this by giving them and their work a much wider audience globally, by writing about them, and by giving them personal support (Center for World Religions, Diplomacy, and Conflict Resolution 2020). The classes have been the venue in which I have been able to implement the power of perspective-taking with both students and local activists of very different backgrounds. The class essentially is about the active experience of perspective-taking with victims of war, their stories, and their heroic efforts to be peacemakers in impossible circumstances.

Let me step back for a minute. Long before 2017, living and teaching in Washington, DC, I had personally struggled during the years of genocidal war crimes in Bosnia, 1991 to 1995. I was particularly traumatized as a Jew because it was for me a re-traumatizing experience to watch a battered, defenseless minority in Bosnia being hemmed in on all sides, driven from their homes, and placed in concentration camps. We saw constant scenes from Sarajevo, an entire cosmopolitan population composed of Bosnian Muslims, Serbs, and Croats, slowly and steadily shot at every day. For me it felt awfully familiar to scenes from the Warsaw Ghetto, World War II, for example. I felt physically ill many days watching the scenes. Since the 1990s I have come to understand that there were war crimes on several sides in Bosnia, and that many innocents were caught in the middle from all the ethnic groups. But in the 1990s, from a distance in America, I wanted to stand up to genocide, especially for the Muslims who suffered the most murders of unarmed civilians. I felt a strong sense of helplessness that weighs on the brain in the face of war's victims, especially when this was televised and felt so close.

I fought for a time in Washington to organize attention to war crimes in Bosnia and to stop the slaughter, but in all that time I had never actually been to the former Yugoslavia. In the years since then, my professional attention was focused on peacebuilding in the Middle East, and so the student trip in 2017 was the first time I went on the ground to Bosnia (Center for World Religions, Diplomacy, and Conflict Resolution 2020). At the Center which I founded and directed at George Mason University, we look on these educational trips for students as a way to support heroes of peacebuilding by visiting, telling their stories, learning from them, and calling international attention to their work. We want to meet those who sacrifice, who struggle, and who have done heroic work for the sake of peacebuilding.

Kemal

We visited people on all sides of the conflict in 2017, from Muslims to Jews to Serbians to Croats, with an emphasis on heroic nonviolent activists during the war. One day, our class bus in Bosnia found its way to a tiny village called Kevljani to meet a 44-year-old man by the name of Kemal Pervanic, a survivor of the infamous Omarska concentration camp.[19] Kemal sat us down to the most harrowing unpublished half-hour film I had ever seen. We saw everything that happened to him and his community. We saw him confront his Serbian college professor who, during the war, turned up as his interrogator during his time at the concentration camp, a man who had sent hundreds to a terrible death after torture. I had heard of the round-ups. I saw the emaciated bodies in the camp on films before, so familiar to me from a lifetime studying the Holocaust of my own people. But to see it through the eyes and narration of a young Kemal with his beautiful blue eyes and a very far-away, haunted look—that was far too immediate for me.

When we finished watching, Kemal stood before us with the most peaceful and plaintive eyes, a survivor of everything we had just seen. Kemal was a survivor of torture by his own teacher, who led the interrogations that the concentration camp—an unimaginable double wound for Kemal. We sat with Kemal in his Muslim village house that had been destroyed during the war and since rebuilt; it was his ancestral home from before the war, and now he lived there alone. The house was dark inside, shades drawn in many places, but outside it was surrounded by beautiful trees, meadows, and flowers. The house was in a tiny Muslim village surrounded by Serbian villages on every side, in a region called Serbska, a part of Bosnia that is dominated by Bosnians of Serbian background who struggle to be part of greater Serbia. It was their forces that surrounded this Muslim village during the war, assaulted it, and killed the men or sent them to camps.

I was broken by the stories in the film, physically drained, haunted sitting in a home bereft of its happy past before the war. My mind and heart were completely and empathically in the past, in the sufferings of the past. But nevertheless, it was twenty years later, and we were there to support him not to mourn. And so I adopted my intervention skills, which should always be focused on compassionate care and on questions more than pat answers. I asked him, "What can we do to help you?" And he responded simply, "You already have, by coming."

This was a stunning answer, and it spoke to us deeply as a group. I have heard it many times before from survivors and witnesses. Presence, care, solidarity, listening. In this way a private hell can at least be shared, understood, its perspective taken, and in that simple but agonizing gesture there comes the smallest bit of healing and comfort.

An Hour Visit to Hell

Nothing prepared me, however, for what was about to come with Kemal. We left with him to travel to the larger town of Prijedor. Everything as far as the eye could see was beautiful, quiet, peaceful, as bucolic a scene as one could imagine. Just down the road he stopped us one last time in his village, and he asked us to get out of the car near the village mosque that was recently rebuilt. He showed us where he is building a peace center, at the very spot where the sports field used to be, the very field where he was forced to gather with every other Muslim man to go to the Omarska concentration camp. The field where his Serb kindergarten teacher, sporting a gun, ordered them all to line up.

Then, turning around, he looked into my eyes and said, "And this is where the mass grave was. Several hundred bodies from the Muslim village, and also from the concentration camp." Of course, this was part of documented history now, but I had not realized the mass grave had been right there.

I was not prepared for a mass grave on this trip. I turned around and I saw the ruins of the old mosque, then I looked at the graveyard, and then I saw it with my own eyes. I noticed the outline of a distinct rectangular depression in the ground going on for hundreds of feet. It was covered over by uncomfortably beautiful grass, and it was a clear rectangular depression in the ground heading off into the distance. I felt instantly what had been there, and I started to shake uncontrollably.

I did not know what to do. I am a professor, I had a class with me, and I was breaking down completely inside. The rage in me, the sheer rage that made me shake. For it is in exactly this kind of bucolic rustic village that three hundred Jews had been rounded up on one day in the tiny hamlet that my Gopin clan originated from in northwest Ukraine, a hamlet 100 miles due east of Cracow. All the Jewish people, most of the town, shot on one day, by Ukrainian fascist militia with a couple of Nazi German officers present, all between Rosh Hashanah, the Jewish New Year, and Yom Kippur, the Day of Atonement, in the year 1943, during the Ten Jewish Days of Repentance in the sacred calendar. It was a beautiful tiny hamlet, my family's hamlet, surrounded by vaulting evergreen trees, just like this village before me, just like Kemal's Muslim village. It was called Troyanivka, and it is the only place where I knew my clan had come from. All the Jews gone now, only a small plaque on the mass grave. It was 1100 miles to the east of where I now stood in Bosnia.

I looked at the scene with the mosque in front of me; I crossed the road, I asked Kemal to accompany me to the mass grave, and I stood next to it with him. Ever since I was little, I had an intense, uncontrollable, and sometimes crippling empathy for those in pain, and here I could not stop thinking about the dead. I imagined and felt the last moments of these Bosnian Muslim men and boys far too much in my mind and in my bones.

The Dark Side of Perspective-Taking: Life in a Mass Grave

I could not help but ask myself a simple question at that moment as I shuddered and wept: "The six hundred people who had been buried there after being murdered, what in their last moments would they want from me, if they could speak?" What in the last moments of my life would *I* have wished for, lying in a ditch, after torture and about to be murdered? It was as if I felt myself beneath my own feet. The answer to my own question that came to me in that moment was that I would want to be remembered, I would want my soul to be prayed for, and I would want to not be forgotten.

And so on that day, in a tiny Muslim village, I walked with Kemal, separated from my class by a hundred feet or so, put on my Jewish head covering which I use for strictly private prayers, and I held my Muslim friend Kemal close. I addressed Hebrew words to Muslim victims, an ancient Jewish chant for fellow Jews who had been massacred in the past. I said the Jewish prayer for the memory of the dead, a prayer for the holy souls of the dead, " . . . that they may achieve eternal rest under the wings of the Divine Presence." Through every word I wept, with Kemal holding me and comforting me, my legs buckling. Jew and Muslim embracing, looking down at a mass grave. Strangely it felt holy, like one of the most sacred moments of my life, like something I was born to do.

I did not want my class to see what I was doing or experiencing. I did not want anyone to see, except Kemal. I needed to bear witness, but I also needed to not make it into a public spectacle in the middle of my professional role as professor. I needed it to be an act of intimacy with the dead. I also needed to be with survivors, with whom I felt as a fellow survivor—and no one else. I needed to share that intimate space where survivors have difficulty separating from the dead, because I sensed this from Kemal from the day I met him, even when he would smile and laugh. And I have felt it too for much of my life.

This compromise separation between my private but intense grieving versus my public role as professor is what my heart felt it wanted to do. But it was also what my reason told me the situation allowed for in terms of trying to keep the class professional. And so I separated from the class but united with the dead, at least in that moment. I struggled there on that mass grave between emotion and reason, despair and determination, empathy with the dead and commitment to the living.

I was not happy, however, that once again empathic distress had overtaken me, even as I was trying to teach healing and peacebuilding. *I knew that excess empathy had a dark side in my life,* and I had just gotten a pretty strong dose of it. And it was not as if I needed this kind of empathy to do my peace work better. On the contrary, it felt somewhat crippling, just as the science of empathic distress would teach me when I read it the following year. The science of empathic distress invaded me as a revelation but also as familiar, like a lifelong partner.

From Empathic Distress to Compassionate Reason: A Personal Journey between Practice and Scholarship

For so many decades, my work in war zones has brought me face to face with survivors, and the pain of what they go through has tended to negatively affect me through what scientists call "empathic distress." I also came to learn that post-traumatic stress disorder (PTSD) is actually contagious when you are continually exposed to war victims who have it.[20]

I remember one moment of my life for which I was completely unprepared. We were up in the north of Jordan, at the height of the Syrian genocide, over a million refugees pouring over the border. My Syrian partners and I were there to help build resilience, skills of coping and rebuilding the lives for survivors. We were there also to bear witness, to express solidarity and care in whatever way we could. I was able to take a large American class with me due to eleven intense years of interfaith peacebuilding work in Syria which I had pioneered as Director of the Center for World Religions, Diplomacy, and Conflict Resolution at George Mason University. I had developed intense relationships with many Syrian friends, fellow travelers, and students, as I have detailed elsewhere (Gopin 2009). The students wanted to come to study and participate in this rare practice of peacebuilding right at the borders of war.

We met mostly refugees who had lost everything, including immediate family, many family members dying along the escape routes as they were hunted and bombed by the Syrian regime, with the full aid of Russia and Iran. My class came to a religious school caring for survivors on March 12, 2016. I came in and saw a middle-aged gaunt man, sitting but sprawled across a table unable to keep his head up; he was one of the parents of the kids. He lost a daughter in Syria just weeks before, and then his wife along the way over the border had bled to death from wounds as they escaped, just a few miles from where we were. His eyes seemed dazed and dead, and I did not know what to do for him, but I saw and felt everything in his empty glazed eyes.

The poor man had his son in the room with all the other kids, a beautiful, tall teenager, fifteen years of age, such a broadly smiling face, and this man's only surviving child. This boy was like a hero to the group in the school and also to my visiting class. He was on crutches and smiling so broadly as he walked. Everyone loved him, everyone cheered him like a hero, and I see his face to this day in 2021 as if he is right in front of me.

As is common in Syria, this boy hugged a lot, and he came to hug me. I hesitated because I know my reactions to empathy, but I hugged him strongly. At that instant something very bizarre happened to me. It felt as if a bolt of lightning went through my body. I saw only white for a moment as I hugged. You see, half his limbs had been blown off, his arm and his leg on one side. When I hugged him, it felt as if the bomb had gone off in *my* body—no pain in me, just an electric shot through me and then blinded for an instant, as I could only see a flash. I could not see in that moment, which made me panic. My heart pounded so hard as if to come out of my chest, and I was unsteady on my feet because I was still feeling like a silent bomb blast. I tried to keep smiling at him, embarrassed by this utterly involuntary response, and then I tried to continue with the visit.

Ever since then I have tried to make sense of what happened to me in that moment. This kind of involuntary empathy is apparently much more common than I ever realized. I could not forget that moment and the hug,

I still feel it, and it still makes my heart beat fast and the tears come. I held that moment in my body, at first with overwhelming shock and now with permanent memory. I tried to process this moment again and again over the years since, and each time it is like a punch in the stomach and a knot in the throat and tears in my eyes. This moment lodged these feelings inside my body, to this day in 2021. I will never forget him, for his face brings me comfort and horror, all at once. Comfort for the resilience of good souls who love and survive and remain so good and kind and hopeful, and horror because I feel inside me permanently the reality of what a small bomb, out of millions, does that lands right on a teenager, right on a family, and how it hollows out the soul of a surviving father. It teaches me why I despise bombs and bomb making.

As I continue to do my work with Syrians in these past years since 2016, I have achieved some degree of greater calm, healing, and recovery. There is a measure of wisdom that can be achieved by the study of health sciences and psychology, as it helps the mind come to know itself better, and this in turn creates more calm, as it did for me. Self-awareness is the critical path to healing, and it does much to overcome emotional roadblocks that would otherwise deter good work for the good of society.

With greater calm, it is also possible to do more analytic work on what is to be done in complicated and emotional situations. Much received wisdom has, over the centuries, addressed the nature of healing processes and the ethics of what is to be done in healing work. This wisdom helps train our minds even more toward higher reasoning and away from involuntary pain and suffering of the caregivers. *Involuntary pain does little good for caregivers or for those they are serving. But the combination of training our minds away from self-destructive pain and more toward compassionate actions will propel the mind of the caregiver, and the society she/he serves, in a healthier direction.*

I now understand, thanks to science and to the wisdom of experience, why my strong empathy with survivors has been less than helpful, causing problems in my personal life, even though so many ethical and religious traditions encourage empathy as a high ethical and spiritual achievement. The moral sense or moral emotion of empathy, whether based on secular ethics or rooted in religious commitment, should come with a warning label for those who become too adept at its practice.

I have come to understand that *the answer to the problematic effects of empathy or empathic distress is the emotional habit of compassion and active solidarity, which is a morally superior response as both care for oneself and care for victims.* Compassion, or solidarity through care, is different from empathy, and in fact it is better, morally speaking. Abuse of the self is just as problematic morally as abuse of others, from the point of view of most ethical schools I have studied. Self-love, self-care, the moral imperative to search for meaning, enlightenment and happiness, these are all givens of most ethical traditions.

Compassion is care of self combined with care of others. In addition, compassion cannot be antisocial by definition, but empathy can be and often is. With the habits of compassion, there are not only good intentions but also practical benefits for recipients who are the object of our empathy, and there is a direct channel of action and healing for our sadness when we feel their sadness. Compassion comes with the clear and loving intention *to do something*, to care, to be kind, to be constructive, but also simply to wish for good and bless others. Good intentions and wishes of the mind are also a kind of action that the mind takes. This is very different from empathic reception of the pain of others, which is largely passive. To be compassionate is to practice an act with deep meaning for the sake of the other but without debilitating over-identification with the suffering of victims. Excessive empathy can cripple the capacity to exercise care, and empathy is therefore far less successful, morally and practically speaking.

Returning to Serbska, it was not my intervention with Kemal that was wrong; it was not wrong of me to bring myself or my feelings into this situation, and it was not wrong to bring my students together with Kemal. On the contrary, care and solidarity with survivors globally is a vital peacebuilding tool for a world that is far too disconnected. Such relationships between strangers from across the world are a critical way to overcome the anger, the alienation, and the scapegoating that dominates politics and international interventions. Such interactions, when done properly, can produce effective and responsible ethical citizens, while also helping victims to recover and be empowered when they are still in danger.

However, it was wrong of me to experience the mass grave near Kemal's home *as traumatically as I did*. It did not help him, it did not help my students, and it certainly was not healthy for me. I am learning from the literature of neuroplasticity and the pioneering experiments of neuroscientists that what we are talking about is a subtle but crucial difference between the experience of empathic distress and the experience of compassionate solidarity. Good ethical and political interventions in life's most difficult challenges cannot be just righteous deeds borne of suffering and grief. Rather, *interventions must be clearly rooted in mental and physical health, and with healthy intentions to act.* For it is only with health that ethical actions build the good society based upon a combination of compassion and reason, Compassionate Reasoning. As we have seen, it is only with an action orientation that the mind and personality can escape despair itself, create meaning, and help others to do the same.

This traumatic moment at the mass grave site in Serbska was a turning point in my life, and it motivated me further to articulate in this book a new approach to pursuing peacebuilding, reconciliation, and relationship building with others, only with a thorough training in Compassionate Reasoning.

Compassionate Reasoning Can Restore the Imbalances Caused by Empathic Distress

The practice of Compassionate Reasoning leads to sustainable and lifelong habits that become an enticing model of health and meaningful happiness. We also set a profoundly positive example for others who come after us, and in so doing, it becomes an epigenetic phenomenon,[21] something embedded in human evolution that we each affect in our own small way. A healthy approach to difficult engagements with others means we live much longer, and we positively affect far more people. Our progeny will need those received habits as they face a deeply challenging environment.

Training in Compassionate Reasoning will help drive the mind toward compassion and away from empathic distress. It impacts both feelings and actions through a reflective use of the higher mind. The reasoning mind, for example, concludes that the self-harm of empathic distress is not prudent or wise for the continued existence of the self or for the self's ability to help others. The higher mind suggests that there are more realistic ways to chart a path toward compassion, without the self-destruction that wears away and harms so many caregivers. Training in this kind of reasoning suggests an embrace of the *positive* effects of compassion but *rejects* self-harm. Then the scientific mind does the empirical research— now that the right questions are being asked, and the right technology is available—to find the best path toward care and peacebuilding that is not self-destructive.

From training our minds and hearts to focus on compassionate action and practical aid, we then build the rational ethical principles necessary for the good society and the good civilization to flourish, and we do it with the mental and physical health necessary to be strong and sustainable.

Journey of a Peacebuilder: How Personal Trauma Led Me to a Theory of Compassionate Reasoning

Some of us who have worked in war and conflict management for decades have come to realize just how debilitating this work can be. We have experienced how constant empathy for those countless victims who suffer in war can deplete you, can make you angry or lost in despair. Empathy can even make you self-harm in unconscious and conscious ways, in order to relieve the distress of impotence, the sorrow of not being able to do a damn thing for those you thought you would help, for those you came to love. And yet there are others among us in this work who seem continually energized and ever ready for more experience. I have asked myself for years, how are these opposites possible in the same field of dedicated practice? What makes for a happy practitioner in war zones?

It was hard for me to understand my own experience of empathic distress as a scholar/practitioner, until I started to reevaluate my field and my practice of conflict resolution. I did this by way of a conscious comparison of my field to the field of medicine and healthcare. In previous books, I have suggested that a comparison to healthcare and public health may be an effective way to discern complicated questions of conflict resolution and the ethics of peaceful intervention (Gopin 2009). Now I want to raise the matter of how and why some caregivers, nurses, and emergency doctors flourish under the worst of circumstances while others fall apart.

I came to some of these conclusions through personal experience with hospitals and emergency care. To illustrate, I want to return to the story I told earlier about the intensive care unit where my sister resided. In 2014 I was immersing myself in my sister's care as she fought for her life, attacked by the H1N1 virus.[22] She is seven years older than me and has cared for me for decades as I grew up, and through adulthood. She was always there to advise me, guide me, and inspire me, and then one day I found myself on the verge of losing her.

I reached out to my rather large social media community and people across the world from so many religious societies whom I had come to know and serve, and I asked them to pray for her as she was on the verge of dying. This was rather uncommon in 2014, as there were few clusters of social media communities that mixed as many religions and cultures as I had in the course of my global career and peace work. I simply had a very unusual mix of people from every continent of the world as friends, and from every conceivable branch of all the major and minor religions. I thought to myself that this fits my sister's global spiritual values, and so I reached out. The response was absolutely overwhelming, and it strengthened my determination to fight for her.

I was living in Washington, DC at the time, but I relocated to Boston. I lived with my elderly mother in order to be in the hospital with my sister. The intensive care unit gave me the chance to observe a very large number of her doctors and caregivers over weeks, weeks that seemed like years. She stayed in the intensive care unit at the edge of life and death every day. I was suffering deep grief and fear in the hospital, long days and especially long nights. Her fate was considered rather bleak, as I described in an earlier chapter.

Oddly enough, in my determination to fight her fate, I became embedded and comfortable in the hospital, often sleeping on floors in empty corridors late at night. I simply could not leave. At some turning point that I cannot pinpoint, I began to find it hard to sleep in beds even when I went home. I could no longer accept the normality symbolized by a bed. It was as if something terrible would happen if I were not in a hospital waiting room or in an empty hallway, lying on the floor. I still feel to this day some strange longing for those places, as if my soul became situated in hospital corridors. It actually took me years to recover from feeling a kind of shaking in my body as soon as I started talking about the weeks outside the intensive care unit. It was empathic distress, and it was PTSD, and I only know that and can accept that six years later.

I learned many things from observing every medical caregiver 24/7 in those crucial weeks, watching all the shifting doctors, nurses, surgeons, and technicians. Then I compared and contrasted their every move with the many grieving families who pass through intensive care units as patients survive and are moved to regular beds or die. The contrast was enthralling to me. I watched as the caregivers focused on the *tasks of healing, using all of their mind and heart in those tasks*, whereas many family members watched passively, empathetically, sometimes looking paralyzed, becoming trau-matized. There were two types of sympathetic actors in this setting: activist caregivers and traumatized observers. It is not that the pain of empathy with the victim did not affect the activist healers. The activist caregivers, most of the nurses and technicians, engaged with minute-to-minute observations and intense care. Watching is passive for many of us; it is a passive act of observation. *But these people watched and engaged as warriors,* as a kind of dramatic battle that they were engaging in with H1N1. What I now call Compassionate Reasoning was the weapon of war that they deployed, the lens of rational medical expertise combined with intense knowledge of the patient's minute-to-minute condition. There was time in their minds only for care, no time for sadness or frustration, since there were so many other patients to care for. More importantly, critical decisions needed to be made hour to hour (sometimes minute to minute) on oxygen levels, fluids, meds, so many variables. They always watched like hawks guarding a nest. In response to this situation, they evinced strength, power. They even seemed exhilarated at every challenge to her survival. To watch the healers at the Mass General Hospital's intensive care unit was a marvel to behold.

There was a young doctor who worked incredibly hard on my sister. One disastrous night he worked for hours, till his hands were numb, in order to stop her bleeding, to save her (as I described in Chapter 1). I was astonished, however, by the emotional difference between me and these caregivers: we both were dogged in determination, both exhausted, but they were exhila-rated and I was in a state of trauma. It all started to make perfect sense years later as I began to intuit the profound difference between empathic iden-tification and compassionate care. This was the exact distinction that the neuroscientists had identified as they traced two radically different neural pathways, one for compassion and one for empathic distress.

This realization led me in the years afterward to strenuous mental efforts to change my own mental habits in international interventions. Every time I felt despair in the company of the victims, overwhelmed by the pain of the victims of genocide whom I was serving, I started in very halting ways to try to redirect my empathic pain to an exclusive focus on what is to be done at the moment. I started to focus only on the moment and without a thought to the enormity of the tragedy I was watching. I especially did so at the moments of my own deepest pain, when I had heard stories of horror from people whom I loved. This gave me strangely a sense of power that I needed in order to give the care that I needed to give.

Later, as I practiced my own intuitive distinctions between the experience of empathy versus the art of compassion, I started to realize something. Many ancient religious traditions and wisdom traditions had often made a fine distinction between empathy and compassion, between *feeling* the pain of the other and the *actions* of care. But very rarely had anyone, either in old religious ethical communities or secular systems of care, nor in my own professional field of conflict resolution, conducted training to help the mind to make this fine distinction in the moment of emergency intervention. There was no training to redirect the mind away from destructive empathy and toward the nobility and power of an exclusive focus on what must be done next, on what are the most compassionate actions to be taken. No training on how to exult in the passion of that practice of love, in the nobility of that moment, in its meaningfulness for one's life, for one's soul.

The subject of compassion was not new to me, and in fact it was a fixation of my scholarship for decades. By 1993, I had finished my PhD dissertation on Rabbi Samuel David Luzzatto, a much-overlooked nineteenth-century philosopher and theologian, as he centralized compassion as the core "moral sense" of Judaism, building on the philosophical moral sense theory of Francis Hutcheson and the Third Earl of Shaftesbury. I published a book in 2017 expanding on that dissertation, entitled *A Compassionate Judaism* (Gopin 2017).

Luzzatto argued, like Viktor Frankl ([1946] 2006) would write over a hundred years later after surviving the death camps of the Holocaust, that the human being can discover the highest experience of meaning through altruism or compassion. Luzzatto asserted that compassion is even a powerful *pleasure* that no one can ever take away from you, no matter how battered you have been by life, no matter what you have lost. You could lose your partner and most of your children—as Luzzatto tragically did—you could lose all of your money and worldly possessions, as he did many times; but no one could take from you the meaningful experience of caring for another who was suffering. *That*, Luzzatto believed, is the essence of true religion, a true embrace of God, through the embrace of the other human being. This message seems to me to echo deeply what Viktor Frankl had experienced and discovered eighty years later in Auschwitz.

Subsequently I wrote on compassion as a core of ethics, but I never practiced this framing and experience of compassion or trained myself in the joy of compassionate care in my field work with survivors. I never made it satisfying and healthy, as there was too much empathic distress all the time. I found work with survivors to be devastating to me personally, to my body, to my state of mind, such was my bodily identification with their pain. I did not realize at the time that some of us need training in this kind of joy of compassion, especially if we have been habituated to empathic distress.

The surprise to me and others is that I persisted in the work of peace in war zones anyway, despite all of that pain I was bringing home from the Middle East, not to mention through students from all over the world. As I look back, I think it was a sense of stoic duty that drove me, in a rather Kantian way. I grew up from early childhood with the influence of a teacher, mentor and friend, Rabbi Dr. Joseph Soloveitchik. He was in many ways the most important Modern Orthodox Jewish theologian of the twentieth century, and he embraced a kind of stoic neo-Kantian legalism as the core of ethics and the core of religion, at least in many of his significant writings, hundreds of lectures I attended, and in countless private conversations with me as I was growing up. R. Soloveitchik's PhD work before World War II had been at the University of Berlin on Kantian and Cohenian logic. The core choice of life for Kant, and I believe for my teacher, was the exercise of the moral will, for duty and principle, no matter what the circumstances, no matter how difficult. In fact, the more difficult the circumstances the more you were exercising your will out of a pure sense of duty to humanity, the Kantian categorical imperative. Meaning and salvation came for Rabbi Soloveitchik from obedience to duty, to law (Soloveitchik 1984, 1998, 2006).

I was inspired by Kant more and more over the years as I charted my own journey of social change, beyond the confines of the religiously conservative world of my youth. I dived into saving lives in war with a dogged determination to fix what was wrong with life on earth, to challenge and fix what was unjust, to champion what universal laws of fairness and dignity for all demand in an increasingly interdependent global community.[23] But my own deeply somatic empathy with pain caught me off guard and hammered away at my ability to function.

It is risky to engage in constant stress, but my risky work trying to prevent global violence came out of a place inside of me of dogged determination— duty, not joy. On the contrary, it often felt like being in hell. I don't regret the work, but I now realize that there are healthy ways to pursue this vital work that need to be carefully and consciously cultivated if the work is to be sustainable. Dogged determination is a good quality, but not in a state of misery.

How Traditional Cultures Can Amplify the Positive Effects of Compassion

Out of this experience of my youth and my unique background in both conservative religion and Enlightenment philosophy, I realized traditional cultures need to be at least a part of the solution to global problems. There must be an invitation repeatedly of inclusion. We must work harder to establish superordinate ethical goals that transcend faiths, moral differences, and lifestyle differences. All the work in the Middle East added up to evidence that with hard work, traditional peoples could be at the table of peace and coexistence with more liberal-minded folks in every culture, and in fact have a great deal to teach. But it would take hard work of relationship building, peacebuilding, and conflict resolution.

I also realized that we need to study the long history of ethics, both secular and religious, in search of what values can be shared and built upon to establish a moral community and peaceful processes of conflict management and resolution. I had seen it happen countless times among people of good will all over the world, but it took painstaking work and far greater global investments (Gopin 2000, 2002, 2009, 2012, 2016). For example, one of the highest experiences of Judaism, with "rewards" promised in this world and "the next world" (Heaven or the World to Come), is called *Gemilus Hasadim*, the bestowal of abundant kindness.[24] Feeling the pain of others is indeed lauded as a sacred quality in the sacred texts of Judaism, but such feelings are not at the same level of spiritual achievement as compassionate *actions*, actions that express or come out of a motive of compassion to help, to care, and to love.

Perhaps this suggests the reason why these ancient sages were so confident that there were "rewards" in this world for compassionate actions. The "compassion" actions are decidedly not empathic distress, which causes so many health problems and so much unhappiness. They were not just making promises to lure the believer into righteous behavior, but rather they earnestly believed that compassionate actions lead to joy and health, that compassionate feelings and behaviors are their own rewards.

From the ancient sages to Hutcheson, Shaftesbury, Luzzatto, and Frankl, we have a clear line of philosophers, ethicists, psychologists, and practitioners of ethics who were offering a pathway to positive social change, health, and happiness through compassion. This path is decidedly *not* through extensive personal suffering and empathic pain with victims, but on the contrary, a victory over suffering through love and compassionate care, even in the most dire circumstances of poverty and premature death, and even in Auschwitz.

In the context of societies where sacred virtues are relevant, the positive impact of training in compassion—a social emotion known to improve health, mood, and socialization—becomes combined with a spiritually or religiously sanctioned emotion of compassion, or religious compassion. This reinforces the positive motivation to be ethical *from several parts of the mind at once*. In other words, part of the mind imagines compassionate action as a positive religious deed, an exalted imitation of God's ways in the world, for example, or even in many traditions as a way to see the face of God through the face of the sufferer whom you are helping (Gopin 2000, 2002).[25] At the same time, science enters with specific methods of compassion training that reinforce parts of the mind known to increase happiness, socialization, and health (Klimecki, Leiberg, Lamm, and Singer 2013). This, it seems to me, puts Compassionate Reasoning training onto a very solid footing in conservative societies, but also on solid scientific footing at the same time. This provides an opportunity for a crucial peacebuilding bridge, an area of collaboration and cooperation between secular and religious constructs that so often keep everyone divided in modern societies.

As I have argued elsewhere, however, the key detriment to ethics in conservative societies is effectively the opposite of Kantian universalism, namely the mandated or militant restriction of an ethical act to a very limited set of believers (Gopin 2000). In fact, such restrictions of moral obligation to only a small set of believers undermines ethics altogether as a binder of multicultural and multi-religious society. When this happens, the observer will notice that broad ethical principles and practices become suppressed in militant societies. In their place you will notice that obscure rituals, clothing, tribal markers peculiar to the group become the markers and tests of piety, the markers of who is in and who is out, who is deserving of moral behavior and who is shunned, even who deserves salvation and who deserves bigotry and aggression.

What I am arguing, however, is that the stronger and more powerful we make compassion training in conservative societies, the more health benefits it offers, and then the more it will become a natural bridge to others *beyond* the conservative community. It will be the same for those who find it difficult to tolerate conservatives. Reasoning based on compassion will ineluctably lead, then, to reasoning out and debating shared principles, values, and public policies. We need to create the context for shared superordinate moral values and shared habits, and then the higher mind uses reasoning and planning for compromise, strategy, and joint principles.

As opposed to empathic distress—which makes people, including religious believers, angry and withdrawn as they mourn the losses of their beloved group—the expansive and happy quality of compassionate socialization is our best contribution to inducing conservative societies to ethical engagement with others. I have seen this work in global interfaith work for thirty years. I continue to be amazed at how much compassionate work with children and other victims binds very conservative and very secular people, across all boundaries of conservative and liberal ideologies.

Out-of-Control Empathic Distress Can Be a Danger to Peace

There is an additional reason to shift our minds and our ethical systems toward compassion. If empathic distress is debilitating, then it prepares the mind more for despair and apathy. If those feelings cause a desire to withdraw from society, then this is the opposite of what we need to establish an ethical society. We need the mind moving *toward* people not away from them. We need the mind to embrace prosocial emotions that lead to a reasoned reflection on how to construct universal laws and practical public policies that apply to all. The *motivation* to even conceive of universal laws applying to all requires some significant degree of compassionate interest in the good of all others and society as a whole. It is hard to do that if your brain is stuck in anger, withdrawal, and apathy. This goes for both secular and religious people, left-wing and right-wing political ideologies. Empathic distress that gets out of control, turning into excessive anger about victims, is an equal opportunity destroyer of universal values.

Empathic distress can even breed rage and hatred. For example, I certainly fought this in myself working with thousands of war victims near the battle front in Syria in the terrible years of 2012–2016 (Center for World Religions, Diplomacy, and Conflict Resolution 2021; Gopin 2009). I definitely felt rage and hatred for those doing the hospital bombings and the regimes supporting it, as I dealt with outrageous stories of torture and destruction. There were people smuggling blood for transfusions in their cars because every hospital had been targeted and every doctor. That can fill you with rage very quickly.

By contrast, the exhilarating experience of compassionate action prepares the mind and heart for rational reasoning. The first thought coming out of compassion is the rational question, "How can I help? How can I cultivate the best of intentions and the most intelligent help for those who need us?" Compassionate feelings extend to all, even adversaries. The habits of compassionate action, extended to all, leads the mind and group thinking to the creation of shared rules of behavior for a peaceful society, rules that necessarily apply to even those you find to be morally culpable, such as criminals and prisoners. Even as you need at times to resist, defend, or fight, if you train your mind in Compassionate Reasoning you can prepare for the day after fighting. But if you are lost in rage, then nothing can stop your descent into hate and violence that is often self-destructive and self-defeating.

From the point of view of the field of conflict resolution, positive experiences of compassion and healing across enemy lines, across lines of diversity, encourages the mind in the direction of a reason-based approach to coexistence despite obvious religious and political differences between many peoples. Compassion and conflict resolution practices lead the mind to discover public policy that must benefit and protect everyone. Compassionate care is the foundation of public policies and social covenants of commitment.

The question of why empathic actions lead to positive change sometimes and not at others, in some places and not others, has always been a mystery. In some places and times, reactionary adherents to multiple religions in close proximity will harm each other, but in other eras and places conservative communities exist side by side and flourish.

The answer I am proposing is the manipulation of empathic distress, or its manufacture, for the sake of political or demagogic power. Politically induced excessive empathy for one's own people, combined with induced hatred of others, is often to blame. Empathic distress may not only be bad for the health of the individual, it may also be deadly for the health of a society. Many pogroms against minorities have deflected crimes by majority-member perpetrators onto scapegoats. One group is made to feel excessively bad about their own misery, and then a chosen scapegoat redirects the group's rage, and they become a mob, a herd that unscrupulous leaders can drive.

Religious demagogues can always inflame the passions of empathy for victims from their own group. A child dies in a medieval town, and she is mysteriously brutalized in the woods. You can convince your own mob that it must be some devilish foreigner or a Jew, but certainly not child abuse that would implicate the beloved in-group. You can inflame empathy, you can turn it into a weapon, and you can turn empathy into a lynch mob.

Good habits of compassionate action and shared practices of compassion, however, are harder to corrupt because they extend to all. Compassion habits have provided crucial bridges across the world and at many times of history, compassion habits that actually prevented outbreaks of violence and created beautiful integrations of religious communities. In other words, an excessive experience of pain for one's own can be a dangerous political tool, whereas compassionate action, such as for the poor, for children, or the environment, can more easily build a bridge between competitor groups. It all depends on generating cognitive frames that move the mind into becoming a tool of healing and resilience, even if scarcity or tragedy strikes.

From Mental Maps to Habits: Coherence, Habitual Thoughts, and Enlightened Practices

This last point raises the question of exactly how Compassionate Reasoning may help us create a society of common values across religious and secular lines. One way of framing the challenge is that we would want to coordinate a religious response to violence and hate with a secular response. This may be done by examining more deeply the basic question of how we human beings determine reality, or how we construct our mental maps.

Epistemology, the philosophical study of knowing, makes the basic distinction of "correspondence" and "coherence" theories of truth.[26] A *coherence theory of truth* expresses the assumption that we construct our reality in a rather subjective way based on our limited purviews and the sum total of what we know. We come to know the world by shaping all of the bits of what we know into some coherent and intelligible reality. A *correspondence theory of truth*, however, focuses on a reality "out there," a reality that is independently true and knowable, while we, as knowers, do the best we can with our senses, our powers of inference, our abstract reasoning and scientific abilities, to come to know that elusive but existing independent reality.[27]

The effects of the Enlightenment from its inception have been to move us away from coherence systems of truth that were not able to be challenged by science and independent inquiry. Religions, by contrast, have prospered by creating attractive systems of coherent truth for their believers, truths that cannot be undone by scientific discovery. A frequent insistence of religion on coherence approaches to truth—including a centuries-long assault on those who would challenge the Ptolemaic, earth-centered construction of the universe—created a perpetual conflict with scientists for many centuries. Especially in the last few hundred years, millions of people have been breaking free from fundamentalist religious systems of coherent truth, even as basic freedoms offered by democratizing trends of many societies have led to these defections. This war between two epistemologies, correspondence and coherence, remains for many adherents of science and independent thinking—and for millions of religious leaders and followers—a war that brooks no compromise, where only one side can win.

To add further complexity to this, many secular academics and contemporary intellectuals began to embrace their own postmodern critiques of correspondence approaches to positivist truth. Arguments in favor of so-called "objective" descriptions of reality, they claim, reek of race interests, imperial interests, monied interests, class interests, and gendered interests, so the argument goes among postmodernists.[28]

This ongoing conflict about positivist correspondence theories of truth versus coherence theories has a strong effect on the exploration of ethics. On the one hand, this conflict makes it difficult to build consensus on basic ethics, but on the other hand, the postmodern critique has deepened the quality of secular empirical analysis of moral decision-making. Let me explain how.

Postmodernism provides important and broad critiques of earlier ethical discussions that did not consider the unique moral trajectories and contexts of individuals and groups facing complicated situations across the world's cultures. We have the potential in inquiry and in the search for ethical principles to be much humbler due to this debate. We can do better at the challenge of discovering truly universal moral principles when examining individual circumstances, class and economic interests, and a vast diversity of cultures within and between countries. We have also understood how many biases went into previous critiques of cultures and civilizations around the world. But the search—albeit with more humility—for a more truthful approach to ethical deliberations remains what it has always been: an intention to identify ways of deciding what is most ethical in complicated situations of life for all human beings in all their unique cultural contexts.

Compassionate Reasoning and Moral Calculus
across Cultures: Confronting Reality

The task remains to identify moral principles, moral inferences, moral senses, and forms of calculation of the good, which can cut across cultures and religions, across lines of secular and religious devotion—that can unite rather than divide humanity. We can learn how to engage a diversity of cultures and values systems in search of what is common, what is higher, what builds rather than destroys the fabric of society. We can evolve to be more consensus-driven, universally condemning some behaviors that are beyond the pale of cultural, regional, or religious differences. In a postmodern context, we have been empowered to learn from science, but we also need to draw from many religious and cultural systems of coherence as to their essential values. In the process, we discover much in common, and we can thus honor diversity and commit to common courses of action.

We must not give up on the critical role empirical research has always played in the history of ethics and philosophy. The more we know scientifically about ourselves, the more we know about the brain, then the better position we are in to appreciate how cultures throughout history have cultivated compassion, for example, and how their best practices make sense. Also, the more we know about the impact of emotions and verbal communications on ourselves and on others, the better we can formulate principles of ethical interaction. Psycholinguistic theories about the power of every word will be fascinating to test in the years to come through fMRI and other technologies.

Similarly, the more we empirically learn about cultures and lived religions, the better position we will be in to discern moral practices that may be shared across dividing lines. The more we know scientifically, we can also emphasize principles, virtues, and emotional habits that are confirmed by research as having a healthy effect on the human being and human relations. The more we learn about the human brain in the context of ethics, emotions, and higher reasoning, the more it will aid us to establish best practices and habits that are durable and sustainable, practices that have the potential to be shared across cultural differences that occur globally within intelligent life. In other words, the more we come to know each other, both in our internal mental realities and biochemical constructs, and the more we study our interactions, the better we can be in a position to establish a workable universal ethics that appeals to all cultures.

The goal for the joint explorations of the mind sciences and cross-cultural/ inter-religious studies is the evolution of a common ethics that corresponds to the best we can realistically elicit from our nature as humans. From Aristotle to Kant, there has been a search for practical ethical principles or habits that could apply to all human beings. Contemporary science and the postmodern analysis of multicultural approaches to values can help us move that universal aspiration closer to the lived reality of billions of humans. With the aid of neuroscience and contemporary studies of the brain and behavior, we can stimulate in all people an ethical way of being and interacting.

Political Ways of Knowing and Thinking

Some psychologists have taken a hard look at what humans actually do politically with knowledge, or how language is used to frame and shape our political contexts. This has far-reaching consequences for the future of human ethics, for the political structures we live in, and for the kind of leaders we promote or accept. For example, Dr. George Lakoff has argued, based on analysis of psycholinguistics, that relatively impenetrable neural nets govern worldviews and reasoning of billions of traditional people (Lakoff and Johnson 1980). Traditional neural nets strongly resemble "coherence" as truth, and these nets frame the way in which people "know" their world and how they make political choices. They frame a rather closed approach to inquiry and empirical investigation.

Whatever enlightened thinkers may hope in terms of human rational behavior, the fact is that most of us are quite drawn to a coherence approach to truth in the context of politics and the frantic fears and regressive biases that are so often associated with the search for leaders. This has serious consequences for the challenge of ethics applied to politics. Lakoff is a passionate progressive who clearly aligns himself with the epistemic structures of the Enlightenment. He believes in the priority of universal social justice and compassion in human ethics, governance, and political evolution. But he believes that democracy is in peril due to the overwhelming power and appeal of coherent epistemic structures imposed by authoritarian institutions and inherited structures of obedience. There is also the persistent danger of demagogues to democracy, proven so well by the Stanley Milgram (1974) experiments that have been confirmed time and again.

Lakoff confronts what is to be done today about the fragile nature of democracy, and of elections, due to the manipulations by demagogues of millions toward selfishness or cruelty. He argues that we must accept a coherence theory of truth as the most prevalent way in which the minds of millions of people work. He further argues that if you are trying to persuade millions of people to be reasonable, self-controlled, and compassionate, it can happen, but it generally does not work through logical argumentation. The only real way to break authoritarian neural nets and open people up to independent thinking is *through care for the lives of those you are trying to affect, and then engagement in rational inquiry with them as you establish more trust*. In other words, Lakoff is proposing the critical importance of compassionate care followed by shared reasoning.

It is not easy to demonstrate compassionate care when you are attacked and demeaned. Champions of human rights and democracy tend to feel this way around the world. They feel attacked, often are physically threatened, and certainly are demeaned by forces of intolerance. What Professor Lakoff advises is hard, but I have seen this work in thirty years of experience in war zones walking in between adversaries. And the truth is that the feelings of being attacked and demeaned are often felt on all sides of culture conflicts, as I have discovered in 2020 going deeply between enemy groups in the United States. But there is a way out of these feelings.

The people who gain the most entry into the worlds of enemies and who build the most trust are the ones who show the most personal care and compassion. It is only after that effort, which can take months or years sometimes, that the spaces of compassion give rise to spaces of reasoning and logical inference as to the best way to live together and the best ways to govern.

We must do the opposite of what our instincts tell us to do when we are attacked. We must care for those with grievances against us or hostile approaches to us, or those who have become hostile to democracy and civil rights for all. The qualities of care and compassion break into the cognitive universe of the other and provide some basis for creating new worldviews, new moral opinions, and fresh reevaluations of what is right in politics. In plain English: *The only way to open up minds is to open up hearts.* Thus, the ethics of Compassionate Reasoning would have a strategic value in breaking up coherent cognitive nets of intolerance.

Furthermore, if progressives like Lakoff and others open their own minds to it, their best allies in this journey toward universal rights will be enlightened religious representatives in every major religion. Millions of them are quite accustomed to struggling on behalf of religious principles and practices of compassion, of care, and an embrace of others. It is true that there are places of tension between strident individualism and strident traditional religion that must remain a contest. It is also true that every major religion in the world has now and in the past been hijacked by distinct subunits of the religion for nationalist and nativist militancy, or sometimes for naked greed and power.[29] However, this is a danger that many mature believers know very well, are quite afraid of themselves, and it is quite easy to engage in constructive discussions about this with them as Compassionate Reasoning is employed. I have been doing this on every continent for forty years, and I can bear witness to innumerable and extraordinary alliances across religious and political lines when people are heard, honored, and cared for.

There is more that unites rather than divides humanity, in terms of moving masses of people away from violence and the closed neural nets of suspicion and hate. But there are very intentional efforts to keep everyone divided on these matters, as it is good for the business of politic, for the business of war, and for the business of extraction industries such as fossil fuels that depend on weak government institutions and weak democracies. But, in fact, millions of religious adherents are actually quite adept at harmonizing modern ethical values of human rights, for example, with a commitment to their sacred traditions. Even if we as outsiders might find their interpretations and efforts at harmonization to be quite strange at times, it actually does not matter what we think. What matters is trust-building and compassion as we build common values.

Secular people do not need to adapt religious narratives or accept their validity in order to find common cause, common moral causes. Our stories do not have to be the same, and indeed the vast majority of us seven billion humans have different stories, cognitive trajectories, and frames for our identity (Avruch 2012; Cobb 2013; Korostelina 2007; Rothbart 2019). But we nevertheless can and do find common cause every day on many issues, and it is these superordinate ethical values and goals that we need to cultivate as a fundamental component of Compassionate Reasoning. This is the way to build a more effective and common political order for all citizens.

The best in science and the best of our spiritual habits can work together to build a better society than we have inherited. Compassion, whether it is based on a natural gift or ethical philosophical training or religious training, is the core ingredient here. *Compassion, strengthened by good habits, thoughtful and creative training and education,* unites with shared reasoning to generate principles and policies adhered to by all citizens as they each feel included and empowered by Compassionate Reasoning. We will turn in Chapter 5 specifically to Compassionate Reasoning habits, as well as concrete suggestions for training and education. But first, in Chapter 4, I want to strengthen the case for Compassionate Reasoning through important and instructive parallels between Compassionate Reasoning and public health approaches to social change.

4

Violent Ideas Treated as Disease and Compassionate Reasoning as Treatment

A Public Health Analogy

In the previous chapter, we explored the relationship between Compassionate Reasoning, schools of ethical thought, and developments in neuroscience. Until now I have framed Compassionate Reasoning as a tool of personal and interpersonal change. Insights from classical schools of ethics, as well as from neuroscience (most notably the recent advent of research into neuroplasticity), helped formulate specific ways that Compassionate Reasoning can lead to intrapersonal and interpersonal transformation. The cultivation of Compassionate Reasoning leads to new ways of feeling, thinking, and doing. It also translates into a form of service to others, healing both those who practice it and also its recipients. The next stage of inquiry, then, needs to move from intrapersonal and interpersonal articulations of Compassionate Reasoning and toward a method of affecting society as a whole. For this we turn to the history of public health transformations as a guide (Goldsteen, Goldsteen, and Dwelle 2015). I propose in this chapter that Compassionate Reasoning should draw critical lessons from modern public health innovations and institutions. The goal of Compassionate Reasoning ultimately is to take personal change and social change to the level of mass social change. This is the proper goal of ethics in general as it moves toward law, policy, and political evolution.

Public health innovations in recent centuries have lengthened the human lifespan dramatically and have also substantially lessened the violence of human society as a whole.[1] Doctors and public health experts have wisely emphasized that the violence of murder, rape, and aggravated assault are not just immoral phenomena or unwise ways to live. They are public health hazards, and from a health standpoint their roots and causes need scientific investigation. They also require treatments, as it were, that reduce these crimes substantially through a variety of interventions. My lifelong

Compassionate Reasoning. Marc Gopin, Oxford University Press. © Oxford University Press 2022.
DOI: 10.1093/oso/9780197537923.003.0004

passion has been the treatments, because clearly in the history of individuals and societies these treatments are occasionally found—or stumbled upon. Compassionate Reasoning is intended as a method of consciously and painstakingly inducing such treatments inside the human being, and provoking them for society as a whole. Let's explore this based on the insights of public health analysis.

Public health analysts wisely note the dangers of poor ideas to human life and wellbeing—malignant ideas such as racism, bigotry, or social Darwinist punishment of the poor (Nairn, Pega, McCreanor, Rankine, and Barnes 2006). Violent ideas are public health hazards they create or exacerbate civil and global wars.

For example, the Spanish Flu of 1918 was a public health catastrophe, but it was spread massively by convoys of soldiers. The absurd thinking and frame of mind that gave rise to the futile battles and mass slaughter of World War I exacerbated the casualties of the Flu of 1918, a novel flu for which humanity had no defense. The "war to end all wars," World War I, was based on what turned out to be the false notion that this war could be won quickly in a few months, that the systematic machine-gun slaughter of almost all of Europe's young men lined up in rows against each other, combined with poison gas, was a terrific idea. This "idea" or frame of mind turned out to kill an entire generation of young Europeans, 20 million. They fought in the trenches with machine guns and mustard gas and accomplished little except mass casualties. This was a stupid war, fought stupidly by out of touch aristocratic elites, and with horrific effects for generations.

The most important point is that "the war to end all wars" actually left virtually all of humanity defenseless against an utterly new virus for which their bodies had no defenses. This is the stupidity that often afflicts major wars, the lack of reasoning through and foresight of consequences. Every man marched off to defend their women, and ended up getting them killed well behind the front lines by a virus spread by the stupidity of the war. The 20 million dead paled in comparison to the flu that it spread, and that is exactly the nature of the public health consequences of stupid ideas and stupid wars. This is very rarely acknowledged by people who would rather lionize and romanticize wars but fail to see the true and full consequences. About one-third of humanity, 500 million people, caught the flu from 1918 to April 1920, and at least 50 million souls perished, over double the actual battle casualties.

World War II is an even more horrifying example: 40 million dead due to absurd and destructive ideas of Aryan and Japanese racial superiority, and the idea that fascist bullies make great heads of state. The racial superiority myth and its genocidal fantasies spread across many countries, well beyond the hosts. Fascism and National Socialism as ideas were responsible for tens of millions of civilians murdered across the world in those terrible years: 90 percent of the Jewish people of Europe, and 25 percent of European Roma.

These were violent, diseased ideas, having no basis in science or research, that led directly to several genocides as well as killing the majority groups that spawned those diseased ideas. The violent idea as a disease literally destroyed the host, as diseases often do. Whereas reasoning and compassion strengthen the mind to save lives, the amygdala and constructs of fear can poison the mind when out of control; they can direct the mind to conduct levels of mad violence not seen in any other species. The human mind is an awesome thing, perhaps the most powerful thing in earth's history, but it is up to us whether its ideas are poisonous and genocidal or compassionate and reasonable.

The Cultural Revolution of China from 1966 to 1976 wiped out as many as forty to eighty million people with fundamentally violent ideas of brutal reorganization and absurd planning (Strauss and Southerl 1994; United States Holocaust Memorial Museum 2021a, 2021b). In Cambodia from 1975 to 1979, the Khmer Rouge murdered at least one-third of their own population, two million people, insanely targeting cosmopolitans, the educated, and city dwellers, as demagogues and totalitarians often do. In fact, it is a common marker of mass murder to target those who have independent reasoning capacity, for it is they who present a clear and present danger to absolute obedience and submission. Anyone educated was killed, as they were thought to be carriers of the "disease" of thinking. Inspired by the Maoist "cultural revolution," Khmer Rouge extremists came up with an insane idea to empty the cities and kill all the educated. A poor idea of the mind unleashed massive murder (Becker 1998; Joffé 1984; Short 2005).

This is exactly how diseased ideas of mass violence are a direct danger to health. Such ideas are examples of the opposite of Compassionate Reasoning, as they are flawed and illogical inferences combined with cruel feelings and murderous intentions. The list of the history of violent ideas leading to mass murder is quite long. These poor ideas, and the negative effects that emerged from these ideas, should be considered among the greatest of public health hazards in human history. Therefore, antidotes to such ideas are essential methods of intervention for public health. Destructive, murderous ideas, such as racism and hate, are a disease, and they cry out for treatment (Bushman 2017; David-Ferdon and Simon 2014; Slutkin 2013, 2020; Violence Prevention Alliance 2021).

A public health perspective is an essential tool of understanding not only what goes wrong and goes right inside the human body in terms of contagion, but what goes wrong and goes right inside the human mind in terms of contagion.

From Nightmares to Hope within the Compassionate Reasoning and Public Health Frames

Let's frame this more positively in terms of public health. The institutionalization of effective rehabilitation from alcoholism and drug abuse, for example, has been a clear factor in increasing the health of families and children in recent decades (Wickizer et al. 1998). Correspondingly, good ideas such as human rights have led to the saving of millions of lives in the following sense. This "good idea" has become embedded in the rule of law of many nations. But the first step was for that good idea to become embedded in the minds of individuals, and then in small progressive communities, slowly and steadily over time and across the planet. Then those groups germinated contagion through education and through inspiration. The idea was socialized more and more until it started to become law.

The amazing thing about the mind and its powerful ideas is that the more setbacks to the idea of human rights, the more that victim groups came to champion the simplicity, the depth, and the potential for legal power of this idea. I remember marveling in recent decades at the times in which human rights seemed to be set back badly, such as for women in India. But the more that outrageous crimes against women were exposed, the more it led to mass mobilization and the power of the few to inspire the many to change the laws, to evolve as people and nations (George and Suri 2018).

In dozens of countries, human rights has now become a dominant way of thinking, a way of thinking so natural as to become a pervasive worldview, especially among youth. The list of human rights extensions to different minorities grows every decade, and they keep turning into new laws. There are setbacks and backlashes, but the march of this idea when viewed over the last couple of centuries is astounding (Viljoen 2021).

Compassionate Reasoning argues for the training of the mind in new thinking that embodies compassion for all, leading to reasonable and rational institutions to safeguard and protect all, such as human rights. It argues further that this entails an emphasis on new habits of thinking and acting that embed compassion into consciousness, into the body itself by way of the mind and its neural pathways, and ultimately into the rule of law, strengthening obedience to such laws. This transforms the structures of society and the very conception of the good society.

Confronting the opposite of compassion is equally important. Rehabilitation from poor ideas—such as bigotry, misogyny, racism, the glorification of rage or hate, humiliation and punishment of the poor—should be vital to the progress of public health. Confronting and challenging these ideas should be seen as essential to lengthening the human lifespan in terms of public health (Menakem 2017).

National systemic improvements along these lines would lead to longer lifespans just as much as the introduction of public health measures such as hygiene and vaccines. In other words, *mental* and *moral* hygiene is as important as *physical* hygiene in the steady improvement of the quality and quantity of human life.[2] Compassionate Reasoning is thus equipped to interact creatively with public health ideas and institutions, as we will explore below.

Contemporary institutions of public health can contribute to new forms of prosocial thinking, prosocial behavior, and peacebuilding. For example, frequent experiences of compassion lead to the habituation of one's own compassionate feelings, resulting in new habits and practices. The more compassion I receive, the more I see and understand compassion as a healthy part of my life. The more I see it as a healthy part of my life, the more I am prone to pass compassion on to others, especially if the public health system in my life—the doctors, nurses, and health authorities—*tell me* that it is a part of my health plan. For it is in the telling, with the authority of medicine and public health, that the mind begins to self-reflect and internalize the importance of compassion not only as an ethical experience or a religious experience but as an act of healthy responsibility.

Equally as important, the more I treat myself with compassion, the more I tend to extend this toward loved ones, toward community, toward strangers, and even toward those with whom I profoundly disagree. Just as with family, my brain learns how to make normal disagreements coexist with compassion and care; so too I learn to extend this to strangers. In this way, with enough encouragement and education, personal habits can lead to society-wide practices.

What we are describing is the opposite of the destructive negative spirals of political polarization and an antidote to political demagogic manipulation of our fears and angers. In other words, *this is a strategy to make compassion into a positive contagion.* This kind of positive contagion is something we can generate through training in thinking and actions, as well as by eliciting supportive cultural ideas and customs that reinforce these values and actions.

It is essential to promote compassion training not just intrapsychically but interpersonally, or both inside one's mind and heart as well as between oneself and others. Compassion in this way becomes a larger society-wide institution, complete with cultural affirmations, religious affirmations, and educational curricula at all ages. This is the way compassion affects the whole of society, the way that Compassionate Reasoning advances the habits of society as a whole.

Public health is a modern human endeavor, a compassionate effort to save as many lives as possible and cause as much human flourishing as possible, and it has been working on habits and rules of behavior for centuries now. It is an important nexus of the personal and the interpersonal on the one hand, and on the other hand a social contract to make all of human life flourish. Public health is both practice and theory, the commitment to care combined with the commitment to think through policies leading to changes in thinking and behavior. It is at its best an embodiment of Compassionate Reasoning, a combination of prosocial sentiment and the reasoning that proliferates that sentiment into the consciousness of the individual and the community.

Public health is focused on disease prevention and lifespans, but it is equally about the ethics of commitment to society as a whole. Compassionate Reasoning should play a role in helping every citizen to see her *right* to health connected to everyone else's right to health, but also her *responsibility* for health as connected to everyone else's responsibility. This is based on training in compassion, but also training in ethical thinking about compassionate and compassion-based policies for society as a whole. This is the essence of universal rules and the social contract, which are essential to human adaptability and human flourishing.

Training in Compassionate Reasoning can save many lives. For example, in 2020, Japan suffered minimum casualties of COVID, whereas the United

States suffered massive casualties (Wingfield-Hayes 2020; Nippon.com 2020). One of the key differences was a long-standing Japanese tradition of great care for public health that each citizen is brought up to believe in and firmly internalize in their every daily habit. This is sufficiently true that if the average Japanese person felt the slightest bit ill from a cold, *decades before COVID* (Burgess and Horii 2012; Rich 2020), they would don a mask that day, *all day*, in public. This was not seen as a violation of their freedom of expression or opinion; this was a moral habit and a commitment to a social contract. This was also compassion, as the mask was a logical outgrowth of the wish for others to be healthy and unaffected by my virus. This was the basis for understanding that everyone must think and feel this way for it to work for all. And that is why hundreds of thousands of Japanese are not dead from COVID and millions debilitated, but over 600,000 Americans have died from COVID-19 as of June 2021.This is compassion and reasoning in one's thought and behavior pattern that leads to the good society *and* the healthy society. This is also a bitter lesson for some societies, but we all must learn from each other in order to morally evolve as humanity. Sometimes Americans have great things to teach humanity, and sometimes they have much to learn from others if they want to survive.

The importance of healthy habits as a moral imperative has also predated contemporary understandings of science and disease prevention (Stroumsa 1993; Alimohammadi and Taleghani 2015; Segal and Blazer 2020; Bar-Sela, Hoff, and Faris 1964). Many old religious traditions and philosophical traditions embraced healthy habits as an essential human obligation, even if what they knew at the time about health itself was limited. Similarly, the cultivation of compassion and even the cultivation of reasoning have been moral, spiritual, and religious paths to enlightenment going back centuries (Condon and Makransky 2020; Gopin 2017; Rosner 1965; Tomasino, Chiesa, and Fabbro 2014; Twersky,1989; Wilhoit 2019). Compassion, therefore, is not only a healthful experience or an ethical virtue; it is a fulfillment of deep cultural traditions that can buttress the neuroscientific basis of compassion as a healthful path for the individual and society. Compassionate Reasoning will become a bond between traditional and secular wings of the same society.

Society in all of its diversity needs to become committed to compassion as a yardstick of health in a community. Given the weight of evidence in favor of compassion's impact on personal health (Cosley, McCoy, Saslow, and Epel 2010), we should encourage the evolution of global metrics on the state of compassion in each society. Just as today some countries have moved toward a Gross Happiness Index (Centre for Bhutan Studies & GNH Research 2016), we should institutionalize a Gross Compassion Index (perhaps as a component of the Gross Happiness Index) as a way of measuring progress and change (De Neve and Sachs 2020; Musikanski and Rogers 2021). Compassionate Reasoning (1) extends the experience and practice of compassion through reasoning, and (2) envisions the construction of the compassionate society as a whole. It takes the best of our reasoning mind to take a positive emotion and turn it into a community and national institution. This evolution takes hard intellectual work and collaboration with other minds, since it must grapple with complicated moral dilemmas and equally valid but contradictory moral arguments. Compassionate Reasoning becomes a tool to work through moral dilemmas in a way that leads collectively to the most amount of compassion for the greatest number of people. A sophisticated integration of the diverse and competing schools of ethics, as we outlined earlier, is essential to steer society away from violence and toward sustainable and healthy forms of interaction and flourishing. This is best done through a combination of self-reflection and active engagement and debate with others trained in the same way.

The analogy between disease and hateful violence and between health and prosocial relations suggests that we should draw from basic assumptions of public health and medical discourse as we apply Compassionate Reasoning to society as a whole. This will lead in turn to a deep dive into lifelong education programs for habits of feeling, thinking, and behaving. Let's now explore this analogy in depth.

A Public Health Model for the Compassionate Care of Society: Neuroscience, Ethical Habits, and the Mind

It is fair to say at this point in history that we have made an astonishing level of progress in the hard sciences, with astounding technological advances as a result. But what about advances in ethics? Has advancement been significant or negligible? In recent centuries we have dramatically decreased the average number of murders and other violent acts in domestic society (Pinker 2011a). We have reduced torture rates, and we have also significantly reduced the number and frequency of wars, when comparing the last fifty years to all previous centuries on a per person or per capita basis (Gurr 2000; Gat 2013;

Human Security Report Project 2014). This is a significant achievement for the progress of human ethics, at least on average.[3]

Even if, statistically speaking, our progress in lessening death through war and violence is significant, the actual hard numbers of violence-related deaths across the world have increased and are horrific, due to our vastly greater global population today. Thus the sheer amount of suffering due to war has increased in the aggregate. Humanity as a whole may have advanced, but cycles of violence, and particularly the uses of hate and violence for political and economic gain, are as prevalent as ever. The indirect effects of the politics of hate translate into cultures of endless greed, with hatred as a perfect political distraction for corrupt enrichment. This combination of greed and politically deflected hatred is degrading the planet's vital resources and threatening life on earth.

We may have avoided nuclear war, but we have not avoided a process of brutal competition for resources currently undermining the future of sentient life on earth. Where are the scientific recommendations as to how to combat this social descent into self-harm? Why can science understand what is happening at the ends of the known universe, or what happens inside chromosomes, but not what can undo the harm of a sadistic, sick, and morally bankrupt political leader? Where are the great universities of the world— or my home country, the United States—on that question? Where are the billions of dollars invested to discover an answer to this threat, considering how many billions of lives and trillions of dollars in resources have been lost over the centuries due to dangerous political demagogues?

The failure to advance in politics and ethics as rapidly as we have in the physical sciences is due to many well-understood issues of power, systems of power, and the inconvenient truths buried by political and economic systems of power that influence what research is heavily funded and what research is barely funded. We understand the relationship between the hard sciences and immense profits to be reaped. Nevertheless, when large numbers of thoughtful and compassionate human beings have willed themselves to overcome systematic suppression of truth, they have steadily done so in history. Thus, those few with excess resources will tend to suppress what may eat into their exclusive systems of power, but we have the will collectively to persist in change. My field of peacebuilding is not suppressed so much as ignored. There is no serious money in stopping wars, but plenty of money for making them.

Sometimes, however, we are not thinking the way we should about a subject, and this contributes to why thoughtful people fail to progress. The great luminaries of my field of conflict analysis and resolution understood this, and that is why they called upon us to *think* differently about problem solving when it comes to conflict, about basic human needs when fulfilled that reduce violence, about the role of contact between strangers that reduces violence, and many other insights. They called upon us to think differently in order to change the course of human conflict and violence (Mitchell and Banks 1996; Kelman and Fisher 2016; Allport 1979; Buber [1947] 2002).

We have been too focused on just a few sciences for human improvement and positive social change. Our good and bad behavior, our failures and accomplishments, our progress and regress when it comes to politics and ethics, are intimately related to how we are thinking, how our minds are functioning within us and between us (Bastian [1860] 2016; Montville 1990; Volkan 1997). We are individual biological organisms forming larger units of socialization. As we move from an understanding of what predisposes us to compassion or, alternatively, to violence, and what influences any shifts or evolutions in society as a result, we need to pay close attention to what kind of thinking and planning forms the basis of prescriptive recommendations for both ethics and politics. We need to mine the depths of past wisdom on this subject, from ancient times to the present, and then bring it forward with experimentation, a multitude of experiments in practice, and learning from practice. This too creates progress, despite the lack of funding.

What scientific analogies and ways of thinking are being employed to describe and prescribe human interaction and political interaction? Which sciences can help us understand better when societies become more ethical, more fair, and less violent? When do they fail to be ethical, and which society becomes hateful, violent, or even genocidal? Are the sciences that can help to best understand this the ones we have actually employed to build the institutions of the state, the foundations of the democratic state? Let's explore this more.

Political philosophy that forms the basis of states and how they run has, from its very inception, tended to see its mission along the lines of *engineering* society, of *building* something, like a skyscraper or a dam. From Aristotle to Confucius, Sun Tzu to Hobbes and Kant, these wise people have contemplated the *structures* that may be built in order to create the good society, or the peaceful society, or the happy society, or the strong and invincible society. We move, therefore, from imagined political structures to imagined constructs of law that will become the backbone of the *structure* of society. The "science" of this creation moves to the "technology" of creation, from political philosophy to economics and engineering, as if we are building a physical house to live in.

Political philosophical literature over the centuries is complex, varied, and fascinating, and it has inspired me since my teen years to further study and reflection. I take personal pleasure in opening up a volume of political philosophy when I want to take a deep breath and step back from a chaotic and disappointing world. I love the visions of the good society from Plato to Locke, and it is true that this literature has stimulated centuries of well-intentioned political movements.

The progress toward those visions, however, has been miniscule when compared to the scaffolding upon scaffolding of scientific genius and technological advance that has been produced by the hard sciences. Today we are geniuses when it comes to exploring the farthest reaches of time and space but absolute pygmies when it comes to political cooperation in a small religious parish or an academic department, let alone a complex society of hundreds of millions.

Science is also quite dangerous when it turns into technology, as is well understood in the nuclear and fossil fuel age. We take scientific genius accumulated over centuries, and then we figure out how to use that science to kill millions of humans by advanced weapons, which we have accomplished progressively, from the machine gun to the hydrogen bomb. We accomplish mass murder *with the gifts bequeathed to us by our own higher minds.* In other words, our higher mind delivers diamonds and rubies to us, but our lizard brain—with its penchant for fight, flight, fear, polarization, demonization, and endless cycles of mutual plunder—turns the diamonds and rubies into filth.

We are, in essence, the physicist who by day is discovering the most magnificent ends of the universe in all its raging beauty, and who by night gets drunk and gets his head bashed in from fights that he himself started at the local bar in his drunken, self-hating stupor. This pattern of contradiction within the human brain, and how this contradiction shapes our social constructs, has set the most advanced civilizations back generations and killed millions throughout the twentieth century. This contradiction is wasteful, sad, and ominous, and the historians know very well that it just keeps repeating itself, except our weapons get much, much deadlier.

This is the puzzle of the brain that has stumped the greatest minds and led to them to predict a short lifespan for the species (Rincon 2018). Science is in the hands of the neocortex, but technology can be, and often is, controlled by the worst paranoia of the brain stem. Why does this happen repeatedly in advanced societies? What goes wrong between the neocortex's astonishing capacities and the rest of the brain? And what does it say about our capacity to handle technology ethically and politically? Most importantly, is there a better way?

It defies logic that the higher mind ends up empowering armies of engineers to spend endless sums on fossil fuel extraction, currently choking life out of the planet and causing mass extinctions, and soon leading to all our demise. One part of the brain enables the most profound understanding of the magnificent and delicate balance of life, while the technical mind is then called upon to find the cleverest ways to upset those balances and destroy the natural world. We have mastered laws of relativity that gives us an understanding of the farthest ends of the universe, but as a species we are still infants when it comes to mastering our minds right here within everyone's reach.

I refuse to accept Arthur Koestler's (1978) diagnosis that there is some primeval mistake in the human brain, though I sympathize with his despair. This is but a more blunt version of what many shell-shocked thinkers of the twentieth century observed, from Freud (Einstein and Freud [1923] 2016) all the way to the late, great pessimist Stephen Hawking (Criss 2016).[4] In the contemporary era, we have had to add to the reasons for pessimism the new ability to destroy all in an instant from tens of thousands of nuclear weapons, and now the certain path of degradation if not destruction of the atmosphere for life on earth by the greed-based fossil fuel folly, mass destruction of tree cover, the suffocation of too much CO_2, and the poison of ubiquitous plastic (Ritchie and Roser 2018).

Previous generations of psychologists and scholars asked what is wrong with us. But I was influenced at an early age by Viktor Frankl, who searched throughout his career for what was also right with us and how to foster it, in order to save human beings from a life of meaningless despair and aggression (Frankl [1946] 2006, [1955] 1986, 1967). I have extensively utilized in my peace practice the lessons of positive psychology. We should not continuously and endlessly overstress what is wrong with us, lest we create a self-fulfilling prophecy (Seligman 2012; Gopin 2015).

I noticed in my intellectual history studies as an undergraduate, and then in my field of peace and conflict, an obsessive focus on the negative. I realized how easy it is to get stuck in what is wrong to such an extent that you never see and focus on progress, successes and resilience.[5] In our struggle today to engender a humanity that is peacebuilding rather than suicidal, we must be careful to not create what we fear most by obsessing about failure and becoming enslaved to it as inevitable.

We must be careful with condemnatory language, with negative diagnoses and prognoses. There is an addiction in intellectual circles to predictions of doom, as if it necessarily works to shame and frighten people into better behavior. If we focus exclusively on the negative, with no way out and no vision of alternatives, then we do tend to become what we fear in a fatalistic and morally irresponsible way. Lakoff's work on psycholinguistics also affirms the power of suggestion through our every word, and the outsized power we have to determine with repetitive words and themes the course of our collective thinking (Lakoff and Johnson 1980).

Despair is an especially important psychological asset to dangerous narcissistic leaders who bully subjects as a way to control and manipulate a population. Hitler and Stalin did this, and a number of the worst global antidemocratic leaders today do the same though various forms of social media manipulation. We humans are healthfully adapted to hone in on danger, but sometimes that survival skill becomes a burden, as we can be easily manipulated by fear mongerers. We need to focus instead on engendering the life-giving qualities that the vast majority of human beings actually possess. This is not in order to evade hard truths as much as it is to build upon the good within human nature and human potential, the good that led to so many spectacular advances for human life on the planet.

Common sense, scientific honesty, and basic decency require us to examine ourselves truthfully, in all our goodness and our destructiveness. We do not necessarily have to insist with Koestler (1978), however, that we are *fundamentally* flawed. We may not want to infect our brains with deterministic constructs of inescapable fate. But we can ask hard questions in a constructive way at this point, more along the lines that Jared Diamond (2019) has framed so well in his life's work. We must ask about where we do well and where we fail, when we rise and when we collapse. We can ask where and when we have evolved to less violence and more sustainability and where we have not, and why. This seems to be a better question, a more resilient question, before we accept the death sentence from the late Stephen Hawking. I truly am sad for anyone, from billionaires to physicists, who ignores the historical evidence for human adaptability, resilience, and learning from catastrophe.

Instead they put all their hopes and resources into outrageous schemes to escape planet earth costing obscene amounts of money that redirected could actually help achieve carbon neutrality at a much faster pace.

I therefore want to ask two questions: (1) Where have we made astounding progress, and where has our progress and evolution been far too slow; and (2) what is the best intellectual frame to utilize in order to make substantially more progress? I want to explore answers by way of logical inference from the following analogy.

When building a skyscraper, you must count on a very precise set of technologies rooted in the most advanced sciences. The complex technologies involved in building a skyscraper, from the design of the smallest bolts all the way to the chemistry of every single substance employed in construction to the exact effect and uses of wind, all rely on the relative predictability of variables in the use of material substances and physical conditions. The predictability of these substances and conditions are essential in order to design and build a skyscraper that will never collapse and never falter. Tragedies can occur when just one variable was not anticipated in design. Therefore, all future designs of every industry involved in construction must incorporate lessons learned from the construction of buildings all over the world.

There are also many failsafe technologies in advanced construction, designed to compensate for unanticipated variables in the physical sciences and the technology of production. When it comes to accidents, whether it be an airplane takeoff or a skyscraper construction error, it takes several interactive *unanticipated* variables to overcome built-in safeguards. That is why there is a steady advance of technology and capacity to anticipate and overcome the confluence of several negative variables. This is why there are fewer and fewer airline disasters as the decades of airline travel have proceeded, because the confluence of four or five negative events is already anticipated. This is the genius of the physical sciences working in concert with technology that gets better and better, anticipating several negative variables. And it is this genius that saves lives as it makes products and buildings safer and safer.

Now let's go to the other extreme of human events, such as the outbreak of war, or even something as simple as the outbreak of a small fight in a playground. When you truly add up every contributing factor to why and when peace, joy, and love break out among friends or in a community versus a brawl on a playground, the mathematics of variables would be staggering and basically impossible to calculate as to why it went one way in one situation and the opposite in the other. Why? *Because the variables are far greater than when calculating the physics of a skyscraper.* There is every single person in-volved, directly or indirectly, in the peaceful and joyful day in the playground versus the conflict day. They each had a completely different trajectory of experiences that particular day, variables of health, mood, and accidental encounters. Every teacher's state of mind in any school is always different every day, and even every hour. They all interact with each other with great frequency in complex ways that influence the atmosphere of every moment. Also, the weather, the noise levels, the heat, the illnesses, the parental fights back home, to name just a few—these are just some of the many contributing factors that I can think of as a conflict analyst that every teacher, every child, every administrator, and they all interact and affect each other constantly. There is so much contributing to peace or war in a playground. The same is true in cities and nations, and the variations are infinite the more people in-volved, which is exactly why conflict analysis and conflict resolution are so difficult. That is not to say it is impossible, but the variables are astounding.

You simply cannot construct peace in a playground on any given day like a skyscraper, therefore. But you don't *have to* construct peace like a skyscraper, and here is the most important point: *The same infinite complex of variables found in the playground are also a challenge for a completely different set of sciences, namely the sciences involving emergency medical care for saving lives.* Emergency services and public health sciences are indeed sciences, but their technique is entirely different from the science of engineering skyscrapers. One cannot save a life in an emergency room on any given day like building a dam—and I am not trying to be snarky here, or disrespectful of dam and skyscraper building. I mean for us to take a moment and think about this dis-tinction, for there is no disparagement of dam builders whose engineering feats hold the lives of thousands in their hands. But if doctors planned out their lifesaving activities every day like building a skyscraper or a dam, then I propose that their patients would die in droves. Why?

Their expertise requires an entirely different set of professional skills, as they prepare for the *uniqueness* of each patient, and the time of year, and the prevalent illnesses of that city, and that moment in time. This is all despite the similarity of human bodies that govern doctor and nurse training in school years before. Doctors and nurses must prepare for similarities *and* unique-ness of circumstances and human bodies. They must make snap judgments *at every minute*, which is impossible for building skyscrapers and dams. There are certain common tests for all people, such as blood pressure, but these are mere baseline indicators that help them make much more complicated calculations as tests proceed and as *interactive interviews* and research continues, and then they must retest as soon as new circumstances arise.

This having been said, if a doctor built a skyscraper in the same way that she figures out what is right, wrong, or needs adjustment in her intensive care unit, then the skyscraper would fall down, or could never be built in the first place. Why? Because medicine represents a completely different approach to preparation and problem solving, involving a constantly changing entity, the human person, that is a million times more complex than a building as it moves through time. The variables and unknowns, the combinations of causal connections at any given moment for the health of a single human being—these stagger the imagination. By contrast, given the physical sciences of a skyscraper being built over a number of years, you cannot possibly leave decisions up to moment-to-moment circumstances. Physical laws of construction are far more predictable, but they too are very intricate. Therefore, it requires a precise level of planning that takes years to execute plans in the proper sequence. Nothing like a patient on ten different lifesaving interventions, any of which could cause a sudden allergic reaction requiring an entirely different set of drugs administered in minutes, or seconds.

Physics and medicine are entirely different, *and so is the construction of the good society.* Physics, medicine, and engineering meet at the level of research on chemistry or device construction, but that's it. Serving patient x or y is an entirely different scientific undertaking. That is why the science of healthcare for the human being has to be utterly different from engineering.

That is not to say that there is nothing in common scientifically. Experimentation, and the assertion of theories that are falsifiable through testing, are critical to truthful analysis in each field. But when it comes to the actual human being and the actual doctor deciding on what to do about their health, when it comes to diagnosis and therapy, things become very interesting and categorically unlike constructing a building or preventing it from falling down.

Let's explore this more as we move toward possible analogies between medicine and healthcare on the one side, and on the other, personal change, the evolution of society, and Compassionate Reasoning. Medicine and public health represent a crucial middle ground of science and reason that addresses not hard objects subject to straightforward laws of physics and chemistry, but the single human mind and body in its infinite interactions. Medicine and public health stand as a challenge for science that is in between the human world of infinite variables and the inanimate world of skyscraper technology. Here are some of the variables: (1) the interaction of lifesaving drugs and each and every patient's different history, genetics, and current life circumstances; (2) lifesaving instruments in experimental or established phases of use; (3) the state of hospital and surgery environments; (4) the state of delivery times for critical information and test results; (5) the number of physicians on call; the day of the week and state of personnel on that day; (6) flu season or not flu season, et cetera.

At the same time, the level of attention and the type of attention to the patient of nurses, doctors, and family are critical factors in what happens on any given day or moment of illness and health. This includes stress-related events of all kinds, as it is well known how interactive stress is with most illnesses, their course and direction (Levenson 2019; Groër, Meagher, and Kendall-Tackett 2010). Even something as elusive as prayer and good intentions seem to play some role (Brown 2012). Many things have yet to be studied regarding the circumstances of illness and recovery, such as the quantity of visitors to conscious and unconscious patients with the same conditions, the role of positive and negative feelings and attitudes of visiting family members, or the state of family peace or conflict injected verbally and nonverbally into the patient's environment. Then there is the power of touch, or the deprivation of touch. There is music and soft sounds versus jarring sounds, and the power of light and mood (Auais, Al-Zoubi, Matheson, Brown, Magaziner, and French 2019).

The list of possible impacts on health in life-and-death situations is endless. None of this would matter, however, to a skyscraper standing or falling. No matter how much stress skyscraper residents have on any given day, it will not matter one bit to the viability of the building's structure. Music won't matter; human moods won't matter; how nice or obnoxious the building inspector is will not matter. He is not a caregiver whose every move either comforts or terrifies a patient and thus changes the neurological and biochemical variables of physical and mental health, physical and mental care.

Thus, when it comes to health, to "building" healthy people and building a healthy society, we need a very particular kind of talent. We need the kind of talent that is deeply immersed in knowledge of the human being and of society, but that is also skilled in the application of that knowledge to each and every peculiar situation—with compassion. Each situation can turn from sickness to health, or health to sickness, in an instant—for a number of reasons, but the overriding importance of compassion and reasoning on the best course of care is indispensable.

Transitioning now back to our subject, this kind of care takes great flexibility of training and practice, and training in Compassionate Reasoning will help considerably. The key is not just to build society, but to build a sustainable moral society with less hate, less violence, and more rational planning for the safety and care of all. A key element of this training is learning to truly *listen attentively* to the uniqueness of each situation of communal health or sickness, and even the condition of each individual, just like an excellent nurse or doctor.

This skill takes extraordinary training in patient compassion and persistent investigation, specifically in the skill of perspective-taking. Perspective-taking, an essential ingredient in peacebuilding but in all work of a social nature, is essential for successful engagements with others. It is the embodiment of a deliberate act of reasoning based on a compassionate understanding of the other.

The next step is to integrate that knowledge into a flexible approach to right and good paths of policy and practice, which is where training in the ethical schools of thought, addressed in previous chapters, becomes quite helpful. Let's explore this by delving into public health policy and frames of thinking, and then we will apply that to Compassionate Reasoning for the betterment of society.

The Medical and Public Health Analogy to the Task of Personal and Social Change

Medicine and healthcare involve skills requiring us to expect and anticipate thousands of variables—to expect surprises, in other words—and then to adjust therapy. Building our character or building society is much closer to the methodologies of medicine and public health than engineering in this regard. The infinite variables making humans unique, and every situation unique, requires many flexible health interventions and adjustments in order to expect the unexpected and have the skills to deal with that. Medicine combines theory and research with a regular therapeutic need to *listen* to everything about the one patient in front of you, adjust medicines, adjust short-term treatments and long-term therapies, and even work on psychological approaches to positive change.

Health involves an integration of (1) great technical knowledge stored in the mind, and (2) skills of empathy and compassion through listening and attention that will better inform all decisions of therapy and healing. Compassion and reason unite in this way, and hence what I have called Compassionate Reasoning is the key. It is for this reason that the medical and public health analogy is the most apt for generating personal, social, and global change through compassion and reasoning, not engineering or physics.

It is not that engineering and physics are not vital for the world we have built and the world to come, but rather that engaging the human being in healthy and evolutionary improvement requires excellence in Compassionate Reasoning for the sake of the health of the society as a whole. Compassionate Reasoning has good roots in medicine and public health, in addition to roots in wisdom traditions, philosophy, and ethics. It also is rooted in the importance of narrative, in the telling and in the listening, the power of story and narrative to transform us (Cobb 2013).[6]

Thus, Compassionate Reasoning forms a bridge across many cultures and subgroups of society as they listen to and learn from each other, which is essential to truly moving the health of society as a whole in a positive direction. People in all their great diversity require deep motivations to behave rationally. They need to feel listened to, loved, and cared for, like they feel with a good doctor. Only then can they take a hard look at changing bad habits and learning better habits of coexistence with others: habits of the mind (cognition), habits of the heart (affect), and habits of behavior.

The Opposite of Compassion Is a Disease Called Hate

"No one is born hating another person because of the color of his skin, or his background, or his religion. People must learn to hate, and if they can learn to hate, they can be taught to love, for love comes more naturally to the human heart than its opposite" (Mandela 1994).

The opposite of health is disease, and the opposite of compassion is hate. Compassionate care has its opposite in humiliation and bullying, which are directly derived from hate. Compassionate Reasoning also has its own opposite in the diseased way in which the mind can be warped into bizarre theories, logic, pseudoscience, and investigations that all turn out to be phony. This is the "reasoning," for example, of scapegoat thinking, conspiracy thinking; that is, the search for scapegoats to hate, to demonize, and to victimize.

Public health as a field has always required building a sophisticated and organized system of intervention, but it is not built without a deep attention to the opposite of public health, which is disease that is endemic and sometimes pandemic. I am proposing that it is the same with public compassion and reason versus public hatred and victimization. Let's explore this proposed analogy by examining the public health model for its lessons. From this we may be able to see how to embed Compassionate Reasoning into every facet of society and thus evolve a more solid foundation for peaceful and sustainably compassionate societies.

Public Health Defined and Applied

Public health has been defined as "a set of organized interdisciplinary efforts to protect, promote, and restore the public's health. It is the combination of assessment, policy development and assurance that is directed to the maintenance and improvement of the health of all the people through collective or social action." The mission of public health is to "promote physical, mental and environmental health and prevent disease, injury and disability" (Institute of Medicine 1988; Blueprint for a Healthy Community 1994).

There is a simultaneous focus in this definition of public health on tracking and promoting *health*, as well as tracking, suppressing, or curing *disease*. I propose the same should pertain to Compassionate Reasoning. We need a systemic approach to (1) promote society-wide compassion, (2) identify the kind of reasoning that leads to compassionate policies for all, and (3) network this approach and embed it in society, so that its contagion envelops a society.

Correspondingly, this approach requires tracking and preventing the contagion of hate, humiliation, and bullying. Its origins must be analyzed, and its means of spreading understood. Finally, we need to develop *antidotes*,[7] including thoughts, feelings, and actions specifically to address and treat these diseases of the mind.

Disease Prevention and Management

Public health terminology, frames of references, and institutions can be helpful as a paradigm for how to take Compassionate Reasoning and make it an indispensable feature of a healthy society. Henceforth, I am going to italicize public health terminology for the reader to see an analogy to crucial lessons of public health.

Public health frames of reference define and address the opposite of health, namely, *disease*. In this case, we need to identify the closest opposites to healthy compassion and the reasoning that it positively influences: hatred and bullying. Abuse and aggressive crimes often emerge from a disturbed state of mind and body characterized by hate. Hate as a disease is something that needs greater attention and debate as to the advantages and disadvantages of declaring it to be a disease. Disease is in many ways a socially defined phenomenon. For example, non-medical mind-altering drug use was seen as an immoral act by most people originally, except of course alcohol, which almost always somehow escaped moral rebuke by most people in the West; thus a social definition of drugs in one moral category and alcohol in another category, despite the obvious destruction of alcohol addiction. But drug addiction is now commonly seen and medically viewed as a disease that can be treated. When something is acknowledged to be a disease with addictive and compulsive patterns, it does not lessen the disapproval of crimes under the influence. But it does open the door to clinical approaches to prevention and treatment (Livingstone n.d.).

When it comes to hate, it is not an either/or proposition. We can consider hate to be a sin religiously, an immoral act in the secular sense, and of course a crime when it results in injury to others. But as a more constructive long-term approach to change, we need to see philosophies of hatred as a diseased state of mind, with dangerous behaviors associated with it. Thus, the first step in developing the strength of Compassionate Reasoning in society is to cultivate an understanding of its opposite, hate, as a phenomenon in need of observation, understanding, analysis, and treatment.

A public health perspective focuses not on sin or immorality, but on a disease that has origins, roots and a great capacity for *infection*. Infection is its inherent danger to society. Therefore, tracking its *incidence* is a crucial public health necessity in order to engage in effective responses. This is often referred to as an *incident rate* that will measure *morbidity*, the death rate, as a way to track *prevalence*. In the case of hate that harms compassion and reasoning, morbidity may have its counterpart in a hate crime or an incidence of bullying, since reaching this level of abuse starts to create permanent damage in victims, but also a level of contagion among other members of society prone to this disease. One act of bullying or abuse emboldens the next and the next, and that is the very definition of contagion. If we want to develop the opposite trend, namely healthy contagion of compassion, we need to confront, prevent, and treat the contagious aspects of its opposite in hatred and bullying.

The *prevalence* of disease in one family or community means it has become endemic, and the disease must be contained before it becomes an *epidemic* across many communities, or a global *pandemic*. Interventions take a very long time, because diseases like hate and bullying become deeply embedded and require a level of *disease management* with a long-term strategy. In fact, premature talk of eradication, promises of "never again" for mass atrocities are actually dangerous in that they suppress evidence of a chronic condition in need of constant care. Indeed, many societies backslide to racist violence or fascism because they pretended that all the bad was in the past and gone. Denial is a natural human tendency to create a sense of calm, even when this is delusional. But healers need to know what they are up against in great detail. They must pay attention to the microscopic and the hidden, if they want to prevent the outbreak of disease and present the appropriate measures to ensure health.

Many people have treated acts of hatred or bullying only as civil rights violations or crimes that require punishment, ignoring the medical analogy to this phenomenon. Therefore, the mentality is: remove the bully from the school, remove the person from the society, sue the hate group into bankruptcy, and the problem goes away. That turns out to be based on a misunderstanding of hate as a chronic disease in need of intervention, management, and treatment. Furthermore, there is little to no attention to investigating treatments, such as compassion and reasoning, in order to test and disseminate the discovered treatments. Compassionate Reasoning is meant to fill that void.

Epidemiology and Risk Management

Extensive efforts to study and treat hate and violence are at the core of fields such as genocide prevention, conflict analysis, conflict resolution, ethics, neuroscience, and peacebuilding. But the view of hatred as a disease and its opposite, such as compassion, as a treatment has not been sufficiently appreciated. The evidence we have presented in this book is the extraordinary power of compassion as (1) a foundation for ethics, and (2) a foundation for a healthy mind that proceeds from compassion to ethical reasoning and planning. Both suggest that we need to invest more in treatments for the disease of hate. What I propose is that public health and medicine provide a well-trodden pathway to follow as we invest more in "hate treatments." The path of health sciences and its accompanying life-affirming ethic of lifesaving and compassionate care makes for a good fellow traveler to Compassionate Reasoning treatments for hate.

Prevention of Hate

There are three forms of *prevention* in the health sciences that can be applied to our subject. *Primary prevention* involves reducing susceptibility to hate and bullying, such as by working on nurturing and compassionate relationships between classmates, teachers and pupils, and family members. *Secondary prevention* will entail early intervention for emerging negative symptoms, whereas *tertiary prevention* involves alleviating the effects of hatred and the *injury* that it inflicts. *Protection* entails examining the circumstances of injury and preventing those circumstances from arising again wherever one can intervene.

There is also an approach to prevention focused on the analysis of risk, such as engaging in analysis of *risk factors*, leading to *risk assessment* and *risk management*. We need to apply this approach to hatred, bullying, and abuse. This entails finding where the greatest risks exist, then directing energy and attention to those places. It involves studying what personal qualities and societal conditions lead to the increased probability of hate arising.

Public health also focuses on identifying *pathogens* and engaging in such actions as *isolation* and *quarantine*. A pathogen is a microorganism that can cause disease. Identifying the pathogen of hate is an important subject to analyze for every intervention and every deployment of Compassionate Reasoning, and it will take the combined efforts of observant people to figure this out *for each situation*. What is it in a situation that is the hidden source of the beginning of the disease of hate? Is it a pervasive thought or habit within a particular group of people? Is it one person with a troubled background who aggressively shifts the atmosphere of a classroom or a school or a community? Identifying the hidden pathogens is a worthwhile pursuit in every situation.

To some degree schools, and society as a whole, do this often regarding hate and bullying. Authorities do have a moral and professional obligation to protect other students or family members from bullying. But this too often devolves into finding one person to eliminate from the situation. It is understandable why this is tempting, but it is often oversimplified and sometimes downright prejudicial.

In public health you want to kill a virus, but we do not want to kill bullies. We try to heal and to treat, not make matters worse by creating more abuse, by isolation of the "problem child," or by various forms of humiliation and punishment. All of these failed approaches to hate and bullying simply deepen the existence of disease. Unfortunately, too much of our approach to bullying, bigotry, and abuse is to destroy and eliminate the pathogen, but if you do that with bullies as "pathogens," then you actually spread the pathogen even more. Here is why: When you shame and isolate bullies, then they just get worse, even if you have engaged in some immediate protection of innocents. Further, whoever follows those bullies will just get worse as you humiliate the bully, and thus you will spread the disease. You cannot cure the disease of humiliation with humiliation, and therefore we must dig deeper for answers in every situation and with every person and group.

Following the analogy to health sciences, we need to look at *protective factors* that could change the atmosphere of hate, and reduce the circumstances and behaviors that give rise to hatred and abuse. There are *pathogens* of hatred, such as dangerous websites that pretend to be news sources, and they are designed to inflame hatred and demonization of others. A serious approach to the disease of hatred must address this with better and equally attractive sources of information, for example, in order to put citizens young and old on a better path of reason and compassion as antidotes to the pathogens coming at them.

Another way of making this point is that we need *screening* and *surveillance* of the sources of hate and abuse so that we can identify *vectors* that carry the disease of hate. Then we engage in *vector control*. Vector control means that we limit the transmission of pathogens by reducing or eliminating contact with the offending vector. Let's say, for example, that the vector of hate is a certain kind of manipulative and false social media, and there is also a vector of hate due to emotional neglect of kids that is common among those who are attracted to such social media. Then we work on cognitive and affective ways in which any recipients of hate vectors at any age are given the tools to resist such mind manipulation or to heal from emotional neglect. We intervene with compassionate emotional support from parents, teachers, peers, fellow congregants, or community members.

When a person becomes hateful, our instincts are to move away from such a person. But that precisely eliminates protective factors against the disease of hate. The goal is the opposite of moving away from the person. The goal is to mitigate the emotional neglect that the person may be experiencing that drives them into antisocial media. Antisocial media are faux virtual communities for those starving for real community. Compassion and reasoning need to find ways into real community with those who have sought false community in toxic places.

These are just a few examples of applying Compassionate Reasoning with the help of a public health perspective. The full analysis of systems of practical intervention would need to be worked on through intensive case study and specialized applications of Compassionate Reasoning to the uniqueness of each situation, each city, each school, each community, even each person.

The Economics of Hate as a Hidden Vector

It is vital to point out how easy it is to miss vectors of hate that are subtle and several steps removed. In our field of conflict analysis and resolution, we are particularly sensitive to the strong association between violence, hate, and economic deprivation. Most poor people never act out violently, but some do across every culture, especially among the young and jobless. There is a fine line between gangs, hate ideologies, and the simple need of highly energized young men to make money, in many conflict zones around the world. Furthermore, the after-effects of deprivation are often a perfect and fertile ground for surrendering to hate ideologies (Burton 1979; Rubenstein 2017; Staub 2011). Thus, the vectors of hate against which Compassionate Reasoning will struggle are not just inside a person or a community but inside a system that creates desperation and rage due to economic injustice.

Systemic Prevention

The evolution of public health in recent centuries has led to a dazzling increase in the human lifespan and also has provided a roadmap for work in positive social change and wellbeing. Public health has taught through example that it is not enough to work on prevention and intervention at the level of individuals and families, for example. It is certainly inadequate to be merely reactive to problems, as opposed to systemic and proactive construction of better systemic alternatives. The true source of increasing the human lifespan through public health has been *systemic* prevention of disease, institutionally, as a fundamental part of local and global *governance*.

In a similar vein, *systemic prevention of hate and violence requires making compassion and reasoning fundamental to the human future.* We need to make training in Compassionate Reasoning an institutional component of modern governance. Specifically, just as there are *safety-net providers* for health, there must be safety-net providers for compassion and reasoning that support families and communities, but especially those that have exhibited risk factors. Just as there are safety-net providers that include hospitals, clinics, doctors, and emergency services, we need to think about such services to combat the diseases of callousness, hate, mental abuse, and bullying. Conversely, these are the same services that can provide antidotes by inculcating the skills and methods of compassion and Compassionate Reasoning; this will prevent outbreaks of these illnesses. This includes the public health practice of *assurance* which means a systematic process of communications that ensures everyone's *access* to care.

A true concern for a moral value and moral practice of society that you want to be universal and sustainable is that there are mechanisms in place to make sure that no one gets left behind when it comes to compassion and care—but we do not do this at present. For example, our systems of education, heavily focused on STEM and basic skills to keep moving children through the system, leave behind most people when it comes to intentional expressions and demonstrations of compassion. We have not made this into a systematic and skill-based form of intervention for every grade level and stage of life. We have also not engaged in a systemic development of moral reasoning capacities that are essential to apply compassion to the building of the good society. There are countless individual teachers who do engage Compassionate Reasoning as a part of their natural talents and their moral code. But we do not train all teachers in this, we do not yet make it an essential part of the social contract, nor do we see it yet as essential for the health and wellbeing of society.

This can change if we internalize Compassionate Reasoning into our personal development as human beings and as agents of positive change. Internalizing the practice of Compassionate Reasoning, applying it to ourselves and our families, will lead us by inference to the natural conclusion that only society-wide institutions for compassion and Compassionate Reasoning can make it a common reality for everyone.

Compassion and Care

Let us focus now on several questions involving public health categories applied to the development of compassion:

(1) What are the *determinants* of compassion? More specifically what personal, economic, and environmental factors contribute to a life of compassion?

(2) What accounts for compassion *disparities*? In other words, why do compassionate actions and words manifest themselves often in some classrooms and workplaces but not others?

(3) What would compassion *promotion* and compassion *education* look like in order for compassion to be a pervasive condition of society?

We also need to develop a conception of best compassion *outcomes*, *outcome standards*, and compassion *status indicators* for compassion to be firmly established in the psyche of citizens, families, and communities. The development of *social norms* for the encouragement of compassion becomes critical, something to be researched and taught in secular and religious institutions from the youngest age. These norms then need to be socialized throughout the community through *social marketing* and public education. Messaging matters, and promotion of *best practices* matters.

In order for this to be done properly, we need to investigate and expound the core compassion *competencies*, just as public health cultivates core health competencies. This includes *cultural competence*, meaning that compassion education and promotion needs to raise up and incorporate the competencies of many cultures and traditions. Cultural traditions contain many resilient resources for promoting and practicing compassion, and it is important that the variety of these cultural approaches are honored and included.

Determinants of compassion examine direct causes of a more compassionate set of behaviors and attitudes. There are *upstream* factors influencing compassion, including the social environment and economic systems that either promote or depress compassion. The *environment* in its totality, therefore, needs to be evaluated in terms of what promotes compassion and what depresses it. This is where the environment of racism or systematic deprivation of schools due to unjust distribution of city and state tax resources are a deep challenge to education in compassion. It is hard to emphasize the subtle skills of compassion and Compassionate Reasoning when institutions and communities lack the most basic necessities and job opportunities, or become militarized due to rampant gang violence. Compassionate Reasoning is a skill and an ethic that must include more creative approaches to promoting justice and equality and resisting unfair distribution of resources.

An example to draw from in a systemic look at what promotes compassion in the environment is the public health program, Healthy People 2030 (Office of Disease Prevention and Health Promotion 2020, 2021). This is an ongoing long-term project beginning in 2010 and extending at least 20 years, with a national objective for improving the health of all Americans. Effective campaigns create long-term and short-term goals, as well as *benchmarks*. If we are to truly tackle the state of hate versus the state of compassion in the United States and globally, we need a Compassionate People 2030 set of goals with achievable metrics and benchmarks for each year.

Benchmarks are important in terms of evidence of progress and success, but also in terms of the psychology of social change. People tend to get depressed when (1) goals are too lofty, and (2) achievements are too puny. There is a learned helplessness that can set in (Maier and Seligman 2016; Trindale, Mendes, and Ferreira 2020). Compassion indicators that are measurable, goals that are achievable, and benchmarks that are reachable can have a remarkable effect psychologically. This is how to take lofty ideals and turn them into concrete reality over time in terms of steady metrics of positive change. This is good for the mind, good for the reinforcement of ethical behavior, and good for the whole of society.

We also need to draw on the *social capital* that can make this happen and identify the *surge capacity* to accelerate these efforts, particularly in moments of trial and crisis. This refers to the capacity to accelerate interventions when dramatic turning points and opportunities arise. One way to do this is by integrating the goals and practices of Compassionate Reasoning into everyone's lives.

This is why *vital events* is a fascinating category of public health. Vital events is a critical public health concept that also has ancient roots in religious traditions. True positive change happens especially through attachment of positive teachings and messaging to the cycle of life, to birth, death, marriage, divorce, graduations, jobs, and job losses. We need Compassionate Reasoning to be taught and equipped in such a way that it constructively interacts with the full range of human vital events, both in terms of celebrating gains and coping with losses. This is the way it can become embedded in the mind and heart of all as they work to transform the life of society.

Triage and Ring Inoculation

There are two related institutions from medicine and public health, *triage* and *ring inoculation*. "Triage is the process of sorting people based on their need for immediate medical treatment as compared to their chance of benefiting from such care. Triage is done in emergency rooms, disasters, and wars, when limited medical resources must be allocated to maximize the number of survivors" (Shiel n.d.). "Ring inoculation" means creating a ring around infected people by inoculating everyone with whom they might have a connection. A corollary of ring inoculation is the *strengthening* of people who have a natural immunity to the illness at hand, either by nature or by recovery, and having them contribute to the health and recovery of society. This, I argue, has its exact analogy when it comes to hatred and violence. Let me explain.

What I tried to do in many of my experiences of peacebuilding for twenty years was to identify those people who had a natural ability to overcome violent situations with compassion, with care, and with love, who managed to create impossible bridges between enemies. They often had an uncanny charisma to influence very toxic situations for the better and transform enemies into friends by their example and by their leadership (Gopin 2012). For me, this was a version of ring inoculation. I knew it was a toxic situation, a diseased situation, but I also knew that a number of people in these situations had an innate ability to inoculate those around them from hatred and infect them instead with love and care that opened up the basis for very reasonable forms of conflict prevention, management, and resolution. In addition, such people also generated numerous moments of reconciliation between enemies.

These peacemakers managed to overcome the understandable hatreds of the situation through compassionate care that they displayed across enemy divides. Their practices also involved a great deal of dialogue and Compassionate Reasoning. It is exactly from them that I started to develop the early notions of how compassionate care leads to a higher form of nonviolent reasoning in dangerous situations. Once the compassion set the stage for relations, they helped a very special kind of dialogue, not one of debate but of reasoning *and imagination* in order to create systems of care across enemy lines. Whereas most "dialogue" was actually angry debate about the past, the compassionate contexts that they generated and the moments of extraordinary reconciliation that they inspired would often be followed up with deep and reasoned imagination about possible futures.

Quite often this was not enough to overwhelm the fatal toxicity of the situation as a whole, since the latter would require a much larger scaling up of Compassionate Reasoning among much larger amounts of people in the conflict zone. But for the people with whom they came in contact, their use of compassion and reasoning was working and spreading. There was clear contagion. In other words, the metric of their successes was how many enemies became friends through their interventions and through the social networks they created (Gopin 2009). When we think of how to increase this kind of healthy change, we must look to such people as exemplars of public health through inoculation. This is the public health of Compassionate Reasoning, a moral health of the mind, of affect and cognition, and of their habits that lead to less violence and a flourishing set of moral relationships.

The role of "triage" in such situations was important to my own practice. I was constantly choosing where to focus my energies and interventions in such complicated and dangerous situations (Gopin 2009). Sometimes I focused on which people could be the most impactful, who had the greatest gift for Compassionate Reasoning. But other times, especially when war was at its height, my colleagues and I would focus on those who were most deeply involved in the war and how we might become a bridge between them in order to make a ceasefire more possible. The greatest amount of lives could be saved by any bridge we could make between active enemies, and that is what we pursued often. This is what the ethics of the moment demanded, namely a search for the way to save the most lives possible. At the same time, I believe that the seeds of nonviolent social change and human flourishing lie in extraordinary agents of change who seem to have the capacity to spread the opposite contagion to hate, the contagion of Compassionate Reasoning.

None of these interventions were literal ring inoculation or triage, but these public health approaches were very much on my mind as I witnessed and helped create extraordinary care between enemies. War and violence very much feel like a disease when you are facing the thinking of enemies on all sides. You have to make triage decisions as you try to save lives in the moment, and attempt to stop the descent into total war. It caused me great trauma to be in between enemy groups, but I also found the greatest insights as you participated with extraordinary peacemakers in dire situations. You got to examine their talents up close, why they were so beloved by good people on two sides of a bitter war, what it said about effective bridges between enemies, and what materials make such bridges. It was compassion combined with reasoning that always gave us the best method to succeed with our interventions.

Placebo, the Power of the Mind, and the Impact of Compassionate, Inspirational Leadership

What struck us was the power of the mind in these situations, the power of extraordinary individuals to guide others who were confused and frightened by conflict and war. The effect on groups in dialogue of charismatic, calming individuals expressing a great deal of patience and kindness had a striking effect on the ability of groups to reason (Foroughi 2016). It greatly enhanced the capacity of reasoning between strangers (Mercier and Sperber 2017).

This effect reminded me of the work of my old friend Dr. Ted Kaptchuk. He is one of the world's leading authorities on the power of placebo for healing. Ted is a Professor of Medicine at Harvard Medical School, and Director of the Harvard-wide Program in Placebo Studies and the Therapeutic Encounter (PiPS) at Beth Israel Deaconess Medical Center in Boston, Massachusetts.

Put very simply, the placebo effect is detectable generally in studies where patients think they are getting a real pill, but it is actually a fake pill, and they still show some measurably positive health effects. This is generally evidence of the power of the mind over the body, and the power of anyone in authority with instructions; this a very oversimplified explanation but suffices for our purposes. I remember sitting in Ted's living room one evening as he described, to *his own* utter amazement, that a doctor could actually *tell* patients that this pill that he/she is about to give them is a sugar pill, but they should take it anyway. They would take it, and it would *still* have a measurably positive impact on the patient! I was amazed too, and I realized right there and then that the power of our minds, when properly directed, can help us heal in amazing ways.

The real question, however, is how to move the mind in the direction of healing. As a peacebuilder, I drew parallels immediately, and I wondered how we can utilize the power of suggestion to move people in a less violent and more peaceful direction. I was deeply impressed with the enduring authority and power of doctors as healers of both the mind and the body. I was impressed with the fact that for billions of people, other forms of authority such as from religious leaders was waning in the modern period, but that the average mind was still deeply impressed with the authority of the doctor, that their simple directions were enough to push the mind to heal.

This, by inference, suggested to me that the main challenge we have not yet tackled concerning the persistent fatalities from hatred and war is the mind itself. We still have not harnessed the power to shift the mind toward less violence and toward more healthy ways of pursuing one's needs and goals. I was also keenly aware, due to the work of psychologist Stanley Milgram (1974) and genocide analysts such as Ervin Staub (1989), that it seemed far too easy to take normal people and make them into monsters through various means, all centered in the final analysis on the power of obedience over the human mind. In other words, the bright side of placebo is that it suggests the power we have to heal beyond physical medicines, but the dark side was how easily authority figures could manipulate us and convince us to believe almost anything and do almost anything.

The Competition for Leadership Is the True Test of Compassionate Reasoning

I longed in that moment for a simpler stage of my life when I believed war criminals are just exceptional human monsters, but they are not. The Milgram and Zimbardo experiments demonstrated that any uncharismatic prison guard, anyone in a booth giving authoritative instructions, could turn many normal people into obedient monsters (Zimbardo 2007). Just as astonishing, so many soldiers who have committed unspeakable crimes go back to civilian life and never harm a fly again, obedient once again to civilian rules.

This is a constant reminder about how much work we still have to do to inoculate the average human being against the contagion of organized political hate and violence, the ease with which political authority turns into mass killing in war. I wanted to search for ways of cognitive, affective, and social resistance to violent authority, as well as to promote the *alternative* contagions of the mind for compassion and for reason. I realized we needed to do more to generate leadership and role models of Compassionate Reasoning. It was quite fortunate that I had witnessed many such leaders over the decades, even in the worst circumstances of war. Thus, our challenge is not with a hopelessly violent and flawed human nature following Koestler. Rather we are in a fierce competition for influence over a very malleable human nature, a competition for leadership over populations, and a race to inspire and train people who can demonstrate leadership through compassion and reasoning.

Obedience as a Unique Political Disease and Existential Threat to Humanity

I began searching for a treatment for *the disease of obedience*, a disease that had taken otherwise great cultures, such as most recently German and Japanese culture, and turned them into genocidal monstrosities for a limited and catastrophic decade of history. I found fellow travelers in this search, and the work of psycholinguist George Lakoff seemed to help with answers. I had grown up with an ancient religious tradition that centralized the spiritual power of words to change reality, to curse or to bless and to cosmically affect reality by carefully chosen words. Words are indeed central to the brain's construction of reality, and I became aware of how easily manipulated we are through the use of the word by political leaders and movements. Each word constructs reality, and when repeated enough times, words establish hardened neural networks that are difficult to undo.

But if mind construction and manipulation could be done for the sake of obedience to violent wills, there had to be a way to undo it and also do the opposite. If something as simple as a doctor telling you that a sugar pill was good for you could change your health and mental state, there has to be a way for us to help people change for the better through words, to direct people to be less violent, more despite violent orders from authorities.

If the mind is so powerful that it can induce obedience to genocide, it can also be directed just as easily toward love as an essential treatment for hate, administered consciously and collectively. If doctors and authority figures were to diagnose hate as a disease—along with compassion and compassion training as a treatment—then perhaps there is enough psychological and cultural power in that health directive to generate less violent societies. This means that training and habit formation becomes essential for not only personal change, but more importantly for political change.

The Disease of Obedience as a Unique Political Affliction and Its Antidote

There are two vulnerable aspects of the mind that Compassionate Reasoning seeks an antidote to: violent emotions and violent ideas. A violent idea, like the racist idea of natural superiorities and inferiorities, is not based on a violent emotion but a mistaken idea with deadly consequences. First there is the idea, and then there is the raw emotion and violent speech and behavior. There is an aspect to the mind, and even locations of the mind that correspond to violent emotions, to paranoia, and to fight and flight. This is a pretty established finding, especially associated with the amygdala (da Cunha-Bang et al. 2017). It seems natural to assume that fearful and violent emotions can also be contagious, affecting crowds very quickly, as we see in every drunken brawl (Chartrand and Lakin 2013; Kelly, Iannone, and McCarty 2016).

Contagion of emotions is not the deeper danger, however. There is also the contagion of "violent ideas," such as racism or supremacy based on skin pigmentation or supremacy based on money or ideology or religion or gender. Toxic ideas become the foundation for millions of people to be persecuted, enslaved, and murdered. Toxic ideas are also the basis for the simplest act of hate. You see countless videos of the moment of a recorded hate crime that culminates in an attack on someone of a different skin color. You think it is just raw emotion that somehow causes the hate, but it is the other way around. I have watched this countless times. First, a toxic idea occurs in the mind of the hater. He says to himself and then out loud, "That guy shouldn't be here in front of me in line. He is Black. I should not be behind him in line." In his mind, he is repeatedly thinking that it is wrong "morally" for a Black man to be in front of him in line. To him in his toxicity, an ethical norm has been violated. He cannot get the thought out of his head, he repeats it and repeats it in his head, and then out loud, and then his amygdala is finally moved by the idea and righteous outrage to start cursing and then provoking a fight. He loses control, and he will end up in jail, but the thought has now unleashed the amygdala that knows no self-control when triggered by such a toxic thought. These thoughts of "righteous" indignation lead the amygdala in this case to an emotional assault and destruction, but it all begins with a false and toxic thought.

Toxic thoughts endure as false ideas all over the world, and have for many centuries. It is extraordinary how universal racism is, no matter how patently stupid it is at the most basic level of investigation and science. Prejudice on shades of skin color afflicts most major societies on earth, with the most absurd, unfair treatments based on shades of color or slight differences that one can hardly see or are simply delusional.

The problem is that a violent idea has no specific place in the brain itself, and is much harder to isolate than say a violent or fearful impulse. But we can see the effects of violent ideas, patently false ideas, and outrageous conspiracies that can take hold of millions of minds and stay lodged in the mind as if it were fact, as if it were science.

The hopeful aspect of neuroscience of the brain is that just as there is a contagion of negative emotions and ideas, there is also the contagion of positive emotions and positive ideas. These are the positive lessons of neuroplasticity in terms of its ethical and political implications (Hatfield, Bensman, Thornton, and Rapson 2014; Kuang, Peng, Xie, and Hu 2019). But these potential evolutions of the mind need nurturing through education and habit formation that impact both the mind's affects and its cognitions, its emotions and its ideas. Both diseases of feeling and diseases of thinking need to be countered by the contagion of positive emotions and positive ideas that captivate the mind, ideas such as human rights and emotions such as compassion. Positive ideas and visions merge together with positive emotions due to reasoning and debate.

Compassion and mutual aid are especially enticing because they are highly adaptive survival characteristics. When nurtured well they lead to many good conclusions of the reasoning mind, such as the logic of public health as a common and essential good, and the reasonable evolution of human rights.

I am proposing that good and sustainable ethical ideas, arrived at through reasoning among many people over generations, are treatments for the diseases of the mind involving hatred. For example, human rights itself is but an idea—a novel idea in recent centuries, but just an idea. However, it is a very powerful one that brings with it much evidence for its health as a sustainable innovation for human survival and flourishing.

Like all diseases, diseases of the mind and of the emotions have warning signs. Excessive obedience, regression in the face of narcissistic leaders, the search by some when stressed or insecure for leaders who evoke fear and hate and spout conspiracy theories—these are the symptoms or warning signs of incipient disease of the mind that have major political, economic, and military consequences. These negative ideas and cognitions lead to contagion and epidemic, unless antidotes are found and administered in the same way that public health regimens are administered and distributed.

By contrast, habits of compassion, moral education of a particular kind that emphasizes prosocial emotions and reasoning, the encouragement of joint reasoning with others, discussion, active listening and debate, perspective-taking, these are antidotes that must be administered through in-depth and broad interventions. This can lead to a contagion of political health rather than a contagion of political disease. When something afflicts many people at once, and it is transmitted rapidly, the logic of medical and public health models should be drawn upon and extrapolated from in order to counteract its effects. If habits of feeling and thinking lead rapidly to political disease, then habits of feeling and thinking will be the basis of a treatment. This too is at the core of Compassionate Reasoning as a social and political methodology of peacebuilding.

As in all good disease and contagion research there must be attention to *carrier hosts*, vulnerable individuals who are susceptible to rapid reception and rapid transmission. But just as there are optimal carrier hosts for disease, there are optimal carrier hosts for recovery and health, people who are particularly adept at compassion, at love, at care and service, at reasoning and education, at moral leadership of society. They carry within themselves the capacity to both model and rapidly transmit good feelings and thoughts that are contagious.

We need to strengthen those with viral potential for Compassionate Reasoning. By contrast, we need to understand and identify who is particularly *immunocompromised* to political authoritarianism and social violence. We need to devise effective interventions by families, by peers, by communities, and by professionals.

This is where both secular and religious constructs of society can collaborate as we single out those with talent for the positive viral contagion of compassion, and jointly intervene with those who have the opposite tendency. We need to understand who has *natural immunity* due to their social environment or their strong natural abilities for compassion and reasoning. We need to encourage them to take leadership roles for the public health of the society.

Democracy is a grand human experiment, an experiment in evolution of the mind as well as of society. If we want democracy to survive and be victorious over authoritarianism, we are going to have to generate more invincible mental/political "immune systems" in a much larger swath of the general public. What I mean by mental/political "immune systems" is the capacity of individuals and collectives to be resistant to personal and political manipulation and demagoguery, through a stronger capacity for public engagement in compassionate behavior and reasoned debate.

This is a political solution going far beyond voting rights, elections and human rights, these being undoubtedly core institutions of democracy that strengthen and preserve justice and peace. We need deeper and more effective treatments, however, than the legal and the institutional foundations of democracy and fair governance. We need mental health and strength of moral character generating *political* mental health, *political* savvy, and resistance to manipulation. And we need new delivery systems of that political mental health, which is why I have conceived of Compassionate Reasoning as a personal and social methodology of positive change.

We cannot counter phenomena like social hatred and bigotry with our current forms of higher education. We need habits of thinking, speaking, and doing that are frequently repeated throughout one's life and communal interactions. This repetition needs time in order to change the chemistry and anatomy of the brain. This will strengthen the hippocampus and several other areas proven now to be strongly associated with generalized compassion and reasoned thinking (Immordino-Yang and Singh 2013; Zeithamova, Schlichting, and Preston 2012).

Hate: A Disease and a Treatment

To recap, hate is a disease that has killed billions of people in history. Hate has been utilized by leaders since the dawn of time to motivate theft, plunder, and countless wars. It is a powerful tool of control, suggesting that the human brain is deeply vulnerable to this social disease. The very plasticity of our brains means the corrupted or disturbed few can come along every so often and induce obedience of the many through repeated lies, baseless accusations, bizarre conspiracy theories, and scapegoating frames; all of these project all corruption and evil into one person or group (Lakoff and Johnson 1980; Milgram 1974; Pinker 2011a). This is the dark side of the human brain in particular, as no other species pursues mass murder and genocide. The power of suggestion to the human brain, especially by those who have any kind of authority (even your doctor), suggests how much lifetime work we have to do with our minds and our habits in order to protect our minds from participation in this kind of destruction.

This kind of hate inducement is akin to a *breakout infection*. Whether it be a pogrom, a crusade, or a lynching, sometimes groups are so driven by hate that it is as if an infection overtakes them. It is a breakout infection through mass obedience. It is a massive escalation of the human capacity for violence that has no parallel in other species. Certainly, no other species has managed to combine technical capacity and genocide.

What is the opposite of a breakout "obedience infection"? *The infection of independent thought, independent moral reasoning, based on compassion for all life at the core. It is a compassion infection, and this too happens. Mass rallies of resistance against tyranny and cruelty to the vulnerable, these are disobedience outbreaks.* The worldwide demonstrations of unprecedented scale that broke out in support of Greta Thunberg's call to action in 2019 on global warming, for example, encompassed millions of youth. These were collective actions against obedience to outmoded and destructive systems of fossil fuel energy production. This was an example of a global mass movement based on compassionate ideas and emotions, a compassionate embrace of future generations especially.

These too are breakout infections, but they are infections of thoughts and feelings of compassion for all of life, for the future of all life, and they are based on deep and collective reasoning about what this earth needs. This does not mean that positive breakout infections are perfect in their ideas or visions. Good ideas need constant revisitation, cross-examination, debate, compassionate understanding of other points of view, and compassionate inclusion of all for due consideration in the pursuit of reasonable courses of action. Compassionate Reasoning means that the heart and mind are continually open, searching, reflecting, and self-examining (Gopin 2016). These are traits that political movements on all sides of the political spectrum need in order to qualify as being rooted in Compassionate Reasoning.

Equipped now with the public health analogy for Compassionate Reasoning, let's explore in the next chapter how to inculcate habits of Compassionate Reasoning from the playground to the university and at every stage of human development. Positive habits of thinking and behaving have been a key component in public health's success with the radical increase in human lifespan, such as washing hands and making sure that water is potable, habits that were far less prevalent centuries ago. Habits of thinking, feeling, and doing are the best way to transform societies composed of hundreds of millions of individual people. We need to explore the same transformation of habits of thinking, feeling, and behaving that will promote Compassionate Reasoning.

5

The Applied Ethics and Habits of Compassionate Reasoning

Habits of the Body, Habits of Thinking, Habits of Feeling

Ethical habits are essential to the betterment of human life, habits of thinking, habits of feeling, and habits of doing. Cognition, affect, and behavior are the essential building blocks of the good person and the good citizen, the family member, the national citizen, and the global citizen. Habits are the foundations for how we move society in a better direction. There are many other building blocks of the good society in terms of necessary social, political, legal, and economic structures, and these structures all must be engaged as we imagine a better future. This book, however, has been focused on the cultivation of the good person, the good citizen. We are interested in what kind of skills are necessary to help the good citizen become a vehicle of positive social change as she builds greater and greater collaboration with strangers and society as a whole.

Compassionate Reasoning is the key tool we have been exploring in order to discover and implement those habits of the person, the group, and the community. In order for Compassionate Reasoning to become instilled in society, we need to explore exemplary habits of cognition, habits of affect, and habits of behavior. These, in turn, steer the individual and, through many individuals, the whole of society toward compassion and ethical reasoning. This, in turn, leads the whole of society toward less and less violent directions. We seek the kind of habits that generate collective commitments to civil behavior and collective policies. Thus, individual habits become the basis for family habits, city habits, regional and national habits.

Compassionate Reasoning. Marc Gopin, Oxford University Press. © Oxford University Press 2022.
DOI: 10.1093/oso/9780197537923.003.0005

Two Diseases of the Mind to Confront

The human mind contains within it the basis for that which can steer toward or away from violence, toward or away from prosocial emotions, toward or away from reason-based constructs of society that serve everyone's needs and interests. Finding the right habits for Compassionate Reasoning to become embedded in the person and in society can be compared to public health efforts to influence habits. The ultimate goal is to affect the way people think about health and disease prevention and the corresponding habits that cause lifesaving changes in behavior. The ethical and political realms of human interaction are every bit as important in terms of lifesaving behavior, however. Habits of thinking, feeling, and behaving constitute a reinforcing loop that is essential for real social change that promotes life and discourages violent destruction.

There are two distinct dangers to the human mind in this regard: diseases of thinking (cognition) and diseases of feeling (emotion/affect). The relation of diseased emotions to violence is self-evident, and the resulting destruction of health is clear. Impulsive anger leads to violence, leading to injury and death. Compassion and compassion training are vital as correctives to hateful habits of the emotions, such as rage, fear, and an aggressive reaction to enemies or strangers.

It is true: Fear in proper measure is necessary for the survival of animals and humans, as all organisms confront real dangers. But fear and rage that are out of control and over-subscribed get people killed. This also leads to paranoia, inventing enemies everywhere and living a life of perpetual rage and violence. This disease requires an antidote in the cultivation of habits of compassion.

There is another disease of the mind that also kills, and that is the disease of bad or false ideas, false constructs of reality.[1] Racism is such an idea, for example. False, simplistic stereotypes are tempting because they lure a person in with a coherent set of truths that give the *appearance* of plausibility. The idea and its partial evidence seem to cohere into a complete truth, and this sends the brain into a self-justifying loop with very limited evidence and false reasoning. By contrast, a correspondence approach to truth, a search for rational correspondence to reality, *in all of its complexity*, is the only antidote. Here is the problem, however. You have to be ready *emotionally* to pursue truth in all its complexity. Truth-seeking and commitment to evidence-based understanding of reality is not just an intellectual journey; it is also an emotional one. You need to be ready to deal with complicated realities that may be uncomfortable, that may provide a great deal of cognitive dissonance (Festinger 1957; Harmon-Jones 2019).

This is why I have put compassion and reasoning together as Compassionate Reasoning, because the self-justifying loop of bad ideas is comforting for a troubled mind, a mind that is in terror of a confusing world. Thus, the desperate need for bad ideas and conspiracy theories is based on an emotional wasteland of fear, the very opposite of a compassionate embrace of the world. Compassion training and reason training need each other, therefore, in order to heal the troubled mind *and* the troubled society from both diseases of the mind: diseased ideas and diseased emotions.

The key to understanding this challenge is that there are two different dangers: diseases of reason (a coherence approach to truth that becomes completely removed from reality) and the emotional diseases of rage, fear, and impulsivity. Compassion addresses the problem of diseased emotions, and training in a correspondence approach to truth, to reason, to calm debate, learning, and questioning, cures unhealthy approaches to ideation, idea formation, that remove one from reality. The checks and balances of human communication and persuasion in a free context promotes a greater openness to facts, but only if done with a compassionate understanding of every party. The free political context is critical, for it is only in the free context that fear does not upend the value of any communicated forms of reasoning.[2]

Cures of the Mind

Emotions

In terms of habit formation for emotions, Klimecki's (2013) work cited earlier demonstrates that the brain has identifiable neural pathways for compassion that can be strengthened through compassion training. These trainings and resulting habits, which have their parallel in many traditional cultural and religious habits of compassion, can provide a counterbalance to other parts of the mind that foster fear and impulsivity. Anger (Beck and Fernandez 1998; Blair 2013), fear (Lange et al. 2020), and impulsivity (Yang et al. 2020) are also amenable—with the right skills in place—to good training methodologies. The shift through habits of the mind and body of destructive feelings has been well established.

Ideas

The challenge with poor ideation, bad ideas (e.g., racism), is more compli-cated, however. The formation of ideas involves many parts of the mind, and thus poor or cruel ideas and constructs of reality may not be subject to correc-tion by the simple training of angry impulses, for example. To be blunt: You can be a very calm, educated racist or practitioner of genocidal policies, and the history of genocide has proven it time and again. As I mentioned above, an idea that coheres in the mind with its own body of evidence is difficult to dislodge. Cognitive therapy does, in fact, work on the whole of mind by challenging the logic of each of our ideas and their correspondence with re-ality, especially thoughts that are destructive (Beck 2011). This is a form of therapy and approach to healing that takes habitual thoughts very seriously. A poor idea involving violence and cruelty needs a persistent and consistent approach to shifts in thinking. The combination of inculcating habits of com-passionate attitudes and behaviors, following the theory of Compassionate Reasoning, sets the stage to challenge ideas that, by definition, will lead to cruelty. One way, then, to think about this is that compassion training is not only a therapy for anger or hate; it is also a preparation for shifting entire ways of thinking about the world and interpreting its reality. Challenging poor ideas in this way is one method that needs to be explored more in all of our interactions, including the ubiquitous effects of social media on our future. We may need to completely rethink how we interact, how we set up deep listening in our society, including in our virtual global interactions that have such a deep impact on opinion formation (Rafi, Bogacz, Sander, and Klimecki 2020).

Ideas and Active Listening

Poor ideas get challenged not only through personal therapy but through ha-bitual social interaction, including deep conversation and interaction. Social institutions of informal conversation become an important asset in lessening violence and increasing the decency of any society. This is especially the case when the art of active listening is practiced well, namely by expressing au-thentic interest and curiosity about another person's thoughts, even if you think them to be abhorrent. The story of Derek Black, former white suprem-acist, and his interfaith friendships at New College of Florida illustrates this idea of the embrace of extremists with great compassion, deep listening, thoughts challenged, and then lives changed (Stevenson et al. 2019; Saslow 2018). It is not debate that shifts the mind's way of thinking; rather, it is the sense of validation that comes from *being listened to*, which in turn leads to deep listening by the person with poor ideation.

Deep listening often leads to real transformation of poor ideas because poor ideas leading to violence cannot stand up to investigation and reasoning. In effect, the art and habit of respectful conversation prompts exploration by the person as to whether their own ideas truly correspond to all of reality. As they listen to others and enter into *their* realities, their own *evolved* set of ideas begin to better correspond to *all* of reality. This leads to less violence, more compassion, and better thinking.

Ideas and Cognitive Reframing

As has been explored throughout the text, a central aim of Compassionate Reasoning is to empower all peoples to better deal and cope with ongoing stressors in their lives. *"Stress modulation" is the term psychologists use to describe the many processes we use to help us minimize, mitigate, and prevent stress.* Stress modulation is steeped in neurological, behavioral, social-cultural, and spiritual processes or practices. Relevant to our study is the process of "cognitive reframing," a practice of identifying challenging experiences in life, then intentionally changing or altering how we view these experiences in such a way that we are better positioned to cope or deal with the challenge.

Cognitive reframing is largely associated with the ventrolateral prefrontal cortex (a region of our brain that is responsible for complex *reasoning*), the anterior insular cortex (emotions and regulation of homeostasis), and supplementary motor areas of the brain (Chialant, Edersheim, and Price 2016; Heatherton and Wagner 2011). Further research should be pursued to indicate whether these and other ancillary brain regions are activated during the practice of Compassionate Reasoning.

Furthermore, cognitive reframing (as a core component of Compassionate Reasoning) offers distinct and powerful psychological benefits for its practitioners, including increases in psychological resilience (the broad process and ability to overcome challenging times, including stress and trauma), increases in prosocial behavior, decreases in violent behavior, decreases in impulsive behavior, and increases in altruism, gratitude, and compassion toward others (Averill et al. 2018; Jiang, Chen, and Wang 2017).

A key factor shaping the effectiveness of cognitive reframing lies in its relevance to the cultural mores of the person practicing this form of stress modulation. Here are two examples. First, at the familial level, children are more likely to engage in prosocial behaviors, including cognitive reframing during challenging times, if their parents (especially mothers) use adaptive, interactive emotion modulation strategies; this trend holds stronger if children live in higher-income, less chaotic households (Kao, Tuladhar, and Tarullo 2020). Second, in addition to social developmental context, spiritual practice (i.e., mindfulness in Buddhist tradition) is a core aspect of cognitive reframing (Mills et al. 2019).

Freedom's Essential Role

Reasoning that supports a less violent, more compassionate approach to reality requires additionally a *free social context*. The rule of law guaranteeing freedom of thought and speech for all provides the important legal foundation of such a society, which in turn allows for the kind of open interactions that encourage better reasoning (Mercier and Sperber 2017). The rule of law in this regard sets the stage for at least the potential to uproot violent ideas like racism. But clearly the legal foundations of freedom do not by themselves root out racist ideologies, as the history of United States law and attempts at democratic institutions has demonstrated. Much more is needed to help the mind, and the whole of society, to become a vehicle of compassion and peacebuilding. Put another way, perhaps, the rule of law and the right to free and open debate would have generated more rational thinking in the United States only if those freedoms had been universally applied from the beginning.

The goal, in terms of dynamics of the mind, should be (a) to shift the brain's heightened states of emotional activation away from fear and anger and toward the compassion centers of the brain, and (b) to shift the mind heavily toward the kind of reasoning capacity that successfully corresponds with the real world in all of its complexity. Compassion has been identified with specific parts of the brain that can be strengthened and whose neural pathways can be reinforced; this is also the case with fear and rage.[3] Habits of all kinds create stronger neural pathways that become second nature and hard to undermine. The strengthening of parts of the mind associated with compassion and the weakening of those parts associated with impulsivity, anger, and paranoia is the goal. This then sets the stage for a better capacity of the mind as a whole to independently and freely evolve rational plans for the self, for loved ones, and for society, plans that are less violent, more kind, and more universal. This is the essence of a mind prepared for Compassionate Reasoning.

Reflection upon One's Emotions Is an Essential Step in the Evolution of Compassionate Reasoning

I also want to argue that reflecting on negative emotions, such as reflecting upon one's own fears, is indispensable to the evolution of Compassionate Reasoning. The reflection itself already begins to shift the mind *away* from raw and inciting negative emotions and instead *toward reflection upon those emotions*. When I *think* about my emotions, the fear and rage are already less in control, whereas my rational cognitive and speaking capacities are increased. This, combined with cultivating compassion through exercises, shifts the mind and the body toward Compassionate Reasoning.

Focusing the mind on the idea of a thing lessens the passion associated with the thing itself. The feeling of racist hate, when confronting the hated person in a bar, is far more dangerous and intense than reflection upon that experience. Analyzing the idea of anger and its articulation by the mind transfers the energy of the person toward the mind and away from raw impulses; this is already a first and essential victory for Compassionate Reasoning. This has parallels in talk therapy, which shifts the mind toward the *idea* of an emotion, rather than the emotion itself (Ladd 2018).

As I was reflecting on this train of thought, I compared notes with the extraordinary American philosopher Professor Heidi Ravven and her classic work based on Spinoza, *The Self Beyond Itself* (Ravven 2013). Here is the relevant passage from Spinoza that stimulated my interest in Ravven's thinking:

> When the mind regards its own self, and its power of activity [i.e., its own thinking, reasoning, causal and ever broader contextual understanding], it feels pleasure, and the more so the more distinctly it imagines itself and its power of activity. (Ethics, Part III Prop 53)

Here is Ravven's comment on the Spinoza citation:

> This is the key to everything. Rational self-understanding and world understanding heals the self and heals one's relationships and social worlds. It creates compassion and cooperation, calm and joy.[4]

I am arguing here that we can build a formidable and new approach to a *mind-centered* form of social change and peacebuilding that begins with the brain through reasoning and positive affect. We can go deeper into a *reason-and affect-based* methodology of human personal and social evolution. What has been missing from American culture is a way for the best practices of philosophical thinking to have a practical effect on how people *ethically operate their minds* on a day-to-day basis, especially in terms of their long-term goals and visions.

The Self Evolving with Other Selves through Self-Reflection

The next stage of proper habit formation of Compassionate Reasoning is to do this reflecting *in concert with others*. The embrace of diversity of meaning systems that is created in good conversations and debates prevents narrow and bigoted ideas from capturing the higher mind. The more this shifting toward reflection is done while brainstorming with others, the more the mind gets used to less aggressive approaches to human problems. Furthermore, people of great diversity debating in a supportive, free context creates powerful advantages for the evolution of the compassionate mind. This militates in the opposite direction of obedience to groupthink and mob behavior, both of which lead toward aggressive actions against outsiders. These tendencies of the mind are thus depressed and subject to more scrutiny by the community. Increasing the habits of *reflection in social contexts* depresses groupthink and mob behavior (Turner and Pratkanis 2014; Baron 2005).

My PhD student Naomi Kraenbring makes the following argument in response to this proposal:

> Getting to this truly "supportive, free context" to allow for the kind of reflection you describe is incredibly difficult, however. Baron (2005) identifies Stasser and colleagues' research (1985, 1995), which demonstrates

the power of the hidden profile effect to potentially limit groups' ability to be completely authentic, safe spaces for reflection. From Janis (1972, p. 207): "For constructive thinking to go on, a group must have a fairly high degree of like-mindedness about basic values and mutual respect. The members must forgo trying to score points in a power struggle or to obtain ego gratification by deflating rivals." Further, I believe Janis (1972) would suggest that the "reflection" you describe must include not only the invitation but demand for doubts and critical dissent.

From a semantic standpoint, then, is that truly "free," unbound, unfettered group reflection? Or are there certain requirements on group reflection that are necessary in order to avoid groupthink, and that, therefore, prohibit the use of the word "free"?[5]

This is a very important critique that cuts to the heart of what we mean in this book by Compassionate Reasoning. On one level, the major point is that by "free" I mean basic freedoms of speech and thought that are quite helpful to the evolution of collective human reasoning, though not always essential. Many great ideas have caught on in history by systematic conversations in many places despite severe restrictions on freedom of speech. Reasoning among people is remarkably resilient despite external repressions.

The deeper critique is that many conversations do not allow for freedom of reasoning because there is far too much confirmation bias, bullying, scoring points, hierarchies, and vested interests at stake. There are myriad reasons why most human conversations are more akin to combat or authoritarian rallies rather than serious exploration of facts and conclusions. Much of the field of conflict analysis and resolution analyzes good versus bad forms of dialogue for this very reason. This is precisely why Compassionate Reasoning insists that the most powerful prosocial emotion, compassion that creates a sense of generosity and perspective-taking, is so crucial to steering reasoning in the right direction.

Kraenbring also notes that Janis (1972) states, "The greater the threats to the self-esteem of the members of a cohesive decision-making body, the greater will be their inclination to resort to concurrence-seeking at the expense of critical thinking." This too is important in that it points to the importance of prosocial affect for better reasoning. Self-esteem is a critical need, skill, and ethical value that requires cultivation. I am arguing that Compassionate Reasoning practiced by everyone in a particular group will enhance self-esteem because the compassionate intention and style honors everyone in a group by its very nature. The compassionate foundation of intentions and communications makes the reasoning an exercise in discovery of truths rather than an exercise in domination or virtual combat. I am arguing that compassionate intentions and communications are essential to effective higher reasoning between human beings.

From the Communal Formation of Ideas to the Structures of the Compassionate Society

Following this line of reasoning, it is also clear that external structures of justice and compassion should reflect internal commitments of all. A marriage of public structures and private responsibilities is needed to generate (a) the good citizen, (b) the good community, and (c) the good society. Therefore, there is supreme value in making compassion and *compassionate service* to community and society into the ultimate act of citizenship. We are now in a position to buttress compassion training and compassionate service with warrants from science, warrants from ethics, and warrants from religion. All three foundations of human thinking and believing—science, ethics, and religion—can work together in the good society to induce most citizens to a path of compassion and reason. Health sciences support this direction by drawing upon the many demonstrated physical and psychological health benefits of compassion training and cognitive therapy (Klimecki et al. 2013). Moral conscience and religious conscience can be drawn upon to further strengthen the centrality of compassion in human life. Rational self-interest, a common foundation of some ethical systems, also yields the inherent value of more reason and more compassion in a fulfilled and happy life.

Habits of the Mind

I want to now delve into an exploration of habits, focusing first on habits of the mind, then habits of the emotions, and finally habits of the body. In previous chapters, we explored how recent neuroscience studies are critical to our capacity to coexist going forward as a species and how we can make better collective ethical decisions. The study of the mind has always been critical to our moral evolution, however. For thousands of years, wisdom literature, philosophy, and both sacred and secular literatures have all explored our minds and our motivations, and I doubt we would still be here without this accumulated wisdom. However, contemporary psychology and neuroscience explorations have revolutionized our understanding of who we are at our worst and who we are at our best. We know more about when and why we are free, courageous, independent, and creative human beings, and when and why we are obedient serfs to tyranny which turns us quickly into monsters, war criminals, and shadows of humans. The more we understand this paradox in our capacity, the more we have the foundations for new strategies of personal and social change.

What is revolutionary in the contemporary period is the discovery of the extent of our neuroplasticity. This means the way in which every thought and every action we take, *even every word we think or speak*, triggers pathways in our brains, laying down new pathways or strengthening old ones. It is hard for me to fathom how this is going on at every second, with every choice I make on what to think, what to articulate, what to imagine, and what to do. But fathom it we must, because in the very act of reflecting on this, internalizing it, we are beginning to take more control over our own minds, as well as becoming more independent and creative. This is the path we should take if we are to escape obedience to either anarchic mobs or authoritarian demagogues, if we do not want to succumb to oligarchies, demagogues, secular and religious alike. We see millions of people around us who still fall into terrible traps of psychological subservience that rob them of independence of mind and the empowerment they deserve. But with the right training of affect and cognition, of our minds and hearts, we have the ability to be obedient only to a moral compass consisting of our capacity to experience and express compassion, to reason with others, and then to act meaningfully as individuals and communities.

The extent of neuroplasticity of the brain that has been uncovered by contemporary science suggests a strong embrace of human cognitive flexibility that the great moral philosophers like Socrates anticipated. Socrates knew well that the proper exercise of the mind *through questioning* could change the way we are and how we behave. Aristotle understood the power of habitual thoughts and deeds to interact with our potential for excellence and enlightenment, all of which improves our ability to be good at citizenship.[6] It was also anticipated by the great Biblical prophets such as Ezekiel, who is an early Jewish philosopher of independent ethical action and personal responsibility (Ezekiel 33).

The commitment to generate an independent human mind that takes responsibility for actions has both secular and religious roots. There would be no democracy or human rights theory and experimentation for centuries without ancient forbearers declaring our responsibility for our own thoughts, for our own words and actions, and for the necessity to change the world for the better. Theories of democracy and human rights assume the human capacity to change for the better, a process that begins with individual commitment to work on one's own mind.

This rootedness of progressive political philosophy in the individual choice to work on one's own mind is often overlooked. But this same literature also recognizes that morality is not the same as moralistic preaching. Morality entails a series of social justice criticisms of contexts that force people into destructive ways of living, thinking, and feeling (Ravven 2013). The commitment to habit formation recognizes that many bad habits come from destructive situations embedded in unjust cultures, and that those bad habits coping with unjust situations deprive people of the freedom to excel in many ways.

Socrates understood that political or religious tyranny stood in the way of the freedom to question; he defended that right to question, and then paid for it with his life. Aristotle understood that the life of balance in moral character required a reasonable political environment in which to flourish. Prophets such as Ezekiel, Amos, and Isaiah understood very well that humans need and deserve a socially just environment in order to call themselves to their best natures. These prophets assumed that personal moral habits of the decent human being, when assaulted by unjust structures, can only take her so far in terms of a good life before God. When leaders created a corrupt system, these prophets predicted the destruction of the society, regardless of personal habits of etiquette or civility. The biblical legacy, to be sure, has endless advice on personal moral habits, such as in Proverbs and many other works, but the overwhelming message of the biblical social prophets is political and social. You can be righteous in a disastrous and violent kingdom, but that, in itself, will not create the good society that survives and flourishes. Only justice for the most vulnerable can do that (Rubenstein 2006).

The Art of Moral Reflection with Compassionate Reasoning: The Question Is the Answer

Social justice is essential to the good society, but it is still the case that the individual is the building block of social justice movements. Therefore, mastering the mind is essential to the individual citizen's evolution in a more compassionate and rational direction. What, then, is the contribution of philosophy and philosophers toward this great journey of mastering the human mind? It is not the answers they provide, many of which are the subject of endless debates for thousands of years, debates hardly even understood by the vast majority of humans. *It is rather philosophy's passionate embrace of the open question.* Open questions liberate us, not the answers, and it is open questions that philosophy has raised for thousands of years. It is the open question that is scandalous to closed systems of control, to power hunger, and to tyranny of one human over the other.

There are many possible answers to open questions, and these answers do contradict each other. The ethical schools of thought we have been applying to Compassionate Reasoning, for example, clearly suggest divergent answers to complex moral dilemmas. It is clear: Sometimes a deontological approach to right and wrong utterly contradicts a consequentialist conclusion about the same situation. One might think, therefore, that philosophical ethics cannot be helpful to Compassionate Reasoning, but that is not true for the following reason. It is the open question that drives the mind to its best capacities for reasoning endlessly, until the best possible paths of action can be found. It is the open question, therefore, that liberates us, that gives us knowledge of ourselves and the world. And the longer the question stays open, the more it liberates us from facile ideas; it protects us from fool's gold meant to suppress the greatest gift we have, the human mind. The longest questions in the history of philosophy, such as the question of free will and determinism, are the best questions precisely because they spur us on to more inquiry, more learning about the world and about ourselves.

Finally, philosophy takes us one crucial step further into ultimate questions of destiny: not the question "What is?" but the open question "What ought the world be?" Not only "Who am I?," not only "Who have I been?," but the moral question "Who could I be?"

I grew up in the Bostonian shadow of the immortal John F. and Robert F. Kennedy, who both quoted George Bernard Shaw regarding taking a visionary path in life: "Some men see things as they are and say, 'Why?' I dream things that never were and say, 'Why not?' "[7] These powerful words changed me forever when I heard Bobby's brother Ted quote them in his eulogy for Bobby. Such words and visions from slain heroes changed an entire generation as to the way we think, even in the way we frame our hopes. Such is the power of the word upon the human mind, when the word is spoken in the right place and the right time with the right emotional impact.

The open question is the key to knowing ourselves and knowing the world. Questions are also the key linkage between neuroscience and the practice of ethics, specifically the ethics of Compassionate Reasoning. This is the way in which understanding the mind and using it toward perfecting the art of ethical questions is a key to our mental health and the health of our society.

The critical moment of health through ethics is being able to ask a question rather than involuntarily emote. This is the move from raw emotions of fear, longing, or desire, to reason. Some emotions such as compassion clearly engage several places in the higher brain, as we have seen on fMRIs.[8] Compassion is a tantalizing area of research precisely because its expression has been seen to engage many parts of the brain. Future studies should compare the fMRIs of ethical reasoning exercises and the pathways of compassionate exercises.

I argue that the truly interesting moment is when a person articulates a base feeling and says, for example, "I am enraged." I find the words and the self-control to say, "I am enraged" instead of throwing a chair, instead of feeling a burning sensation all over the body, instead of shouting and becoming red with rage. In that moment of saying, "I feel rage" that there is the hope of human beings to be less violent, less destructive. For it is in that moment the higher mind of self-awareness and speech is stronger than the base level of rage being driven by the amygdala (Barker 2020). It is in that moment that a person begins a journey of victory over raw impulse. Finding a path of victory over the raw impulse of rage has been the great holy grail of ancient philosophical ethics and religious wisdom traditions, from Plato to Proverbs and the Talmudic *Ethics of the Fathers*. Why is this moment of articulation and confession the ultimate desideratum? Because this moment of self-reflection, self-awareness, and self-control prepares the way for the mind to seek a pathway of coexistence with family, friends, and society.

It is not that throwing chairs destroys one's life permanently. I threw a chair once in rage, once in my life, when I was so overcome with frustration and moral indignation with a group that was concealing from me a deeply anti-semitic past in a portion of its community. They were ashamed, but the concealment over many months set me into a frenzied and uncontrolled sense of betrayal and terror when I found the truth; I never will fully recover from the Holocaust that my families experienced. Thank God almost no one saw me throw the chair, because it would have removed my ability to be an ethical leader. I did learn something in that moment, however, and that is that I needed to find words, many, many words, until the rage in my heart could subside and be controlled by the more constructive, rational, compassionate side of my social self and my mission in life. In the end, the words made me into a person, into an ethical being with agency, with the agency to teach, to rebuke, to inspire, and to lead.

Contemporary brain science helps us see exactly the power of words. Some words are words of harm, batter, and abuse, but such words express a kind of servitude of speech to the raw rage and fear centers of the brain stem. Words of self-reflection, however, are different. They represent the victory of thought, reflection, and reasoning, and signify a very broad use of multiple brain centers and capacities. It is the reflective word that is a critical response to long-standing open questions and journeys of the mind. This is a critical path to becoming less violent. Naming emotions with words, and doing it again and again and again, every day—if necessary, every hour—changes the structure of the brain. Neural pathways of great strength emerge, pathways that make it easier to be reflective, kind, forgiving of oneself, and forgiving of others. This is an important foundation of why talk therapies in psychology for the past 130 years have helped countless people to escape their own worst impulses. The precise form of talk was less important than the ability to artic-ulate, express, and communicate (Ladd 2018). This approach may have been substantiated by what we can see now in the brain after compassion training, but it has old precedents in the confessional methodologies of many religious and wisdom traditions. Articulating the good in us, the bad in us, the com-plex reality of our struggles through words has helped millions of people es-cape their own violence, become more reflective, more self-controlled, more evolved as ethical beings.

But if self-control were so easy, then we would not be facing a climate catas-trophe of our own making that is already wiping out billions of animal lives, whose species can never be recreated, and bringing closer the end of human civilization. We have stumbled as a species into killing our future even as our domestic violence rates steadily have decreased. If we could simply talk our way into nonviolence and rationality, we would not be facing the fatal earth consequences of unparalleled human greed that is demonstrated by the out-of-control global energy industry in the twenty-first century. And this is after we were supposed to have learned the lessons of the twentieth century, which saw the worst effects of technology and rage combined in its unprece-dented mass murders and world wars. The twenty-first century is witnessing the worst mass murder of sentient life, the worst die-off of animals in all of human history, the loss of our precious bees, our gorgeous species on land, in the air, and deep into the seas. On a religious level, we have already begun to fail the great Abrahamic biblical mandate to tend and guard the garden of life on this earth, which is fragile and unique in the entire galaxy, as far as we can tell thus far. As a species, we may have progressed in STEM but we need more self-control than ever before if we are to have a future.

Cognitive and Moral Habits Are Central to Our Thinking and Behaving

Let us return for a moment to the life of the individual and his/her psyche, the basic building block of social and global change. If you are like me, you may wonder often, "What am I going to do next? How am I going to act in the situation that is coming up?" My mind is sometimes a jumble of thoughts and feelings coming in rapid succession. It is even harder to figure out not just *what I am* thinking but what I *should* be thinking about and how I should be thinking about it.

Beyond that whole jumble of internal questions are my actions, or more precisely the essential ethical question: "What should I be *doing*?" When I am truly honest with myself about my day-to-day and hour-to-hour behavior, my actions and behaviors are not always the result of a well-planned course of action. I can think confusedly, reacting to a complicated string of events over hours or days, some set of complex stimuli, and then I act in reaction to those stimuli.

With all that impulsivity flowing in and out of me, why am I not in trouble all the time? Why do I not end up stepping out of line constantly? I do not, but it is not always apparent why.

I would like to suggest the centrality of habit. The force of good habits keeps most of us decent every day *without* us having to put too much clear or consistent thought into that effort. But the reality of jumbled thoughts and jumbled impulses to act makes it amazing to contemplate how and why we are good, how we make right choices when we make them, how and why we so often choose to be good despite all those muddled feelings and thoughts.

For this reason, I have come to love simple meditations focused not only on breathing or thoughts but on the sequencing of my actions. Yoga helped me with this, but extensive reading in neuroscience and then my own experiments led me to distill the essence of what I was learning from yoga that I had engaged to heal lifelong backaches. As a mental exercise, I take something very simple, like getting ready to go out the door in the morning, and I make it into a mind practice together with slow breathing. I sit doing nothing for a mere moment, and I think for a few seconds to myself the following, for example: "I am going to take the toothbrush out, then I am going to remove the cap and place it on the sink, then I am going to put the toothpaste on the brush, brush teeth, rinse, then I am going to wash my face and use this particular towel to dry, then I am going to take only this brush to comb my hair in this mirror, then . . . " I am lucky if I get five steps in before I get distracted by a thought: "Oh, God, need to bring with me the phone charger to the car before I leave; oh, damn, forgot to text my daughter, better do that; wait, did I email the class about that reading I forgot to assign?" It takes all my energy to resist jotting those distractions down or dropping the sequence with which I started. I resist, I resist, and something changes in me when I do, which I cannot clearly define. Resisting the interruption to my focus and intention is the point of the mental exercise, and I know I calm down as a result of the procedure. I become more alert, more methodical, more at peace, and I feel some kind of gentle or compassionate disposition emerge. In other words, reasoning and compassion are somehow strengthened in my mind by this one simple practice.

Why is this simple practice a good discipline? Because when I insist on the sequence I planned, I am getting my brain used to following through on my will, on my rational vision of my immediate future, even if that future is only ten seconds from now. I find that throughout my day, *once I do this*, I tend to react less impulsively on much more serious matters, like anger about the news, like anger about old age and illness affecting people around me, like the wars I cannot stop. There are many sad things that I am powerless to stop that leave me with what Klimecki (2013) identifies in neuroscience as empathic distress. It may seem strange to the reader, but with these practices I start to have less anger, more compassion, more intention, more plans, more hope, more of a sense of duty anticipated and duty filled.

In other words, my toothbrush becomes a training for ethical decision-making, for compassionate engagement with myself and the world, and for a deep sense of respect for myself and for others. I do not completely understand this, but I know that fashioning my own mind with the simplest of things seems to have the most profound implications for the very core of my moral existence, my moral hopes and intentions for myself and for the world.

I focus on a silly toothbrush precisely to jar the reader, following the inspiration from Thich Nhat Hanh (1987, 2001, 2005) and his take on Zen

Buddhist practice. It does not matter what the object of discipline is for the mind, but the more disciplined the brain is, the more you become in charge through your will and habits formed. This leads to an integrated mind better attuned to your best moral feelings, such as compassion, and your most organized reasoning.

There is also the matter of intentionality of order, especially with breathing, planning, and visualization of each step. This discipline is a deliberate effort to break a deep cognitive habit of (1) associative thinking, and then, as a result, (2) impulsive shifting of behavior. What I mean by "associative thinking" is the random way in which minds rapidly go from one object of thought or imagination to the next. This is especially acute in some people more than others, and I have it very strongly. There is a long literature on this mind challenge. In meditation literature, it is often referred to as "monkey brain," based on the image of the monkey jumping back and forth endlessly from branch to branch and tree to tree.[9] I call this "associative thinking," which is a more neutral term than the pejorative "monkey brain," as I will explain.

Associative thinking has many benefits in terms of creativity (Koestler 1964; Benedak, Könen, and Neubauer 2012). The creative process itself depends on linkages made between images, ideas, and information that are not normally connected. All of my best ideas for every book and every speech came about through associative thinking. But *in excess*, endless associative thinking encourages anxious impulsivity, and this leads to personal and social ills, as well as a loss of focus and productivity. My mind is constantly associating and moving from one thing to the next on a constant basis, as I have described. When I intentionally keep the order of actions that I planned, however, I am fighting off many impulsive thoughts to shift my action and priorities toward things I can see in front of me that need attention (e.g., "Was going to put on my shirt, but I forgot to clean that countertop. Was about to fix that footnote, but I forgot that corner when I dusted. Going out the door for a walk, but I forgot to write down that insight about meditation in Chapter 5."). I then stop what I was doing and run to the thing that came into my mind. I stop and answer the text in the middle of another important task, *even though* it is not urgent, because I become *addicted* to associative thinking, to associative doing, and addicted to the stimulus of immediate sound and sights and reactivity itself.

I think this addictive behavior is sometimes a displacement of anxiety, but the important point is that when I do this frequently, I run the risk of killing my capacity for intentionality. It leads to frustration and even anger as I fail at my most important intentions, and then this in turn leads to a loss of patient compassion for myself and for others. In other words, this kind of behavior, as the meditators and spiritual traditions rightly noticed, has implications not just for happiness and misery but for ethical patience, ethical compassion, and their opposites. Excessive associative thinking makes it harder and harder to follow through on reasoned thinking, reasoned action, as well as the ethics of compassionate care of self and others.

The kind of very simple meditational training through sequential acting that I have outlined may occur naturally in anyone who has taken on skilled disciplines. From piano to tennis to Tai Chi to systematic thinking and focus on dishwashing sequencing, the possibilities are endless for training in focus, for a more assertive control over the mind. Whatever gets a person to that space of order and follow-through tends to have a powerful effect on the power of the mind to be less controlled by fear, anger, and paranoia. There is then more control by the intentionality inherent in reasoning, dialogue, and purposeful acts of kindness and generosity. It is especially true if these trainings are a self-conscious, deliberate intention for the sake of your life's goals and your moral commitments.

When I endlessly indulge associative thinking, however, I find that I may have increased my productivity in a certain sense of not forgetting these other tasks, but I have now lost the original tasks and I have felt a certain defeat in the ordering of my actions according to my mind. More importantly, I have lost a vital way to build a good habit, to train in intention and will, to do what my higher mind tells me to do. Instead I have strengthened the power of my impulsive lower brain over my will, over who and what I had willed to be that day.

I feel often in these impulsive moments that I am not in control, not embodying my higher sense of self, my sense of who I am and who I want to be. I have allowed these thoughts and impulses, no matter how creative, to undermine what I had planned that day, or that hour. More importantly, in excess it undermines who I had intended to be in that hour, on that day. Compassionate reasoning thus depends on a moderate degree of intention training through focus and habits of the mind and body.

Now this is where morality comes in. At least one vital and ancient approach to morality is commonly called deontology, as referred to in Chapter 3 and most often associated today with Kant, but in reality it has ancient roots in all rule-based moral disciplines across many cultures. Deontology focuses on the power to assert your will. Morality in this sense constitutes the will to do an act that is categorically good, even when you may not want to do it at that moment, even when there are a thousand excuses not to, even when your impulses say no.[10] It takes great energy and self-control to do the right thing very often, and it needs practice. Put another way, "monkey brain," the constant shifting of the brain in one direction after another based on sight and sound and stimulus, leads to entropy, a dispersal and loss of energy. It is the way in which the pent-up energy of doing an act of will is lost through many impulses misdirecting the human will. Being scattered as a person is easy, but being focused takes energy, practice, and control.

Focus and Practice Are Essential, but Ethical Life Requires More

Being focused with good will and good habits is essential, but an ethical life cannot be achieved only through habit and focus. Compassionate Reasoning seeks to cultivate the good mind, the ability—through reasoning, inference, and training—to implement self-controlled steps of action in one's life and in the life of the community. Meditation on small actions can help with this, and this has been the great lesson of cultural disciplines the world over, such as the Japanese tea ceremony (Sakuae and Reid 2012; Cross 2009).

The higher mind's reasoning does control impulses, but it does not make the focus of one's actions into something *nonviolent*, into something profoundly ethical, namely an act that is good for you and for all others. Only kindness and compassion do that. Kindness and compassion are essential to direct the focus of reason toward what is good for all, and it requires training in a moderate degree of empathy, and most importantly compassion and kindness. This is the essential combination necessary for Compassionate Reasoning to function.

Compassion Is Essential to Correct Flaws of Reasoning

The good will is cultivated mentally by three components:

(1) a trained mind,
(2) a mind geared toward seeking out kindness and compassion in oneself and others,

(3) both 1 and 2 functioning together so that they eliminate poor ideas of the higher mind that can be abusive, bigoted, or even genocidal.

In other words, even after you have lessened anger and loss of control in human feelings and behavior, many people—and many civilizations—have self-destructed on simple, stupid ideas: "slavery is good," "slavery is destiny for some," "the x race is superior to all other races," "the y religion is the only one that should dominate," "when you fail to make it on your own financially, nature lets you die and we should not interfere." All of these simple, poorly conceived ideas are not just cruel; they are also mistakes of thinking disproven by science, not just the result of an angry impulse or an overactive amygdala.

Thus, Compassionate Reasoning and its mental discipline is certainly the opposite of anger, the opposite of fear, the opposite of impulsivity and cruelty. But Compassionate Reasoning is also the opposite of poor ideas that have consistently led to massive violence and misery. Bad ideas masquerade for a time as logical, but they are inevitably unkind to all, unkind to the earth, and self-destructive for society.

It is for this reason that compassion and reasoning need each other. They balance each other and strengthen crucial parts of the mind as they work together. Compassionate Reasoning is a "whole of brain," or "whole of mind" experience. The compassionate resources of our mind and our nature need constant cultivation in order to attend to the occasional flaws of bad reasoning and bad thinking that prove destructive over the long term and that violate basic universal ethical norms.

Training the Mind in Positive Growth:
The Great Schools of Ethics

The other aspect of the training in intentionality that I described above is that it is decisively *not* focused on mistakes, negative behaviors, or existential failings as a human being. Those do exist, but the training focuses quite simply on training for positive focus. Too much time of moral inner life in a variety of wisdom and religious traditions, as well as therapeutic processes, has focused on the negative, on failure, on diagnosis of illness, on why we do stupid things, or, in the moral frame, on the evil things we do as human beings. *We do not focus enough on the "how" of what we do, the mechanics, the biology, the chemistry of doing the right thing.* If we want to cultivate the exact *how* of doing things right, we have to look at not just the negative but at the mechanics of the positive.

The training described above is in sequencing of behaviors that lead to improvement of the mind. I have pointed out its net positive effect on moral decision-making as well, and a better balance of affect and cognition. This makes a good transition to training for a moral way of thinking and acting in terms of Compassionate Reasoning. An immersion of the mind in open moral questions, in moral questions more than the answers, is the key to Compassionate Reasoning as a critical bridge between self and others. Asking core questions regarding our choices and actions is at the heart of philosophical ethics going back thousands of years, but it is also an essential training for the moral evolution of the self and the moral evolution of society.

The key to the practice of ethics is not the answers but the questions of the various schools of ethical training. It is the questions that stimulate creativity in the higher mind, and that give the mind a pause for reflection. It is the questions asked in earnest that liberate the mind from uncontrollable and negative impulses of the lower brain, and it is the questions that are at the core of the genius of schools of ethics which have been debated for centuries. The more questions asked about conflict dilemmas, and the more that scenarios are built in the mind, the more that we engage others in earnest exploration of ways forward. The puzzles posed by questions have the effect of leading us to inquire of ourselves and others in search of answers. The more we do this with our minds and conversations, the less we assume that others who come to different conclusions are somehow evil and othered. We see the complexity with our higher minds and thus become less driven by violent emotions to demonization. Let us explore what this looks like.

"How can I be good?" and "How can we be good?" are essential questions of morality that we all ask from time to time. The hardest question throughout history, however, is not "what is good" or "what is right to do," but rather *how to be good in the moment* and *how to do what is right in the moment*. It is much easier to agree on what is good, but far more difficult to agree on how to be good in the complexities of actual life. "How to be good" triggers engagement with the infinite variables and complexities of life, all the grey areas that make moral decision-making so challenging.

Pursuing the answer to these questions entails a much better engagement with the mind itself, with our capacities for reasoning and intuition, as we will explore shortly, and then for engaging others in imaginative debate and brainstorming. This was the desire of many of the greatest philosophers of history, as well as wisdom traditions throughout the world, both secular and religious. But they were not able to build consensus between the conflicting schools of ethical thought as to how to morally engage the complexities of serious conflict and the incredible diversity of human opinions.

We need each other, then, secular and religious, North and South, East and West. We need our brains pondering ethical dilemmas together, in open-ended and respectful ways. We need more consensus on how we can fulfill our needs as humans while *not* consuming and destroying all the other life on the planet upon which we ultimately depend. We need each other's minds, correcting us, provoking us, to save all of life on earth.

This need for each other's minds means that we must be in dialogue over what is to be done. A way to begin our discussion of this process is making an earnest inquiry into how the great philosophical schools would *in theory* debate questions of how to be good and then build a path forward together. Compassionate Reasoning draws upon the best thinking of all the schools of ethical thought, especially regarding open moral questions that stimulate the mind and heart, cognition and affect.

For the purposes of this inquiry, I am going to simplify complicated schools of ethical thinking. The way that I frame their essential teaching in terms of questions is meant to stimulate a more integrated and simplified approach to moral inquiry. Compassionate Reasoning will be shown to be a subtle combination of the best of ethical schools of thinking while avoiding the pitfalls of any one approach by itself.

Here are the questions and the ethical schools:

(1) Deontological ethics, or the ethics of principles: Is the action fair? What is the universal principle at stake? What is the right thing to do for all people finding themselves in this circumstance? Is this moral principle being developed and executed with the best of intentions? Is there a good will at work here? What is the policy for all people?

(2) Virtue ethics, or character ethics: Will it make someone a good, balanced human being? Will it make character better? Will it make the human being more virtuous? What are the habits of the mind, of the heart, and the body that lead to the best character and the best ability to act virtuously?

(3) Happiness ethics: Will it bring the most happiness?

(4) Consequentialist ethics: Will it have the best consequences and outcomes for the greatest number of people? Alternatives: Will it save the most amount of lives? Will it cost the least amount of suffering? Will it produce the greatest amount of true happiness?

(5) Moral sense ethics: Will it be the kindest thing to do? Is it generous? Is it compassionate? Does the action emerge from prosocial feelings of compassion, love, generosity, care?

These schools can also be framed in terms of competing ethical goals with different emphases. The essence of ethical life can be any of the following:

to protect life,
to act compassionately to all,
to act justly and fairly to all,
to create the best possible outcome for the most amount of people,
to generate the most amount of happiness,
to generate the least amount of suffering,
to generate the most amount of love,
to become the most virtuous human being you can be.

Framed as either goals or as questions, these alternative emphases clearly may lead to competing opinions and conclusions in many specific and complex situations. Thus, these schools and approaches lead to greater depth of thinking and reflection, but they do not lead easily to consensus. On the contrary, they can lead to endless argumentation, and we know now that endless confusion and argumentation can lead to despair and withdrawal from engagement with others (Wong et al. 2020).

Compassion Is Indispensable to Correct the Flaws of Human Reasoning

Here is the most important point as to why Compassionate Reasoning is necessary. These alternative ethical approaches do not by themselves suggest a way to resolve differences or come to consensus on a common course of action. In other words, conflict management and resolution are not built into philosophical ethical analysis, debate, and practice over the centuries. Thus, the practicality of ethical schools can be seen as limited or even irrelevant when it comes to resolving competing ethical interpretations by countless people engaged in serious conflict and competition. This lack of practical ethics leads to a great deal of pandemonium in human relations.

As if this is not enough to explain destructive human conflict and even wars, there are also flaws in each ethical school's approach *when these approaches are not considered in some combination* with the other schools. For example, the focus of deontology on universal principles sounds excellent and rings true to our sense of justice and equality. But this approach fails the test of what I call the "psychological fallacy." How do you know that what *you think* is universally right for all people is actually valid for all? How do you know that what you think is universal as an imperative is not governed by unconscious biases, motives, needs, and desires of your own tribal community? How do you get at an objective sense of one's duty that can be translated into a duty for all of humanity? How do you know that you are actually extending a universal human right or obligation to all people?

Immanuel Kant was a great champion of the universal human imperative, perhaps the greatest in the history of philosophy. And yet he fell into traps of terrible bias when it comes to most of the world's population, regarding indigenous people as savages (Kant [1797] 1991). How then was his categorical imperative supposed to actually work? How *did* it work in practice in the minds of enlightened Europeans? We have a clue in how all the civilized empires of the time treated people of color and indigenous people around the world. True savagery was revealed in reverse, as is well known by the sad history. The categorical imperative was nowhere to be found, even though it had been integrated into so many democratizing movements for white male rights across the European continent.

Now, taking the long view of history, Kant's theories have been critical to the development of universal human rights for people of color, for all people, the foundations of many constitutions in every continent, and the United Nations itself. But, practically speaking, if Kant were sitting in the room with indigenous tribal members, I would not want him to be the one to figure out how everyone should get along. Of course, he never left his native region of Prussia, and I cannot predict how his attitudes to others would have evolved if he had the chance to do the global work of learning from all peoples the way that some of us have. Thus, I respect what his mind came up with, as far as moral principles are concerned, and I have built much of my theory and practice of peacebuilding on them. But when it comes to complex global cultural situations of war and conflict, there I would want his school of thought to be tempered by other ethical approaches, such as moral sense theory based on compassion, and also consequentialism. Human bias needs many correctives and many checks and balances, including inside the human mind itself.

Consequentialism by itself has major flaws as well, falling into the same problems as deontology. How do you know that your intended consequences are based on an objective analysis? How can you make a judgment of the ethics of the moment based on your estimation and guessing about what the likely consequences will be? Can you trust your own biases in evaluating what, out of the range of possible outcomes, are the most important to value? How do you know that the good outweighs the bad that you do in terms of its ultimate effects? Most importantly, who counts and who does not count in the calculus of the effects of your actions on others, or the consequences of your actions? Are you calculating what is good for *all citizens* of your country, or your favorite ones? For all of humanity or only some, only the most educated, only the most secular, only the most religious? Do you calculate consequences for all sentient beings, *including animals*, such that you never would have embraced fossil fuels, for example, had you known that it would wipe out billions of animals and threaten the future of all life? Did you really decide that the car was good for everyone, even though so many species face extinction, including the polar bear, the monarch butterfly, the leatherback turtle, the Atlantic cod, and a million other species? What about consequences for your grandchildren as they live on an increasingly uninhabitable planet (United Nations 2019)? How do you calculate consequences of a future that you do not know, or that you are afraid to know, and who is included in that calculation?

Compassion Is the Key Addition to Higher Reasoning That Makes It Optimal for Less Human Violence and More Peace

The pitfalls of moral reasoning that we have just described are why I argue that another school of ethics, moral sense theory, is an essential addition. *I am suggesting that our goal should be for the human being to "check in," ethically speaking, with an additional set of neural pathways of the brain—not just the calculating brain, not only the abstract reasoning brain, but the prosocial compassion brain that motivates you to be kind, generous, and loving.* These are the neural pathways of the brain that ask a simple question of your behavior—short-term and long-term behavior—and the behavior of your community and society: Is this kind? It is that pathway of the human brain that keeps in check other human tendencies to skew our calculations and reasoning in favor of whatever bias, desire, or interest we may have driving our calculus without even knowing it as we calculate. We can mistakenly calculate the moral consequences more for men over women, for example, or white over black, or Christian over secular, or Jew over Arab, or vice versa in every case.

Compassion, however, as a key pathway of the human brain, makes different demands when considering legitimate ethical thinking, feeling, and acting. The mind senses whether you are acting and promoting positions based on a positive feeling of compassion or not. A common argument of moral sense theorists has been that our natural feelings of compassion, the compassion little children have, for example, is less subject to prejudice and cognitive distortion from a young age. We do develop mistaken cognitive views of prejudice over time as we age, biases that skew our ethical calculations of what is right (Gopin 2017; De Keersmaecker et al. 2018; Ziegler et al. 2012).

We think we are making rational calculations for the greater good, and so we rationalize things as barbaric as lynching or forced segregation, for example, even though we know these are cruel and inhuman. But in the moment of choice, people rationalize good consequences for law and order that will come from such crimes as lynching (Carr 2016; Oney 2003). We think that this will preserve the good society, even if this is "unpleasant."

So many war crimes are committed in this spirit, but, of course, the brain has in fact gone haywire in such moments. Thus, the moral sense theorist argues that the best way back from such barbarism is to cultivate and strengthen compassion *before* the rationalizing brain justifies all manner of barbarity. It is not that reason is incapable of goodness but, left to its own devices, it carries some serious flaws and needs help.

What I am proposing with training in Compassionate Reasoning is that these competing ethical schools seem to allude to or depend upon different aspects of the human mind's capacities and perspectives, and that these approaches to ethics in fact need each other as correctives. I am arguing that it is not a good idea to decide complex and fateful moral choices with only one capacity of the mind considered. Some combination is necessary in order for ethics and peacebuilding to become a "whole of mind" enterprise that directs the individual and society as a whole.

This is a safer choice as we try to help the human being to be better in conflict than he has been thus far. The capacity to make ethical decisions that prevent destructive conflict is a very imperfect human capacity. But if we engage the best aspects of the mind *in combination*, in a way that they can check each other's weaknesses, ethical decisions will be made and directions taken that are less violent and more constructive. This is Compassionate Reasoning, and it requires a self-conscious personal, educational, and collective turn in this direction. It will also require a new set of habits and trainings, as we will elaborate upon below, because this is what the mind requires for true evolution and positive change.

Learning from Crimes against Humanity

Let us add another perspective on how to get optimal ethical decision-making. Sometimes when you are trying to evaluate an approach to ethics, it is good to contemplate its opposite, namely how people justify and rationalize crime, and especially the most obviously horrific crime, genocide. Genocide rationalization is good to study in terms of the deluded ethics of groups that engage in mass murder, as it helps to clarify the challenge of human ethical thinking (Staub 1989, 2000; Docker 2008).

Why do genocidal war criminals kill? How do they justify it? They almost always consider what they do to be righteous in some way (Haidt 2012; Klein and Epley 2016). Some kill out of duty, the principle of duty and honor, following orders, a bizarre kind of rule-based ethics, or deontology. Some kill out of a sense of the good of the whole, as opposed to the bad for the few, a bizarre form of calculus of the greatest happiness for the greatest number, consequentialism. This is especially useful to abusing or destroying numerical minorities of any kind.

Millions of people have killed in history, killed innocents *en masse*, thinking they are being good soldiers of deontology or consequentialism. When you ask such people about the universal moral rule they are applying as they stand over thousands of dead civilians, they might say two things: (1) The rules do not include these dead because they are not really human, and here is the "proof." The rational mind is tricked into barbarism by pseudo-science, as happened regarding slavery, and during the Holocaust, but is true of many apocalyptic conspiracy theories (Douglas et al. 2017). Or, (2) This crime was an unfortunate necessity for the good of the majority, or even the good of humanity. Most racial savagery is justified based on some rationalizing combination of deontology and consequentialism. But truly this is a trick of the mind in many large wars that culminate in mass murder of civilians.

The third stream of ethics that we have addressed, moral sense theory, seems to be an interesting corrective to these tendencies of the mind. Many thinkers centralize compassion as the most powerful prosocial sentiment (Smith [1759] 2005; Hume [n.d.] 2003; Gill 2016; Hutcheson [1728] 2002; Klimecki 2019). On the whole, compassion as a sentiment and motivator for action seems far more unscathed by rationalization of crime than other streams of ethics, such as deontology and consequentialism. The neural pathways of compassion seem to stand apart and more immune from distortion. No one tortured and murdered thousands of people and then claimed that it was out of compassion for the victims. But they do claim their actions in the name of duty, and they did it often in the name of the "good" consequences of saving the mythical Aryan race or the mythical white race, for example.

You will see the occasional bizarre rationalization in the name of religion that they are torturing the *body* out of concern for the *soul* that they are liberating. But most often this framing of compassion is considered laughable, even by those perpetrating the crimes (Schweiker 2008). There are also ways in which compassion is redirected by the calculating mind away from the individual and toward the group. For example, you kill the mentally ill and the deformed in order to "put them out of their misery" and "out of compassion" for the whole of society. But these rationalizations are impossible to reframe in terms of authentic compassionate feelings for the victims themselves. The person doing the crime clearly knows that they are suppressing their feelings of compassion in order to commit the crime. Furthermore, those crimes are often put into the hands of willing sociopaths who are missing compassion entirely.

Sociopathy in such crimes against humanity is another clue that compassion is supremely important to the essence of human ethics. Compassion is the quintessential opposite of sociopathy, which in turn, is the opposite of ethics itself. Compassion as a prosocial moral sense emerges as a reliable category of ethical psychological response and a good set of neural pathways to strengthen in the mind. There is also strong scientific backing for compassion's critical role in moral psychology.[11]

Some will argue that compassion misguides you in terms of justice. Unbounded compassion could lead you to ignore and weaken justice, perhaps. But not really, since an unbounded feeling of compassion must extend to *all people in a situation* and thus bring you right back to a desire for justice for all that minimizes or ends violence and cycles of retribution. Justice is considered by many thinkers to be a moral sentiment as well (Hume [n.d.] 2003). More importantly, compassion for all (unlike empathy or solidarity only for some) leads the mind necessarily toward a fair justice system. *Justice for all is the only way that compassion for all can turn into practice when people are in competition or conflict.* In other words, compassion for all is a sister to justice for all.

More importantly, compassion for all never drives you to commit war crimes and crimes against humanity. It would make no sense, and this is significant. A sense of justice for one side of a conflict, however, or moral outrage toward your own victims and empathy with victims you know—*that* could and often has motivated people to violence and even war crimes. But not the deeper sense of compassion as love for all people. Compassion for all is very hard to twist into war crimes, which makes it a reliable building block of ethics.

Compassion is also the approach to human ethics that best aligns with ethical animal behavior, which Luzzatto and other moral sense theorists knew well (Gopin 2017), and this suggests its deep roots in human psychology as Homo sapiens. Often I reflect on the concentration camps of the Holocaust where 90 percent of European Jews, millions of men, women, and children, among other peoples, were tortured to death, gassed, and burned. People say blithely and without thinking that the Nazis behaved like animals, as if animals behave like that, as if humans are good as long as they do not behave like animals.

It is manifestly untrue that genocide is animal-like. Animals are capable of massive displays of altruism, compassion, and solidarity with others in pain (Wohlleben 2017). Compassion is an animal behavior to be emulated, but this only makes sense for ethics rooted in compassion, not ethics rooted in higher forms of principled thinking that animals cannot do. The human being, and the brain of the human being, shares a great deal of commonality with animals that exhibit compassion, and we would do well to root moral habits in that which is oldest and most reliable in our primordial ethical nature.

The Cultivation of Debate: Refining the
Open-Ended Questions

The upshot of this analysis is that clear thinking, the "calculus" of ethical decision-making, can be seen in many ways, but it requires compassion and compassion training in order for the mind to stay on track with ethics that truly is universal in intent, scope, and effect. Compassion is best in combination with the rational calculus and evaluation of means and ends, of principles, and of the weighing in the balance of good and bad outcomes. These taken together, then, are the essential building blocks of Compassionate Reasoning.

Compassionate Reasoning places great importance on the calculus of reasoning and the search for common principles guided by compassion. These reasoning activities are improved remarkably, however, by collective human thinking and active debate. Progress in science is far ahead of other aspects of human progress, due to debate across the world for centuries, but ethics is doing much more poorly in terms of systematic progress. Our ethics as a global community is so far behind our scientific collaboration that the very technology we have collectively created is capable of wiping out advanced civilizations due to our complete failure to advance as quickly and collaboratively in our ethics. We have uncontrollable conflicts, greed, and a refined tendency to kill *en masse* as a technology-driven species.

Unlike in science, we seem unable to work collectively on ethics. On the contrary, we tend to operate as a herd and are very prone to obedience to demagogues when we actually come together as groups. Imagine what science would look like if the rules of empirical investigation could be easily overturned by demagogues with gobs of money. Science has created centuries of debate between independent and free minds across the world, and those conversations, debates, and methodologies of inquiry have led to more and more technical advances. We should try to emulate this for ethics, but we have been unable to, unwilling or lacking sufficient courage and creativity to do so thus far. That is why it often feels as though we are in our infancy as an evolving species.

Ethics points the way to answers for our challenge at this moment in time. Put very simply, ethics should stimulate thoughts, feelings, reactions, and actions that try to address the following questions:

(1) What is the universal principle you are proposing?
(2) Do you have the best of intentions for everyone?

(3) Will what you are proposing lead to the best outcomes for the greatest number of people?

(4) Will what you are proposing lead to the best development of human character and society's character?

(5) What are the habits to be instilled based on your recommendations?

(6) Is what you are proposing truly kind?

The question is the key to the open mind, to the mind that is ready to: inquire, learn, be proven wrong, and listen to others. Second, we need compassion to be a final arbiter of our thought processes and debate processes when it comes to ethics. Even the most refined debate and collective thinking can "go off the rails" sometimes when it comes to brutality against minorities or simply benign neglect of the missing and the voiceless.

Habits of Compassionate Reasoning through the Mind, the Emotions, and the Body

We have seen now that compassion is a critical corrective to the thinking and reasoning brain. That is why I want to (1) reiterate the importance of training in habits of compassion for the mind itself, and (2) move toward a more embodied or somatic habit of compassion training, but still inside the person. Finally, I will address habits that involve the body in combination with interpersonal interactions. The power of compassion and Compassionate Reasoning habits are expressed through (a) thinking, (b) feeling, and (c) doing. These stimulate personal growth but also interpersonal growth that, in turn, generates broader social change.

Compassion Meditation Training

First, let's recall the work of Dr. Olga Klimecki, referred to earlier (Klimecki 2020). Recall also the video in which she describes her own training in compassion habits as she thinks of the person in the world who gives her the most joy, her grandmother (Klimecki 2012, video time 8:35). Meditation on compassion takes passing thoughts that we have of compassion, but it makes them into a concentrated mind training. It is a conscious and sustained foray into images, thoughts, and memories of compassion and love. You also breathe deeply, indulging the mind in thinking about places and persons that have given you joy in the past and that make you want to give joy to others.

Instead of such a compassion memory being random, training makes these thoughts purposeful and lengthy, a brain training and a tonic. Doing this over time has led to identifiable parts of the mind becoming heightened in strength, with associated biological changes toward mental and physical health. At the same time, neural pathways on the fMRIs light up with such training, and they demonstrate intense functioning of certain specific parts of the brain. This is how it becomes possible to identify the physical pathways most associated with compassion. Then there are the reported findings of increased socialization, general happiness, and far less stress or withdrawal from others.

From Empathy to Compassion: Breathing Meditation Training

As the scientific case for compassion training becomes stronger and stronger, it is time for compassion mind training to become an essential tool for improving all human interactions. Compassion training will improve the chances of success in conflict resolution efforts, but that is not all it will do. Compassion training will also improve ethical decision-making, because it is compassion together with reason that plays such an essential role in all human positive social change. As opposed to empathic distress and habits of withdrawal and hurt, compassion and compassion training lead the person *toward* others, toward socialization. Compassionate Reasoning training makes it far easier to make ethical decisions that will improve socialization and decrease destructive conflict. For society as a whole, this will increase the chances of human reason developing universal policies truly for the common good. This is the gold standard of policymaking based on Compassionate Reasoning.

Specialized Compassionate Reasoning Training: The Lessons of Tonglen

In this chapter we have emphasized till now the habits of the mind when it comes to ethics. We have explored a diversity of ethical ways of thinking and cognitive constructs that can be molded and shaped through Compassionate Reasoning into a powerful tool of personal change and social change. Our emphasis has been on thinking and feeling, but not as much on the embodied aspect of personal and social change.

Our introduction of Tonglen changes that. Tonglen, an ancient Tibetan practice, involves mind, emotions, and the body. It is a technique of compassion training that deserves special mention here for the way in which it combines mind training with body training. Tonglen literally means "taking and giving," and it is done with the somatic practice of deep breathing. I will oversimplify Tonglen, for the sake of argument, to be essentially this: It is a mind and body practice. Breathe in while you are *taking in* the pain and suffering of others into your imagination. Then breathe out as you imagine the *giving* of compassion to them, as you wish for them compassion.[12]

Repeat this steadily for those you love. When you are ready, do this for strangers, and when you are even more ready, do this even for adversaries. Essentially, as you practice this, you do the opposite of what we normally do with distressing thoughts and feelings about the pain of others. Our engagement with empathy and empathic distress can be involuntary, as many people cannot help but feel pain when they see pain in others (Derbyshire, Osborn, and Brown 2013).[13] Therefore, we try not to think about the pain of others we love, but we do so anyway. We involuntarily feel. We imagine our 97-year-old mother suffering from dental surgery, unable to take painkillers because it will affect her badly. From hundreds of miles away, we feel the pain of the lost teeth, we feel the excruciating gums, and we sense the terror at a bleeding event in the time of COVID for a 97-year-old mother we love. We must love from a distance during COVID, which also causes empathic distress. Or we may remember involuntarily the sight fifty years ago of this mother crying for her only brother, who was killed at the age of four, thirty years before that. An event in your family over eighty years ago, and you still feel it involuntarily.

The pain hurts us as we feel the pain of others, their trauma. If we experience this once in a while then it is okay, but let us say that we feel it often, like every day. Then it starts to eat away at us, at our ability to be around people. We are stuck in empathy, in the past. This is empathic distress, and it has a bad effect on our minds, on our health, on our social skills, on our ability to reason ethically and contribute to positive social change. We retreat into food, into TV, into anything that will distract and take our minds off anxious repetitive memories that now have strong neural pathways. If we are not careful, we will pass these habits and attitudes on to our children, and then they too will have a hard time.

Enter Tonglen, or "taking and giving" while deeply breathing. Tonglen upends all of this in a simple and brilliant move of the human will, of our thoughts and habits, and of our embodied embrace of the opposite of empathic distress. Tonglen says that if you have a perpetual involuntary memory not of a happy, joyful grandmother, but of an unhappy grandmother in tears, and this memory sears you with hurt even in your old age, then dive into the memory. Dive into the memory with a slow and steady deep breath. Do the opposite of what society tells you.

Breathe in all your grandmother's pain, breathe in all the tears you saw streaming down her wrinkled face while sitting on the edge of her bed in your home when she lived with you. Breathe in your own trauma at the adults in your life feeling unbearable sorrow for your great-uncle, long dead, but whose grave you were asked to visit every year of your young life. Breathe in her tears as she looks at your seven-year-old eyes and sees her own killed son. Breathe in as she smiles deeply at you, tears of sadness running down her cheeks, and then mistakenly calls you by her little boy's name. Take it in, breathe in the memory, and then breathe out compassion and love on her, on her memory, and on the little boy, your mother's only brother. Bless her soul as you breathe out, wish for her all good things, as if you are a vehicle, a messenger of compassion. Then breathe in the pain again and again, rhythmically, but breathe out the deepest compassion you have, the deepest love you feel for her, even fifty years after she has died. Keep doing this until slowly the pain of empathy dissipates and becomes pure compassionate love.

This is Tonglen, but I want to present it here as a possible training for Compassionate Reasoning. I have not seen research on neuroscience insights into Tonglen, but there should be research into it as a practice. Steadily counteracting embedded feelings of trauma and withdrawal with alternative feelings and cognitions of connection to others certainly seems to be the kind of transition recommended by trauma therapy, and certainly that is happening here in the Tonglen practice. You take in your memories of trauma and absorption in your grandmother's pain, but you breathe out, focus and train on the very prosocial connectedness of love and compassion for her (Herman 2015). But it bears greater experimentation as to what is happening in *neural pathways* as one experiences painful memory, versus a deliberate exploration of memory along the lines of Tonglen. It would be fascinating to see which neural pathways light up at which stages of imagination and activated feelings. There are some fascinating clues emerging on which parts of the brain are associated with observing pain in others.[14] Such training in compassion may prepare you to love and hold precious everyone around you; it will drive you toward others, not away, and it will heal your broken memories and broken heart. As with all brokenness, the goal of every training and every breath is to remake your neural pathways just a little bit more. You are retooling your neural pathways away from pain, withdrawal, and remorse, and toward love and compassion, giving you more courage and skill for your next human encounters.

Children in the Playground Training: The Buddy Bench

Turning to another somatic, bodily experience, I want to explore the Buddy Bench. The Buddy Bench for the playground is a fascinating intervention designed to eliminate alienation on the elementary school playground. It is introduced by teachers with instructions that if you are not playing with anyone, you sit on the Buddy Bench, colorfully designed and clearly placed at the center of activities, and then other kids are supposed to keep an eye on that bench as they play in groups. When they see someone there, they are supposed to run up and ask them to join. The results have been quite extraordinary (Griffin et al. 2017; Clarke 2018). There was a fascinating study of artwork produced about the Buddy Bench experience *by the children themselves*, and it is quite revealing. Here is how it is described:

The buddy bench, a primary school playground implementation designed to eliminate playground loneliness, provides a potential strategy to ensure more children reap the positive benefits of elementary school recess. Through children's artwork, in-depth interviews, and playground observation this ethnographic study explores the socially constructed meanings of the buddy bench and their implications. This methodology advances the communication field by demonstrating how scholars can use children's artwork to identify and define children's socially constructed meanings. Findings build on a previous study showing that playground buddy benches can offer effective playground interventions and demonstrate that the presence of a buddy bench on the playground creates shared meanings of solidarity, inherent worth, empowerment, and a shift in focus from playground bullies to buddies amongst the children. This leads to a perceived climate change on the playground. These shared meanings reshape children's narratives about themselves, loneliness, and the playground experience in a positive manner. (Clarke 2018)

This is an extraordinary example of how newly formed habits can change the mind of young people.

Habits are regimens in the evolution of humanity. Habits are everywhere: habits of parenting; habits of education; habits, styles, and conditions of peer relations; and even habits built into the intentional structure of playgrounds. These habits are determinative of the universe we see as children, and that then forms us as we see the world as adults. The moral structure of a playground is internalized from the physical universe that is perceived and experienced every day by the child. The child will be the adult with permanent memories inside of the structure of the child world.

It will be important to know more about the Buddy Bench from a neuroscience perspective, how the Buddy Bench, which clearly has had a major impact on many children, may reorder the "furniture" of the brain as to how the universe is viewed and constructed. The forming child's mind is constructing the universe every day, and every aspect of the external world is being internalized into a map of what one day soon will be superimposed onto the map of the adult world. Everything we do and do not do with children is being processed into a map of the adult world. Is it a world of alienation or a world of constant play, comfort, and companionship? Is there a Buddy Bench that steers that world away from alienation, bullying, othering, hurt, and withdrawal? What will be the results in the adult world, and what neural pathways will be created and solidified with such a bench that embodies compassion? What by contrast is the mental map of a child's world drenched in daily bullying on the playground? What mental map will be superimposed on the adult perceptions of reality?

Formative education and brain training for compassion may be seen someday as a cure for all manner of intrapsychic and interpersonal maladies. We are taking the internal processes of training and habit formation and putting them into the physical furniture of our playgrounds and classrooms. This is a reorientation of the mental geography of the universe in formation, the crafting of memory, the construction of the adult world out of the memory of the child world.

Think about it and visualize it for a moment. Stop reading and imagine yourself sitting in the corner of a playground, and you feel the outcast; you play the outcast in the theater of the playground, for any number of reasons that you can imagine or remember from your life. And as you are playing the outcast and feeling it, everyone else sees you this way more and more every week. And this pain begins to fester in you like a cancer and grows inside you year after year, until one day you find yourself intensely playing alone, again and again, a video game where you can blow the brains out of all your classmates. Before you know it, you have fantasies of violently getting even for years of alienation, and one day you explode after never being violent before.

Now think of yourself again, younger this time, in second grade, and there is this crazy thing called a Buddy Bench. So let's say that one of your legs is shorter than the other, or you have a wandering eye congenital defect that frightens other kids, or you come in every day to the playground with a grimace on your face because your father berates you on the way to school, and he berates you every single damn day before drop-off because his own father somehow got the stupid idea that berating kids sets them "straight." Despite all of that, saddled with all those handicaps, you sit on this damn Buddy Bench because the teacher told you to. Then inexplicably in your small and sad universe, within a minute or two, your classmates all have this strange habit, with obedience to the teachers and to the Bench itself. They come toward you, you who are sitting there in isolating and festering sorrow, and they say, "Hey, how about some stick ball?" and you go, "Sure!" hesitantly. And you just come out of your shell, more every day. You are never alone for long. You develop confidence and compassion. Then one day in twenty years, you look back on second grade as the time that changed your entire life, the time you learned compassion for outcasts, including love for yourself as outcast.

And so, when your father kicks the bucket one day and you inherit his massive company as CEO, the company he spent all his time on when he was not berating you, you completely transform the environment of your inherited company. And you make sure that no one, not even the janitors, ever, ever feel left out of anything, all of them even owning a few shares in the company. Because, to you, everything in life that matters is the Buddy Bench. Everything that makes or breaks your world is compassion and connection. That is how a mental universe constructed out of a habit-forming bench, conceived and executed with compassion and reason, changes the world. This is Compassionate Reasoning in practice.

Social habits and rituals such as the Buddy Bench are a preventative cure to antisocial behavior, even as they reorient the way in which the child sees the world every day. I am proposing that this mental map of time and space, where there is always a space for kindness, can become your moral map of the universe through the artful generation of a variety of new habits based on Compassionate Reasoning. This can affect your mental and moral map of the world for a lifetime.

Neuroscience and fMRI mapping may be able to help us more and more to understand why habits such as the Buddy Bench do what they do to us. We will see more and more what lights up in our brain, what compassion pathways become strengthened, and why, as we go through these experiences, we become more rational and more compassionate.

This is the kind of habit that unites four crucial elements: cognition, affect, bodily experience, and engagement with the other people. This combination, especially in the context of the outdoors—the wind, the sun, running, and jumping—engages so much of the brain as to overwhelm the mind with a positive and transformative experience. If we can proliferate these kind of experiences of being beloved and of loving others with all of these brain centers being engaged at once, then we are on the road to less violence and more peace in a way that the child will never forget. In fact, the child becomes the powerful adult and then creates this same environment for others. The child who felt so good because she gave of her time to include another who was lonely on one sunny day in the playground will use that experience for the rest of her life to lead her adult world with acts of kindness. Compassionate Reasoning training such as the Buddy Bench set the child on the road to the adult who does his part to create the kind society every day.

Student Habits: The Peace Corner and Self-Regulation

Peace corners have become a powerful tool of self-regulation in the classroom, but also a place of healing in relationships (Love n.d.; Silcock and Stacey 1997; Hunter 2008; Lantieri 2008; Harrison and Muthivhi 2013; Short 2016).

Just as above, I am submitting that we need to study the long-term effects on the young impressionable mind of growing up with *an image of your world in which there is a corner for peace*, a geographic corner of the world, a designated space, where you can go to work out your problems with a peer.[15] Think of this as setting the stage for a lifetime of adult interactions when they may have the power to rearrange the universe of a work space, or the work of an agency or a company or a city or a country. They will begin their engagements with the assumption that if we will it then there absolutely can be a safe place for peace, self-regulation, reflection, and reasoning. This reframes the world of the young mind and her mental map of the world. This implies a new approach to public health, education, ethical and social habits in the adult world that begins in one childhood classroom.

Peer Therapy Training: The Grandmother Friendship Bench

The Grandmother Friendship Bench created a worldwide movement, and the grandmothers are important in regard to what we have been arguing. Like the Buddy Bench, this method and habit of change also involves sitting on a bench in a physical space of the world that becomes a symbol in the mind of a safe, kind, prosocial space (Abas et al. 2016; Riley 2018). The method does involve the brain functions of reasoning, but also an enveloping act of compassion from friends who practice active listening and support in the context of a safe space. This safe space becomes a new and evolving mental map of one's world. It engages dialogue and reasoning but also compassion and an embodied experience. Mind, feelings, and body are engaged in a specific space and time.

This bench does for adult women what we have seen for children in terms of the Buddy Bench and the Peace Corner, and it marks an exciting revolution of peer mental health engagement. The grandmothers have demonstrated a basic truth about what is missing from therapy, namely the compassionate engagement with basic human needs, and the solidarity that comes from problem solving together. In other words, the peer-based therapy was not only focused on emotional health in a safe therapeutic space. It has been focused also on solidarity with *material needs* and developing strategies to improve life—more akin to life-coaching and aid with social network empowerment. This is an example of Compassionate Reasoning habit formation at its finest, and the results have been remarkable.

We want more and more habits and rituals that bind people together across the lines of strangers and disparate communities. We want more habits and rituals that help people through compassion and sharing of reasoning processes which lead to actual improvement of their lives in a material sense as well as emotionally, their needs met, their feeling of safety enhanced, their self-esteem strengthened to take care of themselves. This is why compassion and reasoning combine so artfully to move the individual—and society—from compassion to principles and policies for all, from deep knowing of the other to deep solidarity in sustainable communal living based on shared values and shared laws as to what is right.

Service to Adversaries as Embodied Compassion Training: Care for Enemies

There are many customs and traditions from cultures around the world that can become vehicles of transformative habits of Compassionate Reasoning. Let me take one example from ancient Middle Eastern Judaism. There is a very strange set of verses in Torah or the Hebrew Bible, namely the instruction in the book of Exodus that if you see your enemy's donkey faltering under its weight, you are obligated as a good deed, a *mitsvah* in Jewish language, to help the enemy with the burden (Exodus 23:5). No explanation is given, but in the book of Proverbs, a much later book of the Hebrew Bible that had a very important influence on the development of today's rabbinic Judaism, there is a very bizarre explanation of aid to the enemy. In the Proverbs text, the aid is more directly to an enemy who is starving and thirsty. The advice is to feed him, and in this way you will pour "coals of fire" on top of his head, and "God will reward you" (Proverbs 25:21–22).

I spent many years amazed and confused by this strange use of metaphor. One usually thinks of help for an enemy as a supreme act of compassion and kindness. Yet the explanatory metaphor of the book of Proverbs implies some pretty adversarial intentions. In some fashion, it is the suggestion that you will really make your enemy burn when you do the opposite of what he expected. Still later in history, rabbinic commentary on this verse by Rabbi Hama the son of Hanina of Judea (third century CE), offers an astonishing explanation that rests on a slight twist in interpretation of the Hebrew, a typical move of Midrash (ancient Jewish hermeneutics). Rabbi Hama argues that the man came to kill you, but with your extraordinary gesture the enemy will be "reconciled" or "in peace" with you. The end of the verse does not mean God will reward you (*ye'shalem*) but rather God will reconcile (lit. "complete" or "make peace": *yashlimeno*) him to you.

What is going on here? The idea seems to be what we call today "cognitive dissonance" or simply shock. Namely, the man who came to kill you will be so shocked by your compassionate gesture that he will lose his entire cognitive equilibrium, his worldview. He will then realize that you are not an enemy but, on the contrary, a friend (Midrash Mishlei 25:5, in the name of Rabbi Hama the son of Hanina). The discomfort of the gesture to him, the shock of it, will upend his worldview, and he will change from enemy into friend. In case one thinks that this was an isolated rabbinic idea, there is this ancient rabbinic saying: Who is a true war hero? The one who changes an enemy into a friend (Avot de-Rabbi Natan 23). Heroism is not murdering your enemy or hitting him when he is down, but making him into a friend precisely because it is one of the most difficult feats any human can achieve. The path to do just that, these rabbis argued, is shock to the brain, the shock to the brain of compassion coming from an enemy.

These biblical verses and the insights of Rabbi Hama have guided my practice of peacebuilding with enemies for almost forty years, in fact it is at the core of my life's mission. To go toward an enemy, the one you fear the most, takes great courage, determination, skills of survival and skills of compassion, and it does feel like a heroic journey. It has never ceased to amaze me how well it works, given the right circumstances and the careful application of this method. I have elaborated on this work with enemies in several other books (Gopin 2002, 2009, 2012). In all of those decades of peace practice, however, I could not appreciate the poetic creativity of the ancient writer in the book of Proverbs until I came across the neuroscience research of Klimecki and others. "Coals of fire" might be an apt poetic foreshadowing of the literal lighting up of the brain that one sees in fMRIs when you surprise someone with kindness.

I have also been struck, following the work of psycholinguist George Lakoff, at how frequently our language is a storage house for our *anatomical* reactions (Lakoff and Johnson 1980). When we say "burning with rage" or "burning with desire," there are, in fact, physical reactions of temperature to desire and to rage at their extremes. When we say we are "tongue-tied," it has quite literal parallels. It dawned on me that this ancient Jewish verse was referring to that feeling of fire you can have when you are about to take revenge on someone. But then they do something nice or something endearing, or you see a side of them by chance that is deeply human, such as their love of a child. It is exasperating! It feels like coals on your head because you were all fired up and then their kindness "melts your heart," a nice metaphor for a lower and calmer heart rate.

Today we can see scientifically in the fMRI how the brain lights up specific pathways through meditative thoughts of compassion. It is possible now to assert that our brain is lighting up in ways that reconfigure our thinking, that forge new neural pathways that did not exist before. This expresses the human potential for changing perspectives, changing habits, and changing the evolution of Compassionate Reasoning in a way that is not only cognitive, not only emotional, but embodied and anatomical. The neuroscience of brain changes and neural pathways should strengthen our argument that *every* thought and *every* habit matter in the evolution of the human being and of humanity as a whole.

In every great culture across this earth there are brilliant rituals and moral deeds that surprise and delight the mind, that cause new neural pathways to develop, that calm down the periodic fires of the amygdala, and that allow for new cognitions and worldviews to grow. *First and foremost, this is the brain talking to itself, remolding itself.* The body does something for an enemy, for example, and this action stimulates a change in cognitive perspective. It is a change in action that leads to a change in cognition that leads to a change in affect, which then leads to a change away from the negative affects of hatred and the embodied actions of hate-based violence. Deeds, thoughts, and emotions are in constant dialogue with each other inside our minds while simultaneously affecting the minds of others. Thus, deeds of compassion, even for those who may not exactly deserve such compassion, lead to changes in cognition and affect inside the self and inside the recipient. This is the mind in conversation with itself leading to internal conversation in the recipients of our actions.

Habits of thinking, habits of perception, and the mind's construction of the world all change our perspective; as they do this, they interact seamlessly with changes in affect. These affects then change the state and condition of the body, namely the state of physical safety. The less violent our cognitions, our affects, and our resulting gestures of goodwill, the safer the body feels and the healthier and calmer it becomes. It is as if we created in many cultures a brain cure through peace and care gestures, a salve for the neocortex to be a natural amygdala suppressant, and also a natural salve for the metabolic system. Another way of saying it is that the mind has its own autoimmune diseases based on bad ideas and bad feelings about others that regularly can come. But through peaceful cultural teachings some minds have their own autoimmune cures, where the mind heals itself and protects the entire organism from self-destruction that can otherwise occur with cycles of hate and violence. This is where universal education in Compassionate Reasoning could tip the minds of millions toward the mind's better capacities for peace, kindness, calm, and health.

I am reminded of the power of Viktor Frankl's testimony from Auschwitz (Frankl [1946] 2006, 1969) and his subsequent lifelong cultivation of logotherapy as a school of psychotherapy. The discovery of meaning and the will to live are intertwined, and in that intertwining lies both reasoning and compassion, especially as he discovered meaning even in the worst of circumstances by giving to others. These cognitions of meaning, will, intention, and feeling become ensconced in the mind so that nothing can budge it, not even a cruel camp guard who wants to kill you at every moment.

When you think about it, Frankl was describing a marriage of the sense of survival instinct with a sense of higher meaning and purpose. This is a fascinating cooptation of the very survival instinct that often gets us into trouble in terms of fighting. If the amygdala's fight and flight instincts are associated so often with destructive behavior, Frankl wisely points out that the person who discovers meaning through giving and compassion in life-and-death circumstances is actually fulfilling and satisfying the amygdala's strong drive to survive—but rather through meaning and compassion, not through escape, which was impossible, and not through fighting, which was also practically impossible. *Survival through meaningful compassion is an extraordinary marriage of the capacities of the higher mind and the lower brain.*

From Question Training and Word Training to the Centrality of Future Vision and Imagination

One could argue that brain training is a kind of therapy for the mind and body. Compassionate Reasoning and the habits that strengthen it can be considered a cure for social ills. It could also be considered a necessary health maintenance practice, post-disease, as well as a permanent regimen of disease prevention for the evolution of humanity.

Compassionate Reasoning needs to also become a mind training in the art of constructive disagreement over ethical differences. It will make the entire experience principled disagreement into an achievement of deeper relationship with fellow citizens on common values discovered through the process of constructive conflict. When you compare principles with others through discussion and debate, when you also explore and compare calculations of the greatest good for the greatest number, your relationship with others can deepen. This is only the case, however, if you engage these explorations with compassion, with active listening, respect, and earnest debate; this is how your relationship with others grows. You are drawn by the debate and exploration *toward* others in community, not driven away in disgust. Principled debate and constructive conflict, when done in a spirit of compassion, deepens relationships (Kriesberg and Dayton 2017; Rosenzweig 2014; Roth 2011, 2012, 2017, 2019, 2021).

Forms of principled debate and habits of engagement that emerge out of Compassionate Reasoning are particularly attuned to the power and importance of each and every word used when engaged with others. Language itself becomes a cure, a power, a healer, as has been seen by sacred religious traditions for thousands of years.[16] Language as a way for the brain to come together in an act of healing is a field that should be explored more. It is in a space between psycholinguistics, positive psychology therapy, cognitive therapy, and sacred ethical and mystical traditions around the use of the word.

Many religious traditions emphasize the power of the word and in general the importance of power as a religious experience. Taoism and many Asian traditions explore the mastery of power (Tzu [n.d.] 2015; Confucius [n.d.] 2014). The search for power is tricky, however, since what the Tao Te Ching meant by it is not at all what Nietzsche meant by it, for example; in fact, quite the opposite. Empowerment through fighting also allows the amygdala to drive us to our most irresponsible and destructive behavior. The beauty, by contrast, of Compassionate Reasoning as it translates into communication skills, is that the word becomes a supreme act of power, a way to become safe but also to protect, to enlighten, to lead, to attract others who otherwise would become adversaries or combatants. As noted above, the power of the word and the deed to make enemies into friends is at the core of Compassionate Reasoning, but this is a very different kind of power than physical intimidation, economic intimidation, or legal intimidation.

Our intentions above to combine the ethical schools of thought into Compassionate Reasoning is a way to empower the mind as a whole. It is to honor each of its functions, but turn them toward something that is healing, life-giving, and that moves away from violence and death. Thus, the marriage of Kantian-style principles with Millian-style calculations, together with the moral sense of compassion, is designed to empower the person to take hold of her world, but without needing to resort to fighting or escape. It is a kind of power redistribution of the mind, where the energy and power of the lower brain, of survival instincts, is redirected toward an integrated plan of action that leads to a safe and viable future that is not solitary or withdrawn but rather in league with others.

Habits of thought and debate that we are suggesting are essentially ethical philosophical reasoning as brain training. The aspect of Compassionate Reasoning involving deliberation on and combination of ethical schools of thought is a way to accept moral dilemmas without panic, without anxiety, and without demonization of others.

Compassionate Reasoning in this sense is an antidote to tribal-induced hatred or the use of it. The commitment to the rule of internal and external law that is emphasized by Compassionate Reasoning creates, in effect, a neural net of internalized law. Some of those laws involve a search for universal principles, and others involve the constant habit of calculus of the greatest good for the greatest number, consequentialism, which I have developed in previous works on social change and ethics (Gopin 2009).

Training in this approach emphasizes questions over answers, as we have outlined above. Questions, rather than dogma, open the mind and deepen dialogue and brainstorming. I want to reiterate and expand the questions we have outlined above as we get closer to the habits and actions emerging out of Compassionate Reasoning. In contemplating courses of action, the mind will be directed to ask many stimulating questions: "What is the principle?" "Will this bring more happiness?" "Will it bring more good to the world?" "Is this kind?" "Will it lead to more kindness?" "Will this make you happy? Everyone happy?" "Will it lead to more justice for all?" "What is the universal rule you are proposing?" "Are your rules consistent?"

Questions are at the core of the mind training for Compassionate Reasoning. Open-ended questions also lead the mind to its healthiest space for nonviolent change, namely imagination, contemplation, and collaborative construction of the future. A focus, for example, of current American peacebuilding work should be on the *future vision* of the ideal America. Positive vision is a habit that the mind can cultivate.

Hermann Cohen, for example, was a neo-Kantian German Jewish philosopher in the early twentieth century who argued that the state of *becoming*, or working toward a future that never quite arrives, is the ideal state of ethical striving toward the ideal society (Cohen [1919] 1995). *Becoming* is the ideal state because it is the end that must be strived for but never believed to be quite achieved. Becoming is in its ideal state as aspiration. Believing that America, for example, is right now the "greatest country on Earth" is precisely how ultranationalism can kill the best ideals of a country. In religious Cohenian terms, it is exactly idolatry. It is the kind of delusion leading to totalitarianism that artificially forces everyone to believe the delusion in order to control minds. But *becoming* is the essential ethical messianic state, argued Cohen.

All ethical work is truly the work of the imagination. It is future-oriented, never completely achieved. In this way, neither the individual nor the state become sick with narcissism, with what monotheism refers to as idolatry. The ideal of Compassionate Reasoning is a tonic for the mind precisely because it is future-oriented and imagination-oriented. It is the skills of imagination and planning, always grounded in and by compassion, that lead to a less violent, more rational, and more peaceful future for the individual and for society as a whole.

Concluding Thoughts on Habits of the Emotions

We have already addressed meditative and visualization habits for cultivating prosocial emotions as a way to steer the mind and feelings away from negative emotions and empathic distress and instead toward universal positive affects, such as compassion. But training in habits for Compassionate Reasoning should include other key emotions, such as gratitude, honor, joy, and care. Religious and secular traditions of ethics throughout the world embrace these positive affects and also inculcate a series of habits, customs, and rituals that orient the mind toward these emotions. From Confucius all the way to Maimonides and Aquinas, habits to form good character, to emulate the "ways of God," are a critical means of training the mind.

Aristotle's virtue or character ethics has set the stage for many centuries of focus on the balance of a character and the cultivation of a personality that emphasize positive emotions and the habits that generate them. This approach to social change raises in the brain an additional question in the moments of complexity and choice, beyond the questions we have already raised. The mind interested in good character asks of each situation: Is what I am undertaking, or being asked to undertake, good for my character? Is this making me a better person? A more enlightened person? A more balanced person?

This approach to ethics I have found quite helpful in dealing with dangerous and difficult places of conflict. For example, you may have assessed that your course of action is right, that you are acting based on principle, that your actions should result in good consequences for most people. At the same time, however, your current course of action may be damaging you personally. Moral sense theory also asks whether a course of action is fair to and loving of *yourself*. Thus, Compassionate Reasoning and its habits must consider care of the self, nurturing of the self, evolution of the self, and evolution of good character. Sometimes, in very complex situations, these questions must be continually asked through habits of self-reflection and emotional self-inquiry.

The habits of Compassionate Reasoning should lead to a way to find goodness in ourselves, and not only the goodness we do for others or for society as a whole. This is an artful combination of self-examination, cultivation of character, cultivation of reason, but always with the guiding eye of compassion. This cultivation of self makes it more likely that your care and love for the world will be authentic and truly expansive and not based on hidden rage and frustration. Healthy public rituals and habits of Compassionate Reasoning need a self that is in good working order, a self that is compassionately cultivated over a lifetime of effort.

Concluding Thoughts on Habits of the Body: Actions More than Words Transform Us and the World

When I was deciding on how to order the steps of *Healing the Heart of Conflict* (Gopin 2016), I put the step of healing involving deeds as the penultimate step, ahead of the step of words and speech. Long ago, I had come to realize that many people cannot find the right words but have found the right deeds when it comes to ethics, when it comes to apologies, and when it comes to repentance and atonement. The primary importance of what we do, as opposed to what we say, is often ignored or missed in ways that lead to tragic human relations. But the fact is that what we do with our bodies not only is a significant way in which we "speak," in which we state who we are and what our intentions are. What we do with our bodies is also formative. We are actually forming our mind, our ideas, and our priorities by the deeds that we undertake, the deeds that become our habits, that become who we are. When you are, for example, an ex-President and your habits of everyday life include building houses for the poor *with your own hands*, then you are forming your life, your future, your philosophy, and your life legacy (Carter 2015, 2018).

Habits of the body and habits of physical service to others is a critical cure for negative emotions and negative cognitions or worldviews. Our body leads, and our ideas follow (Reddy 2020).[17] We referred earlier to the power of helping the enemy when he is suffering. We talked about the shock to his brain and how it can reorient ethics and thinking. The rabbinic source cited above emphasized what such service and aid did for the enemy and *his* brain. But I submit that embodied service changes the one doing the deed even more, as it implants a completely different worldview and intentionality around conquering hate and violence. Service to others changes you, changes your mind, even more than it changes the recipients. *If hatred is an infection, then service is a cure, because compassionate service itself spreads virally from the body to the emotions to the worldview itself.*

The Transformative Power of Service to Others

My own experience is that I have found myself for many years helping those whom I grew up fearing. They were the enemy, and I was in mortal fear of them. When I went to their countries, I found myself feeling very sorry for the oppression they suffered. But ironically, my very visits to their country were already considered by them to be a surprising service from someone like me coming from the United States. I received a shocking amount of gratitude, respect, and warmth. The more I helped them, the more I fell in love with them, with their children, with their war wounded, with their survivors, with their artists, and with the more noble and heroic of their clerics.

Service does strange things to the psyche. The more you give, the more you fall in love, and the more you fall in love with the strange other—even the enemy—the more it expands your worldview and changes you permanently. It did for me, as I have described elsewhere about my Syrian experience (Gopin 2009, 2012). Thank goodness, I did not make the mistakes of empathic distress as I came to feel strongly the suffering of others. I did not choose sides or come to hate the United States as a result, or Israel, nor those who stayed with the regime in Damascus that was killing so many tens of thousands of innocent civilians. I just fell deeply in love with a wounded people, their talents, their sorrow, and their hopes and dreams. It became compassion, and I focused all my reasoning on how to help. Thus, my engagement of Compassionate Reasoning became sustainable to this day, 18 years and going strong. But if I had fallen into only rage at their pain through empathic distress, I would have not been able to be much good to anyone, and I might have just become part of the problem.

This love for a wounded people feeds my soul to this day with projects that have engaged many citizens in several countries, especially women and children. In times of doubt, fear, and danger, when I became unsure of what I was doing and the risks I was taking, I would repeat to myself a mantra from Psalms 89:3, "The world is built upon compassion," "The world is built upon compassion." I would say this to myself over and over again in Hebrew, "olam hesed yibaneh." I would repeat this to myself in the streets of Damascus, in refugee camps, at nervewracking border crossings, and while cuddling traumatized child survivors.

With this mantra I was trying to convince myself that I was not crazy, and that I was there in this terrible refugee crisis for a good and rational reason. It was crazy in a way, but it was also glorious, and I never felt more alive, never more sure of my destiny. It is times like those where I needed my body and my thinking and my feeling to be in sync and deeply unified by compassion. It kept me balanced but also fed my soul. It was not painful in these moments like empathic distress, but rather an exultation.

I remember once being for the day, in 2012, at a school for orphaned refugees. Kids were running around everywhere, but I saw a five year old boy so overtired, eyes glazed over, and so sad, walking aimlessly. I sat on the floor next to a pillar in the middle of the room of screaming kids. I welcomed him over to my arms. He cuddled, lay his head onto my chest, fell asleep, and then I too fell asleep, with dozens of kids running all around us. It was a moment of deep joy for me because I could give him a small moment of peace and comfort. I felt it as a kind of victory that comes with love over hate in impossible circumstances and with a complete stranger whose name I never was able to find out. He is in my mind's eye and in my heart forever.

I have come to realize from such personal experiences that these habits of Compassionate Reasoning can be induced, can be encouraged, can even be trained. I saw myself stumble into such habits and then get addicted to them in good ways. I started to realize that the training could encompass both secular and religious alike, people from many different traditions, and that this made it an important tool of positive peacebuilding. Compassion and helping people reason through what is best for everyone were skills and ethical values that could be shared across religious and secular boundaries. If this was a power of the mind that could work even on the border of war zones near dangerous soldiers and militias, then surely it could be of benefit to life in many circumstances. A loving heart has an unstoppable energy that I observed in so many helpers in such extreme circumstances. But the loving heart can be a wild thing, and thus only when it is guided by reason into good principles, calculations, and plans—only then does it become truly a blessed thing, something that can transform the individual but also society and offer hope for a better future.

As we have seen in the chapter on public health, however, it is essential for good habits of the mind, habits of feelings, and habits of the body to be translatable into policy for violence reduction, peacebuilding, education, community development, and national resilience. As we have analyzed earlier, these habits need metrics to measure progress. Experts need to encourage these habits but also recognize nascent threats, such as outbreaks of hate in schools or on the streets. There need to be protective measures, such as ring inoculation, to surround outbreaks of hate with outbreaks of care on all sides, outbreaks of good habits to counteract destructive ones. A regimen of good habits of Compassionate Reasoning needs to cohere with achievable goals in increments of positive change. The habits of Compassionate Reasoning need to be coordinated with the lessons of public health that we have studied. There need to be demonstrable results that show improvement of the quality of life in terms of psychological health and the general state of relations, from schools to the community and the workplace. In other words, the habits of Compassionate Reasoning for the individual must cohere with a steady expansion outward that transforms the community and society as a whole.

6

Summary of the Argument
of *Compassionate Reasoning: Changing the Mind to Change the World* and Implications for Training

We have explored Compassionate Reasoning through the preceding chapters:

(1) Compassion, Reasoning, and the Urgency of Healing Divided Societies
(2) The Theory and Practice of Compassionate Reasoning
(3) Compassionate Reasoning, the Mind, and Moral Choice
(4) Violent Ideas Treated as Disease and Compassionate Reasoning as Treatment: A Public Health Analogy
(5) The Applied Ethics and Habits of Compassionate Reasoning

Now let's consider a summary of the argument:

(1) Compassion, Reasoning, and the Urgency of Healing Divided Societies
   - An unprecedented planetary danger faces human civilization and puts its future in question, especially carbon emissions climate catastrophe. There is a vital need, therefore, for human beings to make much better decisions together.
   - These decisions must take place across many cultures and civilizations that have conflicting interests, ambitions, and needs.
   - Thinking together with as much diversity as possible leads to far more advanced thinking and problem solving. The future of human life on the planet depends on this.

Compassionate Reasoning. Marc Gopin, Oxford University Press. © Oxford University Press 2022.
DOI: 10.1093/oso/9780197537923.003.0006

- In order to survive and be successful, humans have always had to make decisions informed by two things: (1) a common concern for each other, and (2) a willingness to reason and a capacity for reasoning that supports sustainable life.
- We are capable of this as a species, and we have demonstrated this ability throughout history. But we are also capable of mass suicide, mass murder, and utter destruction of life on earth.
- This is a dangerous paradox of mutually exclusive fates, with the negative fate only circumvented through the cultivation of our positive capacities.
- Our positive capacities for survival require a careful cultivation of compassion and moral reasoning, what is being introduced as "Compassionate Reasoning."

(2) The Theory and Practice of Compassionate Reasoning

- Cultivating a "common concern for each other" entails a complex set of capacities of the human mind that involve prosocial feelings, prosocial thoughts, actions, and habits.
- These feelings, thoughts, actions, and moral habits entail specific neural pathways in the mind that need to be developed and strengthened.
- These reactions of the mind require a strong capacity for moral reasoning.
- Cultivating a willingness and capacity for reasoning that supports sustainable life entails significantly enhancing the reasoning part of the human mind.
- But the reasoning part of the human mind has also been utilized throughout history for the technical execution of war, mass murder, and utter destruction of sustainable life.
- In such situations of extreme violence, the rational mind is subservient to lower brain impulses based on fear or hate.
- The subservience of reasoning to greed, power, selfish, or hateful intentions results in human institutions of slavery, trafficking, wars, mass murder, and ultimately genocide.
- By contrast, it is through the cultivation of the neural pathways of prosocial feelings that the mind can be motivated to utilize reasoning for sustainable life.
- All prosocial feelings have some positive value, but not all are equally useful for the purpose of generating sustainable positive

change and peacebuilding, as has been demonstrated by neuroscience. Empathy is an important example.

- Empathy with the suffering of others is a strong prosocial emotion, but in excess empathy often leads to "burnout" among helpers and social change activists. Burnout can include withdrawal from others, PTSD, physical ailments, and metabolic abnormalities.
- Empathy with suffering can also lead to antisocial feelings and behaviors and even hatred of and violence toward others who have caused suffering to oneself or to loved ones.
- Empathy for a limited number of loved ones in one's family, one's group, one's nation can actually produce great rage and violence.
- Compassion, by contrast, is one of the most esteemed prosocial emotions in the history of ethical theories, philosophy, and contemporary psychology.
- Compassion's extensive reach to all people and all living things makes it a powerful ally of moral reasoning and moral habits.
- Compassion and empathy both have value, but they need to be explored, distinguished, and incorporated in appropriate measures to intrapsychic, interpersonal, national, and international relations.
- Compassion has also been shown to engender short-term and long-term health and happiness, and neuroscience demonstrates that its neural pathways emanate from a completely different set of pathways than empathy.
- Compassion is far more prone by definition to *sustainable* prosocial care for oneself and for others, regardless of skin color or religious, tribal, or national differences.
- Philosophical ethics and ancient wisdom traditions—both secular and religious—have much to offer in the training of the mind for both compassion and for the moral and political reasoning that leads to less violence, less hate, and more sustainable life.
- Compassion as a way of feeling and thinking is demonstrated to be in perfect consonance with the leading schools of ethical thought throughout history.
- Compassion training for the mind is critical as a tool with which to teach a variety of schools of moral reasoning.
- Compassion is deeply embedded in numerous sacred messages and teachings across the earth that can be drawn upon as support from religious traditions of great diversity.

- Compassion is thus embraced as healthy and valuable by secular science, secular ethical traditions, and many interpretations of religious traditions across the globe.
- Taken together, training first in the emotion of compassion, and then in reasoning *that is guided by and motivated by compassion*, constitutes a new and specific approach to human cultivation of the self, cultivation of relationships with others, educational innovation, social policy, and political governance. This is the essence of Compassionate Reasoning.
- Habit and repetitive actions are the essential glue of Compassionate Reasoning.
- Emotion, then cognition, and then habitual action are the essential training regimen of Compassionate Reasoning for the individual and for society as a whole.

(3) Compassionate Reasoning, the Mind, and Moral Choice
  - There are a number of ethical schools of thought that are simplified by this book into manageable trainings in thinking and acting.
  - The schools of ethics outlined guide relationships to the self and others in complex moments of choice that involve many variables.
  - These ethical schools are essential to decision-making for peacebuilding and any forms of positive social change.
  - The directives emerging from diverse ethical schools often contradict each other, however. This is inevitable given the complexity of human life and its often desperate circumstances.
  - This has made it difficult to incorporate moral reasoning into complex efforts at positive social change and peacebuilding and has often led to the sidelining of moral reasoning.
  - Moral decision-making in complex moments of conflict and social ferment can be gut wrenching without better methods of applying ethics to painful circumstances.
  - Guided by compassion training, however, ethical schools of thought can all be drawn upon as legitimate lenses through which to view complex human choices.
  - Taken together, compassion and familiarity with simplified ethical schools of thought will guide reasoning toward less violent, more peaceful, and just societies.
  - The cultivation of compassion is shown to be a glue that bonds a variety of schools of ethics into one enterprise of moral reasoning as

seen through several lenses. These can cohere with the cultivation of Compassionate Reasoning.

- There is extensive evidence that human beings reasoning together are far more adept at problem solving than when reasoning alone, especially if they have earnestly cultivated care and compassionate relationships as a group.

- Moral reasoning in fierce competition with others, by contrast, can actually retard the discovery of solutions to thorny problems. But when seasoned by training in compassion, the collective effort at moral reasoning is far more successful at confronting complexity and moral ambiguity.

- Compassion and training in ethical schools of thought will encourage collective reasoning rather than isolated and selfish reasoning. This lessens the chances that selfish reasoning, or reasoning enslaved to selfish or sadistic impulses, will dominate difficult human moments of conflict.

- Excessive obedience to authority is one of the most dangerous aspects of the human lower brain that has resulted in the perpetual historical stain of demagoguery, mass manipulation, vulture capitalism, totalitarianism, and periodic genocide.

- Democracy is quite vulnerable to destruction at the hands of some citizens who are always prone to obedience, especially those prone to an infantilized search for abusive authority and abusive parental figures in times of stress or uncertainty.

- The search for community and empathy in unstable times often leads some to a blind obedience to unhealthy community, blind obedience to demagogues, and empathic distress.

- A critical antidote to excessive obedience to abusive authorities is extensive training in Compassionate Reasoning, from the earliest age all the way to advanced adulthood.

- Compassionate Reasoning through public education is accomplished through curricula that attract and condition the mind and the body to the pleasures and advantages of compassion and moral reasoning.

- One of the essential ways that compassion and reasoning become dominant and habitual is to continually educate as to its pleasures, joys, and benefits for one's life.

- Unlike the empathic distress of suffering in the suffering of others, often magnified by social media, which leads to destructive emotions and behaviors, habituation to compassion is joyous and addictive in a positive way.
- To take the perspective of others actively and with habitual practice, to listen deeply to and resonate with the story of others, is an essential experience and ethical skill of Compassionate Reasoning. The emphasis is on its joyous experience of aid to others, being appreciated and embraced for that aid.
- Empathy for suffering shifts productively into compassion in peacebuilding by emphasis on an action orientation, such as the extension of care to families and solidarity with survivors of violent conflict.
- Religious and secular people alike can find commonality in moral values and the human experience of compassion and moral reasoning. They can become trained in shared moral habits that build community despite difference in philosophical orientation.
- The work of discovering shared moral habits among diverse religious people, both conservative and progressive, is an essential practice of Compassionate Reasoning. This in turn creates interfaith peacebuilding and the building of a common civic culture for most societies today in which secular and religious must coexist as equals.

(4) Violent Ideas Treated as Disease and Compassionate Reasoning as Treatment: A Public Health Analogy

- Education by itself is not enough to firmly implant Compassionate Reasoning. The cultivation of internalized moral universal laws, secular or religious, are an important antidote to demagoguery, if and only if these laws are rooted in compassion for all.
- The human being needs internal laws to self-regulate, laws that kick in as habits even when one does not feel strong enough for compassion or moral reasoning. This ethical school of thought is especially associated with Emmanuel Kant.
- Internalized laws fulfill the human need to occasionally submit and conform, but they create obedience to something higher than the self, something that applies to all. It is obedience to a higher law, and especially not to a demagogue, tyrant, or abuser. This is essential for peacebuilding and democracy.

- The cultivation of internalized moral universal laws is a great advance, but it is not enough to fight off the human tendency to obey tyrants and bullies *when in group settings*. The cultivation of robust laws of governance for society, from the schoolyard to Congress, are an important source of obedience for the human mind if, and only if, they are rooted in compassion for all.
- The tendency toward obedience can become less destructive if human obedience is not to another human but to the law, to human rights, to constitutions, if and when those laws are morally applied fairly to all human beings. This combines the best insights of deontology and moral sense theory.
- Conflict between humans is inevitable and even essential for moral growth. Conflict management with training in Compassionate Reasoning, informed by the schools of ethical reasoning and training in the emotions and habits of compassion, will minimize the destructive potential of conflict. This will guide conflict in the direction of what is defined as peacebuilding, conflict resolution, and reconciliation. These approaches to conflict require an intentional combination of the ethical and political goals of both peace and justice.
- Elicitive peacebuilding, the preferred methodology of this book, is a specific form of peacebuilding that entails a profound and humble commitment to eliciting the wisdom of each and every person in conflict as a way of building sustainable peace within and between groups. It has proven to be uniquely successful in building durable and equitable change in previously destructive situations.
- Human conflict is infinitely complex. It therefore requires a unique form of reasoning for intervention that cannot be understood by interpretations of causality that are common in the hard sciences of inorganic matter.
- Physics, as complicated as it is, does not deal with the infinite complexity of variables in every moment of human interaction. Each individual changes at every moment of every day through mood swings, biological rhythms of strength and exhaustion, as well as through nonverbal signals that cause humans to influence each other's perceptions and feelings on a constant basis.
- The best parallel for understanding ever-changing human beings and human relationships comes from medicine and public health.

In the latter, science is essential, testing and observation are critical, but it is the helping professional herself—the nurse, the doctor, the epidemiologist, and the health official—who is called upon to make moment-to-moment decisions in order to save lives. This is the model for the peacebuilder and the practitioner of Compassionate Reasoning.

- Compassionate Reasoning and elicitive peacebuilding are better guided by medicine and public health in their best practices. This includes the importance of honoring and listening to each patient, their unique needs, and their self-reporting. But at the same time, it looks at scientific studies of the human condition in the aggregate, across many studies, many cultures, and many circumstances.

- Public health also ideally studies those who are supremely healthy, as well as those who are extremely sick, and then intervenes accordingly. The health practitioner addresses through diagnosis and treatment all the complex variables of individualized medicine, as well as the even more complex variables of family, community, environment, and public health.

- Intervention in health, both physical and mental, has been too guided in modern times by what is wrong, as if humans are machines that need to be fixed. More recent research is drawn upon to steer intervention toward positive health and positive psychology. This requires a deep look at what is healthy, such as compassion, imagination, self-control, meaningfulness, purpose, and a future orientation. It is to seek to strengthen what is healthy as a key component of health but also of Compassionate Reasoning.

- Compassionate Reasoning thus draws inspiration and important parallels from the world of public physical and mental health.

- Contagion and epidemiology can be applied to threats to compassion and threats to moral reasoning, as well as confronting the dangerous spread of misinformation or the intoxicating effects of big lies.

- Contagion, when it comes to public health, positive psychology, and Compassionate Reasoning, needs to be seen as an asset in promoting health, not just containing disease. This is epidemiology applied to positive contagion, as well as identification of dangers to the cultivation of compassion and moral reasoning.

(5) The Applied Ethics and Habits of Compassionate Reasoning

- Positive psychology, and many schools of ethics beginning with Socrates, point to the conclusion that questions are more important than answers. Questions open the mind and strengthen imagination.
- The capacity of the mind to imagine the lives of beloved others, the lives of total strangers, and even the lives of enemies, the capacity to imagine society in better ways—these visions and uses of the imagination are all stimulated by open questions of the mind, far better than dogmatic answers. This is why Compassionate Reasoning and elicitive peacebuilding focus on what can be drawn from persons and groups through creative questioning, relationship building, and listening.
- Spirited debate is also stimulated more by questions than dogmatic answers, and there is a perfect symmetry between the cultivation of Compassionate Reasoning and the methodologies of elicitive peacebuilding. Both encourage close relationships, moral reasoning, and debate in an atmosphere of compassionate care.
- Compassionate Reasoning is designed to work as the essential intrapsychic and interpersonal capacity that will aid conflict prevention, conflict management, reconciliation, and elicitive peacebuilding.
- Habits of feelings, thoughts, and behaviors are essential for the cultivation of the human being and the society that is capable of sustainable life and flourishing.
- The neuroscience previously referred to has demonstrated the essential role of repetition in the cultivation of prosocial neural pathways.
- Modern education has completely failed to invest in the kind of feelings, thoughts, and behaviors that will generate compassion or the kind of reasoning that is in the service of sustaining life.
- Training in science, technology, engineering, and math (STEM) is only as useful as the compassion that it must serve.
- Without regular compassion training in feelings, thoughts, and habitual deeds, from the youngest age to senior adulthood, STEM can and will create monstrous economics and dangerous technology that human civilization can no longer sustain.
- Engineering and technology are only as good as the motivations behind them.

- History and the natural world have ample proof that compassion-based animal and human societies are inherently sustainable, whereas cruel and selfish societies eventually self-destruct. There exists a choice between these two stark fates, and it is in the hands of every family, every community, every nation and community of nations.

- Even when darker impulses surface in democratic societies that have become deeply unequal and in which wealth has become excessive, it is still possible to steer a course away from catastrophe. Education and training in Compassionate Reasoning is designed to entice the minds of the majority to make bold decisions and ethical choices.

- Even when the earth itself and all other nonhuman life forms are suffering beneath the weight of human greed, and global climate destruction looms, it is possible for the minds of individuals and collectives to evolve through compassion and through moral reasoning. The choice is ours.

- A life of service to other sentient beings, to fellow humans, does extraordinary things to the psyche. The more you give with compassion, the more love, and the more you fall in love with the distant other—even the enemy—the more it expands your worldview and changes you permanently.

- Compassionate Reasoning is in this sense a liberation from a purely selfish worldview, and it opens up the mind and heart to a flourishing life of service, health, care, and wisdom.

A Proposal for Training

Recommendations for practice and implementation of Compassionate Reasoning in society have been forthcoming throughout the book. But I want to emphasize in conclusion some practical ways to integrate Compassionate Reasoning into positive change personally, communally, locally, and globally.

Training in Compassionate Reasoning is both possible and essential for the future. The cultivation of compassion will be critical to generating moral reasoning that steers personal and collective actions toward less violence, more peace, and more constructive approaches to sustainable global prosperity.

This will require an unprecedented level of collaboration for which interactive moral reasoning will be essential.

Sentient life on our planet is more interdependent with each passing year, and our legal relationships become ever more interdependent and complex. But little of those interdependencies have been focused on the complex relationship between human affects, states of mind, and states of behavior, especially moral behavior.

The search for happiness has become an interesting exception in that regard. As an interdependent world we have become quite adept at the metrics of our economic relationships but not our emotional and moral relationships. Happiness quotients, however, have become increasingly common as a way to evaluate the state of society.[1] We need to build a system of measuring the cultivation of compassion at the local and global levels. We can no longer assume that educational advancement and the cultivation of reasoning by themselves guarantee the long-term survival of society or a sustainable global civilization. Global measurements of compassion need to be accompanied by global and national measurements of happiness. These two efforts can reinforce each other, especially with more research into the neural pathways of the sense of happiness and the experience of compassion.

Long-term measurements of national and global compassion will create a cultural environment that induces personal and communal life journeys to move in the same direction. Personal, interpersonal, communal, national, and international goal-setting for compassion is a future-oriented behavior that emphasizes imagination and rational planning. This reinforces all the neural pathways most conducive to Compassionate Reasoning.

Specific metrics need to be developed regarding compassion and Compassionate Reasoning.

- In order to assess schools, communities, workplaces, cities, there will be a process of moral deliberation developed to identify compassionate actions that are measurable.
- The experience of feeling compassion toward others or from others will be based on self-reporting measurement systems.
- Observable effects of compassion care measurements will be developed by neuroscience, physical health measurements, and mental health measurements.
- Observable effects of compassionate actions, words, and gestures should be explored.

- Observable and quantifiable effects of compassion can include: quantity and extent of smiles, words of gratitude, stimulus of reciprocal cycles of kindness, measurable mood improvements after experiencing extraordinary acts of compassion, measurable health and attitude improvements in the giver of compassion, measurable health and attitude improvements in the receiver of compassion, tears of joy and appreciation.
- These are all things that, with the planning and moral intentionality of Compassionate Reasoning, will become observable and measurable metrics of progress for compassion's effect on the individual and society, and on compassions effects on conflicts and their resolution.

Training Elements

The elements of training will include but not be limited to:

- Empathy with pain in proper measure through perspective-taking.
- Compassion in a joyous way through training in meditation, imagination, compassionate action, compassionate habits, both internally and externally expressed.
- Compassion leading to advanced moral reasoning that combines and unites the best ethical approaches and practices outlined in this book.
- Moral reasoning that guides the genius of human ingenuity and creativity toward the common good.
- Training in the application of Compassionate Reasoning to rules and policies that need to be applied to all: to the youngest communities in the playground, to the largest of societal interactions at sports games, for example, to nuclear family communities, to senior citizen communal life, to professional communities, to working class communities.

Let's delve into the details of what that training will include and how it might be operationalized.

Techniques

The most basic techniques of training begin with habits of thinking, speaking, and doing. These are the three areas that help the brain strengthen neural pathways of compassion. This will include dedicating reflection time for memories of giving and receiving compassion over the course of one's lifetime. This will involve imagination as well, in terms of imagining about your most ideal scenarios of giving and receiving compassion. This is not only an intellectual exercise of memory and imagination, however, as this meditation is meant to be felt emotionally as well as thought about rationally and imagined. That is why breathing deeply and concentrating only on those thoughts is important, even if it is just for ten minutes at a time.

It is the same with words of compassion and deeds of compassion. These are meant to be concentrated on and experienced intentionally, exclusively, and deeply. It is as if the person is doing exercise and training for sports or fitness, but it is a fitness training of the mind and heart for compassion and for a way of life that is increasingly meaningful, intentional, and happy. This is an intentional methodology to strengthen neural pathways of compassion.

These acts of compassion can be preceded and followed by a mental intentionality to do what one is about to do, such as saying to oneself, "I am about to do something kind. I want to do this, it is important to me, it is who I am, and I hope it has a good effect on others and on the world." This concentrates the mind and makes what one is doing into an affirmation of one's will and one's identity, and it is a conscious strengthening of one's will and identity. This is a methodology that has clear parallels between a secular, psychological intervention and a more spiritual intervention.

This exercise in intentionality can take place in one's mind only, but it is also helpful to be written and spoken. The more parts of the mind that are engaged by one's intentionality and compassion the better. When thoughts, words, writing, and deeds are all geared toward a focus on compassion, it affects the pathways of compassion that much more strongly.

Education

Education from the home to school, from toddlerhood to senior citizenship, needs an age-appropriate set of innovations for the cultivation of compassion that is directed at all living beings. Training in moral reasoning that successfully applies compassion to social life and society as a whole is the second aspect of educational training that is crucial, as we have outlined in previous chapters.

The training in compassion and moral reasoning needs to adjust to the smallest and the largest expressions of society, from the sandbox to the corporate boardroom. A full curriculum for each stage of life and each possible venue of life and work, with frequent repetitions of what needs to become second nature, is critical.

Our earlier explorations into the importance of neural pathways makes it clear that compassion only becomes second nature with extensive repetition. This should be applied to moral reasoning as well, and includes memorization of agreed-upon shared ethical principles, such as human rights, but also the practice of and reflection upon shared moral words and deeds. These can have secular outlets but also have strong parallels in religious literature, thus providing a gateway that unifies cultures across traditional divisions at the current time.

Education in moral reasoning should lead to training in spirited debate on the moral complexities and ambiguities that are inherent in human life. Differing opinions *in a compassionate atmosphere of positive respect and care* will yield far greater areas of agreement on shared values, in addition to clarification of principled differences that require compromise and coexistence. The sophisticated conflict resolution practices of scenario building and role playing, a key to cultivating compassion for different people and differing views, will push the human mind to better and better skills of moral reasoning with others and nonviolent coexistence with difference. This needs to take place at every level of educational engagement, from childhood to continuing professional education and qualification.

A full curriculum concerning civil rights for every stage of education is an important component of applied Compassionate Reasoning. Compassion brings the skills to appreciate every person's needs and the eagerness to apply care to each person. The training in moral reasoning hones the skills to apply these compassionate intentions, emotions, and actions to all people and all expressions of life, despite the inevitable complexity of society and despite inevitable conflicts and difficult human circumstances.

Psycholinguistics, Neuroscience, and Compassionate Reasoning

At the core of education and training is the power of the word to change the mind. The practical upshot of the psycholinguistics and neuroscience that we have studied in previous chapters in relation to the construction of Compassionate Reasoning is that every word we think, say, and repeat has a remarkable effect on our minds, on our cognitions, and on our emotions. Every word triggers various pathways of imagination, various kinds of longing, distressful memory, or joyous imagination of the future. It behooves us then to orient Compassionate Reasoning education at every level to the power of the word.

The moral and spiritual obligation to be careful with words is an ancient tradition going back to the dawn of humankind. This is a primordial recognition that words have tremendous power over us, something that we now understand better as more than mystery and magic. Sciences of the mind may be giving us more clues as to why there were so many warnings and taboos throughout history surrounding verbal curses and the destructive use of words. Conversely, the power of blessings, good intentions, prayers, and hopes may also be given new importance for the development of peaceful society. All of it implies that we can develop a more intentional approach to molding our minds and emotions with more research that helps us build the power of Compassionate Reasoning into the way we learn how to raise children with words, the way we publicly speak, the way we learn how to write, the way we teach, and the way we do politics and public policy.

Training for Conflict Resolution and Elicitive Peacebuilding

Working with people in conflict zones can be quite traumatizing. In this regard we need to return to the subject of empathic distress as opposed to compassion and Compassionate Reasoning. The natural tendency of those morally motivated to do peacebuilding or to engage in interventions of care for others is to overextend oneself with an excess of empathic distress at the suffering of others. Training in compassion, however, will be a boon to the helping professions, to conflict resolution, and elicitive peacebuilding because it will strengthen a person's ability to enter into painful situations without being consumed by the pain of others. Compassionate Reasoning training needs to be experimented with as an antidote to empathic distress or burnout. The training's focus on doing with internal joy and care, as well as external professionalism and care, as opposed to guilt and desperation, will rework completely the effects of the work on both the givers and the receivers.

Similarly, extensive training in moral reasoning will give a person the ability to face the inherent moral ambiguities of each situation without it devolving into personal pain, trauma, and depression. This is the kind of training that will help cultivate compassion even in the most dire situations. The training will guide one in how to exercise compassion, how to extend it, how to wish for it, and how to take actions that express the compassion in one's heart on an ongoing basis. This is the opposite of the distress caused when one can find no way to heal the pain of others. This also allows for the mind to be more ready through habit formation to help through moral reasoning in desperate and unexpected circumstances. Expecting the unexpected is in the nature of good training and preparation of the mind to exercise its highest qualities, not its most base instincts.

Compassionate Reasoning empowers the person or group, and all those affected by them, to move beyond the paralysis of excessive empathy with the pain of others. Compassion training combined with advanced moral reasoning undermines empathic pain by a concentrated and habituated focus on what can be done for the self and others in a way that brings joy and satisfaction even in the most difficult of circumstances. Every day, even in the most peaceful of societies, one is bound to witness someone who is ill or elderly or in pain, and excess sensitivity to those pains is very debilitating to some people. Compassionate Reasoning gives one the ability to rise above that pain and toward a joyful care for others that nurtures oneself at the same time. But Compassionate Reasoning is also a boon to those who do not feel enough compassion for others and thus end up with a variety of moral deficiencies and conflict-ridden problems. The cultivation of Compassionate Reasoning encourages all people toward a centered and balanced altruism that is also satisfying to the self.

Compassionate Reasoning and Ethics Training

We have analyzed the need to become adept at simplifying a range of schools of ethics and moral decision-making in order for Compassionate Reasoning to function well and in an integrated way. In the context of training in compassion, becoming familiar with the principles schools of ethical decision-making will make it far easier to apply compassion to a wide range of situations.

This moral training is as helpful for one's personal life as it is for society as a whole. The combination of ethical approaches is more useful, practical, and integrated in methodologies of decision-making in difficult circumstances, as well as in negotiating the difficult choices of society-wide policies.

Compassionate Reasoning training will enhance health and happiness, but it will also encourage greater freedom of thought. The conscious training in compassion for thoughts, in words, and deeds promotes greater control of the mind and one's behavior. Its tie to moral reasoning further helps to liberate persons and groups from loss of emotional control that often leads to misery, conflict, and violence. Thus, these techniques and trainings can be promoted in society as an offer of freedom for persons and groups. There will be a greater satisfaction with one's best efforts to move from personal wishes, will, hopes, and visions, toward the rational application of the best possible moral principles and moral outcomes applied to complex aspects of interpersonal and communal experience.

Policy

Training in Compassionate Reasoning and policy will be the greatest use of the mind as we apply the lessons of Compassionate Reasoning to the formation of good policies for the most number of human beings and sentient living systems of the planet. This will take an interactive creativity between one's knowledge of policy and policy choices on the one hand, and on the other the basic prosocial emotions and moral principles emerging from Compassionate Reasoning; the latter need to engage those policies in their formation, development, and application. For example, this training involves asking one's own mind, as well as brainstorming with others, regarding some basic questions. Here are some examples: What economic policies allow for the most compassionate behaviors of society? What political systems and legislation promotes the exercise of compassion in society, and what systems and laws make compassion harder? What laws lead to the greatest compassion for the greatest number? What health policies do the same? How can public health systems encourage compassionate relationships and behavior? What emergency care is the most compassionate, and how does one engage in systems of medical triage in a way that maximizes compassion for the caregivers, the patients, and their families?

How can we engage in political competition for office in a nonviolent democracy without it turning politics into a system of hate and demonization? What is the most compassionate way to defeat an adversary at the ballot box? Is it even possible, and what can moral reasoning contribute to the search for how to encourage competition in the marketplace or in politics without that competition becoming destructive or wasteful of resources? How does one engage in diplomacy with dangerous adversary nations in such a way that exhibits sincere compassion for adversary populations while at the same time protecting one's own population? What principles should be utilized in doing so?

The Question Is the Answer

As we have seen earlier in the book, this multitude of questions contain the seeds of the answer. There are few certainties regarding ethics when it comes to human situations of complexity and competing needs, all the way from the sandbox to the ballot box. How can we balance a compassionate care for millions of species steadily disappearing versus the needs of humans? Where does compassion belong? Where is the balance between compassion for fast-disappearing species versus basic human needs? What can moral reasoning teach us about the balance? Where does reason belong in the balance of care for sentient life, especially when losing more and more species is also guaranteeing the steady demise of the human ecosystem as well? That is surely a question whose answer must combine compassion and reasoning.

The best answer we have for all of these questions is the need for a giant leap in the human capacity for compassion and moral reasoning applied to complex, life-and-death struggles. The answer is that we do not have precise cookie-cutter answers to such life-or-death questions, but we do know that better training and preparation and a better intentionality of the mind and heart around Compassionate Reasoning would make what we come up with far less destructive and far more sensitive to the needs of the most amount of people. Better training in compassion and moral reasoning, in a carefully combined way, helps policymakers, diplomats, law enforcement, and military decision-makers to reflect on and confront the open questions we have raised. The more that they do this consciously, with the best intentions and extensive training, the more likely that they can steer humanity away from violence and self-destruction and toward flourishing and prosperity. The human mind can work quite well for the good when we make it our intention to do so. It is the concentration itself, the intentionality itself, for compassion and for taking moral reasoning seriously, that exercises and fashions the mind toward the direction of better outcomes.

In recent years, after seeing the destructive relationship between law enforcement and community in too many American cities, I made it my intention to engage both police and minority communities with great compassion and with a great intention to understand their pain. My wife Christel and I worked especially with both black communities and black police. Out of that work has come the most amazing collaborations on approaches to policing with compassion, to training in self-reflection, in Compassionate Reasoning for every situation, to the compassionate care for families and young people and the defense of human rights of all in every region of the country. All of our interventions focused less on pain and suffering and shaming and more on the compassionate intention to help and to use the best of our reasoning to revolutionize relationships between police and communities, empowering the best people as much as we could. The work is ongoing, but it is quite sustainable as an intervention because creating beloved communities around these efforts is such a joy. It is such a joy to witness the incredible resilience of communities, as well as the incredible courage and sensitivity of forward-thinking, compassionate, and creative individuals who have saved so many lives and changed so many communities for the better.

Training and the Future

A key component of training in Compassionate Reasoning is a future orientation. The question itself, the posing of questions, is the mind opening up to future possibilities. But the future can either be a space of anxiety and nightmare or a place of hope and longing. It all depends on training the mind toward its pathways of compassion and rational planning through moral reasoning. There is no doubt that many things pull us toward fear and anxiety, and the natural path toward fear of future illness and death that awaits us all ultimately. But this is where training in a meaningful fulfillment every day of compassionate thought, words, and deeds leads the mind toward a proper balance of fear and hope, caution and longing.

A Balance of Empathy and Compassion: Revisiting the Ancient Golden Rule

As we have seen earlier, Tonglen is an ancient practice that in many ways is the embodiment of a brain practice to shift the body, thinking, and emotions from empathic distress at the pain of others to the joy of compassionate thinking, reasoning, and acting. This is through a future orientation, a discipline of the mind. It is the breathing in and thinking of the imagined pain of those around you, from your own pain to the pain of loved ones—even extending to enemies. Then it is a conscious and slow breathing out while concentrating exclusively on wishes for blessings of others who are suffering, for comfort to them, wishes for all their body parts to work, for all medicines to work, for all positive emotions to work, for all injustices to be removed, for all love to be felt, for safety to be felt, and for one's own intentions to lead to compassionate words and deeds as a joyful fulfillment of a meaningful life.

You breathe in and imagine a COVID patient in the ICU in the worst and most terrifying moments of isolation. You breathe in their utter sorrow and despair, something that can reasonably leave you paralyzed with sadness. But then you steadily breathe out all the best wishes and hopes for them and their loved ones. Then you imagine the hundreds of thousands of people in pain. What do you wish for each and every one of them? This is a brain exercise to switch from pain to joy, from past and present to the future. It is a conscious process of changing the brain pathways from the paralysis of sorrow and fear toward the liberation of the mind and the body toward the joy of compassion, love, and hope. It is a meaningful application of the mind toward being able to do the most good for humanity in the most constructive and reasonable ways possible.

Some people do not feel the pain of others around them enough, and therefore they suffer a deficient ethics of care. They lack sufficient compassion to be morally responsible, to use their reasoning minds in a way that truly brings benefits to themselves and to humanity at the same time. This results in great suffering, since the human mind and its reasoning capacity is a dangerous tool without the directive of compassion. On the other hand, many who do care for others become enmeshed in an overindulgence in empathy with the pain of others, an excessive sense of responsibility, and a slippage into despair, anxiety, depression, withdrawal, and even hate.

The Golden Rule, to love one's neighbor as one loves oneself, requires a consistent training of the mind, both ideation and affect, ideas and emotions, mind and heart, in the art of caring for oneself and caring for others simultaneously, and doing so in a way that brings joy to oneself and to others. This is the way to make the Golden Rule sustainable in one's own life and in the life of community.

Compassionate reasoning is a discipline to do just that. Compassionate reasoning requires lifelong practice and a public dedication to its essential role in building a sustainable life for all sentient beings on planet earth. This requires an emphasis on training and on a consistent intention to not only care for oneself and for others but to care for the future of life itself.

Notes

Chapter 1

1. This is not an exhaustive list, but some of the most essential texts and authors currently in the field include: Oliver Ramsbotham (with Woodhouse and Miall 2016), Kevin Avruch's (1998) *Culture and Conflict Resolution, Conflict Resolution and Human Needs* (Avruch and Mitchell 2013), *The Handbook of Conflict Resolution: Theory and Practice* (Coleman, Deutsch, and Marcus 2014), *Conflict: From Analysis to Intervention* (Cheldelin, Druckman, and Fast 2003), John Paul Lederach's work (1996, 2005), and *Introduction to Conflict Resolution: Discourses and Dynamics* (Cobb, Federman, and Castel 2020).

2. One promising pathway of research exploring this hypothesis is the recent literature on compassion-focused therapy on survivors of violent trauma, particularly trauma that induced shame within survivors (Au et al. 2017). In many conflict contexts, especially when social psychological processes of depersonalization, dehumanization, and scapegoating are employed to belittle one social group, perceptions of shame contribute to the perpetuation of conflict dynamics—including acts of violence.

3. Steven Pinker's thesis has been subject to many critiques and defenses. I am interested in the rather incontrovertible evidence on the importance of compassion and reasoning for a trend toward less violence globally. Reasoning about universal principles, the moral sense of compassion, and the central importance of education and habit formation have all figured prominently in several ethical theories throughout history. I am arguing that their prominence in global patterns of less violence suggests a revisiting of global efforts to promote a more peaceful and sustainable earth. These are the moral skills and habits necessary to increase the possibility of global survival of sentient life and human civilizations. There is a confluence implicit between long-standing trends in ethical theory that combine nicely with analysis in psychology and neuroscience on critical capacities associated with less violence. This confluence of philosophy and psychology is important to the formation of Compassionate Reasoning as a proposed method of social change.

4. The link between an individual's mental health, and this individual's moral treatment of others, has a long history in the brain and mind sciences. Beginning with the first "clinical psychologist" (Freud), extending to modern-day neuroscientific approaches to psychotherapy, both cognitive (reasoning) and affective (compassion) models are co-jointly implicated in transforming both the individual and the society around him or her. Paul Gilbert (2010) suggests that compassion-focused therapy (CFT) can support individuals as they cope and deal with their own mental health challenges (e.g., eating disorders, bipolar disorder) and to broad patterns of social behavior as well.

This book, in contrast to psychopathological models of compassion and reasoning as boons of mental health, contends that compassion and reasoning—combined—can prove transformative for non-clinical individuals (i.e., people who do not present traits of mental disorder).

5. A recent systematic review reveals a wide diversity of approaches to bolstering compassion in clinical (e.g., therapeutic) settings. One of the most important findings to emerge from this evidence-based literature is the simple tenet that more compassionate people are, generally, happier people (Kirby 2017).

6. It is beyond the scope of this chapter to provide a comprehensive review of interfaith ritual exchange and compassion practices. However, two key exemplars deserve note: First is Friar Ivo Markovic, a reconciler and peacemaker working in post-conflict Bosnia. Among his many peacemaking successes is his creation of the Pontanima Choir, which includes sixty members of various religious and spiritual traditions that represent religious communities within Bosnia and Herzegovina (BBC 2020). This choir, and much of Friar Ivo's work, is a creative outlet for religious peacebuilding (Little 2007). The second figure is Sheikh Abdul Aziz Bukhari, cofounder of Jerusalem Peacemakers and head of the Naqshabandi Sufi order in Jerusalem. Sheikh Bukhari collaborated with religious leaders (Christian, Jewish, and others) to build peace for Israelis and Palestinians (Gopin 2012).

7. For a more detailed account of the link between Compassionate Reasoning, self-examination, and breaking down binaries, see my case studies of Ibtisam Mahameed and Eliyahu McLean in *Bridges across an Impossible Divide* (Gopin 2012). The individuals portrayed each have their own personal methodology of peacebuilding that included compassion at the core, and I begin there to describe the foundations of Compassionate Reasoning.

8. A giant in psychological research, Alfred Bandura (1977, 1997) would support this thesis, based on his prodigious research on social learning theory and the power of "modeling." According to Bandura, and the generations of social psychologists he inspired, some individuals who challenge immoral norms in society (in this example, racism) can inspire others to adopt similar stances as well. Many factors shape the power of modeling, including similar personality- and identity-based traits between the modeler and the modeled, complexity of the behavior(s) being modeled, and trait self-efficacy of the modeled. In the context of this book, individuals who publicly model "Compassionate Reasoning" may inspire others to take up this moral-affective practice.

9. My PhD student Nicholas Sherwood commented here that it is wiser to distinguish two kinds of empathy in the psychological literature. He states, "*Cognitive empathy* describes being able to *understand* how another person feels and what they might by thinking. *Affective empathy* is actually *sharing* these feelings with another person. Sociopaths and other antisocial actors can test very high on cognitive empathy but not affective [empathy]. Wai and Tiliopoulos (2012) have a good article modeling how empathy can track to 'dark personality' traits." This is a very important distinction, and this distinction may point to how, in Tibetan Buddhist practice, for example, there is a place for training to *know* the pain of the other (cognitive), while also trying

to train in prosocial solidarity and *wishes of kindness* (affective) to the person (Burton 2010). This raises two important issues:

(1) We need to train in affective empathy in order for it to lead to kindness and solidarity with others.

(2) Cognitive empathy, on the other hand, may be a method of intervention that is a little cooled down, that is useful as a barrier to *too much* pain experienced from others on a regular basis, such as may be experienced by care professionals in an emergency ward or teachers of child victims of war. For them, an emphasis on cognitive empathy may be useful as a means of providing help while not becoming so invested emotionally that you get sick. Conversely, Baldwin, cited above, exemplified a rare empathy for enemies. We need more *affective* empathy between enemy groups in order to de-escalate violence while escalating the possibility of change. There is mostly a deep absence of affective empathy between enemy groups that is a key reason that they get stuck in cycles of violence. This important conceptual difference between compassion and empathy is further explored within the Buddhist spiritual tradition: (a) *mettā*, signifying "loving kindness" that correlates with compassion; and (b) *muditā*, signifying "sympathetic joy" that correlates with empathy (Yeh 2006).

10. Haidt (2012) is right about the danger of righteousness and self-righteousness for rational politics. But I am delving more in this book into the psychological stressors of legitimate and laudable empathy that triggers a descent into destructive forms of righteousness. We will explore Compassionate Reasoning as an entirely different and alternative engagement with the mind that is better informed by prosocial emotions, reason, and mind training for a more balanced and productive ethics.

11. Our modern-day obsession with STEM (science, technology, engineering and mathematics) as both a pathway to vocational success and an indicator of productive "rational thinking" is being challenged by ideas both old and new. Increasingly, many professionals in traditional "STEM fields" (e.g., scientists) have proposed the addition of "art" to this acronym to create STEAM (Wade-Leeuwen, Vovers, and Silk 2018). STEAM advocates implore the addition of traditional humanities (e.g., language, dance, drama, music, visual arts, new media, and ethics and philosophy) to pedagogy strategies. The history of STEAM can be traced as far back as Leonardo da Vinci's hybrid approach to exploring the human condition vis-a-vis science, art, and religion, but it has deep roots across the globe going back to Confucian education in China as well, and many other ancient examples.

12. The literature on complexity-induced anxiety and frustration is murky, however. According to one theory (Briscoe and Feldman 2011), when presented with ambiguous information, many individuals assume a cognitive space in the middle of simplicity and complexity without reports of psychological duress. At the same time, this "tolerance for complexity" may result from environmental factors as well (i.e., when we are not stressed, we are more likely to accept complexity in the world around us). In contexts defined by stress, conflict, and violence, our tolerance for complexity (and willingness to engage in complex social situations and complex decision-making) may be thwarted, thereby leading to psychological paralysis, rashness, or frustration.

13. There is a large literature on this. See, for example, Timmons and Byrne (2019).

14. This potential source of resilience is linked to the interplay between "resilient personalities" (e.g., hardiness) and seeking social support from "super-copers." Bonanno (with Westphal and Mancini 2011), a prominent theorist and researcher of psychological resilience, contends that resilience-building is a relatively ubiquitous affair—most individuals exhibit some form of resilience when confronted with adversity, stress, and trauma—and that resilience strategies can be modeled, taught, and socialized from individuals who cope exceptionally well in the face of life's challenges. Recent research (Fletcher et al. 2020) examines reactions to prolonged stress and complex trauma and how to build resilience in these instances. In a context of extended conflict and stress, a powerful source of resilience is to learn from "super-copers." These individuals seem to have innate knowledge and wisdom related to resilience-building strategies, and these individuals often take it upon themselves to impart this knowledge to individuals who are new to traumatic and stressful contexts.

15. See Pirkei Avot 1:6 and Ecclesiastes 4:12.

16. The idea of "maximizing goodness" that I am introducing here can be focused in either a Kantian way on the exercise of good principles and good deeds, or a consequentialist way in maximizing the good things that human beings can achieve through fulfillment of basic needs such as safety, or higher needs such happiness or meaning. We will explore later the diversity of the schools of ethics alluded to in this note, and how each school contributes positively to refining Compassionate Reasoning.

17. See generally Mercier and Sperber (2017). I do not agree with the authors' definition of reasoning, but their emphasis on reasoning as a process of convincing others, a negotiation of persuasion, is important for the points we are making. We must empower everyone to be in the business of logical persuasion. This is the only way that reason and compassion can work together for a better society more immune to the manipulations of a few demagogues in concert with unscrupulous media. We need moral argumentation to become a habit of communication by word and deed.

18. Bennett-Levy and Thwaites (2007) are two of many mental health researchers who elevate the power of self-reflection to better oneself and one's relationship with society around one. These authors conceptualize the self-reflection process as the adoption of a cognitive schema that places the individual as her/his own therapist (i.e., the self-as-therapist schema). When an individual internalizes this schema, she/he is able to develop new conceptual and technical skills to enhance her/his moral agency in the world and to teach these skills to others in non-therapeutic contexts. Again, we see the power of self-reflection to act as a social contagion.

19. My PhD student Nicholas Sherwood notes: Zimbardo (2007) and Milgram (1974) are the two most well-cited psychologists exploring this trend. Putting their works in conversation, we see that individuals in positions of authority or leadership can and do exert undue influence over the moral behavior of individuals under the leaders' sphere of influence. Characteristics of the leaders (e.g., material characteristics such as wearing white doctors' coats, and immaterial characteristics such as perceived similarity of values between the leader and those being led) is an especially powerful predictor of how, when, and to what degree human beings can be compelled or

manipulated into violating their own ethical code. Not satisfied with this line of research, Zimbardo (2021) has since pivoted toward understanding how heroism, too, can be contagious between leader and follower. Zimbardo (2021) contends that the combination of the bystander effect, a growth mindset, bias reduction, and heroism training can equip populations to directly challenge leaders who attempt to hijack moral behavior.

20. Psychological research on the impact of fundamentalist/authoritarian beliefs on cognitive and moral functioning is a burgeoning field. Empirical studies suggest that high fundamentalism/authoritarianism correlates with a very low tolerance for ambiguity, cognitive flexibility, and a high need for closure (Kossowska et al. 2018). There does seem to be a marked difference in ethical decision-making between high fundamentalism/authoritarianism and low fundamentalism/authoritarianism samples. The next step of this research, which this book will explore, is how to *conceive, enact and enable* cognitive shifts away from authoritarian tendencies.

Chapter 2

1. There are many concerns raised about empathy that we will explore later. My student Nicholas Sherwood notes: Fritz Breithaupt, Professor of Germanic Studies at Indiana University, has identified at least three "dark sides of empathy" in his recent (2019) book: (1) "vampiristic empathy," intentionally manipulating others to empathically and vicariously experience their successes and joys (e.g., helicopter parents); (2) polarization arising from strong empathic connection to one's own tribe or group (e.g., students learning about the Northern Ireland conflict, terrorism recruitment); (3) burnout and overextending oneself in order to serve others. The last example is most pertinent to the themes explored throughout this book.

2. "*Reason*, in *philosophy*, the faculty or process of drawing logical inferences. The term '*reason*' is also used in several other, narrower senses . . . . That *reason* which gives a priori principles Kant calls 'pure *reason*,' as distinguished from the 'practical *reason*,' which is especially concerned with the performance of actions." (italicized words not in the original entry; Editors of Encyclopedia Britannica 2020).

3. Building networks of positive social change with Compassionate Reasoning necessitates some knowledge of social network theory and complexity science. Networks are highly disproportional and dynamic, and they form connections according to principles that may seem counterintuitive. This stems, in part, from the basis in human characteristics and relationships which leads individuals to make decisions and choices in relation to network connections. Individual and group behaviors may not align (Granovetter 1976, 1978). However, the phenomenon of a global system working together to create a new level of the organization comes through self-organizing. Patterns emerge and become part of systems creating subsystems through the local-level organization that forms broader hierarchies and networks (Bar-Yam 2018).

4. *Talmud Bavli* Chagiga 14a; *Ruth Rabbah* 4:3; Maimonides, *Mishneh Torah*, Yesode Hatorah 2:12.

5. I am indebted to colleagues who have pioneered and innovated the field of Scriptural Reasoning (SR). This field has ancient roots in creative spiritual forms of textual study and debate. My path in this book will be more related to integrating ethics and neu-roscience, but SR has played a critical role in demonstrating the possibility of shared ethical values across the lines of worldviews and starkly different theologies. This is an important cousin to what we are investigating here. For more information on SR, I direct you to (a) Professor David F. Ford's (2020) lecture: "Broader, Deeper, Further: Engaging with Religions in the Twenty-First Century; (b) King's College London's Professor of Christianity & the Arts, Ben Quash's (2020) chapter: "Deep Calls to Deep: The Practice of Scriptural Reasoning"; and finally (c) the University of Virginia's Edgar M. Bronfman Professor of Modern Judaic Studies, Peter Ochs' (2006) article: "Philosophic Warrants for Scriptural Reasoning." See also Dr. Aref Ali Nayed's work, including his (2018) book *Operational Hermeneutics: Interpretation as the Engagement of Operational Artifacts* and manuscript (2010): "Growing Ecologies of Peace, Compassion, and Blessing: A Muslim Response to 'A Muscat Manifesto.'"

6. For more information on consequentialism, see (a) my chapters in *To Make the Earth Whole* (2009) "Confronting the Ethical Dilemmas of Citizen Diplomacy" and "A Global Ethic of Citizen Diplomacy"; (b) Jeremy Bentham's "An Introduction to the Principles of Morals and Legislation" (Rand 1909); and (c) John Stuart Mill's "Utilitarianism" (Rand 1909). For the purposes of this text, consequentialism is an ethical practice that (1) calculates the greatest amount of happiness to the greatest number of humans over the greatest amount of time and (2) prioritizes action that maximizes these three variables (happiness, persons, time).

7. See, for example, Immanuel Kant's "The Metaphysics of Morality" (Rand 1909) and *The Critique of Practical Reason* (Kant and Gregor 1999).

8. The "emotional contagion effect" was formally proposed by Hatfield, Cacioppo, and Rapson (1993) and includes three sequential processes: (1) most people consciously and unconsciously mimic other individuals when engaged in conversation; (2) the mime then experiences subjective emotions as a result of the mimicry process; and finally (3) "people tend, from moment to moment, to 'catch' other people's emotions" (p. 99). Emotional contagion effects are furthermore linked to positive emotions (e.g., contentment, joy) and to negative emotions (e.g., sadness, frustration). The experiences of these emotions then offer the motivation to act, whether in prosocial (e.g., generosity and care-taking) or antisocial (e.g., aggression and suicide) ways (Jollant, Malafosse, Docto, and Macdonald 2014; Jordan, Rand, Arbesman, Fowler, and Christakis 2013).

9. For example, see Smith's chapter "Of Sympathy" in *The Theory of Moral Sentiments*:

> Sympathy, therefore, does not arise so much from the view of the passion, as from that of the situation which excites it. We sometimes feel for another, a passion of which he himself seems to be altogether incapable; because, when we put ourselves in his case, that passion arises in our breast from the imagi-nation, though it does not in his from the reality. We blush for the impudence and rudeness of another, though he himself appears to have no sense of the

impropriety of his own behaviour; because we cannot help feeling with what confusion we ourselves should be covered had we behaved in so absurd a manner. (Rand 1909, pp. 446–447)

10. From Hobbes' *Leviathan*:

And because all signs of hatred, or contempt, provoke to fight; insomuch as most men choose rather to hazard their life, than not to be revenged; we may in the eighth place, for a law of nature, set down this precept, that no man by deed, word, countenance, or gesture, declare hatred, or contempt of another. The breach of which law is commonly called contumely. The question who is the better man, has no place in the condition of mere nature; where, as has been shown before, all men are equal. (Rand 1909, p. 225)

11. My student Nicholas Sherwood notes: The connection between social justice and spirituality is strongly exemplified by the American-led "social gospel" movement, first formalized by Walter Rauschenbusch's (1919) *A Theology for the Social Gospel*. The author concedes the Great War (World War I) presented a tremendous opportunity for spiritual and religious traditions to take up the mantle of caring for society's most vulnerable members. At the same time, this "care" was oftentimes matched with proselytizing and evangelism (e.g., the idea behind many Christian mission trips). However, at the core of the social gospel movement is that members of any society have a moral obligation to care for one another, and the depth of this morality extends into the realm of spiritual and religious "truth." Here we see the power of compassion and compassion-inspired prosocial behavior to sway multitudes, even quite conservative multitudes, especially if framed through a religious/spiritual-moral/ethical lens.

12. For an even-handed review of the evolution from Darwinism to social Darwinism and finally eugenics, see Paul's (2003) chapter in *The Cambridge Companion to Darwin*. To summarize a few points, Paul (2003) viewed the social Darwinian and eugenics movement as a product of the appropriation of Darwinian thought. This appropriation occurred vis-a-via the confabulation of a *language* rather than a *set of coherent ideas* from the *Origin of Species* and other related texts—this language was used to validate old ideas about competition, race, and gender. The most famous of these appropriators are the Nazis. Combating the deleterious effects of the bastardization of Darwinism occurred largely due to the ideology (Ninkovich 1986) and policy (specifically related to the welfare state and "trickle up" economics; Scheurell 2003) of US President Roosevelt and the international advocacy and politicking of Eleanor Roosevelt (Naddeo 2005).

13. See *Report to the Special Committee of the Board of Directors of the American Psychological Association: Independent Review Relating to APA Ethics Guidelines, National Security Interrogations, and Torture* (Hoffman et al. 2015; Seligman 2016; American Psychological Association n.d.).

14. One study, examining bullying behavior in adolescents, contends a higher natural sensitivity to moral issues correlates with an individual's willingness to intervene in situations where moral "laws" are broken. Furthermore, higher reports of self-efficacy ("I will do action because I know I am capable of accomplishing it") further increases a bystander's willingness to stand up to moral violators. In other words, a sensitivity

toward compassion in day-to-day life, and a cognitive reasoning process, both impel moral behavior (Thornberg and Jungert 2013).

15. "But the proposition, the will is in all its actions a law to itself, indicates only the principle, to act on no other maxim than which can also have as object itself as a universal law. This, however, is precisely the formula of the categorical imperative and is the principle of morality; hence a free will and a will under moral laws are one and the same" (Kant and Gregor 1999, pp. 94–95).

16. An easy-to-follow review of the relations between the forebrain (where more complex reasoning occurs) and the hindbrain (where our more primitive instincts are activated) can be found at the National Institute of Neurological Disorders and Stroke (2020) website.

17. I am not idealizing any single author; they all had their flaws. Even as Dickens vastly expanded empathy for the miserably poor, he perpetuated an inveterate prejudice against Jewish people (Meyer 2005). But the expansion of moral concern beyond kings and queens was revolutionary in the nineteenth century.

18. Some interesting work has been done in this area. See Jarvis and Gouthro 2019.

19. Belden C. Lane, *Ravished by Beauty: The Surprising Legacy of Reformed Spirituality* (New York: Oxford, 2011), p. 33. The paradox of abolition of cruelty to animals coming sooner than human slavery abolition is an important indication of the challenges of understanding compassion in the human mind. How and when do we extend compassion to all? What prevents that extension to a human slave of a different color, for example, as opposed to, say, a pet? Greed? Scapegoating? A primal need for bullying and hierarchy among humans? Whatever the reasons, it is clear that training in compassion that challenges forms of structural violence such as slavery or second-class citizenship must take into account the deep barriers to the full extension of compassion in human consciousness. We will extend compassion far more easily to animals before we extend it to all humans. Working toward educational systems and social atmospheres where there is a full extension of compassion to all requires a close collaboration between ethicists and scientists of the human mind.

20. The link between logical development (e.g., mathematical ability) and moral development (e.g., taking proactive steps to prevent or reduce causing harm to others) has been a staple of developmental psychological research since before Kohlberg (Haan, Weiss, and Johnson 1982). As has been demonstrated, moral and logical development often occur in complex and distinct ways—contingent upon biological factors (e.g., health, nutrition) and sociocultural factors (e.g., stress; Haan, Weiss, and Johnson 1982; Chase 2003).

21. An evocative example of this fundamental commitment to ethical behavior can be found in the courageous successes of Le Chambon to protect persecuted Jews from the Nazis (Rochat and Modigliani 1995). Throughout World War II, the Christian "ordinary citizens" of Le Chambon actively deceived their local politicians (who were collaborating with Nazi forces) to protect their Jewish neighbors who were targeted for extermination. Rochat and Modigliani (1995) locate three mechanisms, which they contend actually constitute a "banality of goodness" (in contrast to Arendt's "banality of evil"): (1) a population's immediate choice to resist, (2) a tactical decision

by citizens to never openly speak of their resistance (thereby allowing the authorities to "look the other way"), and (3) the endurance to stay ahead of the authorities throughout the duration of World War II. These three mechanisms were also initiated by local spiritual leaders' calls to protect Jews from the Nazi regime, again echoing the idea that ethical decisions are indeed contagious affairs. Furthermore, it is important to note, there was no overarching organization guiding and directing the heroism of the citizens of Le Chambon. This was, in essence, *a collective decision to do the right thing without support, without guidance, simply because protecting other humans from extermination is the right thing to do.*

22. See the debate below on interpretation.

23. The preponderance of such debates between many religions, and within many religious sectarian struggles, suggests that religious debates about inclusion versus exclusion are less about texts and interpretation and more about the psychological tendency in certain leaders and followers to divide the world into "us" versus "them." See Sapolsky (2017), *Behave,* for a brief summary of the neurological bases of implicit bias against those in designated outgroups.

24. *Genesis Rabbah* 24.

25. We cannot overlook the impact of individual factors on habit formation. Building toward automaticity (e.g., repeating a behavior without the need for prior planning and minimal cognitive investment), whether flossing our teeth or treating a stranger with kindness, is largely contingent on an individual's life history, neurological functioning, and environmental cues (Lally, Van Jaarsveld, Potts, and Wardle 2010). Despite these complexities, here are a few supported assertions we can make about habit formation: (1) earlier repetition has payoff in the long run, rather than trying to "catch up" on repetition later in the habit formation cycle; (2) for each person building a habit, there exists a formation "ceiling," meaning, there are some behaviors that will not become habitual and will require intentional energies to complete; and (3) simple tasks (e.g., flossing teeth) are easier to build into habits than are complex tasks (treating a stranger with kindness). The third assertion is important in this discussion—building a habit of Compassionate Reasoning will likely take a massive investment, both from the individual and from society. This highlights the importance of building Compassionate Reasoning into early education, and then rewarding habits from this education across the entire lifetime. Some religions do this very well, as long as the object of care is a member of an acceptable group of people.

Chapter 3

1. The 80/20 Rule, also known as the Pareto principle, refers to the idea that 80% of a problem or 80% of a solution is often due to 20% of the efforts expended. This was popularized by the work of J. M. Juran (1974) in management theory and quality control research. For my purposes, I am interested in issues of maximization of social change, the efficiencies—and inefficiencies—of social change work that is often

based on very few resources. I am interested in maximization of efficiency also because there is an ethical foundation to maximization of good in consequentialist and utilitarian ethics that we will address below. Another way to put this is that we spend 80% of our efforts on what is not as productive as 20% of our efforts. When it comes to social change and peacebuilding, we need to focus far more on what has worked and strengthen those trends. We ought to recalibrate most of our energies to focus on what works in order to maximize the good, such as saving lives, healing trauma, building compassionate environments, or creating the greatest number of peaceful gestures in conflict-ridden contexts.

2. Italics mine throughout this cited passage.

3. See generally the important work of Dr. Emile Bruneau, an extraordinary neuroscientist who passed too soon. "Empathic failures are common in hostile intergroup contexts; repairing empathy is therefore a major focus of peacebuilding efforts. However, it is unclear which aspect of empathy is most relevant to intergroup conflict. Although trait empathic concern predicts prosociality in interpersonal settings, we hypothesized that the best predictor of meaningful *intergroup* attitudes and behaviors might not be the general capacity for empathy (i.e., trait empathy), but the difference in empathy felt for the ingroup versus the outgroup, or 'parochial empathy.' Specifically, we predicted that outgroup empathy would inhibit intergroup harm and promote intergroup helping, whereas in-group empathy would have the opposite effect. In three intergroup contexts—Americans regarding Arabs, Hungarians regarding refugees, Greeks regarding Germans—we found support for this hypothesis" (Bruneau and Saxe 2012; Bruneau, Cikara, and Saxe 2017; Cikara, Bruneau, and Saxe 2011).

4. By "neural plasticity," I am borrowing from Sharma, Class, and Cohen (2013): "the ability for the central nervous system to adapt in response to changes in the environment or lesions" (p. 3).

5. *Moral sense theory* assumes that ethical behavior is created by our emotions—our sentiments shape our moral cognitions about the world, then driving us toward behavior. Additionally, this pathway works in reverse: Ethical behavior is thus categorized by our moral cognitions, leading us to positive emotional responses. Notable historical founders of moral sense theory include Adam Smith, the Third Earl of Shaftesbury, and Francis Hutcheson, but the roots of this line of moral theory go back to antiquity (Frankena 1955).

6. *Virtue ethics* is the constant cultivation of an individual's character, or ethical "set point" of behavior. Part and parcel of this approach is an individual's prototype of "the virtuous person." In this school of ethics, each person is encouraged to act "as a virtuous person would" in a given moral dilemma. Furthermore, this school is also concerned with the questions: (1) What does being a "good person" really mean, and (2) What is the "good life"?

7. One example of this is the proliferation of "applied behavioral analysis" to empower parents, educators, and mental health professionals to work with neurodiverse individuals (e.g., autism spectrum; Yu, Li, Li, and Liang 2020). This is arguably the most culturally salient form of behavior modification, but it is also strengthening our moral

capacity to deal with the radical diversity of humans in their strengths, capacities, and unique challenges.

8. It should be noted, this influence is plastic in the neural sense of the term (Ressler and Maren 2019). This means that exposure to fear (in a distinctly Pavlovian sense) is distributed across brain structures, much as the entirety of a trampoline uncoils in response to the sudden weight of a child jumping at full force. Just as the trampoline "springs back," launching the child back into the air, the impact of fear on the brain impels behavior to (a) fight the fear stimulus, (b) run from the fear stimulus, (c) freeze in response (i.e., "play dead"), and / or (d) recruit social supporters to help one cope with the fear stimulus. This has been traced in individuals living with generalized anxiety and post-traumatic stress. Finally, though fear does ensconce the amygdala and other neural structures, this *can be reversed* (which, arguably, is a major thesis of this book). Individuals whose minds and brains are warped by totalitarianism, by a dependency on the fear of those in power, can be redeemed.

9. This conceptualization of the nature of childhood has been vociferously defended by many developmentalists (both expert and lay alike). See Maria Montessori's text *To Educate the Human Potential* (1947) for a deeper dive into the origins of positive developmentalism.

10. Also known as *act utilitarianism*: "an act is right if and only if it would have best consequences, that is, consequences at least as good as those of any alternative act open to the agent" (Hodgson 1967, p. 1).

11. Also known as *rule utilitarianism*: "an individual act should be considered to be morally right if it conforms to the correct moral rule applying to this type of situation—regardless of whether it is the act that will or will not yield the highest possible social utility of this particular occasion" (Hasanyi 1977, p. 32).

12. Taking this a level deeper, experiments demonstrate that compassion training impacts social behavior and neural structures *simultaneously* (Weng et al. 2013). This is a critical point for the entire thesis of this book. Strengthening neural pathways of compassion inside the psyche has a dramatic and practical effect simultaneously on social behavior. Therefore social change of society as a whole can result from incorporating Compassionate Reasoning training into private and public education at every stage of life.

13. Barker (2020) states:

> In one fMRI study, appropriately entitled "Putting Feelings into Words," participants viewed pictures of people with emotional facial expressions. Predictably, each participant's amygdala activated to the emotions in the picture. But when they were asked to name the emotion, the ventrolateral prefrontal cortex activated and reduced the emotional amygdala reactivity. In other words, consciously recognizing the emotions reduced their impact.
>
> Self-awareness, self-examination, is a fundamental aspect of increased self-control and also essential to the course of human development through Compassionate Reasoning. The more the mind articulated the emotions, the less the emotions of the amygdala, fear and impulsivity, controlled the mind (Korb 2015). Talk is good; debate is good; articulation of emotions is good. All of this happens as people work at self-examination and at shared rules.

14. In the next chapter we will extensively explore the idea of using the public health education model to rejuvenate compassion in society as a revolutionary method of lessening violence and building peace. This is pivotal to our line of argument for Compassionate Reasoning. Public health education has been successfully used with other pressing social problems, such as gun violence (Butts, Roman, Bostwick, and Porter 2015), but I will take it much deeper into compassion in the next chapter.

15. There is a rich literature describing the transformative power of perspective-taking on intrapersonal, interpersonal, and intergroup reconciliation—within experiments (Barth and Stürmer 2016) and naturalistic settings (Bilali and Vollhardt 2013).

16. Role play has also been used in classroom settings to help students troubleshoot situations involving (a) the outbreak of violence, (b) war games, (c) peacekeeping operations, and (d) reconciliation processes (Shaw 2004).

17. There is extensive research into the range of ways that we automatically identify with those with whom we have direct and intimate contact. Whether it be through mirror neurons or other automatic processes, it is increasingly clear that bringing people into close contact creates many involuntary forms of empathy. The more we watch and listen to others, the more powerful the ability to identify (Neumann and Westbury 2011). Even better, however, is conscious education in perspective-taking through in-depth and sophisticated methods of role-play and analysis of external and internal role-play reactions by all parties. Perspective taking is also accomplished by the study of ethics in philosophy and global cultures, by the study of world literature, through social psychological processes of compassion training, and through service work and personal and group guided reflection upon that service work, just to name a few.

18. The critical task of *envisioning* the world we want, *backcasting* the steps to get there, and *planning* strategic goals to meet this vision has been richly explored in the work of peace anthropologist Douglas P. Fry (2012).

19. The Omarska concentration camp was a site of horrific violence during the conflict (Blake 2002). The United Nations International Tribunal for the former Yugoslavia (ICTY 1995) estimated that thousands of people in Bosnia were abducted, brutally tortured, raped, or murdered. My class stood in the torture room at that camp.

20. In the clinical psychology literature, this is referred to as "secondary trauma" (Elwood, Mott, Lohr, and Galovski 2011). Secondary trauma, most typically, occurs when members of the healing professions (e.g., psychotherapists, counselors, teachers, first responders) are repeatedly exposed to trauma survivors, bearing witness to these survivors' tales of violence and conflict.

21. Epigenetics refers to the process by which our heritable phenotypes are altered by changes to our chromosome **without** changes to our DNA. Oftentimes, this occurs through behavior and socialization—especially in our earlier developmental stages. Singh-Taylor et al. (2018) note that this includes resilience-building mechanisms, including emotional regulation and self-modulation in response to highly stressful events. This trend likely extends to successfully coping from trauma as well. Hopefully, science will one day be able to demonstrate that when we act compassionately in social settings, our children (or other youngsters still in an early stage of development) internalize this behavior vis-à-vis modeling. Therefore, they are more likely

to replicate this behavior, leading to neurological changes, which further reinforces compassionate behavior and resilience.

22. Dr. Lamas was involved with my sister's case as she lay in the intensive care unit due to the pioneering and radical intervention with an ECMO machine in order to save her life. Lamas later recounted the story (Lamas 2014).

23. This is a reference to *tikkun olam*, repair of the world, a principle in Judaism that embodies ancient Jewish prophetic and rabbinic critiques of society when it is unjust, unkind, or violent. Society is in perpetual need of human beings to complete the work of creation of the world by fixing what is not right (Jacobs n.d.; Rose, Kaiser, and Klein 2008).

24. Pirke Avot 1:2 (Jewish Virtual Library n.d.).

25. This touches on the concept of *imitatio dei*, a concept found in many world religions stating that humankind has an ethical obligation to imitate, or embody, God and God's actions.

26. A brief history of correspondence and coherence theories of truth in the sciences may be found in Dawson and Gregory (2009).

27. We share the capacities of inference with many animal species, and we work in tandem with each other to infer more, as do many of our primeval ancestor species. The exact overlap of metacognitive abilities in humans and our most recent animal ancestors (i.e., chimpanzees/bonobos) is a question that has plagued comparative psychologists for quite some time (Smith, Beran, Couchman, and Coutinho 2008). It is also likely we (scientists) may not have the instruments to fully measure metacognition in other species (perhaps even in our own). This issue of measuring metacognition and reasoning is fundamentally plagued by the question: What exactly is reasoning? How much is reasoning a further discovery of truths and more sophisticated inferences, or is it a human form of communication and persuasion to what we already believe to be true? This is one approach to the argument about truth and knowledge in modern and postmodern thinking, and the difference between a "correspondence modern" and positivist theory versus "postmodern coherence" theories of truth. See, for example, *The Enigma of Reason* (Mercier and Sperber 2017). Wherever this debate goes, to the extent to which reasoning is a form of persuasion, this book is arguing that when combined with compassionate feelings and habits, reasoning steers human minds that think together with other minds *away* from violence and toward moral principles of shared society.

28. This critique has been enriched by contributions from identity researchers as well, including folks from the feminist and critical race theory camps. In some regards, anthropologists and sociologists heralded this critique decades ago (Harklau and Norwood 2005).

29. Over time a particular branch of a religion can completely rewrite the script of both the religion and the host society, all in search of aggressive and ultimately violent means of conquest. For example, in the United States, many religious scholars and practitioners have identified a strand of Christian theology called *Christian Dominionism*, seeking three primary goals: (1) Christian nationalism (e.g., the United States should be a Christian nation), (2) religious supremacy at the expense of other

religions, and (3) theocratic visions of law and politics (Aho 2012). But this is a contest, and by dismissing all conservatives as sharing this kind of religious supremacy we push more and more people into a corner of militancy for no rational reason and certainly with no compassionate consideration. Christian supremacy or white supremacy are neither kind nor rational. But lumping all conservatives into one camp to which they do not necessarily belong is also neither rational nor compassionate.

Chapter 4

1. Public health research and innovation has massively increased the average human lifespan across many, many cultural contexts (Pinker 2011a; Geertz 1989). It is beyond the scope of this book to cover adequately the profound changes that public health initiatives have yielded in recent centuries as they built upon the scientific revolution, the industrial revolution, and expansion of human rights. Contributions of health sciences include the innovations in practical mass applications of medicines, massive increase in habits of prevention and treatment, such as simply washing hands with soap regularly, and the *moral ethos* of public health agendas that champion the value of every human life in terms of all hospital, medical, and government policies. These contributions have driven other domains of social and political culture toward a greater valuation of the individual life, regardless of race, class, or religion. When a country invests in public health initiatives across the world, everyone lives longer than they used to, no matter who they are (Aísa, Clemente, and Pueyo 2014).

2. There are two key points here: the imperative values of (1) global *mental* health, and (2) global *moral* health. Regarding the first point, an estimated 70 percent of individuals across the world currently experience mental illness with no treatment from health care staff (Henderson, Evans-Lacko, and Thornicroft 2013). Imagine the world we could live in if we collectively chose to address mental health challenges with the same fervor as we have challenges such as sanitation and drinkable water? With regard to the second point, the challenge of a global *moral* health program is deeply rooted in the tendency for moral boundaries to only reach as far as our "imagined communities" (whether a local community, a clan, a country; Anderson 1983); the challenge is for us to expand our moral boundary to include all of humanity—one beloved community (Morone 1997).

3. For example, the *Human Security Report* (Mack 2005) offers the following hopeful statistics:

   - Since the early 1990s, we have experienced a 40 percent drop in armed conflict.
   - Outside of Rwanda and the former Yugoslavia, the number of genocides and politicides have dropped 80 percent.
   - The period since World War II has been the longest interval of uninterrupted peace between major world powers in hundreds of years.

4. While scanning the literature of fatalism vs. optimism for humanity's survival in the long term, Rifkin (2013), offers his best advice for empowering humanity to

live as long and happily as possible. He notes (at the end of fourteen detailed bullet points): "Plan in detail to quickly produce and administer vaccines and other medical interventions during a pandemic," seven years before COVID.

5. Kathy Marshall Emerson's (2015) review of the resilience literature contends that a "new fifth wave" of resilience research is on the horizon: a wave that accounts for our inner landscape, including spiritual and religious traditions, ethics and morality, and our relationship with ourselves.

6. My colleague Solon Simmons (2020) argues that narrative and power, when combined, are able to impel us toward transformative action.

7. Henceforth in this chapter I am highlighting multiple terms in italics that are from public health terminology as I apply them to Compassionate Reasoning.

Chapter 5

1. Although we note these are "false realities," we are quick to add that these realities *feel* real and *compel real behaviors*. As Berger and Luckman (1966) so presciently argued, from birth, humans undergo a reality-constructed process that is reinforced and reified throughout the home life, education system(s), and beyond. What we are arguing here is that a constructed social reality that is too unmoored from the facts-on-the-ground, and a constructed social reality that compels violence, is a grave threat that methods such as Compassionate Reasoning are designed to overcome.

2. "*Enlightenment is the human being's emergence from his self-incurred minority. Minority* is the inability to make use of one's own understanding without direction from another. This minority is *self-incurred* when its cause lies not in lack of understanding but in lack of resolution and courage to use it without direction from another. *Sapere aude!* Have courage to make use of your *own* understanding! is thus the motto of enlightenment . . . . For this enlightenment, however, nothing is required but *freedom*, and indeed the least harmful of anything that could even be called freedom: namely, freedom to make *public use* of one's reason in all matters" (Italics as in text; Kant [1784] 1996).

3. See our discussion on this in Chapter 3, as well as the work of Ressler and Maren (2019).

4. Heidi Ravven, private correspondence, 7/23/20.

5. Naomi Kraenbring, private manuscript commentary, 10/28/20.

6. This interpretation of Aristotle is complementary with theoretical developments within the realm of existential psychotherapy (see, for example, Georganda 2015). One of the basic tenets of existential psychotherapy contends that increasing our agency comes from deep self-reflection (aided and abetted by psychotherapy, of course). These assertions in agency-building are also congruent with our discussions on neural plasticity and epigenetics in previous chapters.

7. Respectfully Quoted: A Dictionary of Quotations, Bartleby.com, accessed November 3, 2020, https://www.bartleby.com/73/465.html.

8. Functional Magnetic Resonance Imaging (fMRI) is a technique used to examine when, where, and how we use our brain during various activities. The technology uses microscopic, benign forms of radiation (i.e., a "signal") to tell researchers when certain neural pathways are being used in participants (Center for Functional MRI 2020).

9. This concept can be traced back to the Samyutta Nikaya, Nidanasamyutta (*Nidānavagga* 12:95): "But that which is called 'mind' and 'mentality' and 'consciousness' arises as one thing and ceases as another by day and by night. Just as a monkey roaming through a forest grabs hold of one branch, lets that go and grabs another, then lets that go and grabs still another, so too that which is called 'mind' and 'mentality' and 'consciousness' arises as one thing and ceases as another by day and by night" (Bodhi 2000, p. 595). But note, in Footnote 157: "It should be noted that neither the sutta nor the commentary interprets the monkey simile here as saying that the untrained mind is as restless as a monkey; the point, rather, is that the mind is always dependent on an object" (771).

10. This is clearly a neo-Kantian emphasis which I am asserting here (Kant [1797] 1991; [1788] 2004; [1795] 2016). But one can also clearly see this in Aristotelian ethics and moral sense theory's emphasis on habit formation. My theory here of training can be framed either in terms of (a) habits and hardened pathways of the brain, or (b) the willful intention of the reasoning mind to act *in order to* create good habits.

11. These arguments have been explored in previous chapters in this text. Summarizing and integrating the contributions of Steven Pinker (2011a), Jonathan Haidt (2012), and Douglas Fry (2009), the emotional capacities for empathy, compassion, and perspectictive-taking are key factors shaping how, when, and why human beings have the potential for and are evolving toward less violence. These potential trends hold across cultural groups and have been replicated in experimental and naturalistic studies.

12. "On the in-breath, you breathe in whatever particular area, group of people, country, or even one particular person . . . maybe it's not this more global situation, maybe it's breathing in the physical discomfort and mental anguish of chemotherapy; of all the people who are undergoing chemotherapy. And if you've undergone chemotherapy and come out the other side, it's very real to you. Or maybe it's the pain of those who have lost loved ones; suddenly, or recently, unexpectedly or over a long period of time, some dying. But the in-breath is . . . you find some place on the planet in your personal life or something you know about, and you breathe in with the wish that those human beings or those mistreated animals or whoever it is, that they could be free of that suffering, and you breathe in with the longing to remove their suffering.

"And then you send out—just relax out . . . send enough space so that peoples' hearts and minds feel big enough to live with their discomfort, their fear, their anger or their despair, or their physical or mental anguish. But you can also breathe out for those who have no food and drink, you can breathe out food and drink. For those who are homeless, you can breathe out/send them shelter. For those who are suffering in any way, you can send out safety, comfort.

"So in the in-breath you breathe in with the wish to take away the suffering, and breathe out with the wish to send comfort and happiness to the same people, animals, nations, or whatever it is you decide.

"Do this for an individual, or do this for large areas, and if you do this with more than one subject in mind, that's fine . . . breathing in as fully as you can, radiating out as widely as you can" (Chödrön 2009).

13. Involuntary empathic distress can occur as a function of several precipitating factors including personality, prior exposure to trauma, social context, and quality/nature of relationships.

14. "It is unclear as to how much the pain matrix is involved in pain empathy. Some studies have found that when all neural components of the pain matrix are observed together, they are more related to one's reaction to the presence of stimuli than pain in particular. The ability to empathize with the pain of others seems to be correlated only to certain parts of the pain matrix rather than the matrix as a whole. Some have argued that only the affective components of the pain matrix, the anterior insula and the anterior cingulate cortex, are activated when it comes to pain empathy" (Hetu, Taschereau-Dumouchel, and Jackson 2012, p. 100).

15. Other resources for the elementary classroom include: Mindful Schools (https://www.mindfulschools.org/), Little Flower Yoga (https://www.littlefloweryoga.com/), Action for Healthy Kids (https://www.actionforhealthykids.org/activity/calm-down-corner/), Child Mind Institute (https://childmind.org/).

16. For an exhaustive and brilliant analysis of the relationship between sacred laws governing the use of the word and advanced conflict resolution practice, see Rabbi Dr. Howard Kaminsky, *Fundamentals of Jewish Conflict Resolution: Traditional Jewish Perspectives on Resolving Interpersonal Conflicts* (2017). Kaminsky's book is an ingenious paradigm for integration of conflict resolution theory, practice, and advanced hermeneutic analysis of major religions spanning thousands of years, a unique feat.

17. It bears noting, however, the "body first" view is one side of a long-standing and spirited debate in psychological sciences, beginning with the James-Lange theory of emotion (Cannon 1927), stating that our body is aroused from a particular stimuli, which our mind secondarily interprets—this leading to behavior and to affect change.

Chapter 6

1. https://worldhappiness.report/ed/2020.

References

Abas, Melanie, Tarryn Bowers, Ethel Manda, Sara Cooper, Debra Machando, Ruth Verhey, Neha Lamech, Ricardo Araya, and Dixon Chibanda. 2016. "'Opening Up the Mind': Problem-Solving Therapy Delivered by Female Lay Health Workers to Improve Access to Evidence-Based Care for Depression and Other Common Mental Disorders Through the Friendship Bench Project in Zimbabwe." *International Journal of Mental Health System* 10, no. 39. https://doi.org/10.1186/s13033-016-0071-9.

Aho, James. 2012. "Christian Heroism and the Reconstruction of America." *Critical Sociology* 39, no. 4: 545–560.

Aísa, Rosa, Jesús Clemente, and Fernando Pueyo. 2014. "The Influence of (Public) Health Expenditure on Longevity." *International Journal of Public Health* 59: 867–875.

Alimohammadi, Nasrollah, and Fariba Taleghani. 2015. "Health and Healthy Human Being in Islamic Thought: Reflection on Application for the Nursing Concept – A Philosophical Inquiry." *Journal of Education and Health Promotion* 4: 73.

Allport, Gordon. 1979. *The Nature of Prejudice, 25th Anniversary Edition*. New York: Perseus.

Amen, Daniel G., and Tana Amen. 2017. *The Brain Warrior's Way: Ignite Your Energy and Focus, Attack Illness and Aging, Transform Pain into Purpose*. New York: New American Library.

American Psychological Association. n.d. "Timeline of APA Policies & Actions Related to Detainee Welfare and Professional Ethics in the Context of Interrogation and National Security." https://www.apa.org/news/press/statements/interrogations#.

Anderson, Benedict. 1983. *Imagined Communities: Reflections on the Origin and Spread of Nationalism*. London: Verso.

Appiah, Kwame A. 2003. *Thinking It Through: An Introduction to Contemporary Philosophy*. Oxford: Oxford University Press.

Appiah, Kwame A. 2006. *Cosmopolitanism: Ethics in a World Full of Strangers*. New York, NY: W. W. Norton.

Appleby, R. Scott. 2000. *The Ambivalence of the Sacred: Religion, Violence, and Reconciliation*. Lanham, MD: Rowman & Littlefield.

Aristotle. 1999. *Nicomachean Ethics*. 2nd ed. Translated by Terence Irwin. Indianapolis: Hackett.

Au, Teresa M., Shannon Sauer-Zavala, Matthew W. King, Nicola Petrocchi, David H. Barlow, and Brett T. Litz. 2017. "Compassion-Based Therapy for Trauma-Related Shame and Posttraumatic Stress: Initial Evaluation Using a Multiple Baseline Design." *Behavior Therapy* 48, no. 2: 207–221.

Auais, Mohammad, Fadi Al-Zoubi, Alyssa Matheson, Kelcie Brown, Jay Magaziner, and Simon D. French. 2019. "Understanding the Role of Social Factors in Recovery after Hip Fractures: A Structured Scoping Review." *Health and Social Care in the Community* 27, no. 6: 1375–1387.

Averill, Lynnette A., Christopher L. Averill, Benjamin Kelmendi, Chadi G. Abdallah, and Steven M. Southwick. 2018. "Stress Response Modulation Underlying the Psychobiology of Resilience." *Current Psychiatry Reports* 20, no. 4: 27.

Avruch, Kevin. 1998. *Culture and Conflict Resolution*. Washington, DC: United States Institute of Peace Press.

Avruch, Kevin. 2012. *Context and Pretext in Conflict Resolution: Culture, Identity, Power and Practice*. Boulder, CO: Paradigm Publishers.

Avruch, Kevin, and Christopher Mitchell. 2013. *Conflict Resolution and Human Needs: Linking Theory and Practice*. New York: Routledge.

Bandura, Alfred. 1977. *Social Learning Theory*. Englewood Cliffs, NJ: Prentice Hall.

Bandura, Alfred. 1997. *Self-Efficacy: The Exercise of Control*. New York: W. H. Freeman.

Bar-Sela, Ariel, Hebbel E. Hoff, and Elias Faris. 1964. "Moses Maimonides' Two Treatises on the Regimen of Health: Fī Tadbīr al-Sihhah and Maqālah fi Bayān Baʾd al-Aʾrad wa-al-Jawāb ʿanhā." *Transactions of the American Philosophical Society* 54, no.4: 3–50.

Bar-Yam, Yaneer. 2018. *Dynamics of Complex Systems*. New York: Routledge.

Barker, Eric. 2020. "Ancient Wisdom Reveals 4 Rituals That Will Make You Happy." Ladders. https://www.theladders.com/career-advice/ancient-wisdom-reveals-4-rituals-that-will-make-you-happy-2/amp.

Baron, Robert S. 2005. "So Right It's Wrong: Groupthink and the Ubiquitous Nature of Polarized Group Decision Making." In *Advances in Experimental Social Psychology* 37: 219–253, edited by M. P. Zanna, Elsevier Academic Press.

Barth, Markus, and Stefan Stürmer. 2016. "Comparison of the Effects of Individual and Group-level Perspective Taking on Intergroup Reconciliation." *Social Psychology* 47, no. 6: 311–326.

Bastian, Adolf. [1860] 2016. *Der Mensch in der Geschichte*. Leipzig: Verlag Von Otto Wigand. Reprint, Norderstedt, Germany: Hansebooks.

BBC. 2020. "Sarajevo's Choir That Bridged the Ethnic Divide." https://www.bbc.com/news/av/stories-43472897/sarajevo-s-choir-that-bridged-the-ethnic-divide.

Bechtoldt, Myriam N., and Vanessa K. Schneider. 2016. "Predicting Stress From the Ability to Eavesdrop on Feelings: Emotional Intelligence and Testosterone Jointly Predict Cortisol Reactivity." *Emotion* 16, no. 2: 815–825.

Beck, Judith S. 2011. *Cognitive Behavior Therapy: Basics and Beyond*. New York: Guilford Press.

Beck, Richard, and Ephrem Fernandez. 1998. "Cognitive-Behavioral Therapy in the Treatment of Anger: A Meta-Analysis." *Cognitive Therapy and Research* 22, no. 1: 63–74.

Becker, Elizabeth. 1998. *When the War Was Over: Cambodia and the Khmer Rouge Revolution*. New York: PubicAffairs.

Benedek, Mathias, Tanja Könen, and Aljoscha C. Neubauer. 2012. "Associative Abilities Underlying Creativity." *Psychology of Aesthetics, Creativity, and the Arts* 6, no. 3: 273–281.

Bennett-Levy, James, and Richard Thwaites. 2007. "Self and Self-reflection in the Therapeutic Relationship." In *The Therapeutic Relationship in the Cognitive Behavioral Psychotherapies*, edited by Paul Gilbert and Robert L. Leahy, 255–281. London: Routledge.

Bentham, Jeremy. [1791] 2020. *Panopticon: or, the Inspection-House. Containing the Idea of a New Principle of Construction applicable to any Sort of Establishment, in which Persons of any Description are to be kept under Inspection. And in Particular to Penitentiary-Houses, Prisons, Houses of Industry, Work-Houses, Poor-Houses, Manufactories,*

Mad-Houses, Hospitals, and Schools. With a plan of management adapted to the principle. In a series of letters, Written in the Year 1787, From Crecheff in White Russia, to a friend in England. By Jeremy Bentham, of Lincoln's Inn, Esq. link.gale.com/apps/doc/CW0125793319/ECCO?u=viva_gmu&sid=ECCO&xid=44ed5bfc&pg=1.

Berger, Peter L., and Thomas Luckmann. 1966. *The Social Construction of Reality: A Treatise in the Sociology of Knowledge.* New York: Anchor Books.

Bilali, Rezarta, and Johanna Ray Vollhardt. 2013. "Priming Effects of a Reconciliation Radio Drama on Historical Perspective-taking in the Aftermath of Mass Violence in Rwanda." *Journal of Experimental Social Psychology* 49, no. 1: 144–151.

Black, David S., Randye J. Semple, Pallav Pokhrel, and Jerry L. Grenard. 2011. "Component Processes of Executive Function – Mindfulness, Self-control, and Working Memory – and Their Relationships with Mental and Behavioral Health." *Mindfulness* 2: 179–185.

Blackburn, Simon. 2016. *The Oxford Dictionary of Philosophy*, 3rd ed. Oxford: Oxford University Press.

Blair, R. J. R. 2013. "Considering Anger from a Cognitive Neuroscience Perspective." *Wiley Interdisciplinary Review of Cognitive Science* 3, no. 1: 65–74.

Blake, Felix. 2002. "Nusreta Survived the Rape Camp, But Her Torture Is Unending." *Independent.* https://www.independent.co.uk/news/world/europe/nusreta-survived-the-rape-camp-but-her-torture-is-unending-128934.html.

"Blueprint for a Healthy Community." 1994. Washington, DC: Association of County Health Officials.

Bluth, Karen, Patricia N. E. Roberson, Susan A. Gaylord, Keturah R. Faurot, Karen M. Grewen, Samantha Arzon, and Susan S. Girdler. 2015. "Does Self-compassion Protect Adolescents from Stress?" *Journal of Child and Family Studies* 25, no. 4: 1098–1109.

Bodhi, Bhikkhu. 2000. *The Connected Discourses of the Buddha: A Translation of the Saṃyutta Nikāya.* Somerville, MA: Wisdom Publications.

Bonanno, George A., Maren Westphal, and Anthony D. Mancini. 2011. "Resilience to Loss and Potential Trauma." *Annual Review of Clinical Psychology* 7: 511–535.

Bouie, Jamelle. 2018. "The Enlightenment's Dark Side." https://slate.com/news-and-politics/2018/06/taking-the-enlightenment-seriously-requires-talking-about-race.html.

Breines, Juliana G., and Serena Chen. 2012. "Self-compassion Increases Self-improvement Motivation." *Personality and Social Psychology Bulletin* 9, no. 38: 1133–1143.

Breithaupt, Fritz. 2019. *The Dark Sides of Empathy.* Ithaca, NY: Cornell University Press.

Briscoe, Erica, and Jacob Feldman. 2011. "Conceptual Complexity and the Bias/Variance Tradeoff." *Cognition* 118, no. 1: 2–16.

Brown, Candy Gunther. 2012. *Testing Prayer: Science and Healing.* Cambridge, MA: Harvard University Press.

Bruneau, Emile G., Mina Cikara, and Rebecca Saxe. 2017. "Parochial Empathy Predicts Reduced Altruism and the Endorsement of Passive Harm." *Social Psychological and Personality Science* 8, no. 8: 934–942.

Bruneau, Emile G., and Rebecca Saxe. 2012. "The Power of Being Heard: The Benefits of 'Perspective-giving' in the Context of Intergroup Conflict." *Journal of Experimental Social Psychology* 48, no. 4: 855–866.

Buber, Martin. [1947] 2002. *Between Man and Man.* New York: Routledge Classics.

Burgess, Adam, and Mitsutoshi Horii. 2012. "Risk, Ritual and Health Responsibilisation: Japan's 'Safety Blanket' of Surgical Face Mask-wearing." *Sociology of Health & Illness* 34, no. 8: 1184–1198.

Burton, David. 2010. "Curing Diseases of Belief and Desire: Buddhist Philosophical Therapy." *Royal Institute of Philosophy Supplement* 66: 187–217.

Burton, John W. 1979. *Deviance, Terrorism and War: The Process of Solving Unsolved Social and Political Problems*. Canberra, Australia: Australian National University Press.

Bushman, Brad J. 2017. "How Violence Spreads Like a Contagious Disease." *Psychology Today*. https://www.psychologytoday.com/us/blog/get-psyched/201705/how-violence-spreads-contagious-disease.

Butts, Jeffrey A., Caterina Gouvis Roman, Lindsay Bostwick, and Jeremy R. Porter. 2015. "Cure Violence: A Public Health Model to Reduce Gun Violence." *Annual Review of Public Health* 36: 39–53.

Cannon, Walter B. 1927. "The James-Lange Theory of Emotions: A Critical Examination and Alternative Theory." *The American Journal of Psychology* 39: 106–124.

Carr, Jesse. 2016. "The Lawlessness of Law: Lynching and Anti-Lynching in the Contemporary USA." *Settler Colonial Studies* 6, no. 2: 153–163.

Carrington, Damian. 2017. "Earth's Sixth Mass Extinction Event Underway, Scientists Warn." https://www.theguardian.com/environment/2017/jul/10/earths-sixth-mass-extinction-event-already-underway-scientists-warn.

Carter, Jimmy. 2015. *A Full Life: Reflections at Ninety*. New York: Simon & Schuster.

Carter, Jimmy. 2018. *Faith: A Journey for All*. New York: Simon & Schuster.

Cassirer, Ernst. 1945. *Rousseau-Kant-Goethe*. Princeton NJ: Princeton University Press.

Cavallar, Georg. 2014. "Sources of Kant's Cosmopolitanism: Basedow, Rousseau, and Cosmopolitan Education." *Studies in the Philosophy of Education* 33: 369–389.

Centre for Bhutan Studies & GNH Research. 2016. "A Compass Towards a Just and Harmonious Society: 2015 GNH Survey Report." http://www.gross-nationalhappiness.com/wp-content/uploads/2017/01/Final-GNH-Report-jp-21.3.17-ilovepdf-compressed.pdf.

Center for Functional MRI. 2020. "What Is fMRI? Imaging Brain Activity." UC San Diego. https://cfmriweb.ucsd.edu/Research/whatisfmri.html.

Center for World Religions, Diplomacy, and Conflict Resolution. 2021. "Study Abroad Courses." https://crdc.gmu.edu/studyabroad.

Center for World Religions, Diplomacy, and Conflict Resolution. 2021. "Syria Program." https://crdc.gmu.edu/syria-program.

Chartrand, Tanya L., and Jessica L. Lakin. 2013. "The Antecedents and Consequences of Human Behavioral Mimicry." *Annual Review of Psychology* 65: 285–308.

Chase, Alston. 2003. *Harvard and the Unabomber: The Education of an American Terrorist*. New York: W.W. Norton.

Cheldelin, Sandra, Daniel Druckman, and Larissa Fast, eds. 2003. *Conflict: From Analysis to Intervention*. London: Continuum.

Chialant, Doriana, Judith Edersheim, and Bruce H. Price. 2016. "The Dialectic Between Empathy and Violence: An Opportunity for Intervention?" *The Journal of Neuropsychiatry and Clinical Neurosciences* 28, no. 4: 273–285.

Chödrön, Pema. "Tonglen Meditation." Omega Institute for Holistic Studies. https://www.youtube.com/watch?v=QwqlurCvXuM.

Cikara, Mina, Emile G. Bruneau, and Rebecca R. Saxe. 2011. "Us and Them: Intergroup Failures of Empathy." *Current Directions in Psychological Science* 20, no. 3: 149–153.

Clarke, Katherine M. 2018. "Benching Playground Loneliness: Exploring the Meanings of the Playground Buddy Bench." *International Electronic Journal of Elementary Education* 11, no. 1: 9–21.

Cobb, Sara. 2013. *Speaking of Violence: The Politics and Poetics of Narrative in Conflict.* Oxford: Oxford University Press.

Cobb, Sara, Sarah Federman, and Alison Castel, eds. 2020. *Introduction to Conflict Resolution: Discourses and Dynamics.* London: Rowman & Littlefield.

Cohen, Hermann. [1919] 1995. *Religion of Reason: Out of the Sources of Judaism.* Translated by Simon Kaplan. Atlanta: Scholars Press.

Coleman, Peter T., Morton Deutsch, and Eric C. Marcus, eds. 2014. *The Handbook of Conflict Resolution: Theory and Practice, Third edition.* San Francisco: Jossey-Bass.

Condon, Paul, and John Makransky. 2020. "Sustainable Compassion Training: Integrating Meditation Theory with Psychological Science." *Frontiers in Psychology* 11: 2249.

Confucius. [n.d.] 2014. *Confucian Analects: The Great Learning & The Doctrine of the Mean.* Translated by James Legge. New York: Dover Publications.

Cosley, Brandon J., Shannon K. McCoy, Laura R. Saslow, and Elissa S. Epel, 2010. "Is Compassion for Others Stress Buffering? Consequences of Compassion and Social Support for Psychological Reactivity to Stress." *Journal of Experimental Social Psychology* 46, no. 5: 816–823.

Criss, Doug. 2016. "Stephen Hawking says we've got about 1,000 years to find a new place to live." CNN Health. https://www.cnn.com/2016/11/17/health/hawking-humanity-trnd/index.html.

Cross, Tim. 2009. *The Ideologies of Japanese Tea: Subjectivity, Transience & National Identity.* Kent, UK: Global Oriental.

da Cunha-Bang, Sofi, Patrick M. Fisher, Liv Vadskjær Hjordt, Erik Perfalk, Anine Persson Skibsted, Camilla Bock, Anders Ohlhues Baandrup, Marie Deen, Carsten Thomsen, Dorte M. Sestoft, and Gitte M. Knudsen. 2017. "Violent Offenders Respond to Provocations with High Amygdala and Striatal Reactivity." *Social Cognitive and Affective Neuroscience* 12, no. 5: 802–810.

Dalai Lama. 2000. *Transforming the Mind: Eight Verses on Generating Compassion and Transforming Your Life,* Rochester, VT: Thorsons.

Dalai Lama. 2020. "Compassion and the Individual." https://www.dalailama.com/messages/compassion-and-human-values/compassion.

David-Ferdon, Corinne, and Simon, Thomas R. 2014. *Preventing Youth Violence: Opportunities for Action.* Atlanta, GA: Centers for Disease Control and Prevention, National Center for Injury Prevention and Control, Division of Violence Prevention. https://www.cdc.gov/violenceprevention/youthviolence/pdf/opportunities-for-action.pdf.

Dawson, Neal V., and Fredrick Gregory. 2009. "Correspondence and Coherence in Science: A Brief Historical Perspective." *Judgment and Decision Making* 4, no. 2: 126–133.

De Keersmaecker, Jonas, Dries H. Bostyn, Johnny R. J. Fontaine, Alain Van Hiel, and Arne Roets. 2018. "Toward an Integrated Cognition Perspective on Ethnic Prejudice: An Investigation into the Role of Intelligence and Need for Cognitive Closure." *Social Psychological and Personality Science* 9, no. 6: 719–726.

De Neve, Jan-Emmanuel, and Jeffrey D. Sachs. 2020. "Sustainable Development and Human Well-Being." In *World Happiness Report,* edited by John F. Helliwell, Richard Layard, Jeffrey D. Sachs, and Jan-Emmanuel De Neve. New York: Sustainable Development Solutions Network.

de Waal, Frans. 2019. *Mama's Last Hug: Animal Emotions and What They Tell Us about Ourselves.* New York: W. W. Norton.

Derbyshire, Stuart W. G., Jody Osborn, and Steven Brown. 2013. "Feeling the Pain of Others Is Associated with Self-Other Confusion and Prior Pain Experience." *Frontiers in Human Neuroscience* 7: 470.

Diamond, Jared. 2004. *Collapse: How Societies Choose to Fail or Succeed*. New York: Penguin Books.

Diamond, Jared. 2017. *Guns, Germs, and Steel: The Fates of Human Societies*. New York: Morton & Co.

Diamond, Jared. 2019. *Upheaval: Turning Points for Nations in Crisis*. New York: Little, Brown & Company.

Docker, John. 2008. *The Origins of Violence: Religion, History, Genocide*. London: Pluto Press.

Douglas, Karen M., Robbie M. Sutton, and Aleksandra Cichocka. 2017. "The Psychology of Conspiracy Theories." *Current Directions in Psychological Science* 26, no. 6: 538–542.

Dubensky, Joyce S. 2016. *Peacemakers in Action, Volume II: Profiles in Religious Peacebuilding*. Cambridge, UK: Cambridge University Press.

Dunne, Sara, David Sheffield, and Joseph Chilcot. 2018. "Brief Report: Self-compassion, Physical Health and the Mediating Role of Health-promoting Behaviours." *Journal of Health Psychology* 23, no. 7: 993–999.

Editors of Encyclopaedia Britannica. 2020. "Reason." https://www.britannica.com/topic/reason.

Einstein, Albert, and Sigmund Freud. [1932] 2016. "Why War? An Exchange of Letters Between Freud and Einstein." In *Freud and War*, edited by Marlène Belilos. London: Karnac.

Eisler, Riane, and Douglas P. Fry. 2019. *Nurturing Our Humanity: How Domination and Partnership Shape Our Brains, Lives, and Future*. Oxford: Oxford University Press.

Elwood, Lisa S., Juliette Mott, Jeffrey M. Lohr, and Tara E. Galovski. 2011. "Secondary Trauma Symptoms in Clinicians: A Critical Review of the Construct, Specificity, and Implications for Trauma-focused Treatment." *Clinical Psychology Review* 31, no. 1: 25–36.

Erikson, Erik. 1969. *Gandhi's Truth: On the Origins of Militant Nonviolence*. New York: W. W. Norton.

Festinger, Leon. 1957. *A Theory of Cognitive Dissonance*. Evanston, IL: Row, Peterson & Co.

Fletcher, Faith E., Nicholas R. Sherwood, Whitney S. Rice, Ibrahim Yigit, Shericia N. Ross, Tracey E. Wilson, Sheri D. Weiser, Mallory O. Johnson, Mirjam-Colette Kempf, Deborah Konkle-Parker, Gina Wingood, Janet M. Turan, and Bulent Turan. 2020. "Resilience and HIV Treatment Outcomes Among Minority Women Living with HIV in the U.S.: A Mixed-Methods Analysis." *AIDS Patient Care STDS* 34, no. 8: 356–366.

Ford, David F. 2020. "Broader, Deeper, Further: Engaging with Religions in the Twenty-First Century." The 2014 Bevir Lecture, Eton College. https://www.interfaith.cam.ac.uk/resources/lecturespapersandspeeches/the-2014-bevir-lecture-eton-college-broader-deeper-further-engaging-with-religions-in-the-twenty-first-century.

Forde, Steven. 1998. "Hugo Grotius on Ethics and War." *The American Political Science Review* 92, no. 3: 639–648.

Foroughi, Cyrus K., Samual S. Monfort, Martin Paczynski, Patrick E. McKnight, and P. M. Greenwood. 2016. "Placebo Effects in Cognitive Training." *PNAS* 113, no. 27: 7470–7474.

Forushani, Nasrin Z., and Mohammad A. Besharat. 2011. "Relation Between Emotional Intelligence and Perceived Stress Among Female Students." *Procedia – Social and Behavioral Sciences* 30: 1109–1112.

Fox, Andrew S., and Alexander J. Shackman. 2019. "The Central Extended Amygdala in Fear and Anxiety: Closing the Gap Between Mechanistic and Neuroimaging Research." *Neuroscience Letters* 693: 58–67.

Frankena, William. 1955. "Hutcheson's Moral Sense Theory." *Journal of the History of Ideas*, 16, no. 3: 356–375.

Frankl, Viktor. 1955 1986. *The Doctor and the Soul*. New York: Random House.

Frankl, Viktor. 1959 2006. *Man's Search for Meaning*. Boston: Beacon Press.

Frankl, Viktor. 1967. *Psychotherapy and Existentialism: Selected Papers on Logotherapy*. New York: Simon & Schuster.

Frankl, Viktor. 1969. *The Will to Meaning: Foundations and Applications of Logotherapy*. New York: World Publishing Company.

Friedman, Hershey H., and Miriam Gerstein. 2017. "Leading with Compassion: The Key to Changing the Organizational Culture and Achieving Success." *Psychosociological Issues in Human Resource Management* 5, no. 1: 160–175.

Fry, Douglas P. 2009. *Beyond War: The Human Potential for Peace*. Oxford: Oxford University Press.

Fry, Douglas P. 2012. "Life Without War." *Science* 336, no. 6083: 879–884.

Gat, Azar. 2013. "Is War Declining – and Why?" *Journal of Peace Research* 50, no. 2: 149–157.

Gault, Barbara A., and John Sabini. 2000. "The Roles of Empathy, Anger, and Gender in Predicting Attitudes Toward Punitive, Reparative, and Preventative Public Policies." *Cognition and Emotion* 14, no. 4: 495–520.

Geertz, Clifford. 1989. *Margaret Mead 1901–1978: A Biographical Memoir*. Washington, DC: National Academy of Sciences. http://www.nasonline.org/publications/biographical-memoirs/memoir-pdfs/mead-margaret.pdf.

Georganda, Evgenia. 2015. "Throwness, Freedom, and the Will for Authenticity: An Existential/Developmental Approach to Psychotherapy." *Existential Analysis* 27, no. 2: 261–276.

George, Steve, and Manveena Suri. 2018. "Rape Cases Spark Political Protest Movement in India." CNN World. https://www.cnn.com/2018/04/16/asia/india-rape-bjp-protests-intl/index.html.

Gilbert, Paul. 2010. *Compassion Focused Therapy*. New York: Routledge.

Gill, Michael B. 2016. "Lord Shaftesbury [Anthony Ashley Cooper, 3rd Earl of Shaftesbury]." *Stanford Encyclopedia of Philosophy*. https://plato.stanford.edu/entries/shaftesbury/#VirtHappReasMora.

Gladwell, Malcolm. 2002. *The Tipping Point: How Little Things Can Make a Big Difference*. Boston: Little, Brown & Company.

Global Ethic Foundation. 2021. "Declaration Toward a Global Ethic." https://www.global-ethic.org/declaration-toward-a-global-ethic.

Goldsteen, Raymond L., Karen Goldsteen, and Terry L. Dwelle. 2015. *Introduction to Public Health: Promises and Practices*. 2nd ed. New York: Springer.

Goodall, Jane. [1971] 2000. *In the Shadow of Man*. New York: Mariner Books.

Gopin, Marc. 2000. *Between Eden and Armageddon: The Future of World Religions, Violence, and Peacemaking*, Oxford: Oxford University Press.

Gopin, Marc. 2002. *Holy War, Holy Peace: How Religion Can Bring Peace to the Middle East*. Oxford: Oxford University Press.

Gopin, Marc. 2009. *To Make the Earth Whole: Citizen Diplomacy in an Age of Religious Militancy*. Lanham, MD: Rowman & Littlefield.

Gopin, Marc. 2012. *Bridges Across an Impossible Divide: The Inner Lives of Arab and Jewish Peacemakers*. Oxford: Oxford University Press.

Gopin, Marc. 2015. "Peace Steps: One Rabbi's Life Journey into the Heart of His Enemies." TEDx. https://www.youtube.com/watch?v=LMaaWYOckjE.

Gopin, Marc. 2016. *Healing the Heart of Conflict: Eight Crucial Steps to Making Peace with Yourself and with Others*. North Charleston, SC: CreateSpace Independent Publishing Platform.

Gopin, Marc. 2017. *Compassionate Judaism: The Life and Thought of Samuel David Luzzatto*. North Charleston, SC: CreateSpace Independent Publishing Platform.

Goriounova, Natalia A., and Huibert D. Mansvelder. 2019. "Genes, Cells and Brain Areas of Intelligence." *Frontiers in Human Neuroscience* 13, no. 44: 1–14.

Granovetter, Mark. 1976. "Network Sampling: Some First Steps." *American Journal of Sociology* 81, no. 6: 1287–1303.

Granovetter, Mark. 1978. "Threshold Models of Collective Behavior." *American Journal of Sociology* 83, no. 6: 1420–1443.

Griffin, Jr., Andrew A., Paul Caldarella, Christian V. Sabey, and Melissa A. Heath. 2017. "The Effects of a Buddy Bench on Elementary Students' Solitary Behavior During Recess." *International Electronic Journal of Elementary Education* 10, no. 1: 27–36.

Groër, Maureen, Mary W. Meagher, and Kathleen Kendall-Tackett. 2010. "An overview of stress and immunity." In *The Psychoneuroimmunology of Chronic Disease: Exploring the Links Between Inflammation, Stress, and Illness*, edited by Kathleen Kendall-Tackett, 9–22. Washington, DC: American Psychological Association.

Grusec, Joan E. 2011. "Socialization Processes in the Family: Social and Emotional Development." *Annual Review of Psychology* 62: 243–269.

Gurr, Ted Robert. 2000. "Ethnic Warfare on the Wane." *Foreign Affairs* 79, no. 3: 52–65.

Haan, Norma, Richard Weiss, and Vicky Johnson. 1982. "The Role of Logic in Moral Reasoning and Development." *Developmental Psychology* 18, no. 2: 245–256.

Haidt, Jonathan. 2007. "The New Synthesis in Moral Psychology." *Science* 316, no. 5827: 998–1002.

Haidt, Jonathan. 2012. *The Righteous Mind: Why Good People Are Divided by Politics and Religion*. New York: Random House.

Harklau, Linda, and Rachel Norwood. 2005. "Negotiating Researcher Roles in Ethnographic Program Evaluation: A Postmodern Lens." *Anthropology & Education Quarterly* 36, no. 3: 278–288.

Harmon-Jones, Eddie, ed. 2019. *Cognitive Dissonance: Reexamining a Pivotal Theory in Psychology*. Washington, DC: American Psychological Association.

Harrison, Giulietta, and Azwihangwisi Muthivhi. 2013. "Mediating Self-regulation in Kindergarten Classrooms: An Exploratory Case Study of Early Childhood Education in South Africa." *Journal of Education* 57: 79–101.

Harsanyi, John C. 1977. "Rule Utilitarianism and Decision Theory." *Erkenntnis* 11: 253.

Hatfield, Elaine, Lisamarie Bensman, Paul D. Thornton, and Richard L. Rapson. 2014. "New Perspectives on Emotional Contagion: A Review of Classic and Recent Research on Facial Mimicry and Contagion." *Interpersona: An International Journal on Personal Relationships* 8, no. 2: 159–179.

Hatfield, Elaine, John T. Cacioppo, and Richard L. Rapson. 1993. "Emotional Contagion." *Current Directions in Psychological Science* 2, no. 3: 96–99.

Heatherton, Todd F., and Dylan D. Wagner. 2011. "Cognitive Neuroscience of Self-Regulation Failure." *Trends in Cognitive Sciences* 15, no. 3: 132–139.

Henderson, Claire, Sara Evans-Lacko, and Graham Thornicroft. 2013. "Mental Illness Stigma, Help Seeking, and Public Health Programs." *American Journal of Public Health* 103, no. 5: 777–780.

Herman, Judith. 2015. *Trauma and Recovery*. New York: Basic Books.

Hétu, Sébastien, Vincent Taschereau-Dumouchel, and Philip L. Jackson. 2012. "Stimulating the Brain to Study Social Interactions and Empathy." *Brain Stimulation* 5, no. 2: 95–102.

Hodgson, D. H. 1967. *Consequences of Utilitarianism*. Oxford, UK: Clarendon Press.

Hoffman, David H., Danielle J. Carter, Cara R. Viglucci Lopez, Heather L. Benzmiller, Ava X. Guo, S. Yasir Latifi, and Daniel C. Craig. 2015. *Report to the Special Committee of the Board of Directors of the American Psychological Association: Independent Review Relating to APA Ethics Guidelines, National Security Interrogations, and Torture*. Chicago: Sidley Austin.

Hublin, Jean-Jacques. 2009. "The Prehistory of Compassion." *PNAS* 106, no. 16: 6429–6430.

Human Security Report Project. 2014. *Human Security Report 2013: The Decline in Global Violence: Evidence, Explanation, and Contestation*. Vancouver: Human Security Press.

Hume, David, [n.d.] 2003. *A Treatise of Human Nature*. Project Gutenberg. http://www.gutenberg.org/ebooks/4705.

Hunter, Tiffany J. 2008. "Creating a Culture of Peace in the Elementary Classroom." *The Journal of Adventist Education* 70, no. 3: 20–25.

Hutcheson, Francis. [1728] 2002. *An Essay on the Nature and Conduct of the Passions and Affections, with Illustrations on the Moral Sense*, edited by Aaron Garrett. Indianapolis: Liberty Fund.

Immordino-Yang, Mary Helen, and Vanessa Singh. 2013. "Hippocampal Contributions to the Processing of Social Emotions." *Human Brain Mapping* 34, no. 4: 945–955.

Institute of Medicine. 1988. *The Future of Public Health*. Washington, DC: National Academies Press.

Irvin-Erickson, Doug. 2017. *Raphaël Lemkin and the Concept of Genocide*. Philadelphia: University of Pennsylvania Press.

Jacobs, Jill. June 7, 2007. "The History of 'Tikkun Olam.'" http://www.zeek.net/706tohu.

Janis, Irving L. 1972. *Victims of Groupthink: A Psychological Study of Foreign-policy Decisions and Fiascoes*. Boston: Houghton Mifflin.

Jarvis, Christine, and Patricia Gouthro. 2019. *Professional Education with Fiction Media: Imagination for Engagement and Empathy in Learning*. Cham, Switzerland: Springer.

Jewish Virtual Library. n.d. "Jewish Practices & Rituals: Gemilut Hasadim." https://www.jewishvirtuallibrary.org/gemilut-hasadim.

Jiang, Huaibin, Gui Chen, and Ting Wang. 2017. "Relationship Between Belief in a Just World and Internet Altruistic Behavior in a Sample of Chinese Undergraduates: Multiple Mediating Roles of Gratitude and Self-esteem." *Personality and Individual Differences* 104: 493–498.

Joffé, Roland, director. 1984. *The Killing Fields*. DVD. London: Goldcrest Films.

Johnston, Douglas, and Cynthia Sampson, eds. 1994. *Religion, the Missing Dimension of Statecraft*. Oxford: Oxford University Press.

Jollant, F., A. Malafosse, R. Docto, and C. Macdonald. 2014. "A Pocket of Very High Suicide Rates in a Non-violent, Egalitarian and Cooperative Population of South-East Asia." *Psychological Medicine* 44: 2323–2329.

Jolliffe, Darrick, and David P. Farrington. 2006. "Examining the Relationship Between Low Empathy and Bullying." *Aggressive Behavior* 32: 540–550.

Jones, Robert P. 2008. *Progressive & Religious: How Christian, Jewish, Muslim, and Buddhist Leaders are Moving Beyond the Culture Wars and Transforming American Public Life*. Lanham, MD: Rowman & Littlefield.

Jordan, Jillian J., David G. Rand, Samuel Arbesman, James H. Fowler, and Nicholas A. Christakis. 2013. "Contagion of Cooperation in Static and Fluid Social Networks." *PLoS One* 8, no. 6: e66199.

Juran, Joseph M. 1974. *Quality Control Handbook*. 3rd ed. New York: McGraw-Hill.

Kaminsky, Harold. 2017. *Fundamentals of Jewish Conflict Resolution: Traditional Jewish Perspectives on Resolving Interpersonal Conflicts*. Brighton, MA: Academic Studies Press.

Kant, Immanuel. [1784] 1996. *Practical Philosophy*. Translated and edited by Mary J. Gregor. Cambridge, UK: Cambridge University Press.

Kant, Immanuel. [1788] 2004. *The Critique of Practical Reason*. Translated by Thomas Kihngsmill Abbott. Project Gutenberg. http://www.gutenberg.org/ebooks/5683.

Kant, Immanuel. [1795] 2016. *Perpetual Peace: A Philosophical Essay*. London: George Allen & Unwin Ltd. https://www.gutenberg.org/files/50922/50922-h/50922-h.htm.

Kant, Immanuel. [1797] 1991. *The Metaphysics of Morals*. Translated by Mary J. Gregor. Cambridge, UK: Cambridge University Press.

Kant, Immanuel, and Mary Gregor. 1999. *Practical Philosophy*. Cambridge, UK: Cambridge University Press.

Kao, Katie, Charu T. Tuladhar, and Amanda R. Tarullo. 2020. "Parental and Family-Level Sociocontextual Correlates of Emergent Emotion Regulation: Implications for Early Social Competence." *Journal of Child and Family Studies* 29: 1630–1641.

Kellner, Alan J. 2019. "States of Nature in Immanuel Kant's Doctrine of Right." *Political Research Quarterly* 73, no. 3: 727–739.

Kelly, Janice R., Nicole E. Iannone, and Megan K. McCarty. 2016. "Emotional Contagion of Anger Is Automatic: An Evolutionary Explanation." *British Journal of Social Psychology* 55, no. 1: 182–191.

Kelman, Herbert C., and Ronald J. Fisher, eds. 2016. *Herbert C. Kelman: A Pioneer in the Social Psychology of Conflict Analysis and Resolution*. Cham, Switzerland: Springer.

Kille, D. Andrew. 2005. "More Reel than Real: Mel Gibson's *The Passion of the Christ*." *Pastoral Psychology* 53, no. 4: 341–350.

Kirby, James N. 2017. "Compassion Interventions: The Programmes, the Evidence, and Implications for Research and Practice." *Psychology and Psychotherapy: Theory, Research and Practice* 90, no. 3: 432–455.

Klein, Nadav, and Nicholas Epley. 2016. "Maybe Holier, But Definitely Less Evil, Than You: Bounded Self-Righteousness in Social Judgment." *Journal of Personality and Social Psychology* 110, no. 5: 660–674.

Klimecki, Olga M. 2012. Empathy and Compassion in Society Conference. https://www.youtube.com/watch?v=GxH-Oiqz-14.

Klimecki, Olga M. 2019. "The Role of Empathy and Compassion in Conflict Resolution." *Emotion Review* 11, no. 4: 310–325.

Klimecki, Olga M. 2020. "Curriculum Vitae." https://olgaklimecki.files.wordpress.com/2020/06/cv_klimecki_200608.pdf.

Klimecki, Olga M., Susanne Leiberg, Claus Lamm, and Tania Singer. 2013. "Functional Neural Plasticity and Associated Changes in Positive Affect After Compassion Training." *Cerebral Cortex* 23, no. 7: 1552–1561.

Koestler, Arthur. 1964. *The Act of Creation*. New York: Macmillan.

Koestler, Arthur. 1978. *Janus: A Summing Up*. New York: Random House.

Korb, Alex. 2015. *The Upward Spiral: Using Neuroscience to Reverse the Course of Depression, One Small Change at a Time*. Oakland, CA: New Harbinger.

Korostelina, Karina. 2007. *Social Identity and Conflict: Structure, Dynamics, and Implications*. London: Palgrave Macmillan.

Kossowska, Małgorzata, Paulina Szwed, Miroslaw Wyczesany, Gabriela Czarnek, and Eligiusz Wronka. 2018. "Religious Fundamentalism Modulates Neural Responses to Error-Related Words: The Role of Motivation Toward Closure." *Frontiers in Psychology* 9, no. 285: 1–9.

Kriesberg, Louis, and Bruce W. Dayton. 2017. *Constructive Conflicts: From Escalation to Resolution*. 5th ed. Lanham, MD: Rowman & Littlefield.

Kuang, Beibei, Shenli Peng, Xiaochun Xie, and Ping Hu. 2019. "Universality vs. Cultural Specificity in the Relations Among Emotional Contagion, Emotion Regulation, and Mood State: An Emotional Process Perspective." *Frontiers in Psychology* 10: 186.

Ladd, Peter D. 2018. *The Talk Therapy Revolution: Neuroscience, Phenomenology, and Mental Health*. Lanham, MD: Lexington Books.

Lakoff, George, and Mark Johnson. 1980. *Metaphors We Live By*. Chicago: University of Chicago Press.

Lally, Phillippa, Cornelia H. M. van Jaarsveld, Henry W. W. Potts, and Jane Wardle. 2010. "How Are Habits Formed: Modelling Habit Formation in the Real World." *European Journal of Social Psychology* 40: 998–1009.

Lamas, Daniela. 2014. "My New Iron Lung." *The New Yorker*. https://www.newyorker.com/tech/annals-of-technology/my-new-iron-lung.

Lange, Iris, Liesbet Goossens, Stijn Michielse, Jindra Bakker, Bram Vervliet, Machteld Marcelis, Marieke Wichers, Jim van Os, Therese van Amelsvoort, and Koen Schruers. 2020. "Neural Responses During Extinction Learning Predict Exposure Therapy Outcome in Phobia: Results from a Randomized-Controlled Trial." *Neuropsychopharmacology* 45, no. 3: 534–541.

Lanzoni, Susan. 2018. *Empathy: A History*. New Haven, CT: Yale University Press.

Lederach, John Paul. 1996. *Preparing for Peace: Conflict Transformation Across Cultures*. Syracuse, NY: Syracuse University Press.

Lederach, John Paul. 2003. *The Little Book of Conflict Transformation*. New York: Good Books.

Lederach, John Paul. 2005. *The Moral Imagination: The Art and Soul of Building Peace*. Oxford: Oxford University Press.

Levenson, Robert W. 2019. "Stress and Illness: A Role for Specific Emotions." *Psychosomatic Medicine* 81, no. 8: 720–730.

Little, David, ed. 2007. *Peacemakers in Action: Profiles of Religion in Conflict Resolution*. Cambridge, UK: Cambridge University Press.

Livingstone, Bob. n.d. "Is Hating Someone Because They Are Different a Mental Illness?" MentalHelp.net. https://www.mentalhelp.net/blogs/is-hating-someone-because-they-are-different-a-mental-illness.

Lo, Imi. 2016. "The Gift Inside Borderline Personality Disorder (BPD)." Counselling Directory. https://www.counselling-directory.org.uk/memberarticles/the-gift-inside-borderline-personality-disorder-bpd.

Lopez-Claros, Augusto, and Bahiyyih Nakhjavani. 2018. *Equality for Women = Prosperity for All: The Disastrous Global Crisis of Gender Inequality*. New York: St. Martin's Press.

Love, Kelli. n.d. "The Peace Corner: An Essential Classroom Resource." https://www.littlefloweryoga.com/blog/the-peace-corner-an-essential-classroom-resource.

Mack, Andrew. 2005. *Human Security Report 2005: War and Peace in the 21st Century*. https://www.jstor.org/stable/pdf/23773842.pdf.

MacLean, Evan L., Brian Hare, Charles L. Nunn, Elsa Addessi, Federica Amici, Rindy C. Anderson, Filippo Aureli, et al. 2014. "The Evolution of Self-control." *PNAS* 111, no. 20: E2140–E2148.

Maier, Steven F., and Martin E. P. Seligman. 2016. "Learned Helplessness at Fifty: Insights from Neuroscience." *Psychological Review* 123, no. 4: 349–367.

Malvaez, Melissa. 2019. "Neural Substrates of Habit." *Journal of Neuroscience Research* 98, no. 6: 986–997.

Mandela, Nelson. 1994. *Long Walk to Freedom: The Autobiography of Nelson Mandela*. Boston: Little, Brown & Company.

Marshall Emerson, Kathy. 2015. "Resilience Research and Community Practice: A View From the Bridge." Paper presented at Pathways to Resilience III International Conference, Dalhousie University Resilience Research Centre, Halifax, Nova Scotia, June 2015. http://www.nationalresilienceresource.com/Resilience_Research_A_View.pdf.

Maurer, Christian. 2006. "Two Approaches to Self-love: Hutcheson and Butler." *European Journal of Analytic Philosophy* 2, no. 2: 81–96.

May, Rollo. 1975. *The Courage to Create*. New York: W. W. Norton.

McKinley, Nicola, R. Scott McCain, Liam Convie, Mike Clarke, Martin Dempster, William Jeffrey Campbell, and Stephen James Kirk. 2020. "Resilience, Burnout and Coping Mechanisms in UK Doctors: A Cross-sectional Study." *BMJ Open* 2020: 1–8.

Menakem, Resmaa. 2017. *My Grandmother's Hands: Racialized Trauma and the Pathway to Mending Our Hearts and Bodies*. Las Vegas: Central Recovery Press.

Mercier, Hugo, and Dan Sperber. 2017. *The Enigma of Reason*. Cambridge, MA: Harvard University Press.

Meyer, Susan. 2005. "Antisemitism and Social Critique in Dickens's 'Oliver Twist.'" *Victorian Literature and Culture* 33, no. 1: 238–252.

Milgram, Stanley. 1974. *Obedience to Authority: An Experimental View*. New York: Harper & Row.

Mill, John Stuart. 2008. *The Autobiography of John Stuart Mill*. Rockville, MD: Arc Manor.

Mills, Andrew C., Jidapa Poogpan, Choochart Wong-Anuchit, and Darunee Rujkorakarn. 2019. "The Meaning of Acceptance (*Thum-jai*) in Thai People: Letting It Go . . . So Life Goes On." *International Journal of Mental Health Nursing* 28, no. 4: 879–887.

Mitchell, Christopher, and Michael Banks. 1996. *Handbook of Conflict Resolution: The Analytical Problem-Solving Approach*. New York: Pinter.

Mitra, Aniruddha, James T. Bang, and Arnab Biswas. 2015. "Gender Equality and Economic Growth: is it Equality of Opportunity or Equality of Outcomes?" *Feminist Economics* 21, no. 1: 110–135.

Montessori, Maria. 1947. *To Educate the Human Potential*. Netherlands: Montessori-Pierson Publishing Company.

Montville, Joseph V. 1990. *Conflict and Peacemaking in Multiethnic Societies*. Lanham, MD: Lexington Books.

Moore, Diane L. 2014. "High Stakes Ignorance: Religion, Education, and the Unwitting Reproduction of Bigotry." In *Civility, Religious Pluralism, and Education*, 112–126. New York: Routledge.

Moore, Edward Caldwell. 1912. "Modern Liberalism and That of the Eighteenth Century." *The American Journal of Theology* 16, no. 1: 1–19.

Moore, George Edward. [1903] 1922. *Principia Ethica*. Cambridge: Cambridge University Press. http://www.gutenberg.org/files/53430/53430-h/53430-h.htm.

Morone, James A. 1997. "Enemies of the People: The Moral Dimension to Public Health." *Journal of Health Politics, Policy and Law* 22, no. 4: 993–1020.

Mumford, David P. 1991. "On the Computational Architecture of the Neocortex: II, The Role of Cortico-cortical Loops." *Biological Cybernetics* 66: 241–251.

Musikanski, Lisa, and Paul Rogers. 2021. *Planet Happiness*. https://www.our-heritageourhappiness.org.

Naddeo, Jennifer K. 2005. *Twentieth Century First Ladies as Moral Leaders for Education: A Study of Eleanor Roosevelt, Lady Bird Johnson and Barbara Bush*. Ann Arbor: ProQuest Information and Learning.

Nairn, Raymond, Frank Pega, Tim McCreanor, Jenny Rankine, and Angela Barnes. 2006. "Media, Racism and Public Health Psychology." *Journal of Health Psychology* 11, no. 2: 183–196.

National Institute of Neurological Disorders and Stroke. 2020. "Brain Basics: Know Your Brain." https://www.ninds.nih.gov/disorders/Patient-Caregiver-Education/Know-Your-Brain#fore.

Nayed, Aref Ali. 2010. *Growing Ecologies of Peace, Compassion and Blessing: A Muslim Response to "A Muscat Manifesto."* Dubai: Kalam Research & Media. https://www.academia.edu/8897031/Growing_Ecologies_of_Peace_Compassion_and_Blessing_A_Muslim_Response_to_A_Muscat_By_Aref_Ali_Nayed.

Nayed, Aref Ali. 2018. *Operational Hermeneutics: Interpretation as the Engagement of Operational Artifacts*. Dubai: Kalam Research & Media.

Nederman, Cary J. 1989. "Nature, Ethics, and the Doctrine of 'Habitus': Aristotelian Moral Psychology in the Twelfth Century." *Traditio* 45: 89–110.

Neumann, David L., and H. Rae Westbury. 2011. "The Psychophysiological Measurement of Empathy." In *Psychology of Empathy*, edited by Danielle J. Scapaletti, 119–142. Hauppauge, NY: Nova Science Publishers.

Neusner, Jacob, and Bruce Chilton, eds. 2008. *The Golden Rule: The Ethics of Reciprocity in World Religions*. London: Continuum.

Newcomb, Anna B., and Robert A. Hymes. 2017. "Life Interrupted: The Trauma Caregiver Experience." *Journal of Trauma Nursing* 24, no. 2: 125–133.

Nhat Hanh, Thich. 1987. *The Miracle of Mindfulness: An Introduction to the Practice of Meditation*. Translated by Mobi Ho. Boston: Beacon Press.

Nhat Hanh, Thich. 2001. *Anger: Wisdom for Cooling the Flames*. New York: Riverhead Books.

Nhat Hanh, Thich. 2005. *Being Peace*. Berkeley, CA: Parallax Press.

Ninkovich, Frank. 1986. "Theodore Roosevelt: Civilization as Ideology." *Diplomatic History* 10, no. 3: 221–245.

Nippon.com. 2020. "Coronavirus Cases by Country." Accessed July 27, 2021. https://www.nippon.com/en/japan-data/h00673.

Ochs, Peter. 2006. "Philosophical Warrants for Scriptural Reasoning." *Modern Theology* 22, no. 3: 465–482.

Office of Disease Prevention and Health Promotion. 2020. "Social Determinants of Health." Healthy People 2020. https://www.healthypeople.gov/2020/topics-objectives/topic/social-determinants-of-health.

Office of Disease Prevention and Health Promotion. 2021. "Healthy People 2030: Building a Healthier Future for All." https://health.gov/healthypeople.

Oney, Steve. 2003. *And the Dead Shall Rise: The Murder of Mary Phagan and the Lynching of Leo Frank*. New York: Pantheon Books.

Paul, Diane B. 2003. "Darwin, Social Darwinism and Eugenics." In *The Cambridge Companion to Darwin*, edited by Jonathan Hodge & Gregory Radick, 214–239. Cambridge, UK: Cambridge University Press.

Philpott, Daniel. 2012. *Just and Unjust Peace: An Ethic of Political Reconciliation*. Oxford: Oxford University Press.

Pinker, Steven. 2007. "The Surprising Decline in Violence." https://www.ted.com/talks/steven_pinker_the_surprising_decline_in_violence.

Pinker, Steven. 2011a. *The Better Angels of Our Nature: Why Violence Has Declined*. New York: Viking Books.

Pinker, Steven. 2011b. "Taming the Devil Within Us." *Nature* 478: 309–311.

Pritchard, Kathleen. 2007. "Comparative Human Rights: An Integrative Explanation." *South African Journal of Political Studies* 13, no. 2: 24–37.

Quash, Ben. 2020. "Deep Calls to Deep: The Practice of Scriptural Reasoning." https://www.interfaith.cam.ac.uk/resources/scripturalreasoningresources/deepcallstodeep.

Rafi, Halima, François Bogacz, David Sander, and Olga Klimecki. 2020. "Impact of Couple Conflict and Mediation on How Romantic Partners Are Seen: An fMRI Study." *Cortex* 130: 302–317.

Ramachandran, V. S. 2010. *The Tell-Tale Brain: A Neuroscientist's Quest for What Makes Us Human*. New York: W. W. Norton.

Ramsbotham, Oliver, Tom Woodhouse, and Hugh Miall. 2016. *Contemporary Conflict Resolution, Fourth edition*. Cambridge, UK: Polity.

Rand, Benjamin. 1909. *The Classical Moralists: Selections Illustrating Ethics from Socrates to Martineau*. Boston: Houghton Mifflin.

Rauschenbusch, Walter. 1919. *A Theology for the Social Gospel*. New York: Macmillan.

Ravven, Heidi M. 2013. *The Self Beyond Itself: An Alternative History of Ethics, the New Brain Sciences, and the Myth of Free Will*. New York: New Press.

Reddy, William M. 2020. "The Unavoidable Intentionality of Affect: The History of Emotions and Neurosciences of the Present Day." *Emotion Review* 12, no. 3: 168–178.

Regehr, Cheryl, Gerald Goldberg, and Judy Hughes. 2002. "Exposure to Human Tragedy, Empathy, and Trauma in Ambulance Paramedics." *American Journal of Orthopsychiatry* 72, no. 4: 505–513.

Ressler, Reed L., and Stephen Maren. 2019. "Synaptic Encoding of Fear Memories in the Amygdala." *Current Opinion in Neurobiology* 54: 54–59.

Reychler, Luc. 2010. "Peacemaking, Peacekeeping, and Peacebuilding." *Oxford Research Encyclopedia of International Studies*. https://oxfordre.com/internationalstudies/view/10.1093/acrefore/9780190846626.001.0001/acrefore-9780190846626-e-274?rskey=7VOyn8&result=1.

Regas, Rima. 2015. "Transcript: James Baldwin Debates William F. Buckley (1965)." Blog #42. https://www.rimaregas.com/2015/06/07/transcript-james-baldwin-debates-william-f-buckley-1965-blog42.

Rich, Motoko. 2020. "Is the Secret to Japan's Virus Success Right in Front of Its Face?" *The New York Times*. https://www.nytimes.com/2020/06/06/world/asia/japan-coronavirus-masks.html.

Rifkin, Lawrence. 2013. "The Survival of Humanity." *Scientific American*. https://blogs.scientificamerican.com/guest-blog/the-survival-of-humanity.

Riley, Alex. 2018. "How a Wooden Bench in Zimbabwe Is Starting a Revolution in Mental Health." Mosaic. https://mosaicscience.com/story/friendship-bench-zimbabwe-mental-health-dixon-chibanda-depression.

Rincon, Paul. 2018. "Stephen Hawking's Warnings: What He Predicted for the Future." BBC News. https://www.bbc.com/news/science-environment-43408961.

Ritchie, Hannah, and Max Roser. 2018. "Plastic Pollution." Our World in Data. https://ourworldindata.org/plastic-pollution.

Rochat, F., and A. Modigliani. 1995. "The Ordinary Quality of Resistance: From Milgram's Laboratory to the Village of Le Chambon." *Journal of Social Issues* 51, no. 3: 195–210. https://doi.org/10.1111/j.1540-4560.1995.tb01341.x.

Rockwell, Norman. 1961. *The Norman Rockwell Album*. New York: Doubleday.

Romer, Jennie R. 2012. "Single-use Plastic Carryout Bags: An Icon of Waste." *Sustainability: The Journal of Record* 5, no. 6: 341–343.

Rose, Rabbi Or N., Jo Ellen Green Kaiser, and Margie Klein, eds. 2008. *Righteous Indignation: A Jewish Call for Justice*. Woodstock, VT: Jewish Lights.

Rosenzweig, Michael. 2014. "9 Adar: 18 Jewish Ways To Promote Constructive Conflict Resolution." The Wexner Foundation. https://www.wexnerfoundation.org/9-adar-18-jewish-ways-to-promote-constructive-conflict-resolution.

Rosner, Fred. 1965. "The Hygienic Principles of Moses Maimonides." *JAMA* 194, no. 13: 1352–1354.

Roth, Daniel. 2011. "The Peacemaker in Jewish Rabbinic and Arab Islamic Traditions." *Journal of Religion, Conflict, and Peace* 4, no. 2.

Roth, Daniel. 2012. "The Tradition of Aaron, Pursuer of Peace Between People, as a Rabbinic Model of Reconciliation." PhD dissertation., Bar-Ilan University.

Roth, Daniel. 2017. "The Pursuit of Peace in Medieval Judaism." In *Religion and Peace: Historical Aspects*, edited by Yvonne Friedman, 1–11. London: Routledge.

Roth, Daniel. 2019. "From the Diary of a Rabbinic Peacemaker: Case Study of a Traditional Jewish Process of Reconciliation and Conflict Resolution." *Journal of Living Together* 6, no. 1: 43–52.

Roth, Daniel. 2021. *Third-Party Peacemaking in Judaism: Text, Theory, and Practice*. Oxford: Oxford University Press.

Rothbart, Daniel, and Karina Korostelina. 2006. *Identity, Morality, and Threat*. New York, NY: Lexington Books.

Rothbart, Daniel. 2019. *State Domination and the Psycho-Politics of Conflict: Power, Conflict, and Humiliation*. New York: Routledge Press.

Rousseau, Jean-Jacques. [1762] 1921. *Émile, or Education*. Translated by Barbara Foxley, M.A. London and Toronto: J. M. Dent and Sons; New York: E. P. Dutton. https://oll.libertyfund.org/title/rousseau-emile-or-education.

Rubenstein, Richard E. 2006. *Thus Saith the Lord: The Revolutionary Moral Vision of Isaiah and Jeremiah*. Orlando, FL: Harcourt.

Rubenstein, Richard E. 2017. *Resolving Structural Conflicts: How Violent Systems Can Be Transformed*. London: Routledge.

Sakuae, Mari, and Denise Reid. 2012. "Making Tea in Place: Experiences of Women Engaged in a Japanese Tea Ceremony." *Journal of Occupational Science* 19, no. 3: 283–291.

Salinas, Joel. 2017. *Mirror Touch: A Memoir of Synesthesia and the Secret Life of the Brain*. New York: HarperCollins.

Sánchez-Bayo, Francisco, and Kris A. G. Wyckhuys. 2019. "Worldwide Decline of the Entomofauna: A Review of Its Drivers." *Biological Conservation* 232: 8–27.

Sapolsky, Robert M. 2017. *Behave: The Biology of Humans at our Best and Worst*. New York: Penguin.

Saslow, Eli. 2018. *Rising Out of Hatred: The Awakening of a Former White Nationalist*. New York: Doubleday.

Schafft, Gretchen E. 2004. *From Racism to Genocide: Anthropology in the Third Reich*. Champaign and Urbana: University of Illinois Press.

Scheurell, Robert P. 2003. "The Welfare State in the United States." In *Welfare Capitalism Around the World*, edited by Christian Aspalter. Hong Kong: Casa Verde Publishing.

Schnack, Hugo G., Neeltje E. M. van Haren, Rachel M. Brouwer, Alan Evans, Sarah Durston, Dorret I. Boomsma, René S. Kahn, and Hilleke E. Hulshoff Pol. 2015. "Changes in Thickness and Surface Area of the Human Cortex and Their Relationship with Intelligence." *Cerebral Cortex* 25, no. 6: 1608–1617.

Schneider, Brett, and Michael Koenigs. 2017. "Human Lesion Studies of Ventromedial Prefrontal Cortex." *Neuropsychologia* 107: 84–93.

Schweiker, William. 2008. "Torture and Religious Practice." *Dialog: A Journal of Theology* 47, no. 3: 208–216.

Segal, Isidor, and Shraga Blazer. 2020. "The Maimonides Model for a Regimen of Health: A Comparison with the Contemporary Scenario." *Rambam Maimonides Medical Journal* 11, no. 4: e0029.

Seligman, Martin E. P. 2012. *Flourish: A Visionary New Understanding of Happiness and Well-being*. New York: Free Press.

Seligman, Martin. 2016. "'Learned Helplessness' & Torture: An Exchange." *The New York Review*, April 21. https://www.nybooks.com/articles/2016/04/21/learned-helplessness-torture-an-exchange.

Seligman, Martin E. P., and Mihaly Csikszentmihalyi. 2000. "Positive Psychology: An Introduction." *American Psychologist* 55, no. 1: 5–14.

Sharma, Nikhil, Joseph Classen, and Leonard G. Cohen. 2013. "Neural Plasticity and Its Contribution to Functional Recovery." *Handbook of Clinical Neurology* 110: 3–12.

Shaw, Carolyn M. 2004. "Using Role-Play Scenarios in the IR classroom: An Examination of Exercises on Peacekeeping Operations and Foreign Policy Decision Making." *International Studies Perspectives* 5, no. 1: 1–22.

Shiel, William C., Jr. "Medical Definition of Triage." MedicineNet. https://www.medicinenet.com/script/main/art.asp?articlekey=16736.

Short, Philip. 2005. *Pol Pot: Anatomy of a Nightmare*. New York: Holt.

Short, Robyn. 2016. *The Neuroscience of Peace: Creating Neural Pathways for Collaboration to Advance the Human Condition*. https://robynshort.com/wp-content/uploads/2016/02/Neuroscience-of-Peace.pdf.

Silcock, Peter, and Hilary Stacey. 1997. "Peer Mediation and the Cooperative School." *Education 3-13: International Journal of Primary, Elementary and Early Years Education* 25, no. 2: 3–8.

Simmons, Solon. 2020. *Root Narrative Theory and Conflict Resolution: Power, Justice, and Values*. New York: Routledge.

Singer, Peter. 2005. "Ethics and Intuitions." *The Journal of Ethics* 9, no. 3–4: 331–352.

Singh-Taylor, A., J. Molet, S. Jiang, A. Korosi, J. L. Bolton, Y. Noam, K. Simeone, J. Cope, Y. Chen, A. Mortazavi, and T. Z. Baram. 2018. "Nrsf-dependent Epigenetic Mechanisms Contribute to Programming of Stress-sensitive Neurons by Neonatal Experience, Promoting Resilience." *Molecular Psychiatry* 23: 648–657.

Sirois, Fuschia M., and Georgina Rowse. 2016. "The Role of Self-compassion in Chronic Illness Care." *Journal of Clinical Outcomes Management* 23, no. 11: 521–527.

Slutkin, Gary. 2013. "Let's Treat Violence Like a Contagious Disease." TEDMED. https://www.ted.com/talks/gary_slutkin_let_s_treat_violence_like_a_contagious_disease/up-next.

Slutkin, Gary, 2020. "'Violence Is an Infectious Disease' with Gary Slutkin, MD, founder and CEO of Cure Violence Global." Pandemonium U. https://www.youtube.com/watch?v=Dvxl8VU-vpU.

Smith, Adam. [1759] 2005. *The Theory of Moral Sentiments.* https://www.ibiblio.org/ml/libri/s/SmithA_MoralSentiments_p.pdf.

Smith, J. David, Michael J. Beran, Justin J. Couchman, and Mairana V. C. Coutinho. 2008. "The Comparative Study of Metacognition: Sharper Paradigms, Safer Inferences." *Psychonomic Bulletin & Review* 15: 679–691.

Smith, Rhiannon L., and Amanda J. Rose. 2011. "The 'Cost of Caring' in Youths' Friendships: Considering Associations Among Social Perspective Taking, Co-rumination, and Empathic Distress." *Developmental Psychology* 47, no. 6: 1792–1803.

Soloveitchik, Joseph B. 1984. *Halakhic Man.* New York: The Jewish Publication Society.

Soloveitchik, Joseph B. 1998. *The Halakhic Mind.* New York: The Free Press.

Soloveitchik, Joseph B. 2006. *The Lonely Man of Faith.* New York: Doubleday.

Soroka, Stuart, Patrick Fournier, and Lilach Nir. 2019. "Cross-national Evidence of a Negativity Bias in Psychophysiological Reactions to News." *PNAS* 116, no. 38: 18888–18892.

Stasser, Garold, and William Titus. 1985. "Pooling of Unshared Information in Group Decision Making: Biased Information Sampling During Discussion." *Journal of Personality and Social Psychology* 48, no. 6: 1467–1478.

Stasser, Garold, Dennis D. Stewart, and Gwen M. Wittenbaum. 1995. "Expert Roles and Information Exchange During Discussion: The Importance of Knowing Who Knows What." *Journal of Experimental Social Psychology* 31, no. 3: 244–265.

Staub, Ervin. 1989. *The Roots of Evil: The Origins of Genocide and Other Group Violence.* Cambridge, UK: Cambridge University Press.

Staub, Ervin. 2000. "Genocide and Mass Killing: Origins, Prevention, Healing and Reconciliation." *Political Psychology* 21, no. 2: 367–382.

Staub, Ervin. 2011. *Overcoming Evil: Genocide, Violent Conflict, and Terrorism.* Oxford: Oxford University Press.

Staub, Ervin. 2015. *The Roots of Goodness and Resistance to Evil.* Oxford: Oxford University Press.

Stevenson, Matthew, Allison Gornik, R. Derek Black, and Marc Gopin. 2019. "The Journey of a Former White Supremacist: The Power of Community to Effect Change." Washington Theological Consortium, Tachmindji Event for Interfaith Dialogue. https://washtheocon.org/for-the-public/tachmindji-event.

Stone, R. David, Emma Goring, and Conor E. Kretsch. 2015. "Increasing Resilience and Disaster Risk Reduction: The Value of Biodiversity and Ecosystem Approaches to Resistance, Resilience and Relief." In *Connecting Global Priorities: Biodiversity and Human Health: A State of Knowledge Review*, edited by Cristina Romanelli, David

Cooper, Diarmid Campbell-Lendrum, Marina Maiero, William B. Karesh, Danny Hunter, and Christopher D. Golden, 238–250. Geneva, Switzerland: World Health Organization and Secretariat of the Convention on Biological Diversity.

Strauss, Valerie, and Daniel Southerl. 1994. "How Many Died? New Evidence Suggests Far Higher Numbers for the Victims of Mao Zedong's Era." *The Washington Post.* https://www.washingtonpost.com/archive/politics/1994/07/17/how-many-died-new-evidence-suggests-far-higher-numbers-for-the-victims-of-mao-zedongs-era/01044df5-03dd-49f4-a453-a033c5287bce.

Strayhorn, Joseph M. 2002. "Self-control: Theory and Practice." *Journal of the Academy of Child Adolescent Psychiatry* 41, no. 1: 7–16.

Stroumsa, Sarah. 1993. "Al-Fārābī and Maimonides on Medicine as a Science." *Arabic Sciences and Philosophy* 3, no. 2: 235–249.

Su, YouRong Sophie, Anand Veeravagu, and Gerald Grant. 2016. "Neuroplasticity After Traumatic Brain Injury." In *Translational Research in Traumatic Brain Injury*, edited by Daniel T. Laskowitz and Gerald Grant. Boca Raton, FL: Taylor and Francis.

Taren, Adrienne A., Peter J. Gianaros, Carol M. Greco, Emily K. Lindsay, April Fairgrieve, Kirk Warren Brown, Rhonda K. Rosen, Jennifer L. Ferris, Erica Julson, Anna L. Marsland, James K. Bursley, Jared Ramsburg, and J. David Creswell. 2015. "Mindfulness Meditation Training Alters Stress-related Amygdala Resting State Functional Connectivity: A Randomized Controlled Trial." *Social Cognitive and Affective Neuroscience* 10, no. 12: 1758–1768.

Tastakel. 2021. "Tastakel." http://www.tastakel.org.

Thornberg, Robert, and Tomas Jungert. 2013. "Bystander Behavior in Bullying Situations: Basic Moral Sensitivity, Moral Disengagement and Defender Self-efficacy." *Journal of Adolescence* 36, no. 3: 475–483.

Thorpe, Nick, 2017. "The Palaeolithic Compassion Debate – Alternative Projections of Modern-Day Disability into the Distant Past." In *Care in the Past: Archaeological and Interdisciplinary Perspectives*, edited by Lindsay Powell, William Southwell-Wright and Rebecca Gowland. Oxford, UK: Oxbow Books.

Timmons, Shane, and Ruth M. J. Byrne. 2019. "Moral Fatigue: The Effects of Cognitive Fatigue on Moral Reasoning." *Quarterly Journal of Experimental Psychology* 72, no. 4: 943–954.

Tomasino, Barbara, Alberto Chiesa, and Franco Fabbro. 2014. "Disentangling the Neural Mechanisms Involved in Hinduism- and Buddhism-related Meditations." *Brain and Cognition* 90: 32–40.

Trindale, Inês A., Ana Laura Mendes, and Nuno B. Ferreira. 2020. "The Moderating Effect of Psychological Flexibility on the Link Between Learned Helplessness and Depression Symptomatology: A Preliminary Study." *Journal of Contextual Behavioral Science* 15: 68–72.

Turner, Marlene E., and Anthony R. Pratkanis. 2014. "Preventing Groupthink Risk through Deliberative Discussion: Further Experimental Evidence for a Social Identity Maintenance Model." *International Journal of Risk and Contingency Management* 3, no. 1: 12–24.

Turner, Robert. 2019. "Finding Likeness: Neural Plasticity and Ritual Experience." *Anthropology Today* 35, no. 3: 3–6.

Twersky, Yitzhak. 1989. "On Law and Ethics in the Mishneh Torah: A Case Study of *Hilkhot Megillah II:17*." *Tradition: A Journal of Orthodox Jewish Thought* 24, no. 2: 138–149.

Tzu, Lao. [n.d.] 2015. *Tao Te Ching*. Translated by David Hinton. Berkeley, CA: Counterpoint.

UNICEF. 2021. "Religious and Inter-religious Organizations, Networks, and Alliances." https://www.unicef.org/about/partnerships/index_60231.html.

United States Holocaust Memorial Museum. 2021a. "Documenting Numbers of Victims of the Holocaust and Nazi Persecution." Holocaust Encyclopedia. https://encyclopedia.ushmm.org/content/en/article/documenting-numbers-of-victims-of-the-holocaust-and-nazi-persecution.

United States Holocaust Memorial Museum. 2021b. "Genocide of European Roma (Gypsies), 1939–1945." Holocaust Encyclopedia. https://encyclopedia.ushmm.org/content/en/article/genocide-of-european-roma-gypsies-1939-1945.

United Nations. 2019. "UN Report: Nature's Dangerous Decline 'Unprecedented'; Species Extinction Rates 'Accelerating.'" Sustainable Development Goals. https://www.un.org/sustainabledevelopment/blog/2019/05/nature-decline-unprecedented-report.

United Nations. 2020. "The Drafters of the Universal Declaration of Human Rights." https://www.un.org/en/sections/universal-declaration/drafters-universal-declaration-human-rights/index.html.

United Nations International Tribunal for the Former Yugoslavia. 1995. "The International Tribunal for the Former Yugoslavia Charges 21 Serbs with Atrocities Committed Inside and Outside the Omarska Death Camp." https://www.icty.org/en/press/international-tribunal-former-yugoslavia-charges-21-serbs-atrocities-committed-inside-and.

Viljoen, Frans. 2021. "International Human Rights Law: A Short History." United Nations, UN Chronicle. https://www.un.org/en/chronicle/article/international-human-rights-law-short-history.

Violence Prevention Alliance. 2021. "Cure Violence (previously The Chicago Project for Violence Prevention)." https://www.who.int/violenceprevention/about/participants/cure_violence/en.

Volkan, Vamik. 1997. *Bloodlines: From Ethnic Pride to Ethnic Terrorism*. New York: Farrar, Straus & Giroux.

Volkan, Vamik D. 2013. *Enemies on the Couch: A Psychopolitical Journey Through War and Peace*. Durham, NC: Pitchstone Publishing.

Volkan, Vamik D. 2017. *Immigrants and Refugees: Trauma, Perennial Mourning, and Border Psychology*. London: Karmac.

Volkan, Vamik D. 2020. *Large-Group Psychology: Racism, Societal Divisions, Narcissistic Leaders, and Who We Are Now*. London: Phoenix Publishing House.

Wade-Leeuwen, Bronwen, Jessica Vovers, and Melissa Silk. 2018. "Explainer: What's the Difference Between STEM and STEAM?" *The Conversation*. http://theconversation.com/explainer-whats-the-difference-between-stem-and-steam-95713.

Wai, Michael, and Niko Tiliopoulos. 2012. "The Affective and Cognitive Empathic Nature of the Dark Triad of Personality." *Personality and Individual Differences* 52, no. 7: 794–799.

Wallensteen, Peter. 2019. *Understanding Conflict Resolution,* 5th ed. Los Angeles: Sage.

Ward, Jamie, Patricia Schnakenberg, and Michael J. Banissy. 2018. "The Relationship Between Mirror-touch Synaesthesia and Empathy: New Evidence and a New Screening Tool." *Translational Cognitive Neuropsychology* 35, nos. 5–6: 314–332.

Wattles, Jeffrey. 1996. *The Golden Rule*. Oxford: Oxford University Press.

Weng, Helen Y., Andrew S. Fox, Alexander J. Shackman, Diane E. Stodola, Jessica Z. K. Caldwell, Matthew C. Olson, Gregory M. Rogers, and Richard J. Davidson.

2013. "Compassion Training Alters Altruism and Neural Responses to Suffering." *Psychological Science* 24, no. 7: 1171–1180.

Wickizer, Thomas M., Edward Wagner, Allen Cheadle, David Pearson, William Berry, Jennifer Maeser, Bruce Psaty, Michael Vonkorff, Thomas Koepsell, Paula Diehr, and Edward P. Perrin. 1998. "Implementation of the Henry J. Kaiser Family Foundation's Community Health Promotion Grant Program: A Program Evaluation." *The Milbank Quarterly* 76, no. 1: 121–147.

Wilhoit, James C. 2019. "Self-compassion as a Christian Spiritual Practice." *Journal of Spiritual Formation & Soul Care* 12, no. 1: 71–88.

Wingfield-Hayes, Rupert. 2020. "Coronavirus: Japan's Mysteriously Low Virus Death Rate." BBC News. https://www.bbc.com/news/world-asia-53188847.

Wohlleben, Peter. 2017. *The Inner Life of Animals: Love, Grief, and Compassion: Surprising Observations of a Hidden World*. Vancouver: Greystone Books.

Wong, Jessie J., Nickolas D. Frost, Christine Timko, Adrienne J. Heinz, and Ruth Cronkite. 2020. "Depression and Family Arguments: Disentangling Reciprocal Effects for Women and Men." *Family Practice* 37, no. 1: 49–55.

Yang, Cheng-Chang, Laura Mauer, Birgit Völlm, and Najat Khalifa. 2020. "The Effects of Non-invasive Brain Stimulation on Impulsivity in People with Mental Disorders: a Systematic Review and Explanatory Meta-Analysis." *Neuropsychology Review* 30, no. 4: 499–520.

Yeh, Theresa Der-Ian, 2006. "The Way to Peace: A Buddhist Perspective." *International Journal of Peace Studies* 11, no. 1: 91–112.

Yu, Qian, Enyao Li, Liguo Li, and Weiyi Liang. 2020. "Efficacy of Interventions Based on Applied Behavior Analysis for Autism Spectrum Disorder: A Meta-Analysis." *Psychiatry Investigations* 17, no. 5: 432–443.

Zeithamova, Dagmar, Margaret L. Schlichting, and Alison R. Preston. 2012. "The Hippocampus and Inferential Reasoning: Building Memories to Navigate Future Decisions." *Frontiers in Human Neuroscience* 6, no. 70: 1–14.

Ziccardi, M. James. 2014. *Immanuel Kant: A Guide to Transcendental Idealism*. M. James Ziccardi.

Ziegler, Matthias, Erik Danay, Moritz Heene, Jens Asendorpf, and Markus Bühner. 2012. "Openness, Fluid Intelligence, and Crystallized Intelligence: Toward an Integrative Model." *Journal of Research in Personality* 46, no. 2: 173–183.

Zimbardo, Philip. 2007. *The Lucifer Effect: Understanding How Good People Turn Evil*. New York: Random House.

Zimbardo, Philip. 2021. Heroic Imagination Project. https://www.heroicimagination.org.

Index

For the benefit of digital users, indexed terms that span two pages (e.g., 52–53) may, on occasion, appear on only one of those pages.

adaptation, 2
altruism, 66–67, 98, 199, 236
amygdala, 24, 35, 36, 49, 94, 133, 164–65
    and self-control, 52–53
anger, 7, 21, 34, 49, 171
    mitigation of, 34, 36, 91, 176
Aristotle, 180, 181, 216
associative thinking, 187–88
authoritarianism, 32–33, 35, 55, 91, 96
Azzai, Ben, 71–73

Baldwin, James, 18–19
benchmarks, 158
Bosnia, 105–10, 113–14
brain, 174, 213
    contradictions within, 141–42
    higher brain, 2, 21, 36, 48–49, 73, 85–86,
        183 (*see also* neocortex)
    lower brain, 2, 21, 51–52, 86 (*see also*
        amygdala)
    plasticity, 80, 84, 101, 167–68
breathing, 202–5
Buddy Bench, 205–8
bullying, 94–95, 101–2

climate challenges, 25, 77, 92, 143–44,
    168, 184–85
cognitive reframing, 174–75
coherence theory of truth, 124–25, 127–
    28, 172
common good, 45
community, 155
compassion, 6, 37–38, 113, 129–30,
    166, 197–99
    compared to empathy, 46–47, 99, 112–
        13, 118, 120, 122, 236
    depressing self-destructive
        instincts, 45, 46

derived from empathy, 103–5
to enemies, 210–13
as a foundation for peacebuilding,
    83, 128
and moral change, 45
neuroscience connections to, 81–83, 99
the opposite of hatred, 149–50, 151–52
as a positive contagion, 136, 168
as prosocial emotion, 43
and reasoning, 41, 48–50, 62–63, 67–68,
    87, 99, 123
Compassionate Reasoning, definition, 2,
    39, 41, 168, 197
    addressing disease of emotions and
        disease of ideas, 171–73
    and cultivation of the self, 217
competition
    healthy, with compassion, 44–45
complexity of variables, 144–46,
    148, 171–72
compromise, 50
conflict, 5, 44–45
    constructive, 44, 213–14
    destructive, 21, 43–44
conflict resolution, 44, 80–81,
    123, 235–36
    the field of, 140
consequentialism, 41, 54, 56–57, 87–89,
    193, 195, 197–98
contagion
    of emotions, 41–42, 164–65
    of ideas, 164–65
    social, 42
correspondence theory of truth, 124–
    25, 171–72
COVID, 136–37
Cultures
    inclusion in global solutions, 120

Dalai Lama, the, 56
debate, 36, 44, 50, 78, 91, 121–22, 200–1,
   213–14, 234
   and the importance of language, 214
decision-making, 14–15, 17, 21, 23, 25,
   29, 30, 33
   virtue and ethical, 96–97
demagogues, 93–97, 101–2, 136
democracy, 167, 180–81
deontology, 54, 59, 85–86, 188–89, 192,
   194, 197–98
deprivation, 49
dialogue, 159–60, 192
disease, 149–52
   as analogy with violence, 138
divided society, 13, 42, 73

economic competition
   Adam Smith, 44
elicitive peacebuilding, 5–6, 235–36
emotions
   and conflict, 43–44
   emotional skills, 4
   and habit formation, 172, 216–17
   positive affect and compassion, 81–
      82, 137–38
   prosocial emotions and
      reasoning, 43–44
   verbal expression of, 184
empathic distress, 12, 29, 37–38, 47–48,
   80, 82, 99, 110–15, 203–4
   effects on society, 122–24
   manipulated for power, 123
   shifting to healthy expressions of
      compassion, 85, 202
empathy, 7, 12, 37–38, 45
   and antipathy, 38
   compared to compassion, 38, 46, 48, 82,
      112–13, 118
   distinct from empathic distress, 37–38
   leading to compassion, 103–5
   negative effects of, 19–22, 29, 46, 47–
      48, 80
   and social change/policy, 46, 47–48
   that can lead to violence, 47–48
empirical research, 126–27
Enlightenment, the, 52, 53, 75, 77, 86–87
   effects on modern ethics, 65, 124–25

philosophical bias towards non-
      European, non-Christian
      people, 53–54
epistemology, 124–25
ethical deliberation/reflection, 21, 31–32,
   36, 91, 93, 191, 200–1
   and prosocial emotion, 31, 34
   and the shift to political constructs, 50
ethical practice, 41–42
ethical schools, 54–55, 182, 190–95
   integration, 93, 97–98, 100, 137–38,
      196–97, 214–15
ethics education, 33, 65–66, 75–77, 84, 90–
   91, 136, 236–37
   necessity of, 94–95
   and traditional education, 65–66, 156

fear, 7, 24, 34, 49, 133, 171
   balanced with love, 96
   mitigation of, 34, 36, 91
   reflection on, 176
Frankl, Viktor, 67, 118, 142, 213
freedom, 175–78
fundamentalism, 32–33, 34–35, 74–75

genocide, 173, 197–99
Gladwell, Malcolm, 39
Golden Rule, 48, 68–71, 102, 240–41
good society, 51–52, 140–41
   construction of, 146
good will (Kant), 42–43, 51, 67, 189–90

habits, 10, 12, 15–16, 17, 23, 29, 42, 49, 52–
   53, 124–25, 170, 185, 206
   benefits of, 64–65
   cognitive and moral, 185–89
   and education, 75
   formation, 251n.25
   and internal rules, 49
   and neuroscience, 15–16, 49, 90, 179–
      81, 208, 212–13
   and religion, 68
   as repeated thoughts and actions, 41,
      135, 167
   words and actions, 217–18
happiness, 57, 192, 231
   and consequentialism, 87–89
   Gross Happiness Index, 137–38

hatred, 20, 21, 36, 101, 139, 149–55
  compassion as treatment for, 152–
    55, 215
  from empathic distress, 122
healing
  focus on, 116–17
health, 19–20, 30, 101, 102
  and compassion, 81–82
  mental, 12, 102, 113–14, 209
  and morality and ethics, 81, 84–85, 89
  personal, 10, 11, 15, 89
  See also public health analogy
human rights, 60–61, 69–70, 74, 99–100,
    134–35, 165, 180–81, 194–95
  and Compassionate Reasoning, 61–62
  incremental change, 70

Jordan. See Syria
justice, 92, 199

Kant, Immanuel, 86–87, 119, 194–95
  categorical imperative, 51, 59,
    74, 85–86
  and ethical choice, 41
  good will, 42–43, 59, 66–67, 70–71
  Perpetual Peace, 60, 74, 86–87
  See also deontology
kindness, 95, 161, 201–2
Klimecki, Olga, 81–83

Lakoff, George, 127–28, 143, 163, 211
Laws
  based in compassion, 51
  internal law and external law, 48–50, 51,
    86–87, 215
  See also human rights; rule of law
leadership, 161–63, 166
liberalism, 77
listening, 148–49, 173–74
love, 68–69, 72, 73
  balanced with fear, 96
Luzzatto, Rabbi Samuel David, 66–
    67, 118

meditation, 185–86, 188, 202–5
  as part of compassion training,
    83, 201–2
mental maps, 124–25

metabolic responses
  to empathy and compassion, 80
moral agency, 95
moral character traits, 4
moral choice, 21, 22, 25, 26, 28–29, 30–31
  and consequentialism, 88–89
moral genius, 23, 24
moral sense theory, 44, 46–47, 54, 55–56,
    85, 97, 193, 195–96, 198
  and conflict, 217
  and Judaism, 118
  in literature, 55

narcissism, 96
natural morality, or natural law theory,
    54, 58–59
neocortex, 24–25, 35, 36, 83, 99, 142
  and perspective-taking, 103–4
  and self-control, 52–53
  and utilitarian calculus, 57
neural pathways, 10, 11–12, 15–16, 23, 52,
    83, 94, 180, 184, 202
  and compassion training, 83–84, 204–5,
    212, 234
  of empathy vs. compassion, 38, 80, 82
  and habits, 90, 175–76
  and repetition of narratives, 94
neuroplasticity, 10, 11, 23, 180
neuroscience
  and compassion, 10–12, 15, 46–47,
    167, 212
  and ethics, 13, 21, 36
  evolution from the Enlightenment, 54
  and natural morality theory, 58–59
  and Tonglen, 204–5
nonviolence, 5, 13, 32, 34, 52–53, 74, 189
  in human ethics, 45
  through self-regulation, 48–49

obedience, 50, 163–67
  blind obedience as the opposite of
    Compassionate Reasoning, 93–94
  to compassionate laws, 51
  dangers of, 64–65, 94
  and lower brain functions, 51–52

peace and conflict studies, 5
Peace Corner, 208–9

peacebuilding, 4, 5, 9, 14, 39, 81, 120, 162
  between secular and religious, 121
  connected to research on the
    brain, 80–81
  harmful practices based on empathy,
    48, 82–83
  and peacemaker burnout, 83–84
  and positive vision, 215–16
  the suppressed field of, 139
  triaging the disease of hatred and
    inoculating with compassion in, 159–
    61, 162–63
  See also elicitive peacebuilding;
    religious peacebuilding
perspective-taking, 102–4, 108, 148
  in peacebuilding and conflict
    resolution, 105
placebo effect, 161–62
pluralistic society, 63–64
polarization, 13, 47–48, 76, 100, 136
policy, 237–38
political activity, 44, 127–30, 237–38
positive psychology, 142
post-traumatic stress disorder
    (PTSD), 110
postmodernism, 125, 126
prophets, biblical, 180, 181
psycholinguistics, 127
psychosocial skills, 4
public health analogy, 101, 131–32, 134–
    38, 146–47, 148–49, 150–59
public laws, 49

racism, 164–65
reasoning, 39–40, 99, 189–90,
    236, 247n.2
  compared to compassion, 40
  in cooperation with positive
    emotions, 48
  as deep understanding, 39
  practical reasoning, 40–41
  and reason-based behavior, 43
religions, 4, 40–41, 78, 92–93, 99–100
  and compassion practices, 12, 40–41,
    46–47, 121, 128–29
  distinction between empathy and
    compassion, 118
  and education, 66, 68, 77–78

and emotions, 216
and the Enlightenment, 53, 124–25
and health, 137
humans created in the image of
    God, 72–73
and language, 214, 235
and natural morality theory, 58–59
and self-regulation, 48–49
and social practice, 45
and reasoning, 63
and secularism, 63–64, 99–100, 129
  See also Golden Rule
religious peacebuilding, 13, 244n.6
  interfaith work, 122
religions and peacebuilding, 14–15
Rousseau, Jean Jacques, 86, 87
rule of law, 50–51, 134, 135, 175
rules, 97–98, 105
  universal, 100
  See also laws

self-control, 52–53, 75, 183
  lack of, 91
  and mental health, 48–49
  and universal rules, 100
self-esteem, 178–79
self-reflection, 31–32, 176–79, 183, 184
  in social contexts, 177
service, 210–13, 218–20
social change, 46, 47–48, 160
  and consequentialism/
    utilitarianism, 88
social Darwinism, 44, 46
social networks, 39, 160
socialization
  as a result of compassion, 86
Socrates, 180, 181
Soloveitchik, Rabbi Dr. Joseph, 119
STEM, 22, 76, 94–95, 104, 245n.11
Syria, 110–14, 122, 218–19

Tonglen, 202–5
training in Compassionate Reasoning, 9,
    10–11, 12, 15, 25, 29–30, 36, 114–15,
    136–37, 156, 201–5, 219–20, 230–
    32, 236–37
  across conservative and liberal
    ideologies, 121–22

both intrapersonal and
    interpersonal, 136
combined with habits, 53, 66, 75–77
and education, 233–34
effect on the brain, 80
effect on democracy, 97
elements of, 232
future orientation, 239
metrics needed, 231–32
and the role of questions, 215
techniques, 232–33

trauma, 19–20, 29, 81, 115–19,
    243n.2
    secondary trauma, 254n.20

utilitarianism, 54, 56–57, 87–89, 97
    moral calculus, 57, 88, 126–27

violence, 131–34, 138–39, 160–61
    Compassionate Reasoning as an
        antidote to, 164–67
virtue ethics, 54, 57–58, 89, 192